Miss Gladys Sandhagen
340 S. Loomis Street
Naperville, Ill. 60540

P9-DDX-063

EMANUEL SWEDENBORG

SCIENTIST AND MYSTIC

BY

SIGNE TOKSVIG

NEW HAVEN

YALE UNIVERSITY PRESS

1948

Copyright, 1948, by Signe Toksvig

Printed in the United States of America

All rights reserved. This book may not be
reproduced, in whole or in part, in any form
(except by reviewers for the public press),
without written permission from the publishers.

Robert Green

Gratis

15 November 1985

71591

To

SOPHY CARR STANTON

IN EVER-LIVING FRIENDSHIP

"There are marvelous things occurring in the human mind, so marvelous indeed that they cannot be expressed. In number they are indefinitely more than all the things contained in the human body, in the threefold kingdom of nature, and in the universal world, visible and invisible. The sciences have drawn out only a few of them, and these are mere rivulets emanating from an ocean."

SWEDENBORG

ACKNOWLEDGMENTS

It is a pleasure to thank the John Simon Guggenheim Memorial Foundation for the grant of a fellowship which made this study possible.

Especial thanks are due to the Library of the Royal Academy of Sciences in Stockholm, to the Library of Yale University, and to the Library of the Academy of the New Church, Bryn Athyn, Pa., for the facilities offered by them, and to Cyriel Odhner Sigstedt, also of Bryn Athyn, for her generosity in lending the writer new material which she herself had found in Sweden.

The editor of the *Journal of the American Society for Psychical Research,* Mrs. Laura Abbott Dale, has been unfailingly helpful. The late Whately Carington, of Sennen Cove, Cornwall, England, was good enough to read and discuss the chapters largely based on his theories, while Professor Gardner Murphy, The City College of New York, must accept thanks for his great kindness in reading the whole book in manuscript.

Contents

Illustrations

EMANUEL SWEDENBORG

CHAPTER ONE

Why Swedenborg

A MEMBER of one of America's great endowed institutions for scientific research was congratulated on belonging to this modern sanctuary, where he could work, free of material worry, together with men interested in the same subject.

He took the congratulations with a shade of reserve, explaining that he sometimes wished he were working at a university where he could drop into a faculty club and talk over his subject and theirs with men from entirely different fields, and learn their points of view. By contact even with astronomy, geology, engineering, philosophy, psychology, he felt that his section of his own field—that of physiology—could be more usefully related to the rest of the world.

Emanuel Swedenborg was such a faculty club all by himself. It is hard to enumerate all the branches of knowledge with which he made himself familiar, as familiar as the resources of a couple of hundred years ago allowed.

But such "scholars" were not uncommon in the centuries before experimental science demanded monogamous attention in each minute parcel of every field, and, except for museum curiosity, there would be no reason for reading about Swedenborg if he had been only such a gorgeous compendium of untested theories. He was, however, in the words of a modern Swedish historian of biology, "one of the richest and most fertile geniuses known to history." [1]

In 1910, at the International Swedenborg Congress [2] in London, it took nearly a whole faculty club of professors to cover the various facets of Swedenborg's learning and to hail the value of his scientific work. Similarly, in 1938, at the 250th anniversary of his birth, tributes were paid to him by scientists in various fields.

These witnesses, most of whom deplored his later preoccupation with religion, claimed that Swedenborg foresaw even "the lines of development of science." Svante Arrhenius, Nobel Prize winner, vouched for his cosmology which surmised the nebular hypothesis and the existence of galactic universes. Anatomists said that Swedenborg was the first to localize the psychological functions of the brain in the cortex, and that he based this discovery not on vague theorizing, but on clinical and pathological observations, as well as on ingenious synthesis of material provided by others.

He had studied under some of the great anatomists of his day, and he says himself that he based much of his work on that of others. For this he gave a subtle reason: "I found, when intently occupied in exploring the secrets of the human body, that as soon as I discovered anything which had not been discovered before, I began—seduced probably by self-love—to grow blind to the most acute lucubrations of the researches of others, and to originate the whole series of inductive arguments from my particular discovery alone . . . Nay, when I tried to form principles from these discoveries, I thought I could detect much to confirm their truth in various other phenomena, although in reality they were fairly susceptible of no construction of the kind. I therefore laid aside my instruments, and, restraining my desire for making observations, determined rather to rely on the researches of others than to trust to my own." [3]

Then he painted this picture of the true men of science:

"The fictitious depresses them, the obscure pains them; but they are exhilarated by the truth, and in the presence of everything that is clear they too are clear and serene. When, after a long course of reasoning, they make a discovery of the truth, straightway there is a certain cheering light and joyful confirmatory brightness that plays around the sphere of their mind; and a kind of mysterious radiation—I know not whence it proceeds—that darts through some sacred temple in the brain." [4]

From time to time in this twentieth century a bold speculation throws this "confirmatory brightness" into our world. Then it often happens that something which had hitherto been merely another dark patch in Swedenborg's writings turns out to shine with the same brightness, such as the theory of matter as force, and the relativity of space and time.

It has been said that in the eighteenth century "men turned from the attempt to apprehend the whole by reason and began to study the part by experience." No one was more enthusiastic about the beauty of experimental science than Swedenborg. Incredibly energetic, he experimented with such apparatus as was available—and it is worth remembering that not better brains but better technical equipment has produced modern discoveries—but for all his belief in studying the part by experience he did not want to throw the right to generalize overboard.

He said, in 1740, to the Swedish Academy of Science that "some of the learned of the present day seemed to have agreed to let thought rest, and to make experiments to appeal to the senses; yet they did so with the hope and intent that some day experience would be connected with theory; for experience deprived of an insight into the nature of things is knowledge without learning, and a foundation without a building to rest on it." [5]

It was for the object of gaining insight into the nature of things that Swedenborg dug into astronomy, physics, chemistry, physiology, and psychology, not for the dubious joy of being an encyclopedia. He acted on the belief that insight not based on experience would be the building without any foundation. So for nearly two thirds of his life he went on working at this, the meticulous digging and bricklaying of science, fact by fact; but what he cared most for, the real motive behind it all, was the building.

That building was to be his answer to the questions: What are we, Why are we, and What is to become of us? Or, as he put it, If there is such a thing as the soul, how is it connected with the body, and does it survive bodily death?

Not a new question, nor even a respectable one from the point of view of the kind of science which rules out problems that cannot be given laboratory answers. Moreover in this sphere "purpose" and "motive" are suspect words, and most rightly so, unless they can be phrased as working hypotheses.

Worse than suspect, the "soul" has long been ruled out, though of late it has been creeping back quaintly as "psyche," even trying to recommune with the body in "psychosomatic," "psychodynamic," "psychokinetic," but making its most spectacular re-appearance in psychoanalysis, where an aspect of it sometimes even dismisses itself as an "escape mechanism."

Swedenborg was only twenty-six when, in 1714, he noted down his intention to "find a method by which the wills and affections of men's minds can be conjectured by means of analysis."

He became an object of analysis himself, especially when a diary of his dreams at a certain period was found. Some modern psycho-analysts interpreted him, trying to account for the change in him from experimental scientist to the man who believed the experi-ments concluded in favor of the soul's existence. Freudians called his case one of an inverted Œdipus complex, and Jungians opted for a split personality.

But William James says of similar charges against those of great imagination: "In the natural sciences and industrial arts it never occurs to anyone to try to refute opinions by showing up their author's neurotic constitution. Opinions here are invariably tested by logic and experiment, no matter what may be their author's neurological type. It should be no otherwise with religious opin-ions." [6]

James goes on to say that such opinions must be tested by experi-ence in relation to our moral needs and to the rest of what we hold as true. By such tests Swedenborg in his later phase has as great treasure to bestow as many of those millionaires of the spirit we call mystics, even if one reads him strictly from an ethical point of view. And, apart from an interest in distinctions between good and evil—not an unnecessary interest at the present time, one would think—Swedenborg in his life and works can, if one takes a little trouble to understand him, open travel horizons for us far exceed-ing all others for beauty and strangeness.

F. W. H. Myers, the great pioneer in the tremulous science of psychical research, has said that "it was to Swedenborg first that the unseen world appeared before all things as a realm of law; a region not of mere emotional vagueness or stagnancy of adoration but of definite progress, according to the laws of cause and effect, resulting from structural laws of spiritual existence and inter-course." [7]

Swedenborg's God is the God of a scientist. He is the essence not only of love but of wisdom, which is, or includes order. "God *is* Order," he has said. He knew nothing of Vedanta or Buddhist philosophy and Karma's inexorable law, but he stressed as fundamental that man is what he becomes through his deeds, and that those deeds trail their consequences with them, irrespective of "faith." In his insistence on intellectual order in spiritual things, he comes nearer to meeting a lack which people of the East have felt in Christian religions than any other Westerner. If the two aspects of humanity are to understand each other spiritually, it may be through the medium of a Swedenborg, brought up to date, as he would have wished to be, and winnowed of time-bound orthodoxies.

Look at him as you will—as a scientist, ethical teacher, religious philosopher, mystic, commuter to and from another world, bringing with him sober reports of talks with its inhabitants, as well as topographical descriptions, or as a poet who imagined that world so firmly that he believed in it—his life is surely what F. W. H. Myers said it was, "the strangest ever lived by mortal man."

There is, however, one red thread or green line in it which can be seen rather easily: the attempt to fit all he knew and all he experienced into a consistent world picture, one that should be based on law, physical and spiritual. Swedenborg's life is therefore also a kind of map, which shows the successes and failures of a man who refused to accept the prescribed solutions. He had pieces of his own which he wanted to fit in, even if he was not always aware that some of them might be fashioned out of his emotional needs rather than his scientific experience.

Three major factors had to be fitted together in whatever picture was to satisfy him. One was his scientific bent: to observe and to classify, to test theories by experience and then to systematize.

Another was the fact that though most men of his class and education were content to dismiss anything not securely of this world with a bit of lip-service, he could not do so. He felt he had to have religion in his world-picture, even including the Bible as divine revelation. This he managed by means of symbolic interpretation, thus, to his own satisfaction, fitting the Biblical and the scientific pieces together.

That he was able to do this was due to the third major factor of his experience, the nature of which was far from clear to him. In middle age he began to discover that most unusual events were taking place in his mind. Today people would call them either psychic or psychotic, according to their own bent, but he was convinced by the startling character of the events that they were inspired. For him, at any rate, they were the most important of his life.

He thought he knew the difference between what he called "phantasies" and objective perceptions; therefore the psychic part of his experience was real enough for him to make it a crucial part of his world-picture, so real that he used much the same methods to study and describe it as he had used in analyzing and classifying minerals and nerves. This helped neither probability nor readability, yet the result is still one which makes it a great adventure to try to fathom what went on in his mind.

Count A. J. von Höpken, the head of the Swedish Government, one of his shrewdest friends, said of Swedenborg's other-worldly books: "Few people have judiciously read his works, which everywhere sparkle with genius; if I meet with anything unusual or extraordinary and which might indicate a disordered understanding, I do not judge of it. We read Plato with admiration; but there is nothing to be read in his works which, if related by another person, might not be deemed extravagant, inconceivable and absurd." [8]

CHAPTER TWO

Stockholm Shocked

WAS Swedenborg a northern Plato?

Up to about 1760, when he was seventy-two years old, the great majority of his fellow-countrymen would certainly never have thought of him in any such terms. They knew him chiefly as a great authority on metals and mines. Sweden's vital mining industry had been much benefited by his being a member of the Board of Mines. As a member of the Parliament, or Diet, he had submitted some of the most useful memorials on such nonmystical subjects as liquor control, rolling mills for domestic pig iron, and, from time to time, strenuous pleas for a sound national currency. Indeed, in this very year 1760, he submitted a long memorial on finance which was so clear and pertinent that he was soon asked to be a member of a Secret Commission on Exchange.

Yet, early in 1760, shocking rumors were heard in Stockholm about Emanuel Swedenborg.

It is not generally recognized, but the intellect can be as voluptuously scandalized as Mrs. Grundy, depending on the standing of intellect at that period of time. In the eighteenth century its standing was probably the highest it has ever been, hence the town was really upset.

The town—this meant as usual a fraction of its educated elite—was, like the rest of Europe at this time, more French than anything else. To be French meant, briefly, that one was saved from superstition by faith in Monsieur de Voltaire. By his writings about the new scientific discoveries, especially those of Sir Isaac Newton, he had demonstrated with the sure weapon of mathematics that the universe was indeed, as had been suspected, a mechanical affair. Science could and did fully interpret nature. What was natural was scientific and vice versa. What was "supernatural" did not exist except in the imagination of the multitudinous illiterate who were used by a power-loving Church for its own dark ends.

Swedenborg was known to be as keenly active mentally as he had ever been, so sensible people found it hard to believe the absurd gossip.

Baron Tilas, a mineralogist of note and Swedenborg's successor on the Board of Mines, said just that: "Nor would I have lent credence to all this stuff, if I hadn't heard it from Count Tessin's own mouth," he wrote to a mineralogist friend.[1]

And Count Tessin had it from the man himself. Baron Tilas assured his friend that the town was in a state bordering on alarm about it, partly because of the suddenness of the disclosure. "Not a breath was heard, then it spread surprisingly fast. It is Swedenborg, who has intercourse with the dead whenever he chooses, and who can inquire after his former departed friends when it pleases him, whether they are in heaven or in hell or hover about in a third, nondescript place."

Count Tessin, Tilas wrote, had been told of a mutual departed friend, who was taking a walk in his other-world garden when Swedenborg came to ask him for some architectural drawing. Much more sensational news was that the late Swedish Queen had remarried in the world beyond and was said to be happy.

"I am all in a flutter," Baron Tilas continued, "before having a talk with him and learning whom my late wife has married. I should hate it if she has become a sultaness!"

But the oddest thing about Swedenborg was "that all this he reports without a screw seeming to be loose in the clock-work in other respects."

Tilas could hardly wait to peer into the clock-work for himself, and he assured his friend that he wished they might go together, only in that case Tilas would have to try to keep the latter from laughing.

Within a week the Baron's curiosity had been to a certain extent satisfied; he had visited Swedenborg and frankly asked him about the current rumors. Tilas wrote to his friend about it with a slightly modified laugh. "Many consider him crazy, but I desire to scan the matter more thoroughly before expressing myself upon it."

Other people of consequence were also visiting Swedenborg; their carriages waited for hours outside his house while the owners talked, listened, and considered.[2] Now it became known that

Swedenborg for many years had been publishing strange theological works abroad and anonymously. Only a few friends at home
got copies. Baron Tilas could not remember all the names, but they
dealt with Heaven and Hell and the New Jerusalem and one was
about the Last Judgment.

"Just hear this surprising news, the Last Judgment has already
taken place in 1757, and he talks about it as familiarly as if he had
been the Secretary there and taken down the minutes. Since that
time the Judgment Board is constantly in session and parties are
judged as soon as they arrive."

Startling and amusing as these crotchets were in a great man,
Tilas begged his friend not to let the matter become generally
known, although he admitted that thousands now knew about it
in Stockholm. Son of the Voltairean century as the Baron was,
perhaps he thought it better, as he said, "to move carefully in the
matter," when dealing with the Last Judgment.

Perhaps also he had been affected by this private talk with the
dignified old man, straight and spare, with the direct gaze and the
"smiling blue eyes," so that he wanted to shield him against his
own indiscretions, his laying bare so unreservedly of thoughts
which could earn him only a pitying verdict in the world.

Even Count Tessin had succumbed to Swedenborg's charm. He
went to see him, as he said himself, "from mere curiosity for making the acquaintance of a singular man," but though he came away
grateful that his own faith and reason were still sound, he admitted
that he found the man "by no means obstinate, too sensitive or self-
sufficient, but friendly, courteous and open-hearted; he has good
judgment both about the times and the people, explains everything
for the best, and seems to be a philanthropist who spends his life
in contentment, delighting himself in his fantasies for which perhaps no medicine can be given." [3]

These fantasies, especially the one regarding new, congenial
mates in the other world, kept spreading and Stockholmers asked
themselves in much perplexity how they were to interpret this man
whom they had known as a scientist and a practical man.

Perhaps it was all symbolical and poetic. There was a well-
vouched-for story of a little girl who came along to see Swedenborg
with her parents and who no doubt appalled them by a question

she put to "Uncle" Swedenborg. (This is still the delightful way in which nice little Swedish children address a man, as they adopt a woman by calling her "aunt.")

Her question, of a certainty reflecting overheard talk at home, was that she did wish he would show her a "spirit or an angel."

He laughed and said he would. Taking her into a garden pavilion, he pulled a curtain away from a long mirror.

"There!" he said, "you see an angel!"

Count A. J. von Höpken had known Swedenborg for forty years, but not as these casual and curious acquaintances. Höpken, as has been mentioned, held a position in the Swedish Government which would correspond to that of Prime Minister today. He was a subtle and distinguished man, and would have been "modern" in any age. He was characterized later by a Swedish historian as "learned, admirable in writing and speaking, cautious, farseeing, a skeptic in thought and character . . ." [4]

In 1772, soon after Swedenborg's death at eighty-four, Höpken received a letter from a Danish general, asking him for an account of Swedenborg's system as well as of the character of the man. The Count was privately, as he said, much amused and surprised and nonplussed that "the honest old gentleman Swedenborg has spoken so favorably about me in various places that he has even made me his apostle after his death," [5] but he answered the general in a serious, if characteristically cautious, vein.

First he begged him to believe that although his office had often made it his duty to give his opinion and counsel in delicate and difficult matters, he did not recollect that anything so delicate had ever before been submitted to his judgment as that which was here proposed to him.

All he could say was that he had for two-and-forty years known the late Assessor Swedenborg and had for some time daily frequented his company. He assured the General that much as his life had brought him into contact with all types of characters he did not recollect having known any man like Swedenborg.

He was "always contented, never fretful nor morose. . . . He was a true philosopher and lived like one; he labored diligently and lived frugally without sordidness; he travelled continually and his travels cost him no more than if he had lived at home. He was gifted with a most happy genius and a fitness for every science, which made him shine in all those he embraced. He was, without contradiction, the most learned man in my country."

Höpken then praised Swedenborg as a Latin, Greek, and Hebrew scholar, as a mathematician, as a mechanical genius able to solve practical problems such as transporting large ships over rocks, as a mineralogist, and as a physiologist whose discoveries in anatomy had been singular.

"I imagine this science and his meditations on the effects of the soul upon our curiously constructed body did by degrees lead him from the material to the spiritual. He possessed a sound judgment upon all occasions; he saw everything clearly and expressed himself well on every subject. The most solid memorials on finance, and the best penned, at the Diet of 1761, were presented by him. In one of these he refuted a large work in quarto on the same subject, quoted all the corresponding passages of it, and all this in less than one sheet."

But what about the spiritual matters, which were the only ones that fervently interested the Danish general?

Here the Count shied away. He said he had no criterion for distinguishing the genuine from the false in such matters. He did admit that he had once taken Swedenborg rather seriously to task for mixing into his beautiful writings those accounts of things he professed to have heard and seen in the spiritual world concerning the states of men after death, "of which ignorance makes a jest and derision."

But Swedenborg had answered him "that he was too old to sport with spiritual things, and too much concerned for his eternal happiness to yield to such foolish notions, assuring me on his hopes of salvation that imagination produced in him none of his revelations, which were true, and from what he had heard and seen." [6]

Count Höpken, while still deploring such excursions from common sense, wrote later somewhat wistfully to a friend about how he had advised the King that if a Swedish colony were really to be founded in the New World of America, His Majesty could do no better than to establish Swedenborg's form of religion in it, because:

"It properly places the worship of God in useful functions, and it causes least fear of death, as this religion regards death as merely a transition from one state to another, from a worse to a better situation; nay, upon his principles, I look upon death as being of hardly greater moment than drinking a glass of water." [7]

The news of Swedenborg's clairvoyance, or "dabbling in the occult" as it might now be called, which had so shocked Baron Tilas and others, was no news, however, to the inner court circle to which Count Höpken belonged. Without trying to explain it, he was himself later to bear witness to the fact that Swedenborg had, in some strange way, carried out a commission which the Queen jestingly had given him.

She was the intrepidly intellectual sister of Frederick the Great of Prussia. At a court reception she had asked Swedenborg to look up her brother, the Prince Royal of Prussia, in the other world and remember her to him. Then she forgot about it, but soon afterward Swedenborg again appeared and, Höpken declared, "not only greeted her from her brother but also gave her his apologies for not having answered her last letter; he wished to do so now through Swedenborg, which he accordingly did. The Queen was greatly overcome, and said 'No one except God knows this secret.' "

Then there was the story of how Swedenborg had helped out the widow of the Dutch ambassador by finding out from the late diplomat where he had put a receipt for money which the widow would otherwise have been nearly ruined in having to pay again.

Or how he had seen and described a big fire in Stockholm while he was in Gothenburg and could not even have known that there was a fire. Many witnesses attested all these and similar stories, and many others scoffed at them and presented "natural" explanations.[8]

Whether such apparent wonders were believed or not did not much interest Swedenborg himself. While always courteous to candidates for amazement, he usually put them off. He was not including a belief in miracles as one of the pieces necessary in the right kind of world-picture. Nor did he try to proselytize. In fact, when a friend asked him how many he had succeeded in persuading of the truth of his doctrines, he said, after reflection that he thought he had about fifty in this world and about the same number in the other.[9]

Curious evidence, this, not only of spiritual humility but of a kind of essential sanity. The victim of the Messianic delusion never hesitates to claim the whole of the other world; he considers himself the custodian of the whole truth, even if stiff-necked people will not bow to him in this world.

Of course Swedenborg believed that the picture he had fitted together was the right one, but not because he personally would thereby be aggrandized.

With all his stubborn energy he had searched through many sciences, countries, dreams, and visions, caring only for an account of human existence—past, present, and future—which not only would fit his personal religious experience but would have the system and the clarity of science.

This was partly a need of his nature. And partly it was because he was born into one of the most fantastic corners of medieval irrationality that had survived in eighteenth-century Sweden—his father's house.

CHAPTER THREE

Parent Extraordinary

IF ever a man rejoiced in himself and in all his works, that man was Swedenborg's father, Jesper Swedberg. (The family name was ennobled into Swedenborg later on.) Few, sparse, and dry are the direct autobiographical details left by his son Emanuel, and this may have been due to a revulsion from the high fermentation of his father's vanity. Much else in Emanuel's life undoubtedly was a reaction from his father, hence a long look has to be taken at this clergyman, especially at his piety. His life reminds one of "the enormous difference between piety and goodness" [1] noted by Pascal, and of a story told of Swedenborg in which he is reported to have said that very few clergymen could be saved.[2]

To make sure he wouldn't be forgotten, Jesper Swedberg presented each of his children with his "Life," six copies written out by himself, 1,012 pages, folio size.[3] He dedicated it to his "children and posterity for needed instruction in how to pass well through this world." The library at Upsala University was also to have a copy so that the "less envious" might profit by it.

Why did he write his autobiography? Not, as the envious would say, to praise himself, but only because "no one knows me better than I do myself, especially since, by the Grace of God, I am very careful to see that self-love neither blinds nor seduces me." His descendants would thus have a good example to follow, he told them, since he could prove to them how wonderfully God had dealt with him.

God, so the bargain would seem to run, was to prosper Jesper Swedberg in every worldly way, and Jesper Swedberg was to give God the credit and to preach against worldly things.

So, at any rate, it worked out from the beginning with only stimulating opposition from the Devil. At seven Jesper was saved from drowning in a millrace. "And if I'm not mistaken I think Satan meant to drown me as he meant to drown Moses in his tender years or to kill me as he tried to kill Christ through Herod's cruel

and inhuman slaughter of the infants of Bethlehem. Probably he
didn't like it that even in my childhood I was fond of reading the
Bible aloud to the people who came to pick hops and so on. My
greatest joy was to preach to them. I sat up high, but fell down so
that I was lame for some time; that too was his doing."

Jesper was destined to study theology. There is genuine feeling
in his account of his early sufferings with drunken and stupid
teachers and those who believed in hammering in learning "per
posteriora," but once he was grown and his talent for dramatic
preaching could be unfolded, his troubles were over.

Brightly shallow and in constant motion, he pushed quickly
ahead. In 1683, at thirty, he had already been named chaplain to
the Royal Life Guards in Stockholm, and he had secured a wealthy
wife from a distinguished family. She was Sara Behm, daughter
of an official of the Board of Mines, and said to be descended
through her mother from Gustavus Vasa.[4]

Jesper had meant to marry another girl, but "God who takes a
wonderful part in the deals of matrimony" sent a snowstorm. This
caused Jesper's brother to lose his way and arrive accidentally at a
manor where Jesper had just come as tutor. Half the night they
talked, and the result was that Jesper decided to try to marry a
sister of the girl his brother was going to marry.

"With this dear wife of mine God sent me great riches," but he
did not intend to be henpecked. From the start he explained to
Sara that just as he would not interfere in her housekeeping but
would give her the money she required for it the moment she asked
for it, and even a little more, so she was not to interfere in his work.
Pray for him, yes, but no more.

Secondly, he explained, "If I am sitting in good company with
worthy men taking my ease and pleasure without too much drinking, without shocking or angering anybody, that she will then not
grudge me this cheerful ease and amusement after my hard work
and much worry and in no way either urge me to leave it or cause
me to be called."

If one looks at Sara's picture it hardly seems to have been a necessary warning to her, especially as he praises her for her gentle
sweetness. But there is more than sweetness in her face. It has an
inward look, something subtle in reserve. Her son Emanuel was to

resemble her. This is evident in the clear-cut features, and in a lightly hovering expression about the mouth, the lips of which are sensitive and sweetly curved but seem to hint that the owner could be ironic.

Many years later Swedenborg was to write in one of his anatomical treatises that he considered the mouth to be the one feature which man himself creates, since all the muscles of the face are connected with it or lead to it and every expression of the face thus helps to mold this feature, itself so mobile and responsive.[5]

Looking at his father's portrait, one is certain that if there was irony in his wife's smile it was lost on Jesper Swedberg. Low forehead, bulging nose, thick lips that seem to stick out in self-satisfaction, heavy black brows under which alert eyes stare forever outward. In one picture a big broad hand reposes on the perceptible mound of his black-gowned stomach, but it is a hand with long, slender, almost backward-curving fingers. Jesper Swedberg really loved music.

Far from poor himself and now "by God's aid" enriched with his wife's money, he left her during her first pregnancy to spend a year abroad. It was in 1684. He made the obligatory visits to England, France, and Germany. In Westminster Abbey he was pleased to see the stone on which Jacob slept when he was flying from his brother Esau in Mesopotamia. But what most impressed and delighted him was the English sabbath. He tells with satisfaction of a nobleman (he did not like nobles) who got his valet to row him to church along the Thames one Sunday. They were both put in jail for sabbath-breaking.

But Jesper Swedberg didn't like "all the many sects and parties, I mean those that the so-called reformed church is divided into. Not speaking of the biggest party which is called *Thoris* and *Wigg,* of High church and Low church, of Quakers and Anabaptists, but only of the so-called English church."

Taking this posy of traveler's impressions with him from England, he went on to Paris, where all his worst suspicions were confirmed. He said that not King Solomon himself had seen or heard of more worldly vanities than were here displayed. He noted the many foreigners who were there, not to consult the good libraries or the learned men, but to learn to dance or fence and speak the

2. SARA BEHM, 1666–1696

Wife of Jesper Swedberg and the mother of Emanuel Swedenborg. (*Courtesy, Nordiska museet.*)

1. BISHOP JESPER SWEDBERG, 1653–1735

The father of Emanuel Swedenborg. Painted in 1707, by an unknown artist. In Gripsholm Castle. (*Courtesy, Svenska porträttarkivet.*)

language. The last accomplishment he was very dubious of—"God grant it be not at the cost of their timely and eternal welfare."

A speaking example of this he found when he arrived in Strasbourg. The city had just been won without a blow by the French. How? Because the commandant, a Strasbourger, had learned French in his youth in Paris, and when the general of the besieging troops spoke to him in this language, offering him a large bribe to sell out, his soldiers didn't understand what was going on and the city was lost.

Not always edified by the behavior of German Lutherans on the sabbath, "God help us, what didn't I see there and they living in the midst of Catholics," he was enthusiastic about the results of drilling people in the catechism, and he came back to Sweden, and to Albrecht, his first child, full of the returned traveler's desire to improve his own country.

His zeal was tempered by prudence, however. Very early in his career, he says himself, "I laid down two chief rules for myself. Firstly, never to meddle in affairs that had nothing to do with my office, especially not with political or worldly affairs. Secondly, never to speak ill of anyone were he my greatest enemy and persecutor."

Not only in the late seventeenth century would those have been excellent rules for a preacher to follow who desired to leave apostolic obscurity, but Jesper Swedberg had positive ability as well.

This ability was largely dramatic. In those times sermons could stretch to three or four hours of tedious doctrinal disquisitions. Not so Jesper Swedberg's. He could, and did, do that as well, so as to show off his vast (often inaccurate) learning, as he does with battalions of footnotes in his autobiography; but even in the book this man who had "the word" in his power can flash out, and in the pulpit he must have given a stirring performance, revivalist style.

His use of simple, strong-smelling words and pungent, homely similes was not original with him, Luther had authorized that, but in Jesper Swedberg there was a native vein of poetry. He wrote hymns that sometimes had a clear folk-song quality. Above all, he could tell a story.

At the beginning of his Stockholm career, when he had King Charles XI in the church one day, he launched into a vivid poetic account of how he had been walking in a green meadow after his hard work and how he had met two troops of children. One lot was weeping and wailing. Why? No one had taught them how to get to heaven. The other troop was joyful, they had been rightly taught. But why were the first lot in such a bad state?

He said he went to their schoolrooms to find out, and here he became shrewdly realistic. In a grammar school he found the pupils in a state of indiscipline, in spite of plentiful blows from a drunken schoolmaster, when they couldn't untangle the complicated doctrinal puzzles they were given. "Why are you drunk so early in the morning?" "Oh, I am very poor," he said, "at home I have a sick wife and a house full of children with neither bite nor sup. It muddles my head and when I leave the house I'm only too glad to be asked to have a glass of brandy. My salary is small and I hardly get half of it."

Previously, Jesper Swedberg said, he had visited a couple of private schoolrooms in noble houses. They knew their catechism all right, but only by heart, not in their hearts. Grand French finery hung all around, which was all they cared about—that and the French frivolity which was taught them by a French governess. What they saw and heard at table from their elders was such that he wished himself far from there. They even heard reflections on the King—no wonder their souls were lacking in spiritual nourishment.

The picture he gave of a lapdog-kissing, arrogant nobility was full of dramatic detail, it could have gone into any proletarian description of the wicked capitalist, but that was not his animus. The rich children, like the poor, were being deprived of true religion, something which he vaguely summarized as the Fear of God.

Undoubtedly sincere in his charges, Jesper Swedberg was not so foolhardy in attacking the nobles as he might seem, because King Charles XI, clearing the ground for absolute monarchy, was busily shearing them of both property and power. Preferment for the clergy came from the King, and Charles XI was quick to be both entertained and pleased by Swedberg and to see his usefulness. The King was one of those stern and pious warriors produced by Sweden. He took being the Lord's anointed seriously, believing that this entailed more responsibilities than privileges. Jesper Swedberg's childhood acquaintance with poor, drunken teachers had given him sincerity about education, a subject about which the King was no less concerned than about procuring able clerical aid in the reduction of the nobles. It was not long before the chaplain of the King's guards was promoted to court chaplain, then to a rural parsonage, and almost immediately afterwards to be third professor of theology at Upsala University. Quickly, in the twinkling of a royal eye, he was made rector, then first professor of theology and dean of the university. Eventually he was to become Bishop. (In 1702, Charles XII made him Bishop of Skara.)

Never, Swedberg was fond of saying, did he acquire any of his offices through "hopping and shopping." Not a penny did he ever pay. Thus he enlarged on the blessed feeling it was to have such calls come to one through Divine favor only.

King Charles XI made no mistake in his rapid promotion of the miner's son. Almost part of Swedberg's theology was his belief in absolute monarchy. "The King should be King and the subject should be subject." What if the King were bad? That was God's punishment on the subjects for their bad behavior, and to be borne patiently.

His clerical brethren against whom he never ceased fulminating for their "jealousy and backbiting" were to say later that of course Swedberg thought every kind of parliamentary system a nuisance, placing so many obstacles between himself and royalty, whom he was expert in milking for financial favors.

Jesper Swedberg deplored such people at great length. If there was one thing he knew about himself, he very often said, besides the fact that he had no self-love, it was that he was utterly without the money-grubbing instinct. There was no avarice in his soul. He was scornful of the clergy for taking tithes or confession fees, he never hounded his parishioners for them. "I never kept accountbooks. The Bible was, is and will be all the book I want." Of course, he added, if people brought him presents, that was another matter.

Nor did he despise the income from the church properties to which he was entitled, and when, after inevitably becoming a bishop, he gave his son Jesper a parish (that Jesper who had been "rather wild" before he was tamed in America and the British navy), Jesper had to pay him the customary yearly tribute, only being let off during the first couple of years.

Swedberg gained great popularity through not ferreting out all the pennies of the poor, as the majority of the clergy had to. Very few of them had inherited copper mines or had married wealth. Nor did they have his knack of loosening the royal purse strings, whether it was to reimburse him for "giving" the catechism to the royal guards, or to rebuild his house in a bigger and finer style each of three times when his old enemy the Devil caused it to be burnt.

The "incredible sums" which he says he used for the publication of his many devotional books were of course spent only for the glory of God, though Jesper signed them, and he never forgets to remind the reader of the thirty thousand riksdaler he lost on his hymnbook, the one which he says his jealous colleagues prevented from being adopted. (He was able to unload some copies on the Swedish congregations in America, and they liked it.) At the same time he notes with satisfaction that he never really lost any money; somehow it all came back to him. The manner is not specified, but at the end of his autobiography he says he is just wealthy as he ever was. Inconsistency in his statements never worried him; knowing the Bible literally by heart, he had a barrage of scripture to support his most contradictory positions.

It is not surprising that this man, so sublimely self-occupied and self-deceived, should scarcely have mentioned his children in this book that was written for his children. Emanuel hardly figures in it, except as the author of some Latin verses which his father requested him to write on the occasion when a copper plate engraved with the Bishop's picture was "miraculously" preserved in a fire.

But we know that in 1688, while Swedberg was still in Stockholm, his wife Sara gave birth to Emanuel, and that at the age of about two years he was moved to Upsala with the family.

The dean of the University of Upsala (and chief professor of theology) had his dwelling in the town which was dominated by the cathedral in more senses than one. Its Gothic towers rose not only over the medieval castle but over the town of about five thousand inhabitants and above the whole of the undulating countryside. The university had been its child in Roman Catholic times. It was still its child in Protestant times, soon to be restive and wanting to lead a life of its own, but obliged as yet to put theology first.

Protestant intellect had given itself to shaping codes of doctrine and dogma as hair-splittingly futile as any of the medieval ones. Protestant emotion out of which the whole Reformation had sprung—aided by the fervent heart of Luther—opposed this desiccating process, and finally rebelled in the so-called "pietist" movement, which was sweeping Germany about the time that Jesper Swedberg was making his grand tour.[6]

Completely unintellectual, it suited him to absorb the idea that "faith," which had come to mean tediously involved doctrine, was not nearly so important as a direct relationship with God expressed in "works." This relationship was nobly interpreted by believers with a touch of the mystic in them as the carrying into life of Christian principles no matter what worldly objections might be, but their hordes of lesser followers turned the movement into one of such "pietism" as glazed inactivity on the sabbath, disapproval of dancing and cards, and scorn of finery. For them this was the positive side of religion, and far less dangerous and difficult than Christian ethics.

The students at Upsala feared the new Dean might be a "pietist" and that "no student might wear wig or sword." But he went easy at first. "Wear wigs," he said, "especially if you need them." That made the boys laugh; they soon decided the hearty, pungent, booming Dean was a good fellow, and they gave him the deference of the young which makes a university such a cozy hothouse for the egoist with a flair for popularity.

He did indeed like to use pietist language against what was "worldly," against "sin," which showed itself in two things, sabbath-breaking and frivolous modern apparel, especially the wearing of wigs. The fashionable full-bottom wig had spread from France to Sweden, and literally nothing so appalled Swedberg as this. Throughout his whole book he comes back again and again to the virtue there is in wearing one's own "God-given" hair, and the dreadful consequences of the other custom. "My whole body trembles," he said, "when I am consecrating ministers and have to lay my hands on hair which is, perhaps, whore-hair."

He mentions that one theological student who wore such a wig as well as lace collar and cuffs was later mixed up in a murder.

Then as now the extravagance of women's fashions was a good target. Even Swedberg's first wife, Sara Behm, felt she had to be in the fashion. As her husband puts it, "Since every woman in those days wore a sinful and troublesome fontange or top-knot, she was obliged to do as others did and wear it, but, hearing that a cow in the island of Gothland had with great labor and pitiful bellowing brought forth a calf with a top-knot, she took her own and her girls' fontanges and threw them all into the fire."

Worse than these sins which reacted only on the individual (or innocent cows) was sabbath-breaking, of which a terrible instance threatened when the Court proposed a masquerade on a Sunday. From the pulpit Swedberg assured them that such doings were punished by the Lord with pestilence and war, so that the masquerade was canceled. But there was enough sabbath-breaking to account for the pestilence and war which soon did harass the country. So he notes, with the deep and melancholy satisfaction of the righteous.

Jesper Swedberg's God, who ought really to have been called The-Fear-of-God, was an Absolute Monarch, fond of endless adulation, before whom the worshiper groveled, and whom by egregious flattery he hoped to move to the granting of favors. Angels, devils, ghosts, demons, weird omens, and portents were all part of His supernatural cast with which to awe rebellious mankind. Freaks of nature, such as the Gotland calf wearing the fontange, showed His indifference to His own laws of nature. Enthroned above them He seemed indeed to be Caprice Incarnate, rather than the embodiment of eternal law.

Although there is so little information on Emanuel's childhood, there is a scrap which seems to show that, curiously enough, he passed unaffected by this creation of egoism and primitive fancies.

A tradition says that Emanuel (as is reported of other "psychic" subjects) had unseen playmates in his childhood. He would speak of things far beyond his years, and when his parents asked him where he heard them he said that it was from the boys with whom he played in the garden house. As they knew he was alone there, they opted for the marvelous and said that angels spoke through his mouth.[7]

When he was old Swedenborg himself reported to an inquiring Englishman this saying of his parents. The words attributed to the child were marvelous enough, considering his youth. He said that from his sixth to his twelfth year he liked to discuss faith with clergymen, and that he said the life of faith was love and this life-giving love was the love of one's neighbor; furthermore that God gave the gift of faith to everyone, but only those could receive it who had that love. "I knew of no other faith beyond this that God created nature, maintains it, gives reason and character to men and whatever follows from that. The learned belief which is that God credits his son's 'merits' to whom He wants to when He wants to, even to those who have neither repented nor improved, I knew nothing of then, and if I had, it would then as now have been far beyond my understanding." [8]

He seems to have had a happy childhood, brothers and sisters to play with by the shining Fyris River that wound through the town. Upsala was a vivid place to grow up in. It mounted to the majestic, grim, rose-red brick of the old castle on a steep escarpment, and to the cathedral in which the soaring pillars were like many tall slender gray beeches grown together and vaulting out in the high dusk above. Besides the lacquer-red wooden houses of ordinary citizens there were several fine, well-proportioned buildings of a warm yellow and there were wide green spaces. Upsala was not a small town; it had architecture, it had history, going back to pagan times. Emanuel came out of the heart of Sweden.

Years afterwards he wrote about the unconscious innocence of childhood, with an accent of autobiography.

"Children do not take credit for anything themselves, all that they get they thank their parents for; they are delighted with the few trifling things that are given to them; they have no care about food and clothing and none about the future; they do not look to the world and covet many things from it; they love their parents and nurses and the little comrades with whom they play. They are attentive and they obey. Being in this state, they accept whatever life offers and hence, without knowing why, their manners are good and they learn to talk." [9]

One can almost see the polite, quiet little Swedish child, solemnly blue-eyed. It must be remembered that Swedenborg had no children of his own, except the child he had once been.

Elsewhere he describes children playing ball and other mildly competitive games under the eyes of their parents and tutors. He observes how "the least inanimate object seems to them alive, when they're at their little pastimes." Few things so shocked him as when once in London he saw parents egging on their children to fight, for money.

When Emanuel was eight years of age, his mother died. She was in her thirtieth year. She had borne nine children, five boys and four girls. Albrecht, her first-born, died ten days after her. Eliezer died later.

Her husband paid tribute to her sweetness, gentleness, and kindness, and remarried within a year.

God again, Swedberg says, provided him with the right kind of wife, by letting him be the means of bringing a young rake to a deathbed conversion, and thus drawing his attention to the young man's wealthy aunt.

Their marriage was arranged before he had had a chance to meet her, but he had managed to find out that she was "godfearing, pious, generous to the poor, wealthy, handsome, a clever housekeeper, and had no children."

Only he can tell what follows: "Two days before the wedding I arrived in Stockholm where she also had arrived two days previously. I was brought into a room where she was sitting alone, but I didn't know it was she, I couldn't imagine it as nobody had told me. I sit down next to her. We talk for a long while about this and that like the strangers we were. Until at last she asks: 'What does the Professor think of our bargain?' I answer, 'What kind of bargain?'—'The one you wrote to me about.' 'What did I write to you about? I don't know of anything.'—'Aren't we to be bride and groom tomorrow?'—'Is that who you are!' I said. And so we confirmed our friendship with handshakes and loving embraces and such like, with mutual pleasure and contentment."

Sara Bergia was her name, and she had already been twice married. "She was barren," Swedberg records, "and now all of a sudden she had seven children."

To them she was a good mother, and her favorite was Emanuel. In his notebook of "other-world" experiences, he startles one by mentioning "my mothers," with equal affection.

It was an age of dutiful children and strong family bonds. Kinship implied much. Love, or at least the expression of it, was obligatory. A kinship term was hardly ever used without the word "dear" (käre) preceding it, often abbreviated to the first letter. You wrote about d:father, d:mother, d:aunt, unless you were actually going to law with your aunt. D:brother and d:sister extended to in-laws.

Set tributes to d:parents were the thing, and Emanuel made several of them to his d:father.

Probably while he was young he shared many people's belief that his father was the bluff, kind, modest man he obviously felt himself to be, and indeed said that he was. Nor can it be denied that Jesper Swedberg along with feathering his own nest was often willing to help others, especially that extension of himself, his family. He took personal trouble in a good cause, preferably in public, and he had sound, commonsense ideas on educational methods. He advocated better pay and a higher status for teachers. He helped to prepare a better translation of the Bible. It horrified him to have Swedish interlarded with French words. His children must often have heard him speak the ringing words he wrote: "I'll care for our noble mother-tongue while I eat Swedish bread and drink Swedish beer."

His delivery of the obvious was always in the stateliest manner, unhampered by any hesitancy of self-criticism.

Emanuel could hardly at this time have begun his reflections on the tawdriness of good works undertaken mainly for self-glorification, nor on the grim discord which is so apt to exist between the inner and the outer man. But in later life while reading his father's autobiography he cannot have helped noticing many things, illuminated by recollection.

He may have remembered the banquet to the paupers of Upsala

which his father describes twice to make sure it will be clear how much he cares for the poor and how little for the "worldly." When his fine new stone house had been built for him, he gave a banquet for the paupers and hospital patients of the town. Swedberg himself, his wife and children waited on them. Emanuel was ten years of age then. All that was lacking to inform the left hand thoroughly of what the right was doing was a radio commentator and a movie camera.

As a pendant to this story there is one of how a little blackmail was used on the King. When the young hero, Charles XII, was engaged in ruining the poor people of Sweden with his obstinate warfare, he ordered total mobilization, even of the servants of the clergy. Jesper Swedberg insisted to the King's face that he had to be allowed to keep his coachman. But Charles was flintily silent, whereupon the Bishop burst out:

"I've been reading the books of wise statesmen, O most gracious King, and I've found that among the devices for keeping subjects obedient is the one by which the Government takes care to have the clergy on its side. If the common people go mad, nobody except the parson can manage them. But if the parson is badly treated he'll tell everything he knows, even in the pulpit, which is not right. The farmer sits and listens, and he sighs, and so it goes whenever they meet. We hope with the help of God, that God will spare us riot and rebellion. But they have happened and they can happen again. That is why the Government has always thought it wise to keep the clergy in good humor."

To all of which Charles answered not one word.

Still more striking Emanuel must have found the discord between the chapters in which his father describes the excellence of his own disposition, and some of the examples he gives elsewhere of his behavior. The Bishop (as he now is) duly thanks God for his fine mind and beautiful character; how since his youth he had always sought good and hated evil; though to begin with he had some faults, yet he loved to be told of them; how he only hated quarrels and enmities; how he took special joy in forgiving his enemies and doing good to them. He admits to a quick temper, but stresses his gentle and forgiving heart. He was always sober. But always merry and bright. He loved work. Perfectly unhappy if he wasn't working.

That was true, he was in ceaseless activity. As to the forgiving and gentle heart, Emanuel must have thought it odd that in this book his father included the letter to Andreas Hesselius.

Andreas was his nephew by marriage. The Bishop was in charge of the Swedish congregations abroad, one of his most self-mentioned glories, and he had sent Andreas to take charge of a parish in America. Later he recalled him, without having any job for him at home. Andreas sent his uncle a letter in which can be traced a resentment of that, and some veiled reference to the fact that he had been done out of an inheritance. He also mentions that he is sorry not to be able to oblige his uncle in the matter of writing a new history of the American congregations in which the Bishop is to be eulogized.

It is not a very friendly letter. The man is evidently overcome by many troubles, but the retort, printed in full, is a scream of excommunication and anathema. So disproportionate is it that the reader is considerably puzzled, until he discovers that the Queen had enjoyed an account of America written by Hesselius, in which there was no mention of Bishop Swedberg.

"I never asked you for a eulogy," Swedberg declares. "In all my books I never praise myself, but other people have done it in abundance." Nor, he points out, had Hesselius brought him the customary present of furs from America. But the reference to the inheritance stung worst of all. The Bishop had published one of his favorite godly works with money left for that purpose by his second wife, Hesselius's aunt. Didn't she have the right to leave the money as she wished? "Who can justly object, save the unjust driven by the spirit of avarice whose tongue is a fire and a world of injustice and ignited by hell?"

There were thousands of words the reverse of gentle forgiveness.

Only a man like Swedberg who had never taken a real look at himself could have called attention to this. Nor could he have written of various other matters which illustrate his attitude toward physical cause and effect. Material for Emanuel, who was to be concerned about a universe of law.

The Bishop tells how he had been left a silver mug by a courtier whom he attended on his deathbed, but he didn't receive it. "The will was contested, for the silver mug was fine and important. The court preacher who buried him got the silver mug, but also rather a hard death in Bender, Turkey. A lynx ate him up. The silver mug couldn't help him."

Archbishop Swebelius had not, Swedberg thought, stood up for his hymnbook as he should. When the Cathedral of Upsala burned, the Archbishop's corpse, which lay in a copper coffin and was immured in a grave with a stone on top, was all incinerated. "But my hymnbooks which weren't even bound didn't get as much as scorched . . . thus does God preserve in the fire that which evil people do not like."

When Professor Jerfeld, "a bold and arrogant man," told King Charles XI right to his face that Swedberg's hymnbook might lead to much trouble, even to a war of religion, the angry King "pushed him against the wall, because of which he had to take to his bed, where he could think about his bold arrogance. He died in a few days." Swedberg's marginal comment on this is: "Prof. Jerfeld gets into hot water."

Less bloodthirsty miracles were also wrought for him, such as the stopping of rain or the coming of it, as needed. He says furthermore that he was able to heal people by the laying on of hands, to drive out demons, and he claims he even raised a girl from the dead. He expects that the envious and the worldly will jeer at him for this, and for recording it, but he will comfort himself by remembering that the Pharisees jeered at Christ himself, and that Christ had his evangelists put his miracles into writing.

Instead of being crucified, however, Jesper Swedberg was to be made a bishop. In 1703 he left Upsala to live at the episcopal residence of Brunsbo, near Skara.

One of his children he did not take with him; this was Emanuel. Since the age of eleven Emanuel had been entered in the university, and he was now to live with his brother-in-law, the college librarian, Eric Benzelius.

He was in his fourteenth year; his childhood was over. It is doubtful if he continued to see his father as the Bishop imagined himself. Swedenborg's lifelong passion for the genuine, both in religion and in science, has roots so deep that its origin must be traced to his most impressionable years. During them he had always before him a spectacular example of that "love of self" whose many subtle disguises he was to become expert in penetrating, even in himself.

But in 1703 the adolescent youth gave his entire love to a new world, one in which selflessness is quite often found—that of science.

CHAPTER FOUR

Undergraduate at Upsala

NO matter how antiscientific he might be, Bishop Swedberg was interested in one science, that of medicine. Not that he had ever been ailing, according to himself his health was as perfect as his character, but he noted several useful cures. One was for jaundice; it was "swine-dirt, with respects to you, mixed into a beer posset or any thin soup." In general, however, he recommended the sovereign remedy of "good old honest Rhenish wine, but it must be old and it must be honest."

Johannes Moraeus,[1] a bright nephew of his, was sent by the Bishop to study pharmaceutics in Stockholm. Moraeus, so contemporaries said of him, was "a man of equable temper, not much affected by life's ups and downs"; more important still, he was of the science party, enthusiastic about mineralogy as well as medicine. Through him the Bishop was, unwittingly, to open a door very early to the new world of facts for his little son. The youth was about to become the first apothecary of Stockholm when his uncle requested his presence in Upsala for the Swedberg children, holding out the inducement that he would also be able to study medicine at the university. It was the sort of charity plus economy that the Bishop loved, and it was a good thing for the eight-year-old Emanuel, whose mother had just died, that this cousin joined the household in 1696.[2]

Emanuel was fond of his tutor; he had a pet name for him, "Morfee." Many years later when the mature Swedenborg began making his strange journeys to that other world which he considered equally factual, he made brief and often scathing observations on what he now saw people to be like who had put up a fine front in this life. But Moraeus fared well. He must have been rather an ugly man, for Swedenborg said he did not at first recognize him, explaining that according to the laws of that other sphere the beauty of his tutor's inner goodness and truthfulness had now become exterior also.[3]

For several years he was under the influence of Moraeus, so that when in 1703 he went to live with his favorite sister Anna, who had just married the young college librarian Eric Benzelius, he entered no alien realm in the world of science which so absorbed his brother-in-law.

Benzelius, as Emanuel was to write to him from London, became his "father and better than a brother," and Benzelius, as a later dedication was to testify,[4] led him into the paths of science. The college librarian, reported from all sides to have been a brilliant man, a true teacher and a friend of the young, kept Emanuel in his house for seven years. No doubt his influence was crucial. In that "other-worldly" notebook of Swedenborg's, where he tells the truth about his feelings, he describes this brother-in-law as haughty of exterior but full of inner goodness. There is, at any rate, a painting of the young Benzelius which shows him as a quick, impatient man. He looks as if he were about to rush out of the frame, just pausing with his head cocked a bit on one side as if willing to listen to what is being said but with a faint superciliousness, or at least pessimism, as to what it is going to be. It is a "modern" face, not cast in any stiff, traditional mold.

He was to end as Archbishop, but he never lost his love for science. Undoubtedly he had had something to do with the victory which science had won in Upsala about four years before Emanuel was enrolled as a student. Eric Benzelius had been in England where the new ideas were already established, and when the fifteen-year-old boy entered the librarian's household he came into an atmosphere where all his bright curiosity had something to feed on, something moreover that was still upsetting, revolutionary, almost contraband—the right of science to go its own experimental way, irrespective of bishops.

It had not won the right without a fight—one that has to be refought every few hundred years. Sometimes it is called the fight for freedom of speech. In Upsala it lasted from 1663 till 1689, and then it was called, heavily, the fight between Aristotelianism and Cartesianism.[5] It provided the mental climate in which the whole of Emanuel's generation had to live and try to think.

Three hundred years or so later the battle was on again in the United States, but then it was called Fundamentalism vs. the Darwinian doctrine of evolution. Or the literal Biblical point of view vs. that of modern science, exactly as at Upsala.

Aristotle, however, was no hard-shell Baptist, and Aristotelianism in the seventeenth century had little to do with him. Christian theologians had taken what suited them of Aristotle's ideas (badly translated from the Arabic) and had used them in their sacred edifice. This, according to them, was a world in which the earth, the home of sin and imperfection, was the center of the universe. Above it was Heaven, salvation, and perfection. Aristotle, so the theologians said, had studied nature all that was needful; for science it was only necessary to study him. But where he was at variance with the Bible they declared him wrong. Spiritual force, or, as the Christians said, God, governed matter, hence miracles were possible. Before Bishop Swedberg left Upsala he said to the students, "All that you need for time and eternity you can learn in the Bible, let that be your handbook."

But when he said this in 1703 the Fundamentalism of the Faculty of Theology at Upsala had already been beaten.

It had been beaten, chiefly, by René Descartes,[6] the frail Frenchman whom the Swedish winter had killed while he was on a visit to Stockholm in 1650. Although he believed he had "discovered the foundations of a marvelous science" in a series of dreams the night of November 10, 1619, he was essentially a "mechanistic materialist," and mainly responsible for freeing the study of nature from the limits set to it by medieval religion. For him material phenomena were not, as Aristotle had held, the result of indwelling spiritual forces or forms, translated by Christian theologians as God. The universe of matter, including the human body, Descartes maintained, was a vast mechanism ruled by the laws of physics. He did make provision for God and for the soul, but as outside of space and time and thus not interfering with the physical laws.

On this theory science was at last free to demonstrate the laws of nature from natural phenomena.

Not, however, if the Faculty of Theology of Upsala could prevent it. They complained about modern science in 1663, and the fight between the theologians and the Faculty of Medicine continued on and off until 1686 when the theologians succeeded in persuading the clerical part of the Diet to present Charles XI with a written application for measures to be taken against Cartesianism at Upsala.

This contained as many teeth as a harrow, and it was intended to root out the spirit of free inquiry forever. The theological faculty was to be the censor of the whole university. Stipends to be given only to loyal Aristotelians. All "disputations" (theses) to be passed on by the theologians as well as all books from foreign countries. The professorship of physics, the hearth of Cartesianism, was to be taken away from the Faculty of Medicine and given to a good Aristotelian in the Faculty of Philosophy.

But Charles XI, conservative and orthodox though he was, did not yield to the black gowns. In 1689, after letting the controversy cool a bit, he decided that though the Christian faith was not to be criticized philosophy should be free "in practice and discussion." "Philosophy" was in effect everything that did not come in under religion. Science had won the right to live.

It had to live, however, in a garment of Latin, like all other learned subjects. This kept the populace reasonably safe from disturbing ideas and equipped scholars with what was still a world language. In Emanuel's childhood and youth he learned to write and to speak Latin. How natural it finally became to the students is best seen by the fact that when one of the professors at Upsala had braved royal wrath by asserting that popular consent was needed for new laws, the students "rushed out into the streets shouting 'Bene nobis, bene nobis, bene republicae litterariae!' " (Good for us, good for us, good for the republic of letters!) [7]

The students were young. Upsala seems to have registered them, at least, as early as eleven. They were then called "novitiates." At the age of thirteen Emanuel was called a Junior, but he was not listed as a Senior until he was twenty. Of college life as it is thought of today there was at least one feature that had some resemblance to American colleges—the clubs or societies known as the "nations." It was as if fraternities were not by invitation but as if the students from Iowa all belonged to an Iowa club with their own house, those from Virginia to theirs, and so on. Students from the different provinces of Sweden belonged to their "nation." It was organized with officers and laws, strict control was kept of the members, and probably it was a good thing for the students, far from home in those ox-cart days. In any case, the university, which had long fought their establishment, finally had to give up. There were twenty-two "nations" at Upsala in Emanuel's time. He was inscribed in the Vestmanland Dala Nation, of which his father was the Inspector or "faculty adviser." [8]

Official evidence shows that Emanuel, far from being a shrinking introvert, took such eager part in the "national" life that he once had to be slightly discouraged. The chief events in the life of these fraternities were not athletics but intellectual contests called "disputations," in Latin of course. Emanuel's nation had been choosing its subject for debate in exalted realms. In 1704 he had been opponent in a debate on "God's Providence," in 1706 in one on the duties of married people, and later in the same year in one on the duties of parents and children. This seems to have overstimulated him because on the same day he offered to preside at the next disputation which was to be on Natural Law. His offer was praised but rejected. "His Magnificence," that is, the university rector who was faculty adviser of the nation at the time, asked the members if a Junior had ever been known to preside. They answered that it had occurred once or twice although the Seniors, whose privilege it was, never liked it. Such a novelty "might conceivably lead to disorder." Where would the Juniors stop? "So nothing further was done." [9]

The occasional slight stutter which people later noted in the mature Swedenborg was evidently not much of a handicap to him, perhaps not even in existence then. Or perhaps this was the very time he cultivated a stutter, consciously or unconsciously, because with such a handicap he could not enter the church, the only obvious career for Bishop Swedberg's bright son, who even at the age of seven had been given a Hebrew grammar.[10] At any rate, though he studied most of the subjects offered by the university, he does not seem to have taken theology or law.

It is known from his letters that he studied with zest under the professors of mathematics, astronomy, and medicine. The curriculum was not as complicated as at a modern school.[11] A single folio sheet, printed in double columns, held not only the list of courses for the whole year, but each professor's description of what he proposed to do. A look at these sheets for the years during which

Emanuel was at the university shows that though science had intruded, the "ancients" still dominated. The professors of history were not even permitted to use any except classic textbooks. They got around that by compiling their own, with modern instances, and using those in the private tutorial classes which all professors were allowed to have and by which they added to their incomes.

Perhaps for this reason they slipped a little gentle advertising into the catalogue. The professor of philosophy promised "publicly to endeavor to insinuate into his auditors the Art of Logic by a succinct and easy method; and for the rest whatever of his private labor can be of service to those requiring the same, this he will willingly and sedulously contribute."

The professor of eloquence and politics intended to expound Pliny's Panegyric "with that faithfulness and care whereby as he judges both the cultivation of the Latin speech and the study of civil prudence can be most greatly advanced." If anyone desired private help he "would in no way fail them."

The professor of poetry was going to explain Virgil's Æneid. "In this he will first lead his auditors by the hand as it were to a knowledge of the nature and constitution of Epic poetry, and this publicly in the large Gustavian auditorium at one o'clock. Privately, from the more chaste writings of Ovid, Horace and other poets, he will demonstrate to students of poetry the art of making verses."

No scholar and gentleman was complete unless he could write Latin verses, and Emanuel rather fancied himself in this art. For years he now and then sought laurels as a Latin versifier. His efforts are said to be neither worse nor better than many similar ones of the time.

The professor of mathematics after he had "briefly covered music" intended "God willing" to set forth the doctrine of numbers, "that is to say arithmetic, both logistic and specious."

"With the good favor of God," the professor of astronomy was going to go into spherical trigonometry, and other fields, while, equally with divine assistance which but few of the professors dared to omit leaning on, a Greek philologist sensibly proposed to teach his subject "in the measure of his own ability, after the manner of his profession, and according to the grasp of his auditors."

The two professors of medicine, whatever they may have ventured in private, stuck to two guides in public. One discoursed on materia medica as explained in a book written A.D. 78 by the Greek Dioscorides; the other interpreted the theories of "the illustrious Wedelius," "embracing briefly and perspicuously almost the whole art of medicine."

This proponent of Wedelius usually limited himself to the above brief statement in the catalogue, but in 1706 he seems to have been stung by some criticism for lack of novelty, since now he explains that he intends "by the goodness of God to continue with the method commenced in former years, and that he may be of service both to newly come tyros and also to his former auditors, he will not introduce anything unusual and novel as is customarily done to beguile the weariness of delicate and fastidious men, but will set forth the same interpretation of the Theories of Wedelius which he has heretofore found to be fruitful for his auditors."

Wedelius or Wedel had taught medicine at Jena about 1680. He does not seem to have been a very remarkable man. A pupil of his, however, the medical mystic G. E. Stahl,[12] had made a stir in the world of learning. During Emanuel's time at Upsala, Stahl's metaphysics formed the topic of lectures "GOD willing" to be given by Professor Fabianus Törner.

Stahl had made valuable contributions to the sciences of chemistry and biology, but he had crashed into the current mechanistic conception of the human body by declaring that what held it together was the soul. If the soul didn't attend properly to the body, the body fell ill.

Törner was the professor selected for or by Emanuel to preside over his final university disputation or thesis or graduation exercises, so it is probable that he had listened to Törner on Stahl and on the Golden Verses of Pythagoras. Plato and Plotinus were known at Upsala. Along with dry Lutheran theology there was a current of mysticism in the community, but while the seeds may have been stored in the young man's mind they lay dormant there. He flung himself into the exact sciences, those to which everything human is alien, mathematics, physics, astronomy—the measurable, the law-submitting. That way lay freedom.

There is a painting of him,[13] probably from about his eighteenth year, the year 1706 when he had wanted to preside over the debate

EMANUEL SWEDENBORG AS A YOUNG MAN

The tradition that this is Swedenborg was investigated and believed to be correct by Alfred H. Stroh, the fine Swedenborgian scholar. It compares well with the bust made from the skeletal measurements, with the Bernigroth engraving (see page 70) and the Per Krafft (the elder) painting (see page 330). (*In the possession of Mrs. Signe Stroh, by whose courtesy it is here reproduced.*)

on Natural Law. It shows a handsome, half-smiling youth with definite regular features but still boyishly plump. In spite of his father's hell-fire clamor against wigs, he wears a powdered wig, the long, curling and flowing kind, a very becoming frame. One suspects lace cuffs on the long fitted coat, and a gleam of a rapier. Emanuel was rather tall, he could carry this male plumage well. The students insisted on it as their right.

It was a male period in Sweden's history.[14] By 1706 the incredible King Charles XII, then twenty-four years of age, had already been at war for several years and had won battles with the Danes, the Russians, the Saxons, and imposed a new king on the Poles. He had so impressed the world that Marlborough himself came to see Charles near Leipzig to find out if western Europe needed to fear him. Whether the Englishman understood the Swedish Puritan who at least believed that he fought only for his just rights is doubtful, but he was able to reassure England that Charles would need no bribes to attack Russia again—not that it would have been a safe occupation to offer bribes to Charles XII!

The Sweden of that day was twice its present size. The Baltic was its lake. But the population of the whole empire was only about three million, of which half inhabited Sweden proper. The bulk of the people were peasants, freeholders, and the educated classes fell into fairly rigid castes, Sweden being then as it still is the most formal of the Scandinavian nations. At that time industry was immature and commerce not for gentlemen. You belonged to the church or the army or the civil service. Under Charles XI the royal power had been made almost absolute so that those who wanted preferment had to look to the throne. Bishop Swedberg was expert in this but not so his son. What was Emanuel to be? Since the church was out of the question there was always that appendage of the church, the university. Perhaps he could be a teacher or an official of some sort. But first he had to finish his own education.

Education has to finish with a flourish, a rainbow loop of displayed knowledge, to be satisfactory to all parties, teacher and student, family and friends. An essay read aloud was the accepted form.

On the first of June, 1709, Emanuel Swedberg, aged twenty-one, read a very long paper in the large Gustavian auditorium, so there must have been quite a throng to hear him, as well as his two official opponents. The Bishop was also present, so that perhaps Emanuel was not wearing all the finery of laces and knots of ribbon with which academic disputants liked to bedeck themselves, but he was no doubt in his best.

Far from his fields of science, the essay dealt with selections from the sayings of a Syrian slave, Publilius Syrus, who had become a favorite Roman author of mimes or short plays. These sayings would now be called "wisecracks," and the Romans were as fond of them as the Americans. The Romans were not afraid of putting wisdom as well as cracks into them. Probably only a classic subject could have been chosen for the disputation, but Emanuel's choice of this one was neither perfunctory nor accidental. He says himself that he put a lot of work on it. This is evident, since each saying in Latin is accompanied by all the interpretations of it that he could hunt up from the learned of all ages, including Erasmus, Scaliger, and even "Rabbelais." Classic authors had also been combed for similar maxims.

There are about seven hundred sayings of Publilius extant, arranged alphabetically. Of these Emanuel chose the first group,[15] getting no further than through "D," but it contained such topics as Love, Money, Friendship, Avarice. Aspects of human mind and manners were dealt with in the brief black-and-white style dear to youth looking for short cuts to experience; in fact these were pellets of practical psychology, a subject which was always to interest both young Swedberg and the mature Swedenborg. Some of the sayings would reappear many years later in his writings, such as "He hurts the good who spares the evil," and the comments on love he was to expand at great length. In his book on love [16] he was to be very charitable toward hot-blooded young men troubled by early sexual development, and he may have thrown a backward glance to the handsome youth of twenty-one who was earnestly declaiming on June 1, 1709, that "The mind may choose to love but not to cease loving," and "Time not mind makes an end of love," and "Love cannot be wrenched away, it can slip away." As for the malady's origin, "tears of love rise in the eyes, they fall in the breast." The state itself had psychological disadvantages. "To love and to be wise is hardly granted to God." "An angry lover much deceives himself." "He who loves what he is suspicious of is a waking man asleep." "The wrath of a lover is placated by tears." "Love like a torch burns brighter by being agitated." To meet the contention that "An adulterer is a more passionate lover of his own wife" he quoted from Plutarch that concupiscence was not love. Nor would he let woman as such be slandered. To the thrust that "When woman is openly bad then she's good," he remarked that actors had to say outrageous and witty things to get applause, but that in general expressed hatred was the less dangerous. When Publilius said that "Woman either hates or loves, she knows no middle way," Emanuel, while admitting that woman was a creature of extremes, maintained that so were her critics—"not a few of them prove it by their own manners."

The heart of all friendship, he said, was in the saying "Friendship is either between equals or makes them so," otherwise adulation crept in. "Friendship is always helpful, love can be injurious." Or, as Seneca had put it, "He who is a friend loves; he who loves is not always a friend." He was sure that "To injure a friend even in jest is not permissible," in fact he consigned to the devil "those jocular wranglings, that eloquence vomiting baneful poison with which certain men of the utmost urbanity exercise their biting and pointed wit—and seek friendship." Seneca came to his aid again: "To be malignant is not funny."

The young intellectual agreed that "Tension breaks the bow, want of it the mind." He noted that "He who fights with a drunken man fights with one who is absent," and that "He sleeps well who does not know how ill he sleeps"—here Emanuel paused to praise sleep on grass in the forest. The grieving mind, he agreed, was not a credible witness on anything, nor was the desire-dominated mind, see Sallust. And "The memory of wrath is itself a brief moment of anger"; "A good mind is more seriously angry when outraged than a poor one," because, Emanuel said, it does not get angry except for just cause.

"Feigned goodness in speech is worse than malice"—this touched a string in him that vibrated throughout life at the idea of hypocrisy. "Let our lips be consonant with our minds," he exclaimed, in his own words, "not slyly speaking, insidious; let them be unrouged, unveiled, unplastered, not imitating goodness by words!"

"Cruelty is not placated by tears, it feeds on them." "When vices flourish, he sins who does right." "God hasn't much power over a happy man." "Frankness is foolish against impudence." "A fluent companion is as good as a carriage." Ovid too had said that speech shortens the road, and Emanuel would some day bring the dictum into his discussion of space-time relationships.

"Whatever the soul of man demands of itself, that it obtains." He called this the highest point reached by the Stoics.

Emanuel was sure he could get whatever he demanded from himself, but after the disputation he was going to demand something from his father, something the Bishop hated to part with— money. Especially money for the object that Emanuel had in view: a journey to England to study there, and to study science.

The disputation had been dedicated to his father, with a sort of sincere gratitude in advance. And among the maxims he chose to dwell on were a number describing the misery of avarice. "Money only irritates the miser, it doesn't content him." "What ill do you wish a miser but a long life?" "The miser does nothing right except when he dies." Whereas "He receives who gives to a worthy man," and "The benevolent discover chances to give," and "Help is doubly grateful if offered over and above"; Emanuel stressed that even the learned Erasmus had said benefits shouldn't have to be extorted.

And, in a maxim like a sigh, the boy quoted from Publilius that one should "Love a just parent; bear with an unjust."

The disputation came to an end as it had begun, with a little bow to death. Emanuel, aged twenty-one, expatiated on the words: "While life is welcome is the best time for death." He declaimed that "It were best to die before by way of hoary locks, wrinkles and languid powers the transit is made to cold and weary death."

In this year, 1709, it was a transit that a great many young Swedes had been privileged to make. Charles XII, careless of the Publilius maxim that "Twice conquers he who in victory conquers himself," didn't know when to stop, and his luck had turned. In fact it had turned over a year before, when he chose to go south in Russia. His armies had been warring for over eight years. The worst frost of generations came to aid his enemies. His soldiers still followed him, because, as his chaplain said, "He was the last King who didn't say to his soldiers, Go and fight, but who said, Come! and took the lead." [17]

They fell frozen off their horses, they were killed, they died of disease. Charles, illimitably stubborn, sent home for many more men, much more money. The country, never rich, was being drained and depopulated.

Good and sensible men, like Emanuel's brother-in-law Eric Benzelius, must have wondered how Sweden was to be built up again. What about the badly utilized mineral resources? What about building up young scientists? It was the progressive Benzelius who urged Emanuel to follow his bent and go to study science in England.

But the Bishop sat on the money-bags quite contentedly—not a bit so irritated by having money as a miser ought to be, according to the maxims of Publilius.

The "graduation exercises" at Upsala ended in June, 1709. On July 13, Emanuel felt sure he would be leaving for England in fourteen days. But on March 6, nine months later, he was still in his father's house at Brunsbo, writing to his "Highly honored D:Brother-in-Law," Eric Benzelius, "I have very little desire to remain longer in this place, since I am wasting my time here almost in vain. Yet I have so improved myself in music that I can act as organist, but in other branches of science there is very little to offer here, nor do those who are here hold it in any esteem, so that I might be encouraged thereby." [18]

He had watched the local bookbinder and bound three books in leather himself; he had written Latin verses and had them printed at the Skara Press; he had collected everything collectable, including an ancient coin for Benzelius and the bones of a whale for the museum at Upsala. And he had begun a lifetime of methodically making notes. Anything which brought in mathematics, such as astronomy, optics, physics, statics, was then called "mathesis," and mathesis was what he took notes on, turning his intense mind wholly on the exact sciences.

He wrote to Benzelius that since with d:brother's advice and approval he had chosen these studies, he meant to continue the collection of such items in the foreign countries he was going to visit, so as to come to know all about every branch of mathematics. He wanted his d:brother to send him a note of whatever he might come across in this connection. And he wished the great Swedish scientist and inventor, Christopher Polhem, would record his inventions; Emanuel would like them for his collection.

This letter had not long been sent before news came of the defeat of Charles XII at Poltava and his internment in Turkey. The situation of Sweden was bad. The Danes were attacking them. Emanuel's father could say, and likely he did say, that the seas were unsafe—the French and English being also at war—and the English journey would have to wait.

But need he wait in flat, dull, discouraging Brunsbo?

Benzelius took pity on him; it was most likely the brother-in-law who suggested that in lieu of foreign travel Emanuel should become the pupil of the great Polhem. At any rate, in the letter of March 6, 1710, Emanuel said, "It is now my chief desire to get a little information of my plan which is being discussed here, to be with Polhem. If so be it that my foreign journey must wait till the spring [of 1711] then I am quite content to be with him for some time, seeing that I can probably reap more advantage there in summer than in winter, and there everything will be so much more lively and pleasant, and my mind in better condition."

He had already met the salient Polhem and they had been attracted to one another. The older man noted that the youth was capable of helping him in his physics experiments, but the scientist refused a request from the Bishop that Emanuel should be apprenticed to him. Eric Benzelius had better luck when he approached Polhem on the same errand.

But—where was Emanuel?

CHAPTER FIVE

Discovery of England

HE was already in London.

Letters made slow progress and he had probably seized on a sudden chance to sail before Benzelius's letter arrived. Emanuel could scarcely have had a more adventurous journey. First the ship was caught in a fog and nearly grounded on a sand bank, then it was boarded by a French privateer, then it got a broadside from an English warship in pursuit of the privateer, and finally, in the Thames near London, some Swedish friends persuaded young Swedberg to break quarantine and sail with them to town.

But as the English authorities knew that the plague had broken out in Sweden they were morose about Emanuel's impatience, in fact they threatened to hang him, this being the legal penalty. He did escape, with a severe warning, but it must have sunk deep into him that a "health certificate" was a serious thing, for those words were to turn up again in his life's most intense spiritual crisis, puzzling even himself.

For the present a spiritual crisis was far from the handsome youth of twenty-two, independent of family control for the first time in his life, and alone, except for a few Swedish friends, in the world's greatest city.

He had come from the little cathedral town of Upsala, inhabitants about five thousand, to London, whose half million brawled and stank over fifteen square miles. All continentals noticed the smells of London.[1] There was indeed a less infected district in the West End, as John Gay had said in his *Trivia*,[2] "Bear me to the paths of fair Pell Mell, Safe are thy pavements, Grateful is thy smell," the London of face-masks, brocaded hoop-skirts, gold-laced uniforms, Ranelagh and Vauxhall, litters, footmen, linkboys, but the young Swede probably had only an outsider's glimpse of these splendors.

He was not in a position to get much else, however good his academic introductions, since his father had given him a sum equivalent to about $250, which, as it turned out, had to last him for a year and a half in a town which was by no means cheap. Good lodgings, there being no hotels, came to about $7 or $8 a week (£1.10), and even if meals were only a few shillings extra this was too dear.[3]

Emanuel lived in working London, rough, noisy, combative, and highly individualistic, especially in the disposal of what should have been sewage but instead was thrown out of doors and windows to land, if the passersby were lucky, in open gutters. Showers made these overflow and diffuse what Gay called "ungrateful odours," joining the symphony of smells that was orchestrated by the boiling caldrons of the chandlers, open butcher shops, whale oil, piles of antique cheese, fish "long absent from the sea," not to mention the age-old open deposits of "night soil."

The man who was later to describe the stinks of "hell" in such plain detail had plenty of olfactory memories on which to draw for comparison.

In that plebeian London, John Gay warned, "if clothed in black you tread the busy town," you must avoid barbershops where powdered periwigs would shed clouds on you, and the baker and miller likewise. If you were "in youthful colors," look out for the chimney sweep, the dustman's cart, the tallow spots from the chandler's basket, and don't run into the "surly butcher's greasy tray," and, whatever you do, cling to the wall! Hold the hands of "waggish boys that play the stunted besom" on the pavement, watch out for the rotten eggs aimed at the fellow in the pillory, be careful of pickpockets at night, and above all be wary of the "ladies of Drury Lane."

They were as common as the smells, and by no means confined to Drury Lane. Gay speaks of one of those man-catchers with "her livid eyes," whose "hollow cheeks with artful blushes glow." "Beneath the lamp her tawdry ribbons glare. She darts from sarsnet ambush wily leers, Twitches the sleeve—or with familiar airs, her fan will pat your cheek."

They, too, like the smells, were to appear realistically in Swedenborg's visions of hell, but they probably played no great part in the London life of Emanuel Swedberg. His release from home had not been from puritan sex restraint into licence—eighteenth-century

Sweden was no more puritan in that respect than England—it was a release into the freedom of following his chief passion. This was not the passion for women, though he was later to confess it so to his diary in a period of self-deprecation.[4] It was ambition, the keen, complex, all-absorbing and forward-striving ambition of the vigorous young intellectual. He had at last come to the headquarters of the knowledge he was thirsting for, measurable knowledge, exact science, a thrilling end in itself, but also the ladder to fame.

To the furthering of ambition Emanuel brought all his zest and energy, making even his disadvantages serve. Was he too poor to take "good" lodgings in the neighborhood of "fair Pell Mell"? Then he lodged from the very beginning with artisans whose trades he wanted to learn for the sake of science, and perhaps he even got the rent reduced in return for his help.[5]

Besides learning a craft or two that first summer in London, he studied the language and haunted the bookstalls. "I read Newton daily." He went on an orgy of buying scientific instruments, "prisms, various kinds of quadrants, microscopes, artificial scales, a camera obscura," and he hoped to have enough left over to buy an "air pump," an instrument about which he was almost tenderly passionate.

His London life comes to us in his letters to Benzelius [6] to whom he said after about five months, "If you were to inquire about myself, dearest brother, I know myself to be alive but not happy; for I long for you and home. If I chance to see a letter from you, it carries me back as it were to my fatherland, for I love and revere you not only more than my brothers, but even as a parent." And he signed himself, "your disciple and lover even to death."

But that was his only expressed homesickness. Paper seems to have been scarce, and his letters were usually so crowded to the margin with his scientific adventures that there was often no space left even for his signature. Having been in London for less than a year, he wrote in his polyglot Swedish, English, Latin, adding Swedish endings to foreign words, "That my Brother encourages me to Mathesien [exact sciences] is a matter I should rather be *discouragerad* in, since I have an immoderate desire thereto without this and especially to *Astronomien* and *Mechaniken*. I make good use of most of my lodgings that I take here. First I was with a watchmaker, then with a cabinet-workman, and am now with an instrument maker in brass, where I steal their trades, which in time will be useful to me."

He did not have long to wait. While the plague lasted Upsala University had been closed and the science professors had used the time to form a "Collegium Curiosorum," the first Swedish learned society. Part of the time they spent in discussing young Swedberg's letters to Benzelius. They wrote to their former student as if to an equal to get information about how things were done in England. Would he go to Flamsteed, the Astronomer Royal, examine his instruments and find out how they worked at night. Would he find out about the latest celestial globes and try to get the printed paper for them so they could be made up in Sweden. And what did quadrants cost, and were they made "with a screw, after Hooke's method." And much else.

As for the globes, Emanuel answered that "to get the paper for the globes is almost impossible, for they are afraid that they will be copied. On the other hand, those that are made up come quite dear. For this reason I have thought to prick off a couple myself . . . and send the plates over to Sweden . . . I have already so far acquired the art of engraving that I think myself capable of this . . . In addition I have learned from my landlord to make brass instruments so that I have made a large number for my own needs. Were I in Sweden I would not apply to any one to make the meridians for the globes and aught else pertaining thereto."

The young man who, in spite of his stutter, had offered to preside over the debating club at Upsala, had not lost his confidence. He had not only, as he also wrote, daily visited the best mathematicians in the city, he had applied his knowledge in practical mechanics. But he had higher aims. His chief aim was very high; it involved the moon.

In the same letter, writing to Benzelius with the special candor about one's own merits employed only toward a sympathetic member of the family, he confessed: "As regards astronomy I have so far acquired it that I have discovered a great deal which I think will be of use to that *studio,* though in the beginning I had much brainracking therewith. Yet, long speculations do not come hard to me now."

His speculations had an object. The Observatory at Greenwich had specific instructions to work out a better method of finding the longitude at sea, and the English, Dutch, and French had for some time been offering large money rewards for this. Emanuel informed Benzelius, still in the same letter, that he had weighed the plans of all but found they would not serve, and that he had "thought up a method which is infallible, by means of the moon, of which I am sure that it is the best that can be given."

Was it? He continued to work at this, and to believe it the best method, and he quotes Edmund Halley as having agreed with him "orally." At any rate, an astronomer of our own day has studied the question and reported that the method seems entirely correct.[7]

But when young Swedberg finally presented ten copies of his method for the award, he did not win it. He inferred, probably correctly, that it was because the commissioners were prepared to reject any lunar method in favor of the more practical one made possible by Harrison's chronometer. Still it was a good piece of work for so young a man to have been engaged on. His letters bristle with parallaxes and lunar tables. He had many talks with Flamsteed. Longitude by the moon continued to be his chief interest.

Professor Elfvius of Upsala wanted him to be sure to acquire the art of lensgrinding, as well as to find out what the English learned really thought of Newton's theory of gravitation. It seemed to the Swedish professor "unreasonable" that one planetary body should gravitate toward another—something that smacked of "pure abstraction" rather than physics. Many other tasks he confided to his ex-pupil, finishing with the postscript that he recommended to "Herr Swedberg's admirable curiosity" to search out all that could be of service to science in Sweden.

Emanuel was a tireless scout and careful purchasing agent of books and instruments for his former teachers, and these missions also served to bring him in touch with the great scientists of England. He wanted especially to go to Oxford, but August, 1711, came and he had to write to Benzelius: "I am left here in want of money. I am surprised that my father has not taken more thought of me than to let me live on 200 riksdaler (about $250) for what will soon be sixteen months . . . it is hard to live like the wench in Skaane, without food and drink."

The reference was to a girl who was supposed to have lived for years without food and drink, and who had been celebrated by Bishop Swedberg as another proof of the Lord's marvelous powers, along with the misbegotten calf of Gotland.

But Emanuel was entitled to some of the income from his mother's iron furnaces, and money came at last. On January 16, 1712, he took coach for Oxford. He was there about six months. He talked with Edmund Halley here about finding the longitude at sea by means of the moon, but the stay does not seem to have been devoted entirely to scientific studies.

This was another England than noisy, smelly London. Oxford shed its peace on him. He said himself to Benzelius that since his speculations had made him not so sociable as was "serviceable and useful" he had taken up *studium poeticum* "in order thereby to freshen myself," but also in order to publish something later and thus to become "renowned." But he would not desert science, and if anyone would encourage him he meant to make more discoveries "than anyone in our age," but without encouragement "this were to torment oneself."

It was really a good, chastened frame of mind for being lulled in Oxford, for the freshness of meadows by the Thames and for browsing in the Bodleian, to whose librarian Benzelius had given him an introduction. Even if England showed its customary indifference to his coming greatness as inventor or poet he must have had time and chance at Oxford to consider the values for which England stood, values which were to influence his whole life.

There was the England of free speech. This often took a form that strangers could not help noticing. While he was in London Emanuel had informed his brother-in-law that "almost the whole city is witnessing the internal dissensions between the Anglican church and the Presbyterians, who burn with a mutual hatred that is almost deadly. The torch and trumpet of the disturbance is Doctor Sacheverel, whose name is heard from every lip, in all quarters, and his book is read in every coffee house."

This curious form of religiosity did indeed run high. Before going to Oxford, Emanuel had been showing London to his cousin Andreas Hesselius, there on a visit, and they were probably together in the newly completed St. Paul's when Dr. Sacheverel expressed

his disquietude about the Presbyterians in words which the astonished Hesselius noted in his diary: [8] "So many vipers borne in England's bosom which would sting her to death." After which, the
Swede added, the mob broke up the meetings of the Presbyterians
and burned their pulpits and books.

But England's bosom is broad and tough. Anglicans and Presbyterians managed to survive in it, together with a lot of other sects.
The freedom of speech natural to England, and the freedom of
thought due to the new outlook of science, released people into
doctrinal diversities as well as into the atheism that was concealed
under deistic lip-service to an absentee God, who, having started the
machine of the universe running, no longer concerned himself
about it.

This state of affairs, which much resembled that of the nineteenth century, had brought into being a group of men later to be
known as the Cambridge Platonists. They could not hold with the
dry formalism of official religion, nor with the crude combative
theology of the ignorant sects, nor with the universe-machine of
some intellectuals such as Hobbes. The same conditions that led to
the formation of the Society for Psychical Research in the England
of the 1880's led to the drawing together of these men, classical
scholars, who wanted to reconcile reason with religion, without
offending either, and on the highest plane.

They found the reconciliation in the works of Plato as interpreted by Plotinus. Very briefly, the core of their faith was that
reason craved a unified universe, all mind or all matter, all God or
no God. Current religion offered a universe split into two. The
mysticism of Plato-Plotinus, like the mysticism of the Hindu
Upanishads, taught that the world was all God, having emanated
or radiated from that unknowable, uncreated source, matter being
simply the radiation farthest from the center. The Christian platonists were able to explain the Trinity as different emanations from
the same God and thus remain orthodox in theory.

Is it likely that they influenced young Emanuel Swedberg?

He had paid dutiful calls on his father's ecclesiastical friends, he
had paid his dues as a member of the Swedish Lutheran congregation in London, and no doubt he went to church on Sunday. He
had answered the questions his brother-in-law put to him about

various theological works, but the main stream of his energy went into "mechaniken," by that he was intoxicated, not by mysticism. Literal wheels within wheels spun in his head, not those of the first chapter of Ezekiel. Moreover, the Platonists had been centered at Cambridge in the seventeenth century, and Emanuel went to Oxford in the beginning of the eighteenth.

But John Norris, "disciple and correspondent" of Henry More, one of the chief Platonists, was a Fellow of All Souls, Oxford; he lived till 1711, and Emanuel had, even before he went to Oxford, read a little book by Norris which interested him a good deal. It was the *Reflections upon the Conduct of Human Life,* and while Emanuel found it "very subtil and ingenious," yet he was puzzled by it, finding himself "in *suspens* as to what may be his conclusion and as to what he would have."

It was not like Emanuel to remain in suspense for long and, being at Oxford for half a year with the Bodleian Library at hand, he probably continued his reading of Norris and was led by him to look into like-minded works. Perhaps it was only part of the reaching out in all directions of his "admirable curiosity," but one cannot fail to see this little rill as part of the headwaters of the stream that was later to carry him into the ocean of mysticism. The charts he was to use bear too great a resemblance to those of Plotinus for this to be an accident, even though the knowledge he may have acquired at Oxford slept forgotten by his conscious mind.

At Oxford he wrote some poetry. He told Benzelius that he was doing it to acquire fame as well as to recover from his speculations in "mechaniken," but, Emanuel being ardent, handsome, and twenty-four, personal feeling undoubtedly was the real dynamo. It was in Latin. One was translated from English, changing "Chloe" to "Delia." Some Englishwomen had been greatly interested in the Cambridge Platonists, and in any case Latin was part of education and Englishwomen had not yet reached Victorian ignorance.

It was not a remarkable poem as poem.[9] Her breast more white than snow made snow melt into tears and slip down her milk-white limbs, standing "like a string of pearls about her garment's hem."

But some were addressed to a person who had charmed him by her playing and singing, music-loving as he was and brought up in a household where music was part of daily life.

This is what he said to her: "Tell me why the string which is touched by a beautiful maiden sounds richer in nature and delights! Why she instils her songs with a certain Nymphean nectar? Why the voice sounds sweetly from this more beautiful mouth? Whatever she loves to say flows from the mouth of the saying; and she touches with her lips every little word. When love is the twin in singing, not songs alone, nor the lips, but the voice of one sweetly singing is what is loved."

This poem was entitled, "To a Poetess—Why her Songs give me Pleasure." It might have been impersonal. But then he wrote "To the Same That She may Answer me": and said, "Not alone do I love the fingers, the tongue, the lips, of the eloquent one, on which so oft would I bestow my kisses; but whatever thou movest when thou dost utter thy songs. For it is thy whole moving body I love. Happy shall I be if perchance our love shall bring forth a little muse or a short letter."

These are meager clues to Emanuel's emotional life. He was always reticent about himself. Yet here is the beginning of his attitude toward sex, one that he was to carry from earth to heaven. When the flood of gossip burst in Stockholm in 1759 about Swedenborg's visions, much of the hilarious amazement was due to the misunderstood news of arrangements and rearrangements of marriages in the other world. When he was eighty, he wrote a book of his philosophy of sex, *Conjugial Love*. In all its impersonality, with heads and subheads, it was his most personal book. "Other-worldly" only in part, much of it was devoted to the problem of sex for young and ardent men who couldn't afford to marry. The problem as he saw it was how "lust" could become "human love." Not that he altogether condemned the young for the lust which was "love of the sex," even if it took the form of "fornication." He laid down as one of his axioms "That with some men the love of the sex cannot without harm be restrained from going forth into fornication. There is no need to recount the injuries which excessive restraint of the love of the sex may cause with those who from superabundance suffer from intense venereal excitement. Hence are the origins with them of certain diseases of the body and disorders of the mind, to say nothing of unknown evils not to be named. It is different with those whose love of the sex is so scanty that they are able to resist the urgings of its lust."

But there were degrees of fornication, and as he examines them in dry textbook fashion it is hard not to feel that here is the old man looking with kind detachment at the struggles of his former self, struggles that were to continue into his ripe manhood. The ideal he was clear about. It was "when man recedes from wandering lust and devotes himself to one to whose soul he unites his own soul." When that love found its physical expression in the union of bodies, he called it "conjugial love," and if there were a union of bodies without spiritual union, even if it were "licit" as in marriage, he called it "adultery," in his vivid symbolism, raising the former to be the very pillar of heaven and making the latter the essence of hell.

Some time, somewhere, Emanuel had had experience of union with a kindred spirit, perhaps it was with the girl who sang for him in England. At any rate there is in the two little poems a hint of his creed that soul and body need each other for perfection in love. As the old man wrote of these things, he said in effect that wandering lust expressing itself in fornication might turn to either good or evil.

"Natural love which is toward the sex precedes spiritual love, which is towards one of the sex," and "in fornication conjugial love may lie concealed within, as the spiritual may within the natural; yea the spiritual is in fact actually evolved out of the natural, and when the spiritual has been evolved, then the natural compasses it about as bark does the wood and as the sheath the sword, and also serves the spiritual as protection against violence."

The youth, then, whose true ideal was a union of minds as well as bodies, might, so Swedenborg thought, pass unscathed through a period of fornication, "for the intention is the soul of all action," and a man was not to be blamed overmuch while he was in the process of evolving from natural youthful concupiscence into "conjugial" or spiritual love. Too much wandering or varietism, as he called it, might, however, destroy the man's capacity for feeling the love that was "the precious treasure of human life," and therefore Swedenborg excused or at least explained the lesser peril there was to the soul in taking a mistress. It was preferable of course to "reserve the fountain of manhood for a wife," he said, but as in so many countries a man had first to obtain a job and the means to support a family before he could marry, it might be better to live with a mistress than to live in soul-destroying promiscuity. "Pellicacy" (from pellex, a mistress) he termed this way out, but it was not to be taken with another man's wife nor with a virgin. However, a virgin might be taken as a mistress and a man "may indeed cohabit with her and thus initiate her into the friendship of love, but still with the constant intention, if she does not commit whoredom, that she shall be his wife."

Pellicacy, it was to be strictly understood, was a relationship in which the souls of the two kept apart, only conjoining the bodies, "while conjugial love unites the souls, and from the union of souls unites the sensuals of the body also, even so that the two become one flesh." If this kind of love were to develop in the liaison then, so Swedenborg held, "the man cannot by any right withdraw without a violation of conjugial union."

In the century of Casanova this put love on a lofty plane without leaving realism. There is no documentary proof that Swedenborg wrote from personal experience of either the lofty plane or the realism, but his detailed familiarity with both sides of the question, especially as it affected the conduct of the young, might seem to indicate that in some respects at least he had Emanuel Swedberg in mind.

At any rate, perhaps looking backward with the clear memory for things long past of the very old, he affirmed in *Conjugial Love* that a youth's interest in sex begins at the time his voice changes and when he starts to think for himself, rearranging the stock on his mental shelves left there by "parents and masters." "Before he only thought from things carried in the memory, meditating upon them and obeying them; afterwards from reasoning upon them; and then, love leading, he disposes the things seated in his memory in a new order and conformably to this order begins his own life, and successively more and more thinks according to his own reason and wills from his own freedom. That the love of the sex follows this beginning of his own understanding, and progresses according to the vigor of it, is known . . ."

Again he pleaded that it was wisdom to restrain the fornication that might follow the natural "love of the sex," but that this restraint ought finally to be based on a man's own reasoning power rather than on memorized principles, such as it necessarily was in the young. He had no great trust in those. "For a boy at the age of puberty has no thought that adulteries and debaucheries are other than fornications . . . nor has he reasoned knowledge to withstand the enticements of some of the sex who have carefully studied the arts of the courtesans; but in pellicacy, which is a more regulated and saner fornication, he may learn to see the distinctions."

A little one-sided and masculine, it might be said. The old man finished off with a warning, "But it is better that the torch of love of the sex be first lighted with a wife."

The "love" of which he had spoken as inciting the youth to think for himself was no doubt that which he sometimes referred to as a man's "ruling love" or chief interest, or, it might be said in the Jungian sense, his "libido," the psychic energy available. That interest with the young Emanuel was the direct pursuit of science, and fame through science. The Oxford idyl was over after about six months of it. In spite of Halley's "oral admission" that Swedberg's way of finding the longitude by means of the moon was conceivable, the young Swede had at last become discouraged. Not with his method, indeed—if only there were proper lunar tables, he wrote to Benzelius in August, 1712—no other projected method could be better than his, but there was another trouble. "Since here in England with this politely arrogant people I have not found great encouragement, I have laid it aside for other lands."

Emanuel packed most of his books and instruments and sent them home to Sweden. He begged Benzelius in quaint English (having specialized in mathematics) that he would help persuade his father to send him what would be necessary for a "yourney," and "what wil give me new spirits to make further steps in what my business is." Where to? Regardless of the Bishop's warnings against the godless French, "I design within space of three or four months to be in French because I desire the understanding of that fashonable and useful tongue."

About the end of 1712 he left England but he did not go straight to Paris. He stopped in the Netherlands for about five months, undoubtedly still concerned with longitude by the moon. He visited the splendid observatory at Leyden, and in that town he took lodgings with lensgrinders (there were no better men at the craft in Europe), learning the trade and purchasing the necessary tools. It is hardly probable that he remained so long in the Netherlands without looking into the works of that other lensgrinder, Baruch Spinoza, who, like the Cambridge Platonists but in his own austere way, also saw the universe as one Substance, essentially divine, expressing facets of the same Energy in both matter and mind.

What Emanuel wrote home about, however, was his new friend, Baron Palmquist, a Swedish diplomat by trade but a mathematician by preference, "who had me at his house every day; with whom I sat and discoursed on algebra every day." They also talked about founding a Swedish Scientific Society, but on the whole the stay does not seem to have helped the longitude project because in August Emanuel wrote to Benzelius that he had left the Netherlands and gone to Paris in order to study more science and to further his invention.

He was grimly determined. "At this place [that being royal Paris] I avoid the company of Swedes and of all those from whom I have the least discouragement in my studies." He had been in Paris about a year before he went on a sight-seeing tour. "At the end in Paris I made a *universel visitation* over the whole of Paris in company with some others, in order to see all that could be seen there." He also sat in Versailles in the great park, looked at the gods and goddesses in marble, and was moved to write Latin verses about them.

He was ill for six weeks when he first came to Paris, he did not say of what, but except for his last illness this seems to have been the only serious one he ever had. Not only was he remarkably strong, so that even in his old age much younger men couldn't keep up with his pace, but he had no more time to be ill than to go sight-seeing in the ordinary sense. He was greedy for learning. Benzelius had given him introductions to scientists which led to other acquaintances. He haunted mathematicians and astronomers, met De la Hire, Varignon, Cassini and several kind librarians, but although he cautiously gave hints about his method of finding longitude, the French were not interested. For Cassini, the astronomer, had a method of his own.

In Paris he may have met with the writings of Malebranche, whom he was later to quote with so much approval. Malebranche too was a Platonist, and John Norris, whom Emanuel had read, had based much of his work on that of the Frenchman. One can only guess at this. Emanuel was so busy with tracing the laws of physical events that any excursions he may have made into the realm of ultimate causes were probably with hasty curiosity, a little spiritual sight-seeing on the side.

He left Paris in the early summer of 1714 and returned to the Netherlands where he again saw his friend Baron Palmquist. It was a short stay. Baron Palmquist had a letter for him from his father who urged him to prepare for an academic career. The Bishop had also written personally to the Baron begging him to persuade his son to return. The study trip had already consumed four years.

But Emanuel did not hurry. On the way he stopped in Hanover, hoping to meet Leibnitz, probably the great mathematician more than the great philosopher, but Leibnitz was in Vienna. And, having arrived in Rostock on the Baltic Sea, Emanuel settled down there. Writing to Benzelius he said, "I am right glad to have come to a place where I have peace and time to assemble together all my works and *meditata* which previously have been without order and scattered here and there on some slips . . . I promised d:father to give out a specimen academicum, for which I will choose some inventions which I have in Mechanicis."

Already, he said, he had a list of mechanical inventions now reduced to order so that they might be published, including all the calculations necessary, and in astronomy too he had things to show.

"Oh how I wish that I could lay the whole before your eyes, dearest brother, and the eyes of Herr Professor Elfvius! But since I cannot do it with the machines themselves, I will yet in a short time do it with some drawings of them on which I am working every day."

This list, even without the drawings, was startling enough, even though (as has been pointed out) [10] the inventions were applications of known mechanical laws to ideas which other people of the time had already had. They still bear witness to his mechanical genius and also tell something more definite about what he had been studying than the letters had revealed.

1. The construction of a ship which, with its one-man crew, could go under the sea, in any desired direction, and could inflict much injury on enemy ships.

2. A novel construction of a siphon, whereby water can be driven from a river to higher places, in great abundance and in a short time.

3. On the lifting of weights by means of water and this portable siphon, more easily than by mechanical forces.

4. On constructions [locks] even in places where there is no flow of water, whereby a whole ship with its cargo can be raised to a given height in one or two hours.

5. A machine vivified by means of fire for throwing out water; and the way of constructing such machines at smelting works where there is no fall of water, but the water is still. The fire and the forge should be able to supply enough water for the wheels.

6. A drawbridge which can be closed and opened from within the gates and walls.

7. New machines for condensing and exhausting air by means of water; and concerning a new air pump worked by water and mercury without any siphon, which works better and easier than the ordinary pump.

I have also other new plans for pumps.

8. A new construction of air guns, a thousand of which can be exploded by means of one siphon and at the same time.

9. A universal musical instrument whereby the most inexperienced player can produce all kinds of melodies, these being found marked on paper and in notes.

10. A universal sciagraphia [art of making shadows as for sundials] or a mechanical method of delineating hours of every kind and on any surface by means of fire.

11. A water clock with water as the indicator which, by its flow, shows all the movable bodies in the heavens, and produces other ingenious effects.

12. Item. A mechanical carriage which shall contain all kinds of works moved by the going of horses.

Item. A flying carriage, or the possibility of staying in the air and of being carried through it.

14. Item. Concerning new constructions of cords or springs and concerning their properties.

Number 13 on this list was odd, a little arrow pointing in the midst of engineering to Emanuel's future interest. It was: "A method of conjecturing the wills and affections of men's minds by means of analysis."

Except for this and for the wholly hypothetical submarine and airplane, it was a list with practical application to the Sweden of his day. The proper utilization of Sweden's water power was important, and various engines of war were calculated to appeal to the hard-beset Swedes. The Russians were threatening to attack the country; King Charles XII, after having failed spectacularly against Russia and having been an obstreperous prisoner of the Turks, was on his way home, on horseback, with only two companions. But he was still King, an absolute monarch, an undaunted commander-in-chief, and war seemed likely to be the main business of Sweden for some time to come.

Soon after he sent the list of inventions home, Emanuel moved from Rostock to Greifswalde in Pomerania, which was a Swedish province. Charles, still on horseback, arrived in the nearby town of Stralsund in November and prepared to defend it against Danes, Hanoverians, and Prussians. Emanuel wrote a Latin ode to the "Phoenix of the ancient Gothic race," but he took ship home before the siege of Stralsund began, arriving in Sweden at the end of June, 1715. He had been thinking for himself now, for over five years, and his great desire was to encourage the growth of science in Sweden and thereby help the impoverished country. As he had written before he left Greifswalde, if only a Scientific Society could be established in Sweden as in other countries for the study of physics and mechanics, perhaps in time their usefulness to mining works and manufactures might become known and the government might then take an interest.

Emanuel Swedberg meant to be useful. He wanted to be a new broom.

CHAPTER SIX

Engineer and Mining Expert

BUT there was no opening for Emanuel Swedberg in his native country. He had not graduated from a technical school —Sweden had none—nor at that time were there great corporations competing to secure the services of a bright young engineer and inventor. Emanuel had collected his scientific knowledge bit by bit, tracking it down in different countries and collating it laboriously himself, but it was knowledge that had as little official standing as theology in our own day. Yet he could see only too well that his country needed his gifts. After fifteen years of war, bad harvests, famine, pestilence, and never-ceasing conscription of men and materials, Sweden was near a final agony, due to "Iron Head," [1] as the Turks had named Charles XII, and his iron pride which did not permit him to retreat.

Emanuel was passionately ambitious to be useful, to do something practical. Where was he to go?

Immediately after his return from abroad he had nowhere to go but home to his father at Brunsbo. There, while the Bishop was willing enough to try to advance his son, the latter met with a wall of incomprehension. The Bishop listened to Emanuel's account of finding the longitude at sea by means of the moon with such indifference that, in a letter to a favorite of the King's, he said his son wanted to build an observatory "in order to find the latitude on the ocean." But Bishop Swedberg knew that in an absolute monarchy one got as close to the King as possible, and this was a letter written to promote Emanuel. He also mentioned that his son was qualified "in the Oriental and European languages," and "especially in poetry and mathematics." [2] Not a letter calculated to interest Charles XII, if he ever saw it.

Worse still, as Emanuel confided in a letter from home to Benzelius, his d:father had mislaid the drawings and the intricate calculations for the machines he had invented. "He thinks they've been sent to d:brother, from my heart I wish it were so, since it cost me work enough to set them down."

They were not found. Emanuel began again to work on a hoisting machine, but he dutifully begged Benzelius to keep him in mind if there should be an opening at the university. Barnacled though it was with long-lived professors, this seemed his only chance to function.

Far more to his taste was the effort to haul Sweden forward into line with other nations in regard to science. Why shouldn't Sweden have a Scientific Society? Why shouldn't Sweden have a scientific journal, and one not in Latin as usual but in the tongue of the people so that research might be encouraged among them? Did not Sweden have Christopher Polhem, the great inventor, and should not his inventions be published along with those of others, such as Emanuel's?

Benzelius agreed, but evidently the Bishop thought it a waste of time and money, for soon Emanuel was writing bitterly to his brother-in-law: "A single word to my father from you on my behalf will be worth more than twenty thousand remonstrances from me. Without making any recommendation you can advertise him of my project, of my solicitude for studies so that he will not imagine in the future that I would waste time and at the same time his money. One word from another will be worth more than a thousand from myself."

But this highly uncommercial venture turned out to be more practical than the Bishop suspected. Christopher Polhem became interested in Emanuel again. He had met the youth and noticed his genius for mechanics five years previously, and now he was more than touched that this young man wanted to publish an account of the Polhem inventions, and at his own expense.

The first number of *Daedalus Hyperboreus,* Emanuel's magazine, was published in January, 1716, the chief feature being the description of an ear-trumpet invented by Polhem.[3]

At this time there was no textbook of arithmetic in all of Sweden, so Emanuel persuaded Polhem to write one, and he promised to pay for that too, not knowing where the money was to come from. Luckily he inherited a little money from his mother's iron works and was able to pay for both the magazine and the arithmetic, which had the alluring title of *Glorious in Youth, Useful in Manhood, Pleasant in Old Age.*[4]

Still, publishing *Daedalus* was not an occupation. The question came up again of whether he couldn't secure a professorship at Upsala. Writing to Benzelius, Emanuel urged that a Scientific Society would "heal the country . . . both in the establishment of manufactures and in connection with mines, navigation, etc.," and that therefore a seventh of the university income could well be given for this purpose. He said he thought it would be wonderful if the existing professors would donate one seventh of their salary to it; then he could become the first professor of mechanics.

Benzelius was highly alarmed lest the professors get wind of this fine scheme, and Emanuel said he had been joking. Yet, what was he to do? There had been one gleam of hope. Polhem had promised to take him along as his assistant engineer in building a dam and a dry-dock for the Admiralty, but then the irrepressible King went to war again, hammering at the Norwegians this time. In the middle of June, 1716, Emanuel wrote to his brother-in-law that Polhem was not coming after all, that "he thinks all good plans and inventions come to nothing," and "it seems to me," Emanuel groaned, "that Sweden is now laid low . . . when she will probably kick for the last time." With a cautious flicker of his real feeling toward Charles XII, he added, "we have hardly anything better to expect if the Lord permit Him to remain."

Meanwhile he brought out three more numbers of *Daedalus* and was applying desperately for the secretaryship of Upsala University when things suddenly changed. The King came back to his temporary court at Lund and ordered Polhem to attend him there to see about the new Carlscrona dry-dock, and Emanuel accompanied Polhem.

It was in November, 1716, that "Iron Head" and Emanuel Swedberg first met. The King, always avid for science, was charmed by the four published copies of *Daedalus,* nicely bound with a special dedication for him, while Emanuel was charmed by the King's interest in mechanics and his penetrating understanding of mathematics.

Polhem lost no time, he struck while "Iron Head" was hot. In a memorial to the King, he recommended Emanuel Swedberg for the only position in the kingdom where his abilities might have full scope, as a member of the Board of Mines. First flattering the King on his own knowledge of the mechanical sciences, he next spoke of the little honor mechanics was held in, being considered as only "the art of a common workman" when yet "it demands much labor and brainwork." He wanted honor for the engineers. "At this time I know of no one who seems to have a greater bent for mechanics than Herr Emanuel Swedberg." Wouldn't it be better to grant him "some prerogative of honor" rather than let "so useful a subject apply himself to some other pursuit"? Wouldn't it be wiser, rather than let young Swedberg go academic, to have him in a field where he could be of greater service, namely, as a member, or assessor, of the Royal Board of Mines? Especially since one who understands mechanics is needed no less than one "who understands the mining ordinances."

The Royal Board of Mines (known as the College of Mines) was like a department of commerce, having complete supervision over the vital mining industry of Sweden. It consisted of a president, two councilors, and four assessors (members entitled to a seat and a vote). "Extraordinary" assessors, while entitled to a seat and a vote, got no salary until through a vacancy they were advanced to "ordinary" assessorship.[5]

There were no vacancies when Polhem recommended Emanuel Swedberg, but Charles XII appointed him an extraordinary assessor,[6] the only one, an honor which had not been granted since 1684 —with the proviso that he was at least temporarily to remain Polhem's assistant. The King made inquiries about young Swedberg (he was then twenty-eight) but no doubt he chose him first and foremost because he saw and felt the energetic ability and unusual knowledge of the man. Charles recognized and appreciated able men.

But in the bureaucracy where not only seniority but status as a nobleman was necessary for advancement, the King's appointment of a complete outsider met with resentment. It began at once. Baron Cronhjelm, the high official who was told to make out the warrant, wrote it in such ambiguous terms that Emanuel protested to the King. Then Charles ordered his "opposer," so Emanuel wrote to Benzelius, to give him a new and more explicit warrant, and the

King made Cronhjelm sit down at the royal desk and write it in duplicate. "So that they who sought the worst for me were glad they had come out of the matter with honor and reputation, so nearly had they burned their fingers."

Emanuel was to learn that those are expensive satisfactions, no matter how just, especially since Cronhjelm, already powerful, was after Charles's death to become the equivalent of prime minister. But for the present Charles was alive, an absolute monarch, and, although tight about money, delighted to talk science with Emanuel. Nor was there any immediate question of taking up his work at the Board of Mines; there was plenty of other work. Polhem and Emanuel occupied themselves, with royal favor and little salary, in trying to start new industries in the impoverished country.

The King had read an article in *Daedalus* about how to get salt from the sea. Sweden had been importing it. Emanuel was told to establish salt-works. He was also busy with calculations for the great Carlscrona dry-dock. Emanuel had been put up by Benzelius to suggest to Charles that an inland waterway from Stockholm to the Kattegat would be a good idea, so the King had ordered Polhem and Swedberg to look into this, the forerunner of the modern Göta Canal.

The two engineers traveled strenuously about the country, looking at suitable sites, considering financial ways and means, running into endless difficulties, but the Carlscrona dam did get built, and the canal was started. Something might come of the salt-works too, Emanuel thought, "if selfishness does not rule too powerfully."

He was beginning to discover other than material obstacles to his practical work, but on the whole he was so happy in functioning that when Benzelius told him he had a chance to be named the professor of astronomy at Upsala he was "a thousandfold grateful," but declined to apply. "My genius," he wrote to this intimate friend, "is mechanics and shall likewise be chemistry." Furthermore, he could be "of greater practical use to the fatherland" where he was.

As he had told Benzelius once, he thought that for every ten mathematicians there ought to be one practical man to bring them to market. He felt himself to be that man.

But on November 30, 1718, Charles XII was killed by a rather mysteriously fired bullet in the Norwegian campaign. Emanuel's last piece of work for him had been the carrying out of Polhem's plan for transporting some Swedish warships over land, a distance of sixteen and a half miles, so as to prevent their capture by the enemy. It was a great engineering feat, and, like the whole of Charles's life, of but temporary value.[7]

With the King's death, work on the canal was stopped and with it the employment of "Em. Swedberg" as a practical engineer.

He was, however, far from being a narrow specialist. He had already begun to study mining and metallurgy in the district around Starbo, where his stepmother owned property the income of which she had allotted to him, her favorite stepson. As early as April 6, 1717, he had been formally "seated" at the Board of Mines and had continued to attend meetings until his duties with Polhem called him away.

But that was while Charles XII was alive. After his death, although Emanuel had been vigorously qualifying himself for the job, the Board refused to grant him a salary. It may have been some encouragement to him that in May, 1719, he was ennobled, along with the rest of Bishop Swedberg's children, taking the name of Swedenborg. (This was quite commonly done for the children of bishops, though not for the bishops themselves. Bishop Swedberg had been campaigning for it a long while.)

Ennobled or not, Swedenborg began to be further conscious of the obstacles to progress in his country. During that summer he put on paper a description of Swedish blast furnaces, and various inventions in regard to more airtight stoves, but, he wailed to Benzelius: "All such speculations and arts are unprofitable in Sweden and are esteemed by a lot of political blockheads as scholastic matters which must stand far in the background while their supposed finesse and intrigues push to the front."

He attended the Board several times in November, 1719, without being recognized as an assessor entitled either to salary or recognition, so he ceased attendance, but continued to study mining. Other matters claimed his interest. He wrote a booklet on the coinage question, recommending the decimal system, and this, he informed Benzelius, was really to be his last word, he was tired of the contempt shown toward "daily and domestic matters." "I've already worked myself poor with them, and have sung long enough to see whether any one opens up and puts some bread in my hand for it."

His chief income had been his share of the profits from the furnaces and forges left by his own mother, and he had used it generously for the printing of *Daedalus* and other little technical works, including Polhem's arithmetic, leaving so little for himself, when he lived in Stockholm, that "a single stiver [ha'penny] was precious to me." Now, he thought, if he could only get some money he would go abroad to study mining and metallurgy there. "For he may be regarded as a fool who is a free and independent fellow and has his name in foreign lands, and yet remains here in darkness (and freezes to boot), where the Furies and the Envies and Pluto have their abode and are those who dispose of all rewards."

When twice in 1720 vacancies occurred in the Board of Mines, Swedenborg applied for a full assessorship with salary, listing the many genuine accomplishments which warranted his requests, but each time another was preferred.

Meanwhile his stepmother, Sara Bergia, the Bishop's second wife, died, leaving her considerable property to her stepchildren. She had wanted to leave it all to Emanuel, but this the Bishop had prevented, the poor woman being on her deathbed. Even so, the money which Emanuel acquired after the division of the estate was enough for his simple needs to enable him to go abroad in the spring of 1722. Before he left he carefully informed the Board of Mines that he was leaving in order to learn about foreign mines and metallurgy, and that, if they graciously wished to approve of his plans, he would look for their letter in Amsterdam.

He put "Assessor" after his name.

Except for duly filing the letter, the Board did nothing about it. They hadn't the courage to shed entirely this irregular, dynamic individual with whom the late King had saddled them, but they did not intend to encourage him.

In July, 1722, Swedenborg was back, armed with new expert mining knowledge as well as with prestige of the kind that only "abroad" seems to confer. In the Netherlands and in Leipzig he had published several little books. They had received flattering reviews in important German scientific journals. One book was on his favorite subject of finding the longitude at sea, the others were on chemistry and physics with especial attention to mining matters and a sprinkle of philosophy. He had studied geology and mining, the latter in the Hartz Mountains, where he had made friends with a reigning prince and his brother. When he studied in England he sought out only scholars; now he probably realized the need of more worldly support if he were to impress the people at home.

Swedenborg's tussle with officialdom continued, and after new appeals to the Board he was seated as an assessor extraordinary without pay, in April, 1723. About a year later he turned down Benzelius's suggestion that he should allow his name to be put forward as successor to Celsius, the professor of astronomy at Upsala. Even though such a position carried with it a large salary, he did not now, he said, find any inclination in himself toward an academic career, and, furthermore, "to give up something in which I think I am functioning usefully would be indefensible."

At last, after more petty maneuvers by the jealous, all of which he met with great patience, persistence, and dignity, Emanuel Swedenborg was appointed a full assessor of the Board of Mines, though even then he had to begin with a smaller salary than was customary. That was July 15, 1724. (It was 1730 before he received the full salary.)

This was an event of signal importance in his career. He had not only acquired the status which was all-important in a country which he considered so status-ridden as Sweden, but he had got as close as he could to fulfilling his heart's desire—a chance to work in applied science for the building up of his country, worn tragically thin after almost a century of wars.

Assessor Swedenborg, thirty-six, had already accomplished a good deal. He was living now independently at Stockholm instead of at rural Starbo which he had not long before envisaged as his only refuge. He had helped found the first Scientific Society in Sweden, of which the six numbers of his *Daedalus* had been the first journal; he had carried out large-scale engineering works; he had made himself thoroughly conversant with nearly all that there was to be acquainted with in astronomy, mathematics, physics, chemistry, geology, and mining. He had published various scientific brochures or had the manuscripts discussed at the meetings of the Society.

As early as 1719 he had published a little book in which he proved from his own observations of stones, strata, and fossil remains that large parts of Sweden had formerly been under water. (In our own time an eminent geologist has said that this work alone would suffice to gain Swedenborg an honored name in science.[8])

Meanwhile he had been sending extremely commonsense memorials to the Swedish Parliament. In 1723 he was especially active, giving good and mainly unheeded advice. To improve the country's almost nonexistent finances, he recommended an improved merchant marine, a survey of imports to find out what was essential and what might as well be made at home, and how to make better and cheaper goods. In other summaries the same year he dealt with the mining trade, showing how foolish it was to favor the production of copper rather than iron merely because copper was supposed to be a "nobler" metal. He pointed out, moreover, how impractical it was of Sweden to export its pig iron to be rolled in Liége or the Saar, when rolling mills could be established at home. He supported his contentions with excellent drawings and minute technical descriptions.

He could do little with the parliament, but he now had his own work with the Board of Mines, work that brought him into close touch with many people as well as with the most vital physiology of Sweden. Sweden's food, so to speak, was iron and copper, its means of digestion was the charcoal made from its forests. The Board of Mines, directly responsible to the Crown, controlled all mining and allied interests, having every power short of actual ownership. It appointed mining officials and settled industrial disputes involving owners and workers. It regulated prices and imposed or withdrew taxes. It licensed new mines, forges, almost every shack, and it mapped out the distribution of charcoal. Other bureaus were associated with it, such as a bureau of metal testing, charts and measurements, a chemical laboratory and a mineralogical cabinet, so that Swedenborg's many-sided knowledge found full scope. He was often called on to assay the quality of iron produced, and he turned in technical reports, such as those on forest conservation, hoisting machines, blast furnaces, and the market value of sulphur.[9]

The position was no sinecure. The Board met every weekday

from September till the middle of July. There was a roll call, and the reasons for absence were noted. During the summer months some of the assessors went on tours of inspection in the mining districts, and Swedenborg did his share. Reports remain of seven such commissions, often covering several hundred pages. He turned in detailed and meticulous expense accounts. Anyone who has driven through the Swedish forests in a motorcar and even then has felt a certain panic that they would never stop can imagine what it was like for Swedenborg on horseback or in carriage laboring along the roads of his day.

An investigator of the records has written of his "stopping at the inns and farms for food, examining charcoal burners in their lonely huts, or holding meetings with the local agents and owners in a country school house, settling small difficulties, making recommendations as to new appointments, explaining mining statutes to the people, even taking an interest in the establishment of orphanages for the children of miners; often risking his life in steep descents into the gloomy underground caverns, where imperfect shafts and rude ladders made it very dangerous for one not daily accustomed to them." [10]

He had far more than a desk job, but besides this he carried out commissions for the family in Stockholm, even to shopping for his sisters—gloves were much in demand—and, to make it a complete human picture, he had a lawsuit with one of the family, his formidable Aunt Brita Behm. She had it with him, rather; it was about a mining property which had been left to them jointly. Emanuel had been called in to help make other members of the clan see reason in such matters, indeed he often gave the decision against his own interests. But Aunt Brita (probably put up to it by someone else) insisted on the physical division of the property, which would have hurt both their interests. This he pointed out in calm cogent words, no matter how much she pettifogged and blustered. A reconciliation was finally arrived at, but for a long while the affair had dragged on. Whenever all else was tranquil, up turned Aunt Brita with a new twist to the lawsuit.[11]

In Assessor Swedenborg's spare moments, between 1722 and 1731, he had been collecting material for a great work on mineral-

ogy, putting down his theoretical and practical knowledge of
metals and mining. Not only this, but the new work was also to
contain his reflections on the origin of matter. That part of it was
to be a philosophizing scientist's view of the world.

By 1731 Swedenborg had practically finished this work, and by
1733 he was given leave of absence from the Board of Mines in
order to finish his researches for the mining matters in the book
and also to have it published abroad.[12]

He kept a diary [13] for most of this journey through Dresden to
Prague, recording what he saw with such meticulousness that it
must have been intended as a report to the Board. It was mostly
about mining processes and metallurgy, but it also had his observations on the making of arsenic, cobalt blue, mirrors, peat-fuel, salt-
boiling, in fact on any method of manufacturing, anything into
which he could steal a look. He proved himself an acute factual
observer. Having seen a thing once he seemed able to report every
technical detail.

To scenery he gave vague appreciative tributes now and then,
but gardens interested him passionately, especially those with
orange and lemon trees, whose very measurements he took. He
noted buildings and the general condition of people, but he was
even more on the lookout for books. He found one on the kinds
of worms that destroy ships and wooden piles as well as remedies
against them. Into his diary went a résumé, with his own observations attached. In every library of consequence he searched for
scientific books, recording his disappointment when he found
mainly "old codexes." The makers of books he sought as well. "It
would be too prolix to mention all the learned men I visited and
with whom I became acquainted on these journeys, since I never
missed an opportunity of doing so. . . ."

In July, 1734, Swedenborg was home again, with the prestige of a
solid and successful book behind him. While he was in Leipzig, he
had seen through the press, at the expense and with the admiration
of his intelligent friend and patron, Duke Rudolph of Brunswick,
the three big volumes of his *Opera Philosophica et Mineralia*
("Philosophic and Mineralogical Works").

The first volume, *Principia Rerum Naturalium* ("The First

Principles of Natural Things"), was his map of the world. But as for years he had been investigating the ever-lengthening chain of causes behind the visible world, the book really was his account of the origin and structure of matter and of the evolution of our solar system.

EMANUEL SWEDENBORG AT FORTY-FIVE

From a copper engraving in Vol. I of his *Opera Philosophica et Mineralia,* by the engraver BERNIGROTH, published in 1734. Swedenborg's friend J. C. Cuno said of this, "Although finished forty years ago, it is still perfectly like him, especially in respect to the eyes which have retained their beauty even in his old age."

CHAPTER SEVEN

Physicist and Physiologist

IN Bishop Swedberg's house, a condensed Caprice called God was worshiped daily. In his son's *Principia* no deity called sinners to account by letting calves be born wearing French headdresses. As one of the first of his first principles Swedenborg laid down that "Nature operates in the world in a mechanical manner, and the phenomena which she presents to our senses are subject to their proper laws and rules." [1]

For this book Swedenborg, the engineer, chemist, and astronomer, had made use of all the sciences he had not only studied but applied now for many years, as far as his epoch's limited powers of microscopy and measurements allowed. The occult doctrines of alchemy had no part in it; he criticized them sharply in his preface. He based his work, he asserted, on Experience, Geometry, and Reason. Translated into modern terms: on experiments, mathematics, and the resulting hypotheses.

His fundamental ideas were not all original. Descartes and Leibnitz had helped. Even before the eighteenth century nearly everything had been guessed at, but there had been at least as many bad guesses as good ones. Swedenborg chose mainly the good ones, showing what has been called his uncanny ability to put things together correctly, not only from his own but from other people's observations.

The *Principia,* however, belongs largely to the pure realm of mathematics. The nonphysicist is lost in this world of bloodless energies, this "geometrical" world of gyres and vortices and magnetic fields. Here it is for scientists to appraise Swedenborg's work.

Part of it at least has been dealt with by Svante Arrhenius,[2] Swedish Nobel Prize winner. When the Royal Swedish Academy rediscovered that Swedenborg was one of its cofounders and began publishing his scientific works at the beginning of this century, eminent scientists wrote the introductions. Arrhenius wrote the one for the cosmological part of the *Principia*. His conclusions were as follows:

If we briefly summarize the ideas which were first given expression by Swedenborg, and afterwards, though usually in a much modified form —consciously or unconsciously—taken up by other authors in cosmology, we find them to be:

The planets of our solar system originate from the solar matter—taken up by Buffon, Kant, Laplace, and others.

The earth and the other planets have gradually removed themselves from the sun and received a gradually lengthened time of revolution, a view again expressed by G. H. Darwin.

The earth's time of rotation, that is to say the day's length, has been gradually increased, a view again expressed by G. H. Darwin.

The suns are arranged around the milky way, taken up by Wright, Kant, and Lambert.

There are still greater systems, in which the milky ways are arranged, taken up by Lambert.

(Another list could be made, and a much more extensive one, of the creative writers and artists who have used, or praised, or acknowledged their debt to Swedenborg's ideas: such as, for instance, William Blake, Goethe, Heine, Balzac, Ralph Waldo Emerson, Henry James, Sr., Oliver Wendell Holmes, Tennyson, the Brownings, Thoreau, Coventry Patmore, and many others.)

Arrhenius was not so interested in Swedenborg's account of the origin of matter, which seemed to him largely "philosophical," but in these days, since the "indivisible" atom has been dissolved into energy, Swedenborg's views on physics are of great interest.

Modern scientists tell us, for instance, that, in the world of relativity, matter is no longer considered "material" in the old sense, but as a local characteristic of a geometrical field of motion.[3] In the *Principia* Swedenborg wrote: "Although pure motion does not necessarily require anything substantial as the basis of its existence, there still pertain to it both form and space, which are attributes of motion." [4]

Swedenborg's framework of first principles began with positing an Infinite and Indefinable Something beyond our space and time. It might be called Unmanifested Energy. To manifest itself, to start in space-time on the voyage to becoming matter, the "mathematical point" was supposed—an abstraction on which Euclid based geometry, the point "which has position but no magnitude." This was the seed, as it were, which contained the latent energy of the universe. According to Swedenborg it was a particle consisting of pure "urge-to-motion" (conatus), a point of latent force.

The rapid movements of these points of force (which would now be called the wave aspect of the point) eventually produced all the qualities of solid matter. They did this by means of two forms of force, which he called finites and actives, and their primary combinations resulted in the four constituents of the cosmos. These he called the four "atmospheres," or "auras," or, sometimes, the "elements."

The function of the first, or "universal," was gravitation. The function of the second, or "magnetic," was magnetism. The function of the third, or "ether," was to carry light, heat and electricity, while the function of the fourth, or the air, was to carry sound waves.

As for gravitation, modern science still sees it as in a class by itself, "steadily refusing to show any kinship to other physical phenomena."[5] That is, gravitation is universal in its sphere of operation.

As for magnetism, "though closely related with electricity, magnetism is yet distinct," its velocity has not been measured, and it permeates glass, a nonconductor of electricity. Sir W. F. Barrett, in his preface to Swedenborg's *Principia* (London, 1912) mentions Swedenborg's "remarkable prevision of the molecular structure of a magnet," and the latter believed that in a magnetic field lay the inception of all other forces known to science.[6]

As for the ether, Swedenborg's idea of it was the same as that of modern scientists until Einstein, but the fact that electricity, heat, and light have the same velocity has been cited as evidence for supposing "a common cause, plane or atmosphere from or in which they act."[7]

Swedenborg seems to have thought of each of these four elementary atmospheres or forces as being within each other in a causal relationship, even as the atoms are within the molecule, the proton, electron, etc. within the atom, and still lesser units within these, like a Chinese egg.

But, as Sir James Jeans has said, "A mechanical model or picture must represent things as happening in space and time, while it has recently become clear that the ultimate processes of nature neither occur in, nor admit of representation in, space and time." [8]

That would have pleased Swedenborg. It would have seemed to him that we were back at the mathematical or, as he often called it, "the natural" point.

To his father, Bishop Swedberg, it must have seemed a very fine point indeed, if he noticed it. About 1722, when Emanuel had gone abroad in search of improved mining methods, his father wrote to a kinsman about him: "Would to God that he succeed with his many experiments and discoveries and that experience may prove their value." [9] The tone implied that his son ought to be making good in some tangible way, and when he saw the three big volumes of the *Opera Philosophica et Mineralia* that Emanuel had brought back from abroad in 1734, the father may have been impressed, at least by their having been ducally sponsored.

But probably Bishop Swedberg did no more than glance at the tomes before he returned to his favorite occupation, the revision of his autobiography to show how his various predictions had come true—how the grievous sin of sabbath-breaking had indeed brought pestilence and war on the country, and how God had preferred and upheld him, Jesper Swedberg, in every way. He was perfectly serene about the reception that awaited him in the world to come. In heaven, according to him, the "saved" sat at table with Abraham, Isaac, and Jacob, waited on by holy angels; or, if especially distinguished, such as he, they sat on thrones wearing crowns. He noted that on one of those occasions when his colleagues in the Diet had so maliciously misunderstood his motives, he had informed them as follows: "At least I know that God will order my angel to have a crown ready which is to be set on my head in God's triumphant Kingdom. While I go to my seat of honor, which after this I shall continue, with the aid of God, to adorn with still greater courage, renown and honor." [10]

His second wife, Sara Bergia, Emanuel's kind stepmother, had died in 1720 when the Bishop was sixty-eight. He praised her death for being as "quiet, as she herself was quiet and gentle and pious."

Most of her handsome fortune, he noted, she left to enable him to publish his works. (There had been a little pushing here; as mentioned before, Sara Bergia wanted to leave all to Emanuel, but the Bishop persuaded her not to, he said the other children ought to share as well as himself.)

Within a year or so the Bishop had married again, another well-to-do lady, not for his own sake, only for the household, of course. The lady, Christina Arhusia, survived him, but first she had fifteen years of household management. Bishop Swedberg died in 1735, aged eighty-one.

He left nothing to chance, not even the eulogy to be read at his burial. He wrote it himself. It was a not-too-brief abbreviation of his autobiography, with all his virtues and the consequent wonders and favors with which God had showered him. He gave minute instructions for the funeral ceremonies, pointing out the spirit of Christian humility in which he did it.

In 1736, about long enough after his father's death for the inheritance to have been distributed, Emanuel Swedenborg applied for leave of absence from the Board of Mines. He had done this before but never for so long a time. It was to be for a journey abroad that might take three or four years. He did not go into details except that it was for the purpose of "elaborating a useful work" vaguely described as having some connection with the preceding one and to be on "some new principles in philosophy."

He offered to take only half his salary while absent. The King and the Board granted the application. Being a state official, Assessor Swedenborg took solemn leave of Their Majesties at an audience where they were both "very gracious"; of the Privy Council; of the Members of the Board of Mines; of his friends and, probably unknown to them and even to himself, of his old life. On July 10, 1736, he left the city of Stockholm for the city of Paris, where he meant to study anatomy under Winsløv, the famous Danish anatomist.[11]

Whether the family knew of his intention is not clear, but probably Unge, his thrifty brother-in-law, expressed the general sentiment of family and friends when he wrote to Swedenborg, "As much as I was pleased with your former letter in which you wrote me that your journey abroad was given up, so much the more disappointed was I at your last letter in which you say the French journey is again determined upon." [12]

Unge was a man who liked to have a relative in an influential position, and there is no denying that Emanuel was now apparently throwing worldly prudence overboard. At forty-eight, with an assured and envied position, he was taking three or four *years* off—and for what?

For what, indeed! The family, if not the Board of Mines, must have suspected that there was very little trace of metallurgy in his plans. Even the connection with philosophy must have seemed tenuous if it were known that he intended to study anatomy.

A mining engineer, chemist, physicist, to leave his country to study anatomy, a science so disreputable that it couldn't be studied properly in respectable Sweden, a study with the whiff of body-snatching about it. To leave not only his country but his good secure job with heaven knows what machinations likely to go on against him in his absence—it was in truth a very strange project. He did not intend to be a doctor.

If Swedenborg's contemporaries had known what we know, as perhaps some of them did; if they had known that this voyage to France was taken in obedience to a religious impulse, then they might have asked much the same questions that our contemporaries do when they hear that someone who doesn't "need to" has endangered his worldly prospects for the sake of "God."

Was he successful in his work?

There is no evidence to show that he wasn't. He functioned well in the kind of work he had himself chosen; he had the feeling that he was useful to the country, and, though he had annoyances due to envious or stupid colleagues, they were no more than any very intelligent man experiences in the business of working with other men, especially if they are bureaucrats.

Was he unsuccessful as an author? Had the great *Opera Philosophica et Mineralia* been a failure?

This was far from being the case. From scientific journals of the highest standing in Europe came long and grateful reviews, especially of the tomes on iron and copper. [13] The physics of the *Prin-*

cipia was faintly suspected of being "materialistic" and was in any case above the heads of the reviewers, but Swedenborg otherwise received great praise, among the rest, for his attitude on trade secrets. He had stated with engaging candor:

There are persons who love to hold knowledge for themselves alone, and to be reputed possessors and guardians of secrets. People of this kind grudge the public everything, and if any discovery by which art and science will be benefited comes to light they regard it askance with scowling visages and probably denounce the discoverer as a babbler who lets out mysteries. Why should real secrets be grudged to the public? Why withheld from this enlightened age? Whatever is worth knowing should by all means be brought into the great and common market of the world. Unless this is done we can neither grow wiser nor happier with time.[14]

Parts of the work dealing with the manufacture of iron and steel were reprinted separately and even translated from the Latin into French, and, later, into Swedish from the French! He had flattering inquiries from academies of science. Far from being a failure he had achieved a European reputation in his chosen field. The road to further fame was lying open before him. Yet he turned from it and into the unrewarding path of anatomy, not so much for its own sake as because through that study he hoped to acquire greater understanding of the body's relationship to the soul, and through this he hoped to come nearer to an understanding of the soul's relationship to God.

Had he failed in his human relationships? There is no evidence for that. His friendship with Eric Benzelius continued to be warm, and he was a generous uncle to young Eric. Some of his colleagues at the Board of Mines he liked very much. Swedenborg was never considered an unsociable man.

Why had he not married?

There is a tradition that when he was still Polhem's assistant he was in love with Emerentia, Polhem's younger daughter (aged fifteen and known as "Mrensa"), and to have been in such despair when she preferred another that he vowed never to marry.[15]

He may have been in love with Emerentia, but in 1726, two years after he became confirmed as assessor, a certain Pastor Steuchius noted in his diary that this day Swedenborg had asked for the hand of his daughter, Stina Maja, but she preferred a court chamberlain.[16] There may have been other attempts which are not known, still his family thought of him as a hardened bachelor. In 1729 Jonas Unge (his rather unsympathetic brother-in-law) was giving him family advice in a letter:

"Why in the matter of marriage does d:brother let all the good chances go by?" And Unge recommended a pretty girl with a good dowry. She was only eleven, to be sure, but why did Emanuel not put in an application? Yet, though Unge buttressed his exhortation with a long Latin saw about the perils of delay, Emanuel did nothing about the matter.

Why did he let all the good chances slip by?

He neither needed nor wanted to marry for money, and, in eighteenth-century Stockholm, he did not have to marry for sex. His friend Robsahm has recorded that he had a mistress when he was young, whom he left because she was unfaithful to him, and to Tuxen he spoke of having had a mistress in Italy. In a diary, he wrote, no doubt exaggerating, that women were his chief passion. But even there he was careful not to cite names or incidents connected with real people. Very little is known directly about his emotional affairs. But it is known that, far from being a libertine, he grieved deeply over "wandering lust" and longed for a harmonious marriage with an intelligent woman.

It is possible that he did not marry because he had met and fallen in love with a woman who already was married.

An English Member of Parliament, C. A. Tulk, who revered Swedenborg's teachings and whose father had known him in London, said that "Swedenborg was in the habit of saying that he had seen in the spiritual world his future wife who was waiting for him there, and that she had been known in the world as a Countess Gyllenborg." [17]

This Countess Elizabeth Stierncrona Gyllenborg, whom Swedenborg seems to have met in his early thirties, is reported to have been both attractive and fervently religious. Swedenborg was a friend of her brother and her husband, though later on, in his notes from the Beyond, he gives the husband a very bad name indeed. But not enough is known about the pious Elizabeth, herself a writer, to make her seem accountable for Swedenborg's remaining a bachelor.

That he was a handsome man his portraits attest, and that he was vital and magnetic even in old age is asserted by several people who knew him. In 1734, when he was forty-five, the printer of his *Opera* in Leipzig was so impressed by his appearance that he begged leave to have his picture engraved for the book, a picture which those who knew him at eighty declared to be still like him.

This shows him not only in the grandeur of full-bottomed wig and aldermanic splendor of official robes but as keen, determined, and robust, with a hint of the slight corpulence he had in middle age. It is decidedly a clear, strong face, no meagerness in it, no obvious and haunted schizoid elongation.

And still Emanuel Swedenborg was a haunted man.

CHAPTER EIGHT

Dissecting Rooms Abroad

WILLIAM PENN, at the age of about twelve, is said to have had an experience in which an ecstasy that seemed to him of another world left unforgettable traces that ultimately shaped his life.[1]

Perhaps something similar happened to Swedenborg, but he never published his intimate experiences, whether of sacred or profane love. There are, however, his later references to the insensible breathing he said he practiced "purposely" in childhood, when at prayer, and he seems to stress that this brought about a kind of rapt state.

Some such experience may have been at the root of the desire to be rid of his ego, a desire which never left Swedenborg entirely. It can of course be explained in as many ways as there are points of view about existence. Was it for "God," or was it for "escape"? No laboratory method can prove the correctness of either explanation. Some great force there must be, innate or acquired, to make a man choose to travel the narrow road—the "razor's edge" of the Hindu mystics—which seems to be the only way to the complete abandonment of self and absorption in the complete fullness called God by some and Nirvana by others.

It seems less likely that Swedenborg sought God because he did not marry than that he did not marry because he had a need to seek God. With his analytic intelligence it was precisely that need which drove him from his father's egoistic piety and tawdry miracle-mongering, making him so keen to welcome the universe of law which science opened up for him.

Swedenborg was well aware that he had parted from his father. Not only does he date the beginning of his spiritual enlightenment from 1710, the year in which he left his father's house to study science in England, but in 1748 he recorded a dream in which he says he told his father, who had appeared to him in the dream, that "a son need not recognize his father for father after he has become his own master." It was all right, he explained, to do so while the son was in the father's house, but when the son ". . . becomes his own master, so as to be able to guide himself from his own mind and know what to do, then the Lord is his father." [2]

This seems to have been the only instance in which the Bishop had no reply to make, but then it was only a dream.

It was inevitable that commentators in later times would try to explain Swedenborg's quest for religion as a sort of penitence for having "left" his father's orthodoxy. Like absolutely everything else in human experience, the story can of course be forced into a Freudian formula. As William James has pointed out, it is a question in the last resort of whether the need for religious experience is always due to a neurosis or not. Were all the great mystics "compensating"? Who can tell, except the mystics, and they cannot, because all love is inexplicable to those who have not felt it.

If it is true that the mystic strain in Swedenborg was evident in his childhood, it is also true that it went underground during the years when he studied science, but he, no more than Pascal or Newton, ever repudiated religion for science. Until about 1733, however, he seems to have published nothing that indicates more than a decent deistic rationalism. With the important exception of the first chapter of the *Principia* (which was written last), it is hard to find any Biblical God in that work. Not that He was left out. Nature, Swedenborg said, was only another name for the motive forces issuing from the Infinite Being, "to be venerated by every philosopher."

It must be remembered that in the eighteenth century, though God might often be dismissed privately as nonexistent, it was not yet safe to do it too publicly. Voltaire himself put up a little chapel at Ferney to Him, on which, to be sure, the name of Voltaire was put in larger letters than the Deity's. And even in the nineteenth century Renan said that people who were unacquainted with modern Biblical research had no intellectual right to leave the church. In Swedenborg's time that kind of research was still to come.

A kind of Engineer-God was acknowledged in the *Principia*, seen as identical with the "Infinite." How that Infinite was going to produce the finite; how that Eternity was going to produce time,

were questions which Swedenborg at first felt were answered by
the conception of the Infinite releasing the energy of the "natural
point." He says, "[The point] . . . is a kind of medium between
the Infinite and the finite, for it is by mediation of this point that
finite things exist from the Infinite." [3] In short, in the second chapter the nexus or connection between the Uncreated and the created
was this purely mathematical point.

When he went abroad in 1733, he took with him the all-but-
finished manuscript of his book. He corrected the manuscript of
the *Principia* in three days, early in June of that year. And, whether
then or before he left Stockholm, he made a summary of the book.
It did not contain the first chapter of the printed version, the reason
no doubt being that it had not yet been written.

When he wrote it, probably in Dresden in 1733, he now hinted
that the "nexus" or connection between the Infinite and the finite
is "the Infinite and Only Begotten" [4] (Jesus Christ).

This might have been a bit of window-dressing for so rational-
istic a book as the *Principia,* but for the fact that in 1734, probably
in Leipzig, he elaborated this hint into a short, fervent book, *Of the
Infinite* . . . in which he maintains that the nexus is not "mathematical" at all. Reason can only discover that there is a nexus, not
its real nature. Using some dubious teleological sleight-of-words, he
tries to hang on to his rational thesis that the "point" is the beginning of the finite world, and yet that the nexus between that world
and the Infinite is Christ who is both God and man. It is not convincing even to himself, and he takes refuge in the authority of
the Bible.

Why has the deist become a theist?

In the course of his argument he seems to feel that he has some
explaining to do, and he suggests that he has met someone or some
"other minds," which have come to the same result as he has, but
who have gone further, superadding "new results, of which I knew
nothing yet which are nowise at variance with mine," so that, as he
says, he is bound to believe them.[5] So it is from these other minds,
it would seem, that he has found an agreement between revelation
and reasoning.

The clue to their identity may lie in the new word "nexus," which
was a favorite term of the Protestant mystics of the sixteenth and

seventeenth centuries for Jesus Christ.[6] Jacob Boehme, for instance, said that Christ united eternity and time, God and man.

Swedenborg did an enormous amount of reading in Leipzig and Dresden, and he may have come across the works of Boehmists or those of the disciples of similar mystics, such as the Schwenkfeldians. No one can read Rufus Jones's work on the Protestant mystics [7] without seeing the startling likeness between many of Swedenborg's ideas and theirs. And as their ideas stemmed from the Plotinian Christianity of the Areopagite and others, and as Swedenborg had come across the same thoughts when he was in England, in the works of the Cambridge Platonists, familiar echoes must have awakened in his soul had he come across the books of the Protestant mystics in the great book markets of Germany.

But there is greater pressure behind *Of the Infinite* than that of intellectual discoveries. Those would not have sufficed to throw a Swedenborg out of his orbit. A stronger passion than that for knowledge would be needed here, and there are signs of it.

He says that in man who is entirely finite, entirely of this world, even as to his soul, there is still a capacity for receiving what is divine, and it lies in this, "that man can acknowledge and does acknowledge God . . ." But—note well—he says that through this faith man has the further privilege of being aware "in love, or delight resulting from love, of a peculiar connection with the Infinite." [8]

It sounds as though Swedenborg had at some time found in passionate human love that inkling of the divine which other lovers and mystics have found. Indeed he was later to elevate "marriage love," including physical love, to be both an outcome and a symbol of the divine.

He concludes in *Of the Infinite* that the true divinity in man is an acknowledgment of the existence of God "and a sense of delight in the love of God." [9]

That sense of delight, which has nothing to do with theology and everything to do with religion, is the dynamism that makes mystics. From the time when Swedenborg had experienced it, though it may have been only a glimpse, his course was changed.

But not his conscience as a scientist. He had not given up science, his one sure grip on a slippery universe. The second half of the book

Of the Infinite he called *Of the Mechanism of the Intercourse between the Soul and the Body,* because Swedenborg saw the belief in God as linked to belief in a soul, and it was clear to him that unless he could show how the soul influenced the body he could not prove that man had a soul.

He decided to investigate. He wrote: "Only from a knowledge of the soul and of the mechanism of the body can we deduce that there is a God and a creator, but the contrary is the case if we postulate the soul as something most unknowable and secret and something far removed from sense; this is the nearest road to atheism . . ." It must not be "regarded as an object of supreme ignorance and as operating by absolutely unknown laws." [10]

If he stressed the "mechanism" of the soul, this was because the blessed word connoted being subject to law. Descartes had made soul a kind of Cinderella outside the palace of matter; Swedenborg wanted to see if he couldn't invite her in and make her the queen, but a constitutional monarch, subject to the same "mechanical" laws as matter.

But, through his study of physics, Swedenborg had come to see that "matter" need not be material. A magnetic field, for instance, could not be either kicked or handled, and yet it had extension, it could be measured. Why not the soul?

"My end, therefore," he said, speaking to unbelievers and probably also to a side of himself, "is to demonstrate to the best of my ability the nature and properties of the soul, and then to show from these endowments that it can never die without all nature being annihilated; and, such being my end, I do not see how anyone, unless indeed some singularly obtuse priestling, can disapprove of the undertaking." [11]

But in the *Of the Infinite,* he said, he was not going to make any "positive declaration," for "experience and geometry alone have the right to be affirmative and positive, and when they become so, then and not till then, by the consent of the soul, the rationale is declared. The main end of these our labors will be to demonstrate the immortality of the soul to the very senses." [12]

The soul being, according to him, "the last and subtlest part of the body," which he already had located provisionally in "the cortical substance of the cerebrum and partly also in the medullary"

was therefore subject to "mechanical" laws, but he did foresee difficulties in explaining "imagination, perception, reason, memory and
so on . . . ," yet "why may not mechanical laws exist in a super-
lative fashion equal to these offices?" [13]

It was not a new interest entirely, this interest of Swedenborg's
in the mind-body relationship. Even before he left for Germany in
1733 he had written a little piece, *The Motion of the Elements,* in
which he brooded on the means used by the soul to affect the body.
And as early as in his twenty-ninth year he had written a study *On
Tremulations* in which he showed a good acquaintance with
anatomy. In Upsala, since Olaf Rudbeck's day, a little stealthy dissection had been done, which he probably had had a chance to see
something of. At any rate, *On Tremulations* dealt with the means
of sensation. He tried to prove that they were tremulations or vibra-
tions carried through the liquids and solids of the body. Hearing,
he said, might be possible even without the mechanism of the ear,
if the tremulation were caught "by means of the sympathetic vibration of the teeth or the bones of the head." [14] (A modern hearing
aid is based on this principle.)

Similarly he applied "mechanics" to telepathy (as we should now
call it), saying: "It also frequently happens that a person falls into
the thought of another person, that he perceives what another is
doing or thinking, that is, his membrane [the word stood for nerves
also] trembles from the tremulations of the other person's cerebral
membranes, just as one string is affected by another if they are
tuned in the same key." [15]

It will be seen that, though he did not deny the reality of thought
transference, he had a purely mechanical explanation ready. It came
close to a "materialistic" explanation, which is perhaps why the
Upsala College of Medicine lost the finished manuscript.

Yet it was not his intention to deny "soul" any more than he ever
denied "God." But at no time did he imagine "soul" as a simple
night-shirted replica of the earthly self, to be raised on Judgment
Day. Few scholars did, even in his time.

It is significant that when Swedenborg came to Halle in March,
1734, he noted in his diary that Professor Hoffmann was still alive.
Hoffmann, a great doctor, as well as his colleague Stahl,[16] whose

theories were taught at Upsala, believed the human organism to be a chemicomechanical affair, which the soul uses as long as it is usable. Hoffmann subdivided "soul." At the top there was an immortal or God-like part. In the middle there was consciousness which received sense impressions and passed them on to the upper house which translated them into ideas. At the bottom, half part of the soul and half of the body, were the "animal spirits," a kind of ethereal "fluid" which was thought to circulate in the nerves. They were what we should call the electrochemical nerve impulse, bringing the sensations to be perceived by consciousness.

These ideas were far from new. From Plotinus and further back they had been trickling through the Dark Ages and the Renaissance in various forms. Always the immaterial part of man was thought to consist of a part capable of contact with the Infinite or Deity, a lower part which took care of concrete reasoning, and a still lower which gave life to the tissues of the body. These theories were known to Swedenborg; yet he held them as mere "opinion" until he could figure out for himself how such soul elements could function in terms of matter and motion.

During the Leipzig stay, in 1734, he came across a book on psychology by Christian Wolff, which he annotated,[17] his remarks showing how thoroughly gripped he was by his new program of study. Here it is as if one were inside the very furnace of Swedenborg's mind, his ideas sparkling in every direction. Wolff's prim little propositions are taken into it; they often, he says, agree with his own ideas, but he carries them much further, sees many more implications, and finally drops them altogether to fling himself into outlining a work which is to describe what he already thinks about the causes of perception, imagination, memory, dreams, and so on. With diagrams. And his "tremulation" theory.

In his notes on dreams one seems to detect a strong personal interest. For instance, he contests Wolff's assertion that if we are not able to recognize an idea reproduced by aid of the senses we can't do it by force of the imagination. That is not always true, Swedenborg says. "Thus in sleep I can frequently remember a thing, which when awake I have completely forgotten; as for instance Greek and Hebrew words, which I would never have known although I had read them."

Without a doubt several things about his own mind were puzzling him. He agrees with Wolff that "every dream is caused by a sensation," and yet "one may frequently notice that they tend to some definite end." He thinks that perhaps the soul "supplies many additional things and marvelously joins them together."

He has come to the hypothesis that the "soul," the highest rational faculty in man, is of the same "substance" as the second or "magnetic element" of the universe. An idea, he says, is a vibration in this most subtle "membrane" of the soul, and in the case of dreams, "something is wont to come from the soul which directs ideas to a definite end, as though they were directed by one of whose origin we are ignorant—a circumstance which often seems to us a matter of wonder."

He adds that unless the vibration-motion in the soul is strong enough, it cannot reach the senses, but if it is "considerable," then "a phantasy arises which spreads to the senses, with the result that in wakeful moments we seem to see and hear this identical thing, exactly as in dreams." Not a bad description of a hallucination. He was aware of such things. "A man," he says, "has heard in his brain the singing of melodies, which otherwise he would have been entirely unaware of knowing."

In these notes he begins to sketch many of his later ideas. He is interested in Wolff's description of the symbolism of hieroglyphics.

He reiterates his belief in thought transference and in the communion of souls, "because there is an undulation between them." He begins to try to apply his theories of immaterial energy "substance" to the make-up of "angels and spirits," but for the common notion of "spirits" he has scorn. "When they can go no further into nature's work . . . our modern authors take refuge in spirits, where the ancients betook themselves to atoms . . . they have merely clothed the unknown with a new name." Men wrangle about anything we can't perceive with our eyes, "the unknowing disputing about the unknown."

Then with a truly magnificent outburst of confidence, he takes refuge in science: "If we had the microscopes, we might be able to see the entire structure both of the soul and the spirit."

He did not intend to be one of the unknowing disputing about the unknown. From the notes to Wolff it is clear he had already studied a great deal of anatomy from standard works on the subject. Impatiently he complains that it is so difficult during a voyage "because of business and pleasure" to make the necessary researches for this study. But he looks forward to the great work he is planning:

"Why should we not reach forward and establish that which surely our posterity will establish—that this body of ours is mechanical, that its organs are mechanical, that its senses are mechanical, the intellect, the reason, and the soul itself. In course of time the learned world will agree. [Nature is] alike in great and small. There is not another kind of reasoning, not another kind of nature; two kinds of nature are by no means possible."

Concerned as he now was about metaphysical and religious questions, such as the Infinite and its connection with the finite world, the nature of the soul and immortality, he was perfectly certain that the answers could not be reached with any satisfaction to his scientific conscience except by "experience, geometry and reason." For some time he had been meaning to turn this battery on the human body. The bulk of the notes on Wolff, as well as the second part of the *Of the Infinite* show that even before his return to Stockholm in July, 1734, he had made up his mind: he intended to delve for the traces of the soul in the finest recesses of the physical brain.

In his notes to Wolff's *Psychology,* he had regretted our unconsciousness of most of our make-up. "If the cerebellum were rightly joined to the cerebrum, and if there were a communication between their subtle membranes, then we would know all that took place in our body . . . If God had willed so to join the cerebellum and cerebrum, we would have been instructed in all things of our anatomy almost without a master."

Bar such a convenient arrangement between the seat of consciousness and what was then considered the center for involuntary physiological processes, Swedenborg went in search of the best masters of anatomy he could find when he left Stockholm for his long leave of absence in 1736, but he did not put a word of this into the diary he kept during his stay abroad.

With a few significant exceptions, this diary,[18] like his previous travel diary, bristles with facts, mostly topical. Travel guides and statistics were not so conveniently published then as now, hence Swedenborg recorded these things for himself—like most diary-keepers not considering what people in the future would like to have had him write about.

His journeys took him over the ground dreamed of by all dwell-ers in the dark winters of the poor, limited North. On July 10, 1736, he left Stockholm, going through Copenhagen, Hamburg, Am-sterdam and Brussels to Paris, where he arrived September 3. There he remained for a year and a half, leaving on March 12, 1738, for Italy. Dangerously "swimming in snow" over Mont Cenis (or Mont Sini, as he had it, spelling most foreign names by ear) he arrived in Turin and went over Milan and Padua to Venice. He stayed there nearly four months. From Florence, to which he gave a fortnight, he went to Rome, arriving September 25, 1738. He was in Rome nearly five months. He left Italy from Genoa on March 17, 1739, returning to Paris and then going to Amsterdam, where he finished and saw through the press the work for the sake of which the journeys had been undertaken.

At the beginning of each new set of impressions the diary could compete with any guidebook; later on it dwindled and sank under the crowding experiences, yet it is a valuable document through which to look at Swedenborg.

While there was still an engineer in him who noted the new dock being built in Copenhagen and most of the military fortifications he saw en route, he was not much concerned now with manufac-tures or even with mining. He was not a worldly man certainly but a man of the great world, and one of the most tirelessly sight-seeing, extrovert type. Though he had been out of his country before, he had never before had time or money enough. Now he saw every-thing along his way—museums, churches, castles, parks, libraries. He grumbled again at the lack of "new books." Except for Bibles, old codexes did not interest him, nor "old-fashioned" architecture either, except when it was old enough, such as the classic.

His energy was fantastic. One day in Paris gives a sample: "I went through Luxembourg and the rue d'Enfer to the Observatory, then to the Porte St. Jacques, past the Capucin monastery, past the Val de Grace, then along the rue St. Jacques to the Porte St. Martin, where we had entered on arriving in Paris; I went along the rampart and looked, from a distance, at the Hôpital de St. Louis, where there are said to be ten thousand beds, mostly on account of the plague; then I went to the rue du Temple and looked at the old ruins of the Temple; I also saw the chapel and the garden of the Hotel de grand Prieur, which is rather fine; saw also the Church of St. Elizabeth right across from it; on my way back I went into the church of St. Jacques de la Boucherie, and thus home." He was impressed himself; he reckoned he had walked a whole Swedish mile (six and a half English) as well as doing his sight-seeing.

Probably for the reason that he always called on and was cordially received by the Swedish envoys wherever he was, he was given chances to see things not always accessible to the ordinary tourist. In any case, he managed to be on the spot for the picturesque. He was present in Paris at the opening of the Parliament in the Palais de Justice, and admired the altar, the pontifical bishop, the many lighted candles, the beautiful music, and the "gentlemen in their red cloaks." Nor did he miss much in Italy. He was there, in Venice, when the senators, also in red cloaks, "went out to meet their ambassador and salutes were fired, balls were held and fireworks illuminated the canals." He was there too on Ascension Day when the Doge celebrated the marriage of Venice to the sea. "I joined them and saw how the sea was consecrated." Perhaps he was on the state ship *Bucentaur* itself. He noticed the masks so commonly worn in that city of intrigues. And, little as he gives of his personal life, there is a hint that he was not without entertainment and companionship in the note: "Every Saturday there was music in the convent of Incurabile e Pieta; lodged at the Ponte Rialto together with H. Firencrantz"—a Swedish name.

In Bologna he saw the city's annual feast, quite a feast. First they played at storming a fortress; "after that there was thrown to the people a great quantity of chickens, pigeons, geese, turkeys, and after that sheep, and then, by Cardinal Spinola and two others, peacocks, coins and lastly purses."

In Livorno he visited a slave-galley and attended a reception with glorious fireworks, for the Grand Duke. While in Genoa he saw "the Doge who always wears red including his shoes," and he saw

the Genoan nobles voting—"they are all in black with little man-
tles; flat noses and faces."

He conscientiously recorded statues and paintings, but art was
for him, as for most of his century, at its best in lifelike and literal
representation. Like all Northerners he was overcome by the
splendor of marble in buildings and statues, and when, later in
Holland, he had a chance to have an inlaid marble table made,
with a comb, a pack of cards and a fan represented on it, he sent
it home, causing much trouble for his family with the Swedish
customs.

The arts which really moved Swedenborg, however, were music
and the theater.

The Italy he knew was deeply sundered and corrupt, and France
was on its way down a slippery slope, but the stately glitter of the
Grand Monarque was still over Paris, its façades and colonnades
laid out on a royal scale, the city framed by rounding hills that were
green and windmill-crowned. Paris, to use the diary's favorite and
almost only adjective, was "magnifique," but what the man of the
world most admired in it was the theater. Swedenborg went often
to the *Comédie,* and said, "It seems now brought to the greatest
height it ever can reach." He was enthusiastic about the singing
and dancing at the Opera, and had his favorites whose names he
tried in vain to spell, but later when he saw in the Verona opera
house how the Italians could sing and dance, he admitted that "in
those respects, the French Opera seems but child's play."

His father, the late Bishop, had left no doubt as to how he felt
about the theater; for him it was Satan's own workshop and going
to it almost as great a sin as sabbath-breaking or the wearing of wigs
that might be made of "whore-hair." Had he seen his son Emanuel
attending the *Comédie,* undoubtedly in a well-curled wig, with a
sword by his side, and wearing an embroidered coat with lace
collar and cuffs, his words would have been pungent.

Emanuel was not being untrue to *his* convictions. He might be
living in Paris at its most decadent, or in Venice when it had become
Europe's illicit pleasure ground, but he did not condemn pleasure
as such. On this he was to give an opinion many years later, after
his travels had been extended to still another world. "I have met
with many in the spiritual world," he wrote, "who in the natural

world had lived like others, clothing themselves splendidly, faring sumptuously, trafficking for gain like others, attending dramatic performances, jesting about love affairs as if from lust, and other like things, and yet with some the angels accounted these as evils of sin, and with others accounted them not as evils; and these they declared innocent, but those guilty." [19] The difference, as he said it was explained to him, was all in the intention.

Within the man of the world, one might say, was the scientist-philosopher. About him the 1736–39 diary tells little except for its eloquent blankness for over a year in Paris and for almost the whole time in Venice, while he was studying and writing; yet there is a glimpse on October 4, 1736, when he notes that he walked in the *Thyllerie:*

"Next to the *Thyllerie,* on the other side of the river is the Hotel de la Duchesse, which is *magnifique;* there is a pleasant promenade, and I speculated on the form of the particles in the atmosphere."

One can see him in the golden haze of a Paris autumn day, near the gleaming Seine, wandering with an abstracted air among the animated French, Swedenborg the philosopher, there and yet not there—already, so to speak, "in the spiritual world."

There was in him too a man who looked at things more and more from a spiritual or ethical point of view. Like most Protestant Northerners, he had at first been charmed and impressed by the lavishness of gold and silver in Catholic churches as well as by the sensuous service. In the Brussels cathedral, among multitudes of burning silver lamps, he heard mass, reflecting that the main thing about it seemed to be the leading of thought to religion by exterior means, "for it is arranged with so much courtseying, bowing and kneeling devotion which charms the eye," while "beautiful music both instrumental and vocal fills the ear," and "there are fragrant spices for the nose." He allowed, benevolently, that human beings were usually led to reflect by way of the senses, but when he arrived in northern France he saw another side of the picture.

Driving through small towns he saw *"magnifique* convents, poor and wretched people." "In general, the convents, churches and monks are the richest and own most of the land, the monks are fat, puffed up and flourishing, a fine army might be recruited from them without their being missed; most of them take it easy and try to get more and more under control; they give nothing to the poor except words and blessings, yet they are always wanting everything from the poor for nothing, of what use are these Capucin monks? Others again are slim, lean and supple, prefer walking to driving or riding, are sociable, like good living, are witty, etc."

A little later he collected some figures about the Church in France. "In France there are 14,777 convents, three or four hundred thousand religious. They possess 9,000 palaces or manors, 1,356 abbeys, 567 abbesses, 13,000 priors, 15,000 chaplains, 140,000 parishes, 18 archbishops, 112 bishops . . . 16 heads of orders . . ."

The signs that were to lead to French revolutionary enthronement of Reason were already clear, but it was not altogether from economic considerations that Emanuel Swedenborg condemned the fat friars. He saw them as he was beginning to see monarchies, not only as hard on the poor, but as inimical to true religion.

He had noted that Their Swedish Majesties were very gracious when he took leave of them, but he had a very strong feeling against monarchy, and this he now recorded in a diary entry where the innermost Swedenborg for a moment revealed himself, the man who had within the last three or four years acquired an emotional conviction of God's existence, and who did not feel he had to prove either God's or the soul's existence "mechanically" while he was alone with his own thoughts.

The entry was from his three days' stay in Amsterdam in September, 1736, and it expressed the feelings of mingled horror and affection in which he held the Netherlands, a country he already knew well from former visits. Arrived in Amsterdam, he noted that "the whole city breathed of nothing but gain," and later on, after being in Rotterdam, he wrote that he could not understand why it had pleased Our Lord to bless such an uncouth and avaricious people with so splendid a country. (He always appreciated politeness. An uncivil ship's captain depressed him, and he noted in Belgium what a relief it was to meet civilized manners after the Dutch lack of them.)

But why, he pondered, had the Lord protected the Dutch for so long, and let their commerce flourish mightily so that riches from everywhere flowed into their hands?

"It seems to me that the chief reason is that the country is a Republic . . . in which the Lord seems to take greater pleasure than in countries governed by sovereigns . . ." In republics, he dryly wrote, "no one feels in duty bound to accord any human being honor or veneration, but think the lesser as well as the greater just as good as kings and emperors, as indeed is evident from the native bent and disposition of every one in Holland."

Why was this so pleasing to God? Swedenborg thought that if the worship of God flowed from each man's free will, then "fear or caution don't make them lose their courage or free, rational thoughts"; furthermore people who have been oppressed by sovereign power are bred in flatteries and falsities, that is, to speak and act differently from the way they think, then "they carry that into church services and extend their flattery to the Lord himself, which certainly must be most displeasing to him . . ."

Any sincere, simple Christian of a pietist or Quaker tinge might have referred thus personally to his God, but Swedenborg was neither; he did not even know what Quakerism was. After being in Copenhagen, where a dismal form of pietism was then in court favor, he noted that "people here are so infected with pietism or quakerismo that they think it pleasing to God to commit suicide."

Swedenborg's form of worship was more constructive—also much more difficult. He knew that. In 1738, after he had been studying physiology abroad for two years, he wrote:

"To complete the single science of the soul, all the sciences are required that the world has ever eliminated or developed." With less than all, the man who undertook this would founder. "The points which he requires, but of which unhappily he is ignorant, he must perforce obtain from himself or produce by the keenness of his own mind, that is to say, he must use his imagination to supply the place of real knowledge, and how prone to error the imagination is if left to her own guidance . . . is perfectly well known . . ." [20]

He would not leave anything to imagination. "Whatever results we are now to arrive at in treating of the brain must be confirmed by all that depends upon that brain . . . the whole body, including all the viscera, organs, parts, solids, fluids, also by records of the body or of the animus [reasoning mind], and, furthermore, by the details of experimental chemistry and physics . . ." [21]

No scholastic web would suffice Emanuel Swedenborg as proof of the soul's interaction with the body. He required demonstration, the kind you could point at with your finger. To find material for such proof was the object of his year and a half in Paris, at Dr. Petit's school of anatomy, where he studied under Winsløv, the Dane, who was probably the first to examine the organs of the body in the body, dissecting them under water.[22] (Anatomists had hitherto taken the organs out.) For this he studied in Venice, where he wrote about the brain, near to Padua, where the brilliant Morgagni taught, much quoted by him. Italy had long been the foremost country for anatomy.[23]

Of these facts, however, Swedenborg's travel diary tells nothing. All that he conveys is that he went from Italy in March, 1739, by way of Paris to Amsterdam, where, "on the stroke of midnight," December, 1739, he finished the book known as *The Economy of the Animal Kingdom*.

CHAPTER NINE

Anatomy of Mind and Body

THE *Economy of the Animal Kingdom*—never was there a title more misleading to the modern reader! Not one word in it means what it seems to say. Swedenborg wrote most of his works in Latin, and his English translators too slavishly followed it. "Animal" in this connection is derived from "anima," the Latin for soul. The title should be: *The Organization* (or Government) *of the Soul's Kingdom*—that is, the body.

The contents of the two volumes were a result of his researches on the blood, the heart, and the brain, plus two chapters on psychology, interwoven with his reflections on ethics and the relation of mind to body.

This is the work which Emerson eulogized: "By the sustained dignity of thinking," he said, it "is an honor to the human race." [1] That does not make it easy reading. As with the *Principia,* modern scientists with technical language will have to be called in if one wants to try to understand the true grandeur of Swedenborg in his first gigantic effort to understand the human body. And philosophers as well as religious teachers will have to be consulted if one wants to trace the convictions about the world and about God which Swedenborg had reached by the time he was forty-five. Neither is this easy reading. A man with his gifts and culture was not a mere simple devout recipient of emotional religion.

But the *Economy* is a bridge. Its colossal arches span most of the distance between the mining engineer and the mystic. The latter can be understood by those predisposed in his favor even if they do not try to understand Swedenborg's science and philosophy (and skip chapters nine and ten of this biography), but if they give up this effort they will certainly have to be content with a house that has no foundation.

From the modern point of view, did Swedenborg accomplish anything of real value to science with the *Economy?*

The answer is Yes. But the answer tarried for a couple of hundred years, illustrating what Swedenborg sadly asks in the book itself: "What is truth? Will it be the work of ages to discover it, or of ages to recognize it when discovered?" [2]

And he mentions that even the discovery by the illustrious Harvey of the circulation of the blood was for a long time disputed by many. "Still," he adds optimistically, "that fashion of judging of a work cannot be eternal which regulates the approbation of the reader not so much by the truth of the writer's sentiments as by the felicity of the language. The latter is an attainment easy and common among persons belonging to polite society; it is the former that presents the difficulty, which is to be surmounted only by intense mental labor." [3]

Intense mental labor, however, is not enough in physiology. Swedenborg himself stresses that "with diligent study and intense application, I have investigated the anatomy of the body, principally the human . . ." [4]

Was he nevertheless "an armchair philosopher, making easy lucky guesses"? A modern American physiologist, Dr. H. W. Haggard, asks this question and acquits him of such a charge.[5]

"His [Swedenborg's] conclusions were based upon the best medical knowledge of his time; knowledge that he gained in the medical school, in the anatomy laboratory, and from the writings of every scientist of his time."

"It was he," so Dr. Haggard summarized Swedenborg's most important physiological discovery, "who first said that what we call the gray matter on the surface of the brain, the cerebral cortex, is the seat of the psychic functions—of consciousness, perception, sensations, thought. He showed the relation of the parts of the brain controlling the muscles of various parts of the body. He went further and said that gray matter in the center of the brain controlled many of the complicated but unthinking acts performed by the body. He was the first to show . . . that the surface of the brain is in connection through nerve fibers with every part of the body, even as he said with as remote an organ as the foot. And what makes it all the more astounding is the fact that he attributed the primary function of nervous control to little oval particles in the gray matter of the brain. It was a hundred years later that scientists were to prove experimentally that Swedenborg's conclusions from deductions were correct. They were to name the oval bodies cells or neurons. Not one but many men were to take their place as famous in the annals of science for proving what one man had said must be so.

"I do not mean," Dr. Haggard guarded himself, "that he wrote modern physiology with prophetic vision. He did not. He saw the correlation of facts better by far than any other man, but he could not in science go beyond the factual information of his time. Thus, one of his discoveries concerned the vessels that supply blood to the heart. He was the first, as far as I can find, who pointed out that the heart was nourished from the blood, but . . . he had the blood flowing the wrong way."

Yet, "The indisputable truth is that Swedenborg had the intellectual insight that has been granted only to a few men. His was an intellect of synthesis."

Dr. Haggard said these things in an address on the occasion of the 250th anniversary of Swedenborg, in 1938, but before then other medical scientists of the twentieth century had come to appreciate their lay brother of the eighteenth. (Undoubtedly the prolonged lack of professional attention to Swedenborg's physiological discoveries was at least partly due to their having been made by a layman.)

The first was a Viennese, Dr. Max Neuburger, a medical historian. In a congress of scientists and physicians at Hamburg, 1901, he declared his profound astonishment at Swedenborg's discoveries in the physiology of the brain, thus giving the Swedes themselves a shove toward looking him up, since he was not much of a prophet in his own country and many of his scientific writings remained unpublished.[6]

Amends were made by the Swedish Professor Gustaf Retzius, who frankly confessed that his attention had been called to the subject by reason of Dr. Neuburger's assertions. Speaking to an international congress of anatomists at Heidelberg, 1903,[7] he also deplored that he had not known of these works on the brain and the nervous system when he, together with Key, wrote a historical account. Retzius then gave Swedenborg full credit for his discoveries, one of which, later to be called the "foramen of Key and Retzius," Swedenborg had already deduced. Of course Retzius emphasized the great discovery, that of the seat of the psychical functions in the cortex, and the localization of the motor functions, as well as the fact that Swedenborg brought "sure proof to show that the motion of the brain not only exists and constantly presents itself in living conditions, but is also synchronous and closely connected with the motion of the lungs, the respiratory motion."

After praising other discoveries, Professor Retzius asked: "How was all this possible?" He answered, "Swedenborg was not only a learned anatomist and a sharp-sighted observer, but also in many respects an unprejudiced, acute and deep anatomical thinker."

In 1910, at a meeting of the anatomy section of the British Medical Association, the professor of anatomy at Upsala, Sweden, Martin Ramström, read a paper, published in the *British Medical Journal,*[8] in which he underscored Swedenborg's brain discoveries. Not only had he shown the function of the brain cortex in governing muscular action, but he had relegated automatic and habitual movements to the gray substance of the medulla oblongata and the spinal cord as secondary motor centers.

Ramström emphasized, moreover, that Swedenborg in the *Economy* had decidedly opposed the current "pre-formation" theory of the embryo.

To bring the chorus up to date, when the full text of the hitherto unpublished parts of Swedenborg's *Cerebrum* was published in the United States in 1939, scientific reviewers of our own day also greatly wondered. While they deprecated the mistakes (mainly due to lack of knowledge of facts which Swedenborg couldn't have known), one of them[9] was sincerely puzzled as to how Swedenborg nevertheless had found out something "worthy of a Nobel prize" without the necessary modern microscope. It had to do with the nature of the coat with which the arteries enter the capillary ramifications. Swedenborg himself said that "this is a matter cannot be explored by the senses." "From various signs," however, he said, he found it possible to conclude something, correctly.[10]

Another modern medical reviewer of the *Cerebrum* says, "Here as in his other works, he anticipates much that was unknown until relatively lately . . . there are still to be found ideas in this book which a neuroanatomist might find not unsuggestive." [11]

The modern reviewers of course dissociate themselves from Swedenborg's speculations on the nature of the soul's interaction with the body. But as it was to lay a foundation for such speculations that Swedenborg wrote these books, it is not irrelevant to take a look at the kind of house he built on the foundation. The speculations are not out of date. In Swedenborg's own time Stahl believed that the soul formed the body, and Hobbes believed the opposite. In the nineteenth century Vogt was to claim that the brain merely secretes ideas as the kidneys secrete urine, and in the twentieth century Hans Driesch was to assert that "in the modern solution of the mind-body problem everything that is new and important in psychology as well as biology is centered," while, nearly half a century later, Dr. Gardner Murphy asks: "Is it not indeed, somewhat of a paradox that in an era of huge progress in neurology, psychiatry, and psychology, almost nothing new and clarifying has taken shape regarding the mind-body problem?" [12]

The Economy of the Animal Kingdom is primarily Swedenborg's attempt to answer a question put by himself: "We have hitherto been stating what the soul is, but, pray, what is the body?" [13]

He dissociates himself from two unfortunately rather large sections of humanity—those "who stubbornly refuse to stir a step beyond visible phenomena," and those who "prefer to drown their ideas in the occult at the very outset."

"To these two classes our demonstration may not be acceptable," he declared. "For, in regard to the former, it asserts that the truth is to be sought far beyond the range of the eye; and, in regard to the latter, that in all the nature of things there is no such thing as an occult quality; in fact, that there is nothing but is either already the subject of demonstration or capable of becoming so." [14]

Truth could be found by objective methods, he thought, but he did not claim to have found *the* truth in this book. He even feared that he might "have gone beyond the ordinary limits of inquiry, so that but few of my readers may be able distinctly to understand me.

71591

But thus far I have felt bound to venture, for I have resolved, cost what it may, to trace out the nature of the human soul." [15]

At the outset he explained his method. It was to cite in full the greatest authorities in anatomy and medicine, and then to draw his own deductions. Here and there, he said, he had taken the liberty to throw in the results of his own experience, but this only sparingly. We know his reasons for this: first, that he felt his was a synthesizing gift, and second, that he feared the temptation of basing everything on a discovery of his own. He determined therefore to rely mainly on the researches of others.

That this was a real sacrifice is evident from the ardor with which he speaks of what he saw in his own explorations of the body. As engineer and chemist he was fitted to appreciate the "pipes, ovens and little bladders" of the body, and all its ingenious constructions that so "cooperated" with each other. Always an image-thinker, fond of concrete metaphors, he speaks of the "gratework of the ribs," or says of the "old blood" that "it is clad in black garments and hurried away to the tombs of the liver." [16]

He so loves physiology that he writes of the organs as if they had conscious life of their own. "The hungry veins" will "eagerly snatch" at the gastric juices; certain nerves are like "a married pair, the intercostal doing the husband's office and the par vagum the wife's." He was especially fond of matrimonial similes; at times a wedding feast seems to be going on in the body's every nook and cranny.

This was one aspect of his being a man who had the great gift of wonder at the apparently commonplace. He himself warns us that "When a name which is given to any unknown quality becomes familiar to us, we are apt to think, after a frequent use of it, that we clearly understand . . . it." In such cases, he continues, one has only to ask, What is this? Whence is this? to be carried off "to things more unknown." [17]

Hence when Swedenborg asked, "What is the body?" he followed that up by wondering how it comes to be a body. He studied the formation of the embryo of a chick, looking at it with his eyes, through the poor microscopes of the day, as well as through his rational mind, second to none in any day. He concluded (the conclusion, as Ramström had said, being one of his modern titles to fame) that no little doll chick existed in the germ and simply grew larger, but that there was in it "a certain formative substance or force which caused the various parts of the embryo to develop in an orderly fashion, one after the other." [18]

"However obscure our idea may be, yet we shall clearly perceive by a little attention, that the stupendous machine of the animal body could by no means have come together without a positive directing force . . ." and that "such a directive or formative force is not without but within the chick or embryo." Furthermore, "it must exist within that substance that was first in the ovum and that has life or soul within it. Now, if we consult the anatomy of bodies, particularly those of early fœtuses or those that are still in the egg, we shall meet with a certain most fluid matter that from the first stamen by a wonderful determination successively projects, delineates and descries the entire image of the future body. Surely then we must grant that this directive force is seated in this fluid, and, if so, we must conclude from the infinite variety of particular effects that it involves a certain wonderful form in the whole and in all its parts, for if not mighty miracles of formation would result from mere chance." [19]

He could not help concluding that "this substance or force represents to itself the state about to be formed, just as if it were a state already formed . . ." What had seemed "a miniature chaos" in the egg, "a blank, undigested mass, is now seen to involve the most perfect order and accurate discrimination." [20]

What would be the effect, he asked, of "the very least irregularity"? "It would be as if an arrow or ball were shot at some distant mark with an error of only two or three minutes of a degree in the aim, in which case the farther the ball or arrow had to fly the farther it would be at last from the target." [21]

Not less important was Swedenborg's conclusion that this formative force "is identical with that principle which repairs the dilapidations of the body, and when contingencies arise renovates and perfects the system." [22]

He was loath to describe it in words, although of course he did, but groaning that all words must be inadequate. Words give rise to "a thousand sleights of language by means of which books are distended with those equivocal terms that produce such hot dissension in the schools." Again and again he longed (at considerable length) for the precision and concision of mathematical language, for symbols that would be applicable both to First Causes and to these physiological and psychological facts. Indeed, he promised to invent this "mathematical language of universals."

And he wondered at this "mass of miracles" of the body, quoting Grotius: "As well might we believe that stones and timbers come together by chance into the form of a house or that an accidental concourse of letters produce a poem."

Via the embryo, Swedenborg decided that "life is one distinct thing, and nature [inorganic matter] is another." [23] He went further: "Life is what regards ends," or purpose.[24]

For centuries this was to be scornfully dismissed as "the old teleological argument." Matter, dead or living, was considered to be all the same. At the close of the nineteenth century, however, Professor Hans Driesch, the "Vitalist" biologist, was to prove that living tissues did behave in a manner unpredictable by the physics then current, but Swedenborg would doubtless have been even more pleased at the opinions expressed in our own day by Professor Erwin Schrödinger, one of the world's leading nuclear physicists.[25]

Professor Schrödinger, with all the humility of the trespassing specialist, nevertheless approached his study of the unfolding embryo with the idea that anything which developed in so orderly a manner, so according to a seeming plan, must be a "many-atomic" structure, because, as all modern physicists know, the behavior of a *few* atoms cannot be predicted. "Only in the cooperation of an enormously large number of atoms do statistical laws begin to operate and control the behavior of these *assemblées,* with an accuracy increasing as the number of atoms involved increases. It is in that way that events acquire truly orderly features." [26]

But the startling fact about the egg (and unicellular organisms) was this, that: "In biology we are faced with an entirely different situation. A single group of atoms [the chromosome fibers] existing only in one copy produces orderly events, marvellously tuned with each other and with the environment, according to most subtle laws." Professor Schrödinger adds: "The situation is unprecedented, it is unknown anywhere else except in living matter." [27]

Professor Schrödinger returns by way of quantum mechanics to the validity of physics, modern nuclear physics, even for living matter, but, as he says himself, with one big new factor. Asserting that his body "functions as a pure mechanism, according to the laws of nature," he insists that he, his "I," is able to direct and foresee the motions of this mechanism, even if the effects are to be fateful, "in which case I feel and take full responsibility for them." [28]

In his more youthful works, Swedenborg was fond of writing a triumphant Q.E.D. when he thought he had proved his point, and he would no doubt have attached that to the above. Eager as he always was to accord praise when he agreed with another scholar, he would also have declared that the "learned and illustrious" Schrödinger was entirely right in his "golden" treatise *What is Life?* Of course everything in created nature—so Swedenborg would have put it—is "mechanical" and subject to mechanical laws, and the difference between dead and living matter is that the living is purposefully governed by a soul.

Swedenborg's answer about "this earthy loan," the body, was: It is something which is fabricated by the soul for its own purposes. Once the body is made it has a certain reciprocal relationship with the soul, but the latter, besides being the manufacturer, is the maintainer and repairer of the body as long as the thing is repairable.

Many of those at whom he so often had jeered as "occult" had made the same answer, but with Swedenborg it was not quite such a short story. He took years and thousands of anatomical pages to tell it. Essentially, however, the plot began with his trying to track down and analyze something which in his time was called the "animal spirits" or "the spirituous fluid," or similar names.

It was only supposed to be a "fluid" in the way that electricity then was called a fluid, something indicating its spatial though invisible nature. It was an attempt to give a name to the nerve impulse, as well as to the "X" that made the difference between dead and living matter.

This "spirituous fluid," Swedenborg said, must have something to flow in, its channels being the "fibres," or nerves. By his study of the motor impulses in the nerves, he arrived at the idea that these started in the "little spherules" [the neurons] in the cortex of the brain. These little spherules, also called by him with pet-name affection, "little hearts, little brains, little bosoms, most pure and sensitive little wombs," as well as "little factories," he saw as the places in the body where "the spirituous fluid" was perhaps not created but "elaborated" and sent out through the body, not only in the form of nerve impulses, but carried by the blood as that in the blood which was life-giving. He imagined this as a kind of special circulation which he called "the circle of life." [29]

Then his synthesizing mind went to work. Having decided that the formation of the embryo was due to a formative force, he identified that with the spirituous fluid, here busy at its first and most important task of forming the body, according to a preconceived image or idea of what was wanted—or else how could organ follow organ in such an orderly and predetermined fashion?

He had, furthermore, found out experimentally that the "faculties" of "understanding, thinking, judging and willing" likewise resided in the "cortical substance," because if it were injured the mind didn't function, so that these faculties too, he concluded, were functions of the spirituous fluid.[30]

From there it was an easy step to identify the "soul" with the spirituous fluid. He hesitated about terms. Should one not rather say that the spirituous fluid was the "organ of the soul" as the eye was the organ of sight?—"Yet it is no matter whether we call the above fluid itself the spirit or soul, or whether we confine those terms to its faculty of representing the universe to itself, and of having intuition of ends; for the one cannot be conceived, because it is impossible, without the other." [31]

Whether Swedenborg called it soul, or spirituous fluid, or animal spirits, or something else, it was still "immaterial." How could it then interact with the demonstrably material cortical substance, "pure and sensitive" as the "little wombs" within it were? What, in his own words, was "the mechanism of the intercourse between the soul and the body"?

Here, where the anatomist failed, the physicist stepped in, even without benefit of quantum mechanics.

To the question Is the soul then material? Swedenborg had another question: "Pray, what is matter?" [32]

He had already written a book about this, his *Principia*. In it, quite in line with modern physics, he had "reduced" or advanced matter to force. As has been mentioned, he called the first, simplest and most "superior" aspect of force the "universal" aura (or elementary constituent). This, he said, was "immaterial," if materiality be defined as "extension endued with inertia," for inertia is "the source of gravity," and "neither gravity nor levity can be predicated of" this force.

"The first aura of the world is not matter in this sense, but on the contrary active force, the origin of gravity and levity in terrestrial bodies, which do not of themselves regard any common centre, unless there be an acting, causing, directing force." [33]

It was Swedenborg's conclusion that "in regard to substance" the soul-stuff, or spirituous fluid, was part of this universal aura; therefore, unless you defined "matter," it was hard to say whether soul was material or not. Were sense perceptions material? They must be, coming from material things, and being "modifications" [waves and/or frequencies of air or ether]. Then what about ideas based on perceptions?

"I do not understand," he said, "in what way an immaterial modification is distinguished from a material modification, unless by degrees, in that the immaterial is higher, more universal, more perfect and more imperceptible. Is not every created thing in the world and nature a subject of extension, and may not everything as extended be called material?" [34]

But, he added, since the soul substance was capable of receiving life, and life came directly from the uncreated Infinite, or God, the soul might also be called immaterial, and so "the materialist and the immaterialist may each abide in his own opinion." [35]

Among the cacti of scholastic terms so often used by Swedenborg, the layman is likely to be discouraged. It is a help to know that scientists are discussing the same problems today in very much the same terms, some of them coming to the same conclusion—that where there is life there is immateriality.

For instance, an eminent Swedish-American astronomer, Dr.

Gustaf Strömberg, of the Mt. Wilson Observatory, grapples with exactly the same phenomena of life and matter (*The Soul of the Universe*).[36]

Dr. Strömberg reminds us of the immateriality of the pilot wave that guides the electron in space and time, emphasizing that the particle aspect of nature is material and the wave aspect is immaterial. The atom consists of particles which are made units by an immaterial wave structure with certain time and space properties.

Dr. Strömberg could almost be used as a guide to Swedenborg. The Californian says, "There is another world than that of space and time." The two worlds, he continues, are not entirely separated; they interact at certain points. These points he also calls "sources," because through them certain forces enter our world from that other. Through some of the sources "electricity" enters our world; it is associated with wave systems identified with "material" particles.[37]

But from other sources "living wave systems of different degrees of complexity" enter our world. These wave systems are "immaterial."

With confidence, for his biology was approved by Thomas Hunt Morgan, Dr. Strömberg says that such a "source" having caused a "living" but immaterial wave system, the latter is responsible for what happens in a living cell when its chromosomes divide. "The material elements follow the changes in the immaterial structure." [38]

He traces the development of the embryo, showing where subordinate wave systems are as it were commissioned to take charge and "expand in a certain order and gradually become 'fixed' or 'materialized'" in the structure and function of the different organs. The signals of the organizing wave system, Dr. Strömberg says, can be thought of as traveling along definite structural channels, and, he italicizes, *the channels often become observable as nerve fibers.*[39]

Swedenborg thought of the "formative force" as traveling along the nerve fibers after having created them.[40]

In 1734, five or six years before he wrote his *Economy,* Swedenborg had asserted that both soul and body were subject to "mechanical" laws. "There are no two natures." Nature was one, with one set of laws.[41]

Now, by spiritualizing matter it would seem as if he had satisfied himself, but he had not. He saw that there was still a problem in the "mechanism" by which the organic and the inorganic communicated. According to the Cartesian physics of his time, the chain of causation should be continuous, but that did not seem to be so. There was a jump by which dead matter became living, as there was between immaterial force and the material atom. Yet there was, there could be, only one nature.

Swedenborg stuck to that, but he abandoned continuity. Nature, he said, progressed by steps, or "by degrees." This hypothesis of his is so vital for an understanding of his whole future scheme of things that it becomes necessary once more to beg aid of modern science, and to compare its findings with Swedenborg's.

The way has been made easy by Arthur Koestler in the last essay of his *The Yogi and the Commissar*.[42] Modern scientists are not unaware that there is an unexplained "jump," be it ever so small, from the immaterial atom to the living cell and from it again to consciousness and to the higher mental states. Relying chiefly on the biologists Needham and Woodger, Koestler gives a summary of the significance of these "jumps."

He uses the simile of a staircase. On each tread the things or phenomena are of the same nature; what makes them seem to differ from the phenomena on the other treads is the way in which they associate, and "the new properties and values which emerge by this specific type of association." Each level depends on "the laws of the next higher level—laws which it cannot predict nor reduce" to its own level.

But, looking at the staircase from in front, only the vertical jumps between the treads are seen, and "everything becomes unexplained mystery." Koestler quotes Needham:

"What has not yet been done, however, is to elucidate the way in which each of the new great levels of organization has arisen . . . It must always be remembered that though we can chart out quite fully the laws existing at a given high organizational level, we can

never hope to understand how they fit into the picture as a
whole . . ." [43]

This picture was precisely what Swedenborg had always been
searching for, and his "degree" corresponds fairly closely to the
modern "level of organization."

The formidable name of Swedenborg's theory, set forth in the
Economy, was The Doctrine of Series and Degrees.[44] Without it,
he warned the reader again and again, nothing in the whole universe could be properly understood.

It was, he said, that doctrine which nature "in acting has prescribed for herself," her way of "subordinating and coordinating"
things. "Series are what successively and simultaneously comprise
things subordinate and coordinate."

A series, to put it simply, is the modern biologist's staircase.
Swedenborg called it a ladder when he wasn't being pedantic. "The
soul," he said, "does not flow into the actions of its body except by
intermediates, nor by a continuous medium, but as it were by a
ladder divided by steps." Also, "The intercourse between the soul
and the body . . . (is) a kind of progression . . . according to
natural order by a ladder divided into degrees." [45]

These degrees, he said, were of two kinds. Later he was to call
them degrees of height and degrees of breadth.[46] The degree of
height is the modern "jump" in the staircase from one level of
organization to another. The degree of breadth is the surface of the
tread, the things of similar nature on the same level.

Swedenborg's degree of height (also called by him a "discrete"
or a "determined" degree) was separate from the one above and
below it. By "separate" Swedenborg meant separate, even as modern scientists mean it. "We cannot arrive," he said, "from a substance of an inferior degree to a substance of a superior degree,
except by the division and as it were destruction of the unit of the
inferior degree." [47]

On the other hand, by the degree of breadth (also called by him
a "continuous degree" or "degree of composition") Swedenborg
said he meant "an aggregate of things coordinate"—as we should
say the phenomena on the same tread of the staircase. They, he

said, were related to each other as more or less of the same thing or quality, "beyond which you cannot proceed further and yet leave a unit or part of that degree." [48]

He had, so he was now convinced, the principle of the mechanism by which an immaterial soul communicated with a material body. Unlike Needham, however, he ventured to say how degrees (levels of organization) had arisen. He said it happened by "influx." "Those things that are superior flow into those that are inferior, according to the order and suitably to the mode in which the substances are formed." [49]

"The 'destiny' of a level," Koestler says, "is its dependence on the laws of the next higher level—laws which it cannot predict nor reduce," or, as Swedenborg never tired of remarking, it is "against order for the posterior to flow into the prior."

Swedenborg now had, in this "doctrine of series and degrees," a theory, a tool, a sort of universal jimmy, for solving the problems that stood between him and the picture of the whole he wanted to make, the system which he could not help making, any more than crystals can help crystallizing.

"The mind," he said, "never really acquiesces in any system respecting the commerce and harmony of mind and body which supposes the unknown and incomprehensible." [50]

His excursion into physiology was for the purpose of reducing the unknown. For him, as well as for some modern physicists, it was a decisive experience to study embryology, but as Swedenborg had not the faintest fear of trespassing on specialist domains he took the evidence he had obtained and stretched it cosmically. He was convinced that an immaterial force built up the material body; he was convinced in the only way he could have been—scientifically, given his honesty and love of truth for its own sake. He now supposed that he was out of "the shade in which hypotheses dwell," and that the following propositions were true:

The material aspect of the world had been developed from immaterial forces. Living matter had also arisen from immaterial force, plus life, which came from life's source, or God. These changes from one form of phenomena to another did not take place "continuously," but by steps, or "degrees of height" (modern:

"levels of organization" and "theory of emergency"). He supposed
that the manner in which this took place was by something he
termed "influx."

And "influx"?

Now the philosopher and mystic began to fill in the spaces left
by the scientist. "All these opinions combine to form a perfect
unity . . . when we acknowledge the omnipresence and universal
influx of God in all created things according to the modified character and capacity of each." [51]

Giving a name, however, to the creative force was as far as he
intended to go. "To know the manner in which this life and wisdom flow in is infinitely above the sphere of the human mind, there
is no analysis and no abstraction that can reach so high, for"—here
the scientist supremely affirmed his faith—"whatever is in God, and
what law God acts by, is God." [52]

In the ninth century A.D., another spiritual giant wrote, "There
are as many unveilings of God [Theophanies] as there are saintly
souls."

John Scotus Erigena (John, the Irishman), in other words, saw
that the idea of God must break differently through the prisms of
different personalities. Swedenborg's personality and what had
been happening in it must therefore again be considered, as well
as the form of religion he had found he could confess without
being untrue to his science.

CHAPTER TEN

Anatomy of Soul

OF all the references with which *The Economy of the Animal Kingdom* is so liberal there are only four to the Bible. Two of those are in the last lines. They have no obvious connection with what precedes them, but a man like Swedenborg did not finish a book of such importance to him without intending to convey the gist of the matter at its end.

The first reference is to the Second Epistle of Paul to Timothy, chapter 3, verses 1–10. Looking it up, one finds that Paul summarizes the vices of men living in the last "perilous times." Among other things such men are, the Apostle says, "without natural affection, truce-breakers, false accusers, incontinent, fierce, despisers of those that are good . . . ever learning and never able to come to a knowledge of the truth."

Looking up the second reference, from the Acts of the Apostles, chapter 17, verses 18–20, one finds that it describes Paul's sermon to the Athenians about the Unknown God, at which some of the Athenians mocked, but among those "who clave unto him and believed" was one "Dionysius, the Areopagite."

The name of Dionysius was taken by or affixed to a writer of mystical theology, who was probably a Syrian monk of the fifth century A.D. His writings were the chief Christian channel through which Neoplatonism flowed into Christianity. His religious philosophy, a modern scholar has said, "is in fact Neoplatonic philosophy slightly sprinkled with baptismal water from a Christian font." [1]

To prove that Swedenborg knew Dionysius it is not necessary to point to a reference to him in the *Economy*.[2] The whole trend of the book is that of Neoplatonism, down to specific details such as many Plotinian similes. Swedenborg had first met this philosophy when he was young, both in Sweden [3] and in England. In England, as already intimated, he met it through the so-called Cambridge

Platonists, to one of whom, Henry More (Morinus), he also refers in the *Economy*. He had read John Norris, the interpreter of the French Platonist Malebranche, whom he had also read. He knew the so-called *Theology of Aristotles,* really a work of a disciple of Plotinus. Swedenborg quotes St. Augustine liberally, and Thomas Aquinas and other Neoplatonist church fathers; [4] he quotes, of course, Plato, the father of them all, and he weaves in Aristotle (calling him often merely "the Philosopher," as was usual) whenever it suits him. It suits him well, because he uses him to support his saying that "the action of God," the law by which He acts, "is God himself." And he knew Spinoza. [5]

Swedenborg did not invent a religion, any more than he invented the science of anatomy.

His discoveries in regard to the human body were based, he tells us, on his study of what the experts in anatomy had set forth, with only a little of his own experience in dissection thrown in. As far as religion is concerned the order was probably reversed, and a spark of personal experience preceded his study of it, but he would have been the last to deny that in his spiritual search he consulted the experts. He did not always put quotation marks around what he used from them—most of it was well known—and he was not concerned to get a doctor's degree for his knowledge.

He was concerned with harmonizing his scientific conscience and his religious yearning, and with the aid of Neoplatonism he was able to sketch out a system, a picture of the whole, which began to fulfill this purpose.

The Hindu, Buddhist [6] and Greek predecessors of Plotinus and his Christian and Kabbalistic successors saw the created world as having emanated as force or radiated as light from the unknowable, uncreated Source, called God or Law or Light, matter being the radiation farthest from the Divine Center.

Neoplatonism [7] often spoke of this procession as a ladder reaching from God to the material world, but until Swedenborg had convinced himself that an immaterial force directing the development of an embryo could produce a material body he was probably not sure, as a physicist, that the ladder really rested on solid ground. He had identified this force, with the soul, and he saw the soul as created by the divine light and capable of receiving it.

Once when he was young, Swedenborg had tried hard to meet Leibnitz, in vain. Now, in effect, he had accepted what, as Aldous Huxley has told this age, Leibnitz called "the Perennial Philosophy"—"the metaphysic that recognizes a divine Reality substantial to the world of things and lives and minds; the psychology that finds in the soul something similar to, or even identical with, divine Reality; the ethic that places man's final end in the knowledge of the immanent and transcendent Ground of all being." [8]

That metaphysic, psychology, and ethic Swedenborg tried to work out for himself in the last part of his book, but not without grave misgivings. At the beginning of this part he makes one of his rare personal appearances. He speaks of his doubts as to whether the human soul was "accessible to any reach of mind." If it were, he said, it must be either by way of philosophy "or, more immediately, by the anatomy of the human body. But, upon making the attempt, I found myself as far from my object as ever; for no sooner did I seem to have mastered the subject than I found it again eluding my grasp, though it never absolutely disappeared from my view. Thus my hopes were not destroyed but deferred; and I frequently reproached myself with stupidity in being ignorant of that which was yet everywhere most really present to me; since by reason of the soul it is that we hear, see, feel, perceive, remember, imagine, think, desire, will; or that we are, move and live.

"The soul it is because of which, by which, and out of which, the visible corporeal kingdom principally exists; to the soul it is that we are to ascribe whatever excites our admiration and astonishment in the anatomy of the body; the body being constructed according to the image of the soul's nature, or according to the form of its operations. Thus did I seem to see, and yet not to see, the very object with the desire of knowing which I was never at rest. But at length I awoke as from a deep sleep, when I discovered that nothing is farther removed from the human understanding than what at the same time is really present to it; and that nothing is more present to it than what is universal, prior and superior; since this enters into every particular and into everything posterior and inferior. What is more omnipresent than the Deity—in him we live and are and move—and yet what is more remote from the sphere of the understanding?" [9]

In vain, he said, did the mind strive to know the Deity's nature beyond what it had pleased Him to reveal "in proportion to each man's individual exertions."

How should those exertions be applied? Swedenborg scored man's wish to mount at once "from the lowest sphere to the highest." Man, he said, no sooner learns the rudiments of geometry than he wants to square the circle, the rudiments of mechanics than he looks for perpetual motion, the rudiments of chemistry than he wants to make gold. And as for the love of the world, who does not strive for honor after honor and for estate upon estate? "Can you point out any considerable number in civil society who place a check or limit to efforts of this kind . . . ?"

Every son of earth still desires to touch the heavens with his finger, he concluded, but there is an order in these things. The progress must be made step by step, by degrees. When nature seems to have left us altogether in the dark, he reaffirmed, we need science in tracing out her steps. And this science he called his Doctrine of Series and Degrees or of Order. The people who don't know this ladder of nature and make their leaps without it, he said, will be found flat on the earth in some obscure cavern, "for instance in some occult position . . ." [10]

Resolutely rationalist, he admitted that even the doctrine of degrees was not enough with which to understand the reciprocal action of soul and body. "A knowledge of anatomy, pathology and psychology, nay even of physics and of the auras of the world" was necessary, for unless we "mount from phenomena thus, we shall in every age have to build new systems, which in their turn will tumble to the ground . . ." [11]

Uncertain, really, of his scheme, wavering in his terms and filling in blank spaces imaginatively much as ancient geographers used to fill in blanks on the map with fancy figures, Swedenborg nevertheless committed himself to a system.

As a physicist we know he had decided that there were four kinds of "forces of the nature of the universe." [12] (The first, or the universal, and the source of gravity; the second, or the magnetic, and the source of magnetism; the third, or ether, and the source of electricity, light, heat; the fourth, the air.)

Although these forces originally had started through the setting in motion and finiting of the "mathematical point" by the Uncreated Infinite, they were inanimate, but they were the means by which life streaming from the Infinite could embody itself. The "soul," or particle of life from the Infinite, Swedenborg said, must descend into matter by the same number of degrees as there are "auras" or forces—that is, by four degrees—and adapt itself to each, and form a kind of organism corresponding to each.

When he wrote the *Principia,* he had considered the mind as divided into "mens," or the rational mind, and "animus," or a lower, instinctual mind. He still held to that division, but above both minds he now put "soul" or "anima." The soul, and here he agreed with Neoplatonic philosophy, "is a faculty distinct from the intellectual mind, prior and superior to, and more universal and perfect than the latter." He again and again repeats that it is so high above the other faculties that it is "their order, truth, rule, law, science, art." Consciousness belongs to it, so does intuition (he quoted Locke to back him up). "And it flows into the intellectual mind much after the manner of light." [13]

The first aura furnishes the material for the organism of the soul.

"The next organ under the soul" is the intellectual mind, "whose office is to understand, to think and to will." It is developed from the material of the second aura.

The third organ is the animus, or the seat of sensuous desires and sensuous imagination. It belongs to the third aura.

The five external senses are in our material, airborne world. These, with the motor organs, "constitute the body, whose office it is to feel, to form looks and actions, to be disposed and to do what the higher lives determine, will and desire. Although there are this number of degrees, yet the animal system consists of nothing but the soul and the body, for the intermediate organisms are only determinations of the soul, of which as well as of the body they partake. Such now is the ladder, by which every operation and affection of the soul and body descend and ascend." [14]

Swedenborg held to it that the soul was the formative force caus-ing the body, and that it was lucky for mankind it was not identical with man's so-called rational mind. For even in an insane person, he declared, "all the economic functions of the body proceed ac-cording to laws in the truest order. The government would be utterly at an end, if the soul were insane at the same time as the mind." [15]

The mind, he stops to tell us, is really the operation of the soul "in the organic, cortical substance," and, being this, the mind "partakes at once of the soul and of the body," [16] but Swedenborg usually treats it as an independent organism. At birth, he believes, the mind has no innate ideas, it has to acquire them from the ma-terial brought to it by the lower mind, or animus, which "conceives or takes in those things that the organs of the body feel." But the higher mind (mens) is able to recognize and to judge the material correctly only because the soul, being in touch with universal wis-dom, pours "an intellectual light . . . into the sphere of our minds, by means of which we are enabled to derive instruction from our-selves." It is the soul which has the innate ideas. "Unless this soul flowed in from science, while from itself, into every point of our intellect, it would be impossible for us to perceive anything in order, or to reduce anything we had perceived to order, we should there-fore look in vain for understanding in intellect or judgment in thought." [17]

Swedenborg again cites Locke: "Locke has abundantly proved that there are no innate ideas in the mind, not even ideas of moral laws. This author has traced the interior operations of the mind with as much care as anatomists have examined the structure of the body; but, after having pursued them to their origin, he remarks that it must be acknowledged that something flows in from above by which the mind is rendered capable of reflecting upon ideas acquired a posteriori" or by experience. Something perceives "the operations of our own minds within us," Locke says and Sweden-borg triumphantly quotes, "which operations, when the soul comes to reflect on and consider do furnish the understanding with an-other set of ideas which could not be had from the things with-out." [18]

As the rational mind functions by means of the cortical substance, so the lower mind or animus functions through the "common sensorium," or cerebrum, Swedenborg says. He calls it "an inferior or middle kind of intellect." It can imagine external objects and sensations, and therefore it is the seat of desire for pleasant sense impressions. It has passions of joy, anger, sadness, fear, envy, "and the like," but not as the thoughtful, purposeful mind has them.[19]

The bodily sensations (of the fourth degree, or the material world) Swedenborg regards as distinct from "internal sensations." The only question, he says, is as to how the external communicate with the internal, and this he has already explained as taking place by influx through intermediate degrees (levels of organization).

That the sensations of the body are independent of those of the internal sensations of the lower mind is proved, he says, by the fact that when the external impressions are cut off in sleep the imagination is still able to present sense images, thus showing that the internal are awake.[20]

And that the lower mind or animus is distinct from the higher or rational mind is shown in sleepwalkers, "in whom . . . the corporeal machine is set in motion without any light flowing in from the sphere of reason."—"So also in many who may be compared to somnambulists as being led solely by the instinct of the animus and by little or no instinct of understanding." Then, after such people have rushed into action blindfold "from mere lust or cupidity," they "appeal to the mind as judge, and bring reasons from it to justify themselves to themselves and to others from the charge of irrationality." [21] (As we should say, they "rationalize.")

But the mind then may, if "by practice and cultivation" it has kept a channel of communication open to the influx and light from the soul, refuse to justify the animus, may "combat with the animus as with an enemy," and fight for victory.

That the mind is distinct from the soul is evident, Swedenborg says, from this conflict of the mind with its lower self, "also from a certain intimate consciousness that twinges and solicits from principles unknown, very often in merely natural things, originating deeply from self-love."

"One thing is clear," he grimly admits, "there is in us an internal man that fights with the external; a manifest proof that as the mind may be in collision with the animus, so may the soul with the mind, and the essential life that comes from the spirit of God, with the soul." [22]

How can such struggles take place?

Swedenborg founds his system of ethics on his belief that man can choose what he will do; he has free will. Then he hurries to ask and to answer what "the will" is. The will is a function of the rational mind, and the mind's office is to understand, "to revolve what things it has understood," then "to draw a line under its judgments and sum them up," to conclude something. "To say *it is concluded* or *to will* amounts to the same thing." "Will is the closing act of the thoughts." [23]

But what is free choice? This, Swedenborg indicates, depends on man's ability to judge. "Thus, the more intelligent the man, the more free his will." There is only a shadow of free will "in maniacs and idiots, a small share in the lowest grades of mankind; in all a larger measure according to their degree of intelligence . . ." [24]

He does not think it is for lack of mental equipment that intelligent men so often choose evil. The rational mind is well equipped, he contests. It can draw on the soul, which is "essential science and natural intelligence," and which itself is instructed by Infinite Wisdom. From below, the mind has the reports of the senses "which are so many masters to instruct us in the nature of the world . . . And that we may know all things that all men know, speech is given us; also the memory of the past, and perpetual experience; wonders too familiar and too closely environing us to allow us to wonder at them." [25]

But to be able to choose the better side more is needed than knowledge. Swedenborg says there has to be also "a reacting force to enable the mind to turn itself either to the one or the other" side. He sees the mind as sitting in the center of forces that usually oppose each other: "the soul acting on it from above, and the spirit of life acting on the soul; and the animus acting on it from below and the body on the animus."

You can think of it also as the mind holding the balance between the two forces. Then the trouble is, as he sees it, that the physical sensations weight the scales heavily, but not so the "spiritual" weights at the other side—they seem to be incomprehensible and intangible. Not so the "infinitely varied amusements of human societies," or the pleasures of the body, or "the loves emanating from every man's self-hood," or necessary economic cares, "for to seek our bread with anxious solicitude and to withdraw the mind from the body are two opposites." [26] (He had found that out during the years it took him to reach independence.)

Set this, he insists, against the fact that we cannot feel or even be conscious always of what gives pleasure to the subtle body of the soul. Its "supereminent fibrils" which were "delineated by the first aura of the world" are *within* our nerves and vessels, but not *in* them,[27] and hence their sensations cannot be perceived by our senses. We can only sense the soul through the imperfect material medium of the brain.

"Hence it follows that we are more capable of understanding what is true than of willing it, and that the liberty of acting, or the wife, is very easily divorced from the understanding, or the husband. And this separation in the marriage-bed of the mind is often more complete in the intelligent than in the simple-minded, for the former persuade themselves by various intellectual reasons to take the part of the lower senses and speciously cloak the merest vices under the garb of virtues." [28]

Is it a bad thing then that the forces from below are so tangible and strong? No, Swedenborg says. "Victory is estimated according to the number and valor of the enemy . . ." He is thinking here in Neoplatonic terms. The reason for the soul's entanglement in matter is for the sake of experience gained in struggle, so that it may return ultimately to the Source bringing its share of "harmonic variety." The cause of what he calls "equilibration," or the mental weighing business, is that "nothing is acceptable or grateful that does not proceed from free choice—what is done from necessity has no merit." [29]

And, though "high and divine things . . . do not come home to our mental consciousness at all by way of sensation," yet we can still be instructed by teachers, by sciences, "in some measure" by our power to reflect, "but principally from the Holy Scriptures." They provide "the code of rules for obtaining the end by the means." [30]

Man has indeed got free will in proportion to his intelligence, and every kind of knowledge is available for him, but whether he chooses the better or the worse, ethically speaking, also depends on something else. Swedenborg says it depends on desire. "The freedom of willing depends upon the love of the end, which results in desire." [31]

The lower agents, working through "the love of self" in the mind, have great advantage over the higher when it comes to instilling desire. "There are always incentives at hand to persuade it [the mind] to descend, and to dissuade it from rising above itself to something that is incomprehensible, that hides its delights in secret places, and remits them away from the present to the future." [32]

The worse is chosen in place of the better, not for lack of knowledge, but because "the desire resulting from love is not present whenever the mind begins to exert its choice. Although here above all a surpassing love should be present, to put out the flames of other loves." [33]

Rigorously honest, Swedenborg admits that he thinks we have no power to light this sacred fire ourselves; worse still, we have hardly the power to want it to be lit, except with a kind of passive wish.

But from somewhere in his reading or experience Swedenborg finds that which at all times he craves, a law. He says, as Plotinus did, that God will compel no man, but if he finds even the faintest spark of reciprocity in man he can kindle it into the sacred fire. "Granting this, it follows that there is a universal law," and if we obey this we shall at last be able to "desire that which at first we tacitly and coldly wish. This law, of His ordaining, appears to be that our willing should excite His willing . . ." [34]

The struggle between the internal and the external man was in the last instance decided by man himself. He had at least to show a minimum of interest before God could help him without violating the divine principle of freedom.

In this picture of the whole that Swedenborg had drafted, he was sometimes inconsistent, not from lack of intelligence but from a kind of swiveling excess of it. He was able to take in too many points of view; perhaps he was now and then dazzled by too many facets of a subject. In his anxiety to bring out a truth, he often became repetitious, doubling and redoubling on his track like a meandering brook that with each new turn reflects the same sky a little differently.

But it was always the same sky. Slightly wavering as his conclusions and terminology were, a whole and essentially consistent picture does emerge from the wealth of scintillant detail in *The Economy of the Animal Kingdom*. It was not a particularly Christian one. Not one dogma is visible in it. Swedenborg showed himself as caring more for the spirit of Jesus than for Christian dogma. At the end he gave it as his conviction (not as anything he had direct knowledge of) that the soul survives the death of the body, happily rid of all interference from the "non-intellectual spheres," living beyond time and almost free from space. Heaven would be a "society of souls" and the City of God on earth the seminary of it. "The most universal law of its citizens is that they love their neighbor as themselves and God more than themselves. All other things are means, and are good in proportion as they lead directly to this end." [35]

It was the creed of a calm scientist and of a good man. It was really summed up when he said, during the discourse on free will: "If then we strive to the utmost of our power to will and to be able, it follows as a matter of course that a higher power then breathes upon us, and raises our efforts to powers not human; and thereby brings us back into a state emulous of that liberty which we have lost." [36]

Swedenborg was far from believing, however, that he personally had reached this state. Here and there on the pure white snow of his intellectual arguments an odd stain and some scattered feathers mark a struggle. After he had pointed out that anger and revenge consign us from liberty to slavery he admitted that "similar remarks apply to inclination and love, by which we are frequently consigned to chains, and the mind itself sees its own will put in fetters, and sometimes smiles with bitterness the while, but without having the power to shake off the yoke." [37]

Physical passion, we can surmise from his diaries, had galled him, but he did not think of physical pleasure as immoral in itself. From his system it flowed naturally that the soul had not created the body to torment it. The delights of the world and of the sensual part of man served, he said, as "the fuel and incentive of bodily life." He condemned those persons as "somewhat beside themselves who aim not to moderate but altogether to exterminate the pleasures of the senses and the delights of the world as if they were so many deadly and pernicious poisons." [38]

Taste and flavor, he said, stimulated the body to repair its tissues. And "the desire for sexual connection descends from an innocent and burning desire of the soul to multiply the individuals of its kind . . ." [39] By what he seems to deem a fortunate dispensation, he considered that the delights and hence the keenness of desire increased in proportion to the universality of the purpose, so that those delights "which if legitimate are known as connubial" [40] were the most alluringly delightful of all.

He was in no morbid state of hatred of the body. Though he was well aware of its weight in the scales as against spiritual force, he was even more conscious of the power of egoism. "I know not what darkness overspreads the rational faculties when the mind begins to swell with pride . . . it is like pouring a liquor on some exquisite wine, which throws it into a froth, sullies its purity, and clouds its translucence." [41]

An ardent and ambitious man, he had had the normal struggles with body and with mind. But in nothing he had so far written was there any arrow pointing to even an unconscious conflict of the kind that make potential mystics appeal so hard to higher powers for help that they dream strange dreams and see lights from beyond sun, moon, and candle power.

Yet these phenomena had already puzzled Emanuel Swedenborg.

CHAPTER ELEVEN

Strange Dreams and "Temptations"

THE well-set-up, rather plump Swedish scholar who lived in Amsterdam from about May, 1739, to about October, 1740, was anything but an idle dreamer, however. It is doubtful whether he gave himself much time to enjoy the golden, liquid shadows of Rembrandt's city. He was there chiefly because it was one of the few places where books could be published without censorship; because it was a place where he could consult the works of great anatomists, and—at least equally important for him —where he could read the books of those men who, like himself, had been driven to ask the eternal questions about body, soul, and God. Amsterdam had been the city of Spinoza.

The first part of *The Economy of the Animal Kingdom* was published in July, 1740, the second part was in print at the beginning of September and out in January, 1741. Swedenborg left Amsterdam in October, 1740, for Stockholm, but while he had been seeing his book through the press he had not confined himself to this. Besides writing a couple of minor works, he had revised and added to the manuscript of his great work on the brain; he had made many extracts from anatomical works; and he had probably begun to make the collection of extracts from philosophical authors which fill another volume of his manuscript.[1]

Not all the extracts were strictly philosophical—he cites from Aristotle that "men solid of flesh are dull of intellect, while men soft of flesh are gifted." [2] There seems to be a sigh of the sedentary here, but Swedenborg's appetite for work was as great as his powers of sight-seeing, and no man who was soft-fleshed in any feeble way could have done what he accomplished when he returned to Sweden.

He was back at his exacting job in the Board of Mines on November 3, 1740, and in almost constant attendance there throughout the next two or three years, except when he sat in parliament as a mem-

ber of the House of Nobles, or when he went on commissions of
inquiry for the Board.[3]

Meanwhile he was carrying on his studies and writings on psychology and physiology. He was not deterred by the fact that the
learned world had received the first two volumes of *The Economy*
with tepid interest and, so far as his theories of the soul were concerned, with some alarm about his "materialism." [4]

He finished the manuscripts of *The Fibre,* which he had planned
to be the third volume of *The Economy*—about four hundred pages
of anatomical, physical, and philosophical thinking on the human
nervous system; he sketched out several smaller transactions containing his more clarified views on the interaction of soul and body,
and then, feeling he had been "too hasty" in rushing into print with
The Economy, he began to compose a new gigantic work.

In his former published work he had dealt with the "government" (economy) of the soul's kingdom; that is, with the cortex
of the brain, with the blood and the embryo, and with a doctrine
of the soul. Now he meant to go through all the organs of the body
and to take up again, with fuller knowledge, the question of body-
soul relationships. This was to be his final map of the soul's kingdom. In seventeen parts.

No wonder that Eric Benzelius wrote to his son Charles, who
was in Stockholm: "Visit your uncle Emanuel Swedenborg as
often as possible, but at such hours as he may himself appoint; for
he is not always at leisure, and is most economical with his time." [5]

It would indeed hardly seem as if Swedenborg had any time to
ponder on flashes of vision or strange dreams. But these come un-
bidden and make themselves at home. The hard-working mining
expert, the physicist-philosopher, the anatomist, had for several
years been conscious of a rill of secret life—perhaps the very spring
of his present studies—at any rate a messenger from subliminal
regions which was making itself more and more evident.

At least as early as his forty-fifth or forty-sixth year Swedenborg
noted something peculiar about dreams. He annotated Wolff's
Psychology with the remark that although dreams probably rose
from some external stimulus, yet there were dreams which seemed

as if they tended to some definite end, as if they were directed by the soul. A couple of years later, in 1736, he had begun making notes of his dreams (they were subsequently lost).

Then, while he was writing the *Economy*, and puzzling over the problem of how to keep the lower mind (animus) in order,[6] he wrote that the rational mind could keep watch and wake while the body slept; and one gathers he felt he had solved something while dreaming, much as did the assyriologist who dreamed the correct interpretation of a difficult inscription.[7] But, besides this, he said, the mind could in a measure stand away from the senses and thus receive a fuller light from the soul. By this statement he was probably referring to a different experience.

In Amsterdam, it may be remembered, when he came there in late August, 1736, he was shocked at the "spirit of gain" pervading the city, and in his diary he made a long entry about God and the Dutch. It was an unusually "interior" entry in that concrete and guidebook diary, but it happened that in Amsterdam he had had an unusual experience.

Together with what he remembered from his childhood of the effect of inhibited breathing, this was perhaps the very experience which led him to make a special study of the connection between the motion of the brain and the motion of the lungs, one of his titles to fame. While discussing the proofs of this in *The Economy*, he several times referred to the mind's power of cutting off the sense impressions when it desired to think intensely, especially the "olfactory impressions" [8] (no doubt canals smelled badly whether in Venice or in Amsterdam, and his sense of smell was keen).

He insisted that the mind's way of cutting off sense impressions was by breathing very quietly through the mouth, or in any case by breathing very shallowly. He spoke of the breast fearing "by any deep breath to disturb the quiet of the brain," and of its compressing itself and admitting only a small amount of air.

Reduction of the amount of air may help intense thinking; if it is carried too far, however, it may lead to something else. (Six or seven years later, Swedenborg wrote in a very different kind of diary that "in the morning the same kind of faintness or weakness came over me as I had in Amsterdam, when I was beginning the *Economy of the Animal Kingdom*." He continued, "it came when

I saw the light," and he thought it meant "as it meant then" that his mind was being put in order "as it happened then too since it give me penetration with the pen." [9])

Three weeks after his stay in Amsterdam, in 1736, he wrote (as previously cited) that when men of science who have the power of synthesizing "after a long course of reasoning make a discovery of the truth, straightway there is a certain cheering light, and joyful confirmatory brightness, that plays round the sphere of their mind; and a kind of mysterious radiation—I know not whence it proceeds—that darts through some sacred temple of the brain."

Clearly he had had, in Amsterdam, an impression of light which he considered mysteriously helpful, a light which was an "influx" from the soul. But at times he was not at all sure about the origin. Elsewhere he expresses how the soul cannot function if the ways of communication are not open, such as in the infant or the idiot, and "yet for all this we will not cease to pride ourselves above our fellow mortals, whenever we receive a few false rays by influx from the soul; and to judge of the souls of others by their bodies."

Had the joyful brightness become a few false rays? He had said that if the mind had once experienced the cheering light ("for no desire attaches to the unknown") it would be carried away wholly in pursuit of it, despising all merely corporeal pleasures; but still he might only have been a little flowery in describing intellectual satisfaction, and so the falseness might be intellectual disappointment.

However, soon after finishing *The Economy,* in February, 1740, he made a terse summary of his system, and at the end of this he wrote, italicizing the sentence: "These things are true, because I have the sign." [10]

What sign? The "confirmatory brightness"?

We do not know. But a few years later, he wrote, ". . . a flame of divers sizes and with a diversity of color and splendor has often been seen by me. Thus while I was writing a certain little work hardly a day passed by for several months in which a flame was not seen by me as vividly as the flame of a household hearth; at the time this was a sign of approbation, and this happened before spirits began to speak with me viva voce." [11]

In another important reminiscent passage, he wonders that he had not realized before what was happening to him, because for many years, he says, such remarkable proofs existed. "Not only were there dreams for some years, informing me concerning the things that were being written, but there were also changes of states while I was writing: a certain extraordinary light in the things that were being written . . ." [12]

There is no doubt that for a scientifically minded man, as he looked on himself, he was in an embarrassing situation with these "occult" experiences and in a state of painful bewilderment in regard to his sanity. In his work on *The Fibre,* written in 1741–42, he said some things about mental diseases in which may be seen veiled references to the suspicions that most likely beset him.

One form of mental disease he calls fanatic imagination (it clearly means a state of hallucination), and he says that it may be due, among other things, to a condition of the brain in which it is "rigid," and refuses to admit the testimony of the senses, "or else admits them by way of exasperants." It does not in this state, he says, dispel "strange and illy consociated ideas," but may absorb them and thereby "immensely augment the idea conceived . . ." [13]

Various physical diseases may cause this, but also sicknesses of the emotional mind (animus), such as hope deceived, or sorrow, but even the rational mind may originate the evil, he says, if it has been too intensely applied, especially to the problem of life after death.

"But so long as the mind is still sane," he reassured himself, "such illusions can easily be dispelled . . ."

On the other hand, in writing about a state which he termed "ecstasy energumene," he regarded it as possible that, besides the half-dead condition of the partly drowned or partly suffocated, there was a state in which the soul voluntarily separated from the body. As proof he cited the case of persons "skilled in the art of magic" from the northern regions. (The Lapps in the north of Scandinavia have always had a reputation for shamanistic mediumism.)

Such persons, Swedenborg said, "are credited with being able to fall spontaneously into a kind of ecstasy in which they are deprived of the external senses and of all motion, and with being engaged meanwhile in the operations of the soul alone, in order that after resuscitation they may reveal thefts and declare desired secrets."

Physically, he noted, the circulation seems to have stopped in "persons subject to ecstasy," as well as the respiration, and he concluded that "for the leading of an ecstatic life a peculiar disposition is required." [14]

Without at this stage exploring the modern theories that may cover Swedenborg's own experiences, it may be mentioned here that he had himself, unconsciously, stumbled on an old technique for inducing such a peculiar disposition. It was not lacking in significance that he marked the apparent cessation of breathing in the "ecstatic" subject.

Professor H. H. Price, of New College, Oxford, in his presidential address to the Society for Psychical Research (1937), declared one of their great difficulties to be that the investigator of psychic phenomena usually has to rely on hearsay. Not only is a technique wanted by which psychic phenomena can be repeated at will, but the investigator should be able to experience the phenomena himself. Professor Price then with all the diffidence in the world called attention to the fact that for a couple of thousand years certain Hindus have practiced a technique which may lead to psychic phenomena, though this is not the primary object—"yoga," or a conviction of union with God, being the primary object. Professor Price suggested that students might try this, but scientifically rather than religiously.

At least two modern investigators, one a Hindu and one an American, have studied yoga technique scientifically and reported their findings. Dr. K. T. Behanan (on a Sterling fellowship from Yale University) went to India to study the subject firsthand and to practice the exercises.[15] Dr. Theos Bernard also went to India for these purposes.[16]

From both one gathers that besides intense concentration on a serious idea the ability to hold one's breath is of vital importance for reaching the condition in which phenomena may occur. Dr. Behanan says that the pause between inhalation and exhalation is "the main feature of all yogic varieties of breathing which are claimed to have spiritual value . . ." [17] He speaks of the different bright colors seen by him during these exercises and of his consciousness of a change in the level of respiration. It seemed to him that in this condition his respirations were very few and shallow. He noted a feeling of joy.

Dr. Bernard, who also investigated Thibetan techniques, laid more stress on the importance of holding the breath. The yogins were said to be able to hold it for about an hour, and he was told that unless he could keep it in for at least three minutes nothing of any significance would appear. He worked up to five minutes. In the second month he began to see lights and vivid colors, and finally a white light of great brilliance, which he was able to make appear at will by using the technique he had learned. An ecstatic condition of great joy sometimes ensued. Dr. Bernard quotes at length from the ancient yogic texts regarding the marvelous psychic phenomena which the accomplished yogin can produce at will. Seeing other worlds than ours, levitation, etc., are said to be the least of them. Incidentally he mentions one form of the exercises which involved mouth-breathing.

Swedenborg has left minute descriptions of the kind of mouth-breathing, shallow breathing, and "internal breathing" which he at first unconsciously and then consciously practiced when he was concentrating intensely on an intellectual problem, or, later, on a spiritual one. He came, he said, to be able to hold his breath almost entirely for "a little hour." [18]

It is at least possible that his visions and feelings of lights, of colored flames, and of "joyful confirmatory brightness" went with the special kind of breathing which he was to develop even further with even more startling results.

Western mystics of all ages as well as Eastern yogins agree on the overwhelming sense of conviction which their experience of the "light" brings to them, and it has been mentioned that Swedenborg interpreted his light-visions as signs of approbation, while he was writing a work that probably was his new book the *Animal Kingdom* or the "Soul's Kingdom of the Body" (*Regnum Animale*).

Approbation of what? Naturally he took it to be of the system which he had worked out concerning the interrelationship of soul and body. And so he stressed more and more the mastership of the soul, the way in which vessels and organs ministered to its purposes, although those could be foiled and spoiled by selfish instincts in the mind and the animus. But he still solemnly invoked experiment as the only way in which truth could be found. He admitted that faith was better, but he said he was writing his book for those who had to go the way of reason, "who never believe anything but what they can receive with the intellect . . ." [19]

His own intellect had not suffered. Some of his keenest deductions were in his work on the brain, which was meant to be a part of the *Animal Kingdom*. He believed firmly that he was on the right track for finding the soul, because the body was its image "if not exactly, yet quite sufficiently . . . Thus by the body we are instructed respecting the soul, by the soul respecting the body; and by both respecting the truth of the whole." [20]

If he had been, as he said, "too hasty" in publishing the result of his findings after only investigating the blood and the brain, he now meant to make up for that by really going into the body's every detail.

Yet Swedenborg was not really happy. He should have been. He had an official position which gave him work that interested him, and in his physiological studies he had outside interests so great that they were really inside. Most important of all for him, he was convinced he had found the right religious philosophy. He was satisfied with the way he had fitted together the pieces of physical and spiritual information he had labored to acquire. In fact he had the comprehensive hypothesis every scientist craves, and it seemed to him to provide all the answers, bar slight details.

Still, it is known from a diary he began to keep in 1743 [21] that he was far from happy. He had indeed formulated his religious beliefs, but he was now confronted by the struggle to live up to them. He was not mildly dejected now and then as every thinking human being must be at the gap between knowing and doing; it was more than that. Swedenborg was suffering. He suffered in proportion to the joy he had experienced when he perceived "the light"—an experience which, all mystics testify, makes a hypersensitive scrutiny of their own shortcomings inevitable, so that after the first glad recognition of feeling "saved" a period of dark doubt occurs.

Probably Swedenborg suffered equally at the thought that the very light he clung to might be a will-o'-the-wisp, might even be insanity. It is not likely that he had anyone to whom he could talk freely on such matters. Eric Benzelius was away in Linköbing. Furthermore, Benzelius, being now a bishop, was presumably a believer, and believers would merely wonder why Swedenborg had to drag in his reason to be satisfied. As for the skeptics, they would have wondered why he needed to believe. Both groups would have distrusted and rejected his visions and his "informative" dreams, either as from the Devil or as insanity.

Unlike Socrates, Swedenborg was too modern a man to listen peacefully to his "inner voice." He had to find out what kind of voice it was, what kind of dreams those were in which he foresaw things that later happened. As early as about 1741, he had made a list of quotations mainly from Aristotle and Plato concerning presages of the future in dreams.[22] There were no psychic researchers about with tabulated results of mechanically regulated experiments of precognition. It must have comforted the worried Swedenborg that Plato, although relegating the art of divining to madness, nevertheless thought it behooved a man of prudence to pay attention to signs that come in visions or in dreams.

Swedenborg did not doubt that there was a divine light which could flow into the soul from God and from the soul into the mind, but he was not sure about the receptacle. Putting his anguish into scholastic sawdust, he had written, "We cannot say with what power, according to what laws, and in what manner, the subject reflects, infracts, diminishes and intercepts these rays, opposes to them its own mists and beclouds itself; how again when these mists are dispersed it emerges into the light; how it warms with zeal; and, on the other hand, how it cools from want of it . . ."[23]

He knew right well that he cooled from want of it and that he felt dangerously lost in the mists. Then it was, no doubt, that he applied his test for insanity, the test he had formulated when he wrote in *The Fibre* about mental diseases.

He began by saying meaningfully, "There is hardly a mortal who is not in his own way insane. He alone is sane and acts wisely who worships God, thrice best and greatest, and by faith aspires to eternal bliss; and the wisest is he who regards not even this bliss except as a consequence, but the glory of the deity as the principal thing."

From this description of wisdom, it was clear, he said, what the degrees of insanity were, and the test of the insanity's "nature and intensity" could be found out by knowing "the ends the mind has in view and follows up." It was obvious to him that deranged minds might have noble ends in view, but the "follow-up" belonged to the sane. If the following up of the end carried away from wisdom, from the Deity, then it was toward insanity, he declared, but he added that this diametric opposition to the Deity was not what was commonly known in the world as insanity, "because it is universal and is believed to be truly human, and indeed of such nature that the world declares those to be insane who are not insane." [24]

Showing that he knew well enough what the accepted definition was, he said, "Medically speaking, an insane person is one who acts contrary to accepted propriety and the customs of society, or, still more, who obstinately defends his own opinion against acknowledged truths and the judgments of a sound mind, and pursues it to the contempt and derision of the vulgar, that is to say who, deranged and empty of mind, exposes himself to public sport." [25]

He gave himself a clean mental bill of health according to the world's definition. But—was he sound from God's point of view? He was sure he was following up a good end in trying to justify faith by reason, but could the mind ever present us with pure truth while it was entangled with the body? Could it ever be rid of the mistakes of the senses? [26] So he asked at the beginning of the *Animal Kingdom,* and there too he stressed the purity the mind must possess, and the concern for only universal purposes, before it can receive the light of truth from above.

A humble man, Swedenborg was very doubtful about his own purity, and now he had reached a point where his own reasoning did not satisfy him. He had had a glimpse of what he thought of as divine approval, and he yearned for more, for enough so that he could put out of his head the suspicion that the blissful light had been the "weak fires" of the body or of the animus or even of the mind, pretending to be the light of life, as he wrote in the second part of the new book.[27]

The book, the *Animal Kingdom,* had its two first parts nearly ready for the press, when Emanuel Swedenborg again applied to the Board of Mines for leave of absence to consult libraries abroad and publish his new work. He said· he would have preferred to stay at home and attend to his little property and have pleasant times rather than go to so much trouble and expense by traveling "in these unquiet times," and this "with the probability of meeting in the end with more unfavorable than favorable judgments." Yet, he said, he wanted to produce something real in his lifetime, something which might be of use in the scientific world and to posterity, and which might even obtain some honor for his native country. He would as usual give up half his salary to a substitute, and he would even keep a journal to prove that his time wasn't being wasted! But that would not be necessary, for his own intention was to use all the diligence possible to finish his work, return to his country, and in "tranquillity and ease" continue his "larger work, the *Regnum Minerale,*" and thus be "of actual use to the public at large . . ."[28]

On July 21 Assessor Swedenborg left Stockholm for Amsterdam, traveling in a leisurely fashion and doing some strenuous sightseeing on the way. He arrived toward the end of August, 1743.

But the change of scene did not dispel the dark mists that from time to time enveloped him. Most characteristic of the period of strife that now began for him is a little incident which he noted in his intimate diary on April 7, 1744.

He said, evidently referring to something that took place in a dining room, either public or private, that "I heard a man at the table ask his neighbor the question whether any one could be melancholy who had more than enough of money. I smiled inwardly and would have answered, if it had been proper to do so in that company or if I had been asked, that a man who has more than enough of everything may not only be subject to melancholy but to a still deeper kind which is that of the mind and the soul or of the spirit which effects it; I wondered that he brought it up. I can bear witness to this so much the more since I by the grace of

God have been granted an abundance of all that I need temporally; I could live well on my income alone and carry out what I have in mind and still have money left over; therefore I can bear witness that the sadness or melancholy which comes from lack of means is of a lower and a physical kind and in no way equal to the other." [29]

Why was he so melancholy? In his book *The Fibre* he wrote at length about the causes of melancholy, and, consulting Swedenborg on Swedenborg, one may find that the "spiritual cause," the "supreme cause," of melancholy is due to an "evil conscience," otherwise "temptations." Such a disease of the soul, he says, descending into the mind and then into the lower mind and from this into the blood, "perturbs, inverts and robs the whole animal organism." [30]

Now what did he mean by "temptations"?

CHAPTER TWELVE

The Great Vision

IT is hard to lock up a house entirely. Lock and bar and shutter as one may, there will nearly always be a window not securely fastened—to the great joy of the burglar, or even to the householder who forgot his key.

Swedenborg, so watchfully impersonal, did leave an opening leading directly into his inner life at its most difficult period. It was a diary,[1] mainly of his dreams, which he kept in 1743 and 1744, while he was in Holland and in England. The hand, probably a family hand, which tore out the notes he had made of his dreams in 1736–39, did not apparently have a chance to meddle with the record he made in this diary. At any rate, someone discovered and published the diary in the middle of the nineteenth century, causing a full Victorian uproar.

There were people who objected that he never meant such intimate notes to be published, referring to his frank descriptions of sexual dreams. By their attitude they unwittingly lent color to the theory which now would seem all too obvious, the theory that Swedenborg was in a state of melancholy because of "guilt feelings" due to suppressed sex. But that easy explanation has to be examined. Fortunately Swedenborg has left no doubt about his attitude in this matter.

It was not Victorian. He lived in an age when his environment did not compel him to veil or to suppress interest in sex—quite the contrary. One of the commonplaces of history is to refer to the eighteenth century, especially the first three quarters of it, as "one of the most licentious, etc.," of the world's record for licence in sexual matters. Casanova need hardly be mentioned. Now Swedenborg was no Casanova, although he himself said that women had been his chief passion all his life.[2] That admission, made to himself only in a supersensitive state of his conscience, need not be taken too literally—there was hardly time in his life for this sort of thing

—but he had been perfectly ready to publish his views on sex in a book written only a year or two before the dream diary.

It was the draft of a book on "Reproduction" (*De Generatione*), and in it he not only described the objective anatomy of the sex organs, but the subjective feelings associated with "this most pleasant and delicious violence and necessity." He described the psycho-physical pleasures of love with a kind of pure and glowing factual frankness, which was equally far from the ineffable or the lascivious—and from the theoretical; though the still eager mathematician in him quaintly enough wondered whether the number of "tacit titillations" of which certain nerves were capable could not "be reduced to calculation," because they "must equal the sum of the papillae." [3]

So when he set down undisguisedly those dreams in which he had had sexual experience, it was not as examples of something which he held in horror, it was because he had come to look on his dreams as symbolic, quite in the modern way, but from another angle. Instead of seeing his dreams as symbols of striving sex desires, he interpreted his sexual dreams as symbolic of striving spiritual desires, either intellectual or religious, or both. One of his dreams, for instance, was of two women, one young and the other older; he kissed the hands of both, but was in doubt as to which of them he would make love. Having decided that women in dreams represented sciences, he interpreted this dream as referring to his doubt whether he would keep on with his older, intellectual work, or take up a newer and more spiritual work also in his thoughts. [4]

After one dream involving successful physical intercourse, he interpreted it as "love for what is holy," since, he said, all love has its origin in what is holy, "it is a series, in the body it really is in *projectione seminis . . .*" [5]

The key-word here is "series." As early as in *The Economy of the Animal Kingdom* he had placed different kinds of love at the different levels of man's personality. At the level of the body was the physical act, this had its "correspondence" in the unthinking desire of the lower mind, and to this again corresponded, in the higher mind, "a purer love, lacking a name of its own, with the representation of another in oneself and of oneself in another, that is, of an inmost connection." This was as high as man could go, consciously, but on a still higher level the origin of these loves and desires lay in the soul's wish to preserve its own kind for "more universal ends," and, of course, he saw this as an expression of the will of God.

Hence, for him, a dream of physical love, the lowest level of the series, could signify its origin in the highest level, that is, God, or "love for what is holy." No step in this ladder was "impure" to Swedenborg (though he noted that the world thought so), provided it really was part of the whole series, and not the last two bits broken off, unspiritualized by that love "lacking a name of its own." In his draft of the book on the *Soul* (*De Anima*, 1741) he gave it a name, calling it "conjugial love," as opposed to "conjugial hate," which he also described—a state worse than hell, he said, where lovers, who had been merely physically linked and then lost the illusion of passion, now loathed each other and fought like furies.[6]

What he saw as essential in the true union of minds and bodies was the feeling that each wanted to give all to the other. Self-abandonment. For this reason he, and many other mystics of East and West, have tried to describe the sense of union with the Infinite in the only earthly terms they knew which approached it— in Swedenborg's case "conjugial love." One of his dreams shows this.

But it was not really a dream, he said. He woke one morning "and lay awake, but as if in a vision; I could open my eyes and be awake when I wanted to, but yet I was in the spirit—there was an inward and sensible joy through my whole body; it seemed as if in some transcendent way all rose and hid in the infinite as if in a centre which was love itself, and which flowed out from there again and down through incomprehensible circles from that centre of love, around and back again. This love in a mortal body with which I was filled was then like the joy which a chaste man has when he is really in love and in the very act with his spouse, with such extreme delight was my whole body suffused . . ."

He noted, he says, that this real and inner joy lasted for half an hour or an hour, but that as soon as any self-love appeared it ceased, and he felt a chill shiver and a sorrow, and in this way he said he realized "from what the great sorrow comes." [7] That, he felt, was the source of melancholy.

Self-love made him far more anxious than sex-love; indeed he had begun his diary by noting that he was no longer "so prone to the sex as I have been all my days," and that he "so quickly lost my inclination for women, which has been my chief passion." He noted too, at the same period, that his ambitiousness had declined. "I wondered that I no longer wanted to work for my own glory," and "I wondered that since I came to the Hague I had lost the push and self-centered love for my work."

He was in The Hague to see his new physiological work—the first and second parts of the *Animal Kingdom* (The "Soul's Kingdom") through the press; he was doing research; he was dining with his friends during the day; only his diary knew of his strange experiences during the night. As he says, "during all this I went to the same parties as before and no one could tell anything . . ."

About what? His diary mentions "wakeful ecstasies" and reveals that since about October, 1743, he had had preternaturally long sleep, often ten or eleven hours at a stretch. The "Kingdom of God" was first shown to him, he said later, "in the repose of sleep," and he described the joy-dissolved sensation with which he had had a vision of a ladder of angels and saints leading up to the Only Begotten Son of God. [8]

It is clear that in his increasing spiritual bewilderment, troubled by strange psychic phenomena, he had had a dream, so vivid that he felt it was "real." In this dream he had had a vision of Jesus Christ, carrying with it a sense of conviction almost equal to his need. That was in Amsterdam, 1743. He was then fifty-five.

For a man of Swedenborg's strong emotions and concrete mind the Indefinable Creator, the "Nameless Nothing" of the Neoplatonists, was not enough for his heart to cling to, satisfactory as the Supreme Infinite had been to his intellect. Once again as in 1733 or '34 when he wrote *Of the Infinite* he felt Christ mystically, but now it was as far more than the "Nexus" between Infinite and finite. It was as the infinitely compassionate figure of the God who had Himself been tempted, had suffered, had been crucified. The direct experience of this Christ had been greatly emphasized in

Protestant mystical literature with which Swedenborg was certainly acquainted. It was not strange to have that form of the Godhead appear to Swedenborg's distraught soul as his one salvation. All the patterns of his boyhood, all the strong traditions of his early environment rushed to reinforce the "vision," and he yielded himself unreservedly not only to it but, in his present great bewilderment, to the orthodox Lutheran theology of grace and faith and atonement that was associated with it.

More correctly expressed, he tried to yield himself unreservedly. Intellectual habits of forty-odd years are not easily given up. And it was mainly this struggle that the diary portrayed. It was Swedenborg's outcropping scientific self that "tempted" him, especially to doubt the literal truth of the Bible. It was chiefly this which caused the melancholy that made him smile inwardly at mere money worries, and even made him tremble briefly at thoughts of hell, thoughts hitherto foreign to him.

It must be remembered that Swedenborg belonged to a people which had fought fiercely in the Thirty Years' War for the right to appeal to the Bible as the ultimate authority instead of the Church of Rome. In a sense they had fought for freedom, and they had bought the right to the Bible with their blood. To Protestants of that time everywhere and very much so to Lutherans the authority of the Bible was the same as belief in the Revolution to orthodox Bolshevists now. They had secured the Bible for themselves through a revolution, and while the Book was to become a yoke it was still the last court of appeal and source of justification for almost any proposition.

(It is well to remember also that as late as in the 1880's even a man like Henry Sidgwick had to read a great deal of modern Bible history before he could free himself from this kind of orthodoxy.)

Swedenborg was not troubled because he was still writing on scientific subjects; indeed, he noted that he sometimes was impatient and blamed God when his work did not move easily as he thought it should, "since I was not doing it for my own sake." He knew that in his painstaking effort to explain the relationship of mind and body he was really pursuing a spiritual goal, and one of which he still thought as his life work.

But the "new man in Christ" that he wanted to become turned

a chill, analytic gaze on the various shortcomings of his old recal-
citrant self. There were certain signs that, after all, his inclination
toward the other sex had not entirely disappeared; one finds him
hinting that he had been "in certain places" [9] with a Swedish boon
companion, but he also suggests that he did not think God objected to this so much since he had not been warned about it as he
had about some other things.[10] Swedenborg seemed to be more
shocked at another kind of overindulgence, namely that he had
eaten and drunk too much at a banquet; this, he said, was leading
"a pig's life." (He was in Holland, of course, and a sociable man.)

But still worse, he considered, with microscopic scrutiny of himself, was his personal vanity. Once while listening to a medical lecture he caught himself wondering if he would be mentioned as
one who knew more about such things. And then there was the
time when he went past a book store and felt that his books would
do more good than others; something for which he reproached
himself severely, adding that probably every book did some good
in its own way.

Worse yet, he thought, was the tendency he found in himself to
boast of the grace of God. When somebody did not seem to value
him as he felt he ought to be valued he caught himself thinking,
" 'Oh, if you only knew what grace I have, then you would act
differently' "—and "that was impure and due to self-love, which
I at last discovered and asked God's pardon for, wishing that others
might have the same grace, as they perhaps already had it." [11]

But the most persecuting sorrow of all was the fact that he could
not become "as a child," could not simply believe without reasoning. He says he prayed and sometimes fasted and sometimes wept
and beat himself, but it is evident that the rational thoughts, his
lifetime habits, would assert themselves. One night, that between
April 6 and 7 in 1744 when he happened to be in Delft, he was
reading about the miracles God did through Moses. But critically.
"I both believed and I did not believe. I thought that was why the
angels and God appeared to the shepherds and not to the philosopher who brings his own reason into it, which always leads him to
ask why God used the wind to bring up the locusts with, and why
did He harden the heart of Pharaoh and not act directly," and other
such things.

The day before he had taken communion and still he had been depressed about hell, his only consolation Paul's Letter to the Romans, chapter 5, in which Christ's death as an atonement for our sins is stressed. Yet the depression had passed into such a state of indescribably mystic joy that "if it had increased my body would have dissolved from mere joy."

And still, there he was, sitting before a fire in Delft the next evening full of the "temptation" of doubt again. But he "looked at the fire" and said to himself that he might better doubt the evidence of his fallible senses and say there is no fire than to doubt God who is Truth Itself, "and so I passed the hour or hour and a half, and laughed in my heart at the tempter."

The entry for this night of April 6, 1744, Swedenborg has marked with three capital NB's. He might well, for from the experience he records here undoubtedly stemmed both his conception of his mission and his feeling of divine authority for it.

He went to bed early, after laughing at the tempter, and about half an hour later he heard a noise under his head (he was evidently by now used to strange noises) which he interpreted as the departure of the tempter. He says he shivered several times (throughout this diary of 1744 he often notes that shivering precedes the "psychic" phenomena), but then he fell asleep and "about twelve or one or two o'clock I trembled violently from head to foot and there was a great sound as of many storms colliding, which shook me and threw me on my face. In the moment I was thrown down I was fully awake and saw how I was thrown down." (This sounds as though he means that he was "in the spirit" or with his consciousness external to his body.) "I wondered at what it meant, and I spoke as though awake when yet it seemed as if the words were put into my mouth. I said, 'O thou almighty Christ, how canst thou condescend to come to such a great sinner, make me worthy of such grace.' I held up my folded hands and prayed, and then a hand came which clasped mine hard. At once I continued my prayer and said, 'Thou hast promised to pardon all sinners, thou canst do no more than keep thy word.'

"In the same moment I lay in his bosom and saw him face to face. It was a face of such holy mien and everything indescribable and smiling so that I believe this was how he looked when he was alive. He spoke to me and asked if I had a certificate of health, I answered, 'Lord thou knowest that better than I.' He said 'Well, then act,' which seemed to me to mean: Love me really, or do what you promised. God give me grace to do so, I thought, it was not within my own power. I woke, trembling, and came again into the state where I was neither asleep nor awake but in thought as to what this might mean, was it Christ, the son of God, whom I saw?"

First he thought it was a sin to doubt it, then he remembered the Biblical injunction to try the spirits, and he recalled the "series mystica" of blissful gyres in which he had been the previous night, deciding that he had been thus prepared by the Holy Ghost for this night's experience. Then he considered his impression that although he had spoken the words of his prayer himself, yet they had somehow not been his, they had been put into his mouth— that is, he *now* thought, Jesus himself had told him he was Jesus. And he prayed to be forgiven for having doubted it.[12]

In 1710 Swedenborg was very near death for having broken the London quarantine. No doubt it sank deep into him then how important it was to have one's health certificate in order. As for the injunction to *act,* it may not be out of the way to remember that Descartes, who had meant much to the young Emanuel, had had "Fac" (Act) in his brief device.[13]

This need not hurt those who believe in the possibility of divine theophanies to loving and anxious souls. If any such Impulse can come from a Beyond it must clothe itself in material comprehensible to the recipient, and perhaps use material in the recipient.

But why should Swedenborg, who certainly was not a great and hardly even a little sinner, have gone through this concatenation of what would now have been dismissed as "guilt feelings"?

In the dossiers of mystics (those who feel they experience God directly) one often finds that it is some glimpse of mystic joy which has set them on their path. The experience may have come unexpectedly, and, they often feel, undeservedly, but from then onward they only live to taste it again. Withdrawn from them, by that species of coquetry which Divinity seems to practice, they begin to torment themselves to find the reason for the withdrawal, and they usually find it in whatever orthodox idea of "sin" belongs to their cultural background, at least in the case of Christian mystics.

That Swedenborg had tasted this "honey of the soul" before his feelings of sinfulness began to attack him is quite clear. Perhaps it was as early as 1733, but certainly there are more than hints at mystical experience in the *Economy*. And in the prologue to the *Animal Kingdom* (the "Soul's Kingdom") written about 1742, he cites the well-known description (by Plotinus) of how the soul having united itself with a higher world and "feeling his own immortality with the greatest assurance and light" has to descend again into the body, becoming "sorrowful as the light decreased." Very significantly Swedenborg adds, "but this may perhaps appear like a mere fable to those who have not experienced it." [14]

According to his diary of 1744, he continued to experience "the usual state of inward joy" quite frequently, but he had no more visions, not at least recorded, which he placed as outside of himself. He did have "a strong inward" vision of Jesus, he said, when he was bothered in a dream by dogs (he identified them with animal instincts). In another *dream* (definitely distinguished from a vision) he says he again saw Jesus. Here there was a charming touch. From time to time Swedenborg worried a little as to whether he wasn't avaricious, a vice he particularly detested, and in some of his dreams he noted that he wanted to hold on to his money. But in this one, he said, "It seemed as if I were with Christ himself as informally as with anybody. He borrowed a five-pound note from someone; I was sorry he had not borrowed it from me, and I took out two notes, letting one drop and then the other. He asked what was that, I said I had found them and that he had dropped one of them. I gave them to him and he took them—we seemed to live together in such a state of innocence."

Still, doubts kept returning. Even the night after the great vision at Delft, he could not make his thoughts "contemplate Christ whom I saw such a little while ago . . ." There was a constant fight between faith and reason in spite of the fact that he thought he had submitted himself in all humility to faith. The fight went with him to England, where he went in May, 1744, having seen the first two parts of his new physiological work (the "Soul's Kingdom") through the press in The Hague. Sticking close to faith, he had taken lodging with a "pious shoemaker" whom he had met on a Dutch canalboat. The shoemaker's piety was of the crudely literal Moravian brand, and from his house Swedenborg moved to that of another Moravian, a watchmaker, following his old practice of taking lodgings with artisans.

At first he seemed to feel that he had been "led" to these "Moravian Brothers" who "only reckon with the grace of God and the blood and merits of Christ," and this belief was doubtless strengthened by the fact that three months previously he had had a dream in which he had seen their church, "just as I saw it later, and they were all dressed like parsons." [15]

Gradually his enthusiasm for them seems to have cooled (nor were they, apparently, at all keen to have such an intellectual aspirant) and he did not join their community of faith. Emanuel Swedenborg was beginning to find his own way out of his dilemma.

While he was recording his strange dreams and spiritual struggles in his diary, he was very busy by day with entirely different matters in this London summer of 1744. By July 3 he had finished a first draft of his work on the senses, two hundred folio pages in less than six weeks.[16] The work seeped through into the dreams. He wrote that a dream of kissing a girl tenderly good-by was his farewell to *The Five Senses,* while another girl "seen farther off" was the further elaboration of his treatise on the brain.[17] But the dreams also seeped into the work. Here and there in the draft of *The Five Senses,* written in the summer of 1744, he refers to admonitions and instructions that he feels he has received in sleep, regarding what is to be written and in what order. (They are personal asides, not meant for publication.)

It is not strange that he thought he was receiving other-worldly aid, for, together with the epilogue to Part II of the *Animal Kingdom* which he had written in the spring of the same year, this brilliant and remarkable sketch of *The Five Senses* was concerned not only with the very essence of the problem he had been trying to master—the body-mind relationship—but reached out and up still further, to "a principle in which life is involved, and the force and life of which all other things carry out and live, and which causes the sense itself to be and to live: this principle is what we term the Soul." [18]

But for his arguments he used his cherished "analytic way," building up from physiology (he referred to his studies of the embryo and the soul as formative force) [19] through the psycho-physiology of sensation to the "spirituality," one might say, of what it really is that sensates, and by what means, and—for him now most important of all—*to what end*.

No series of conquests were ever planned with such zest as the intellectual campaigns that Swedenborg promised in this draft of *The Five Senses.* Among the volumes planned to complete the *Animal Kingdom* were the ones on reproduction, on the nerves, on psychology specifically; he had drafts ready of these. Of course he meant to finish the drafts he had on the brain; in fact he was adding to his studies of the brain while he was in London in 1744, one of the additions being the localization of the motor centers of the cortex.[20]

He prepared and published part of the work on the senses as Part III of the *Animal Kingdom,* but the rest of that "noble procession" (as he had thought it symbolized in a dream) remained either in manuscript or never even reached paper, not at least in scientific form. He never tried to publish even the important brain discoveries.

Had Swedenborg given up the attempt to try to find "the mechanism of the intercourse of the soul and the body" by means of "experience, geometry and reason"?

He had not. Everything he had written went to show that he felt he had essentially solved the problem, but in the draft of *The Five Senses* he did say to himself, as it were, that as he had written it he felt his theories could not be comprehended by others, and he himself noted that certain points were still obscure to him. But he meant to go on, for the general picture was clear to him. The soul, the life force, had created for itself an instrument in the material body. The rational mind was a kind of sixth sense or chief instrument of the soul, the latter alone having the power to see "the beauty, order and truth of the rose," [21] while for the botanical details the rational mind officiated, instructed by the senses.

Physically the soul was "the principle of active life in the body." Psychologically it organized the ideas the mind had acquired from sense reports. This took place in the cortex. Writing with the awe that nearly made him a poet at times, Swedenborg said: "There [in the cerebrum] the soul resides, clad in the noblest garment of organization, and sits to meet the ideas emerging thither and receives them as guests. This high and noble place is the innermost sensorium, and it is the boundary at which the ascent of the life of the body ceases, and the boundary from which that of the soul, considered as a spiritual essence, begins." [22]

Swedenborg did not think he had shirked "the laws of physics," however. About the body and mind relation he specifically said that "there is a continual influx to be explained by the laws of physics," adding, "This also falls under demonstration, yea, God willing, it shall fall." [23]

And he sketched out discussions of the "changes of state" by which an external stimulus reached the soul as a conscious sensation, first as a "modification" or vibration in the external sense organs, then carried by "the spiritual essence" or energy-stuff in the nerves to the "cortical glands" and/or that inner sensorium where mind and soul interacted and the "field" of the memory could be consulted, that "field" not being anything "material" nor yet separate from "an eminent organism." [24]

But all that, he said, could not be really understood until the brain had been fully studied, also "changes of state." He thought he was on the right track. What dragged him away from continuing to follow it, at least in more or less orthodox scientific fashion, was that he had become occupied with another question: To what *end* have we this mind, this intellect, that may or may not accept instruction from the soul?

All through the draft of *The Five Senses* runs a refrain that seems to have little to do with science—the love of God, reached as a result of the conquest of that which is "inferior and external" in man.[25] Swedenborg here shows himself to be as God-intoxicated as ever Spinoza was, and, like Spinoza, he thought he could demonstrate the things of the spirit "geometrically." Not only true and false, but also good and evil, though he saw the two pairs of opposites as linked. For those assessments, however, sciences were not enough, he now stressed, they involved truths, "wisdom is what also involves goodnesses." [26]

Swedenborg had stopped walking around life and viewing it mainly from the outside, yet he had not renounced reason, he felt he had given its exercise a divine object. Through his mystical experience he had been dragged like an iron filing into a celestial field, and from then on he was still concerned about truth, but even more about "wisdom"—the use of truth in the service of goodness. Our rational mind should enable us to choose the best, to know good from evil. "This is the work of science and wisdom. To the extent that we are affected by the love of the truly good and especially of the supreme best, to that extent are we united to it . . ." [27]

Carefully noting that the love of God should not be for the sake of experiencing "felicity," Swedenborg nevertheless seems to have been so overwhelmed by his experiences that, about three weeks after he had ceased his work on physiology, he began to write another book. The title he felt had been given him when he was in a state "neither sleep nor wakefulness." This state, the forerunner of his later "trances" (or "dissociated" conditions), he mentions often enough in the dream diary to show that he was becoming accustomed to it, at least for the reception of mystical joy. But there were other signs in the same diary that he was increasingly puzzled by certain things he thought he saw, felt, heard, and even smelled, half in dream, half out of it, mostly trivial, but which he did not know how to interpret.

This did not bother him very much. The great experience into which he now wholeheartedly flung himself was the new book.

This book was *Of the Worship and Love of God*. Like a stream long dammed up it poured out of him. This poetic-pedantic allegory of the creation of the world and the creation of Adam and Eve was a kind of summary of everything Swedenborg had been trying to tell in his other books. It was in Neoplatonic terms, with the odd addition of God's Only Begotten Son, while the story of Adam and Eve was far from literally Biblical. Significantly their mental faculties, their "intelligences," were personified as beautiful women who told them how the Supreme communicated via the soul through intelligence.

No more blackening of reason as against "faith." This book was a bright symptom of the fact that Swedenborg had emerged from orthodoxy and melancholy at the same time.

He had used his own tragic emotions as material for the book, always an excellent sign of returning emotional health in a writer. When Adam was puzzled by the same questions as Swedenborg, then "Wisdom," a daughter of his soul, answered them just as if she had read his books. And she used some pretty similes. When he wondered if it were really true that man is governed by his "loves" or desires, and in that sense has little or no free will, his "Wisdom" asked him if he had not noticed the ringdove violently beating the air with his wings. It seemed to the dove that he chose the shortest and quickest way home, but in reality "his loves—his fledged young and his mistress—excited his mind and his mind moved his wings."

"Wisdom" did not miss the chance to note that "it is the life of our love which we live, and that life is of such quality as the love is." [28]

And Swedenborg in a footnote asked, "What are truths without an ultimate regard for goodness! Or . . . the intelligence unless to know how to choose the Good . . ."

Disguising it slightly, Swedenborg wrote even of the vision when he had felt himself to be in the bosom of Christ, who in this book was called "Love Himself." When Adam emerged from a similar experience in which he had, like Swedenborg, heard the divine words "spoken within himself," he too began to wonder what it had really meant. "Where now," Adam asked, "is that Love in whose bosom I was held? . . . Am I fallen down or am I deluded? Tell me, my wisdoms! I entreat you by God—where have I been; rescue me from this darkness." [29]

An honest cry, one not uttered by a man who was longing to be self-deceived for the sake of ecstasy.

Adam was told by one of his "wisdoms" that he was still in "His bosom," that only a thin veil kept him from seeing this. If that veil were but a little withdrawn "He will again appear, for He is in our inmost principles and also in the highest; Himself and His Heaven being in the former and in the latter." [30]

Swedenborg had found his religion again—the spiritual religion or "Perennial Philosophy" that sees the "inmost and highest" principle of the soul as capable of being influenced by the divine and only Reality, even of being identified with it, and that sees the essence of this divinity as love working through wisdom.

But the brimming—and lasting—wave of light, warmth, and confidence which now so evidently bore up Swedenborg was not due to his intellectual agreement with this. He had agreed intellectually long ago, and it had not prevented him from passing through such doubt and sadness that he was on the brink of thinking he had to sacrifice his reason in order to "believe."

Then he had, through his vision, felt the "love of God." And, during the months that followed, he had scrutinized the experience and come through to certainty, with reason intact.

Clumsily made as his new book was, with pedantic interpolations and gigantic footnotes like chunks of science heaved into mystic joy, it was the work of a sane mind, a mind that often flashed into brilliance as when he expressed in a paragraph things he had taken chapters for in other books, while at times there was poetic grandeur in it such as in Adam's and Eve's vision of creation. (Eve was as intelligent as she was beautiful.)

There were also many indications of what it was that had saved the day for reason.

Swedenborg no longer felt he had to believe in only the literal significance of the seven plagues of Egypt and whatever else offended his head or heart in the Bible.

He had freed himself from his compulsion, as many had done before him, by the device of interpreting the Bible symbolically. He had long been interested in symbolism; as early as 1734 he was curious about hieroglyphics as symbols. And by deciding what the symbols in the Bible meant he could make everything fit. In 1741 he had been working out a *Hieroglyphic Key* to the Bible, and in 1744, probably after his vision, he had resumed this work. It consisted mainly of lists of the metaphors, parables and allegories used in the Bible, and of his own interpretations.

Swedenborg had read Philo Judaeus, Origen, and others who had tried to make the Bible more divine by humanizing it, through symbolic interpretation, but the Latin translation which he was using at this time happened to be that of Sebastian Castellio. Castellio, one of the noblest of the Christian Neoplatonists, had also written books, and he had translated the *Theologia Germanica,* that gem of mysticism with which Swedenborg's beliefs have much in common. It cannot be proved that Swedenborg had read these books, and he could have read the same opinions in a dozen other books to which he had access, but it is interesting that Castellio had written that "Divine revelations can be seen in a literal, pictorial, temporal way, or they can be read deeper . . . as eternal and spiritual realities." [31]

It is not likely, however, that Swedenborg had not read the preface to the translation of the Bible with which he was working, and in this preface Castellio expressed an idea that may have been the spark to Swedenborg's tinder. Castellio said: "Only the person who has in himself the illumination of the same Spirit that gave the original revelation can see through the garment of the letter to the eternal message, the ever-living Word hidden within." [32]

Might not Swedenborg feel that he had had that illumination in his Delft vision? There is a hint in his diary in October, 1744. He wrote of a vision of bread "which was a sign that the Lord himself would instruct me . . ."

He hints too that there is something he ought to do which is still obscure, but he will find the right way.

Was it that which he felt he had "promised" the Lord to do at the time of the Delft vision? It could not be the book on *The Worship and Love of God.* He abandoned it about April, 1745, after he had written two parts and begun a third part.

He had wondered and wavered as to what his mission was to be —science or philosophy, but what he did after April, 1745, was to devote his leisure to the reinterpretation of the Bible.

The traditional story of what happened to cause Swedenborg to turn to this work is the one told by Carl Robsahm, a friend of his later years. This, set down by Robsahm in his old age,[33] is to the effect that Swedenborg had related he was having a good dinner in a London inn when a mysteriously appearing man told him not to eat so much, and Swedenborg saw vapor come out of his own body and flash off as worms. That night the same man revealed himself as the Lord and commissioned Swedenborg to explain the spiritual contents of Scripture. He himself would tell Swedenborg what ought to be written on this topic. To convince Swedenborg, the story went on, the world of spirits was opened up to him that night and he recognized many acquaintances there of every class. From that day, he said, he gave up all worldly intellectual work and devoted himself to spiritual matters, according to what the Lord commanded him to write.

This picturesque story has probably done more to cause Swedenborg to be deemed plain mad than anything else. Does he himself tell it as Robsahm said he did in any records left by him from the time the incident is reported to have happened, or even within a few years of it? No such records have been traced, but there are contemporary references by Swedenborg to some of the ingredients of the Robsahm story, references that are complete in themselves yet leave out the main features of the "Lord" and the "commission."

In his "spiritual diary" for 1747 there is a note dated "April, 1745," that is, the date of the Robsahm story. Swedenborg, as was his custom, gave the entry a title: *A vision by day concerning those who are devoted to the table and who thus indulge the flesh.*[34]

Then follows, "In the middle of the day an angel who was with me conversed, saying that I should not indulge the belly so much at table. While he was with me there clearly appeared to me, as it were [note visionary quality] a vapor, exuding from the pores of the body, like a watery vapor, extremely visible, which fell towards the earth where the carpet was, upon which the vapor being collected, was changed into various little worms," which, he says, seemed to burn up in a noisy flash. From this Swedenborg deduced very calmly that it was a kind of purification of immoderate appetite, going to show "what luxuries and similar things carry in their bosom." (Amateurs of modern "ectoplasm" theories would say it was a case of "ectoplasm" being molded by his mind into the shapes that for him symbolized his self-indulgence.) [35]

About a year later, probably less, he again referred to this vision as being symbolic of those unclean spirits which "correspond" to overeating, mentioning the "smoke" that came out of his pores in "April, 1745," but he speaks of this merely as an aside to explain that the "worms" were the same as the "frogs" spoken of as one of the Egyptian plagues.[36]

In neither contemporary reference is there anything about the Lord, although the first is from his private diary where it certainly seems as if he would have mentioned a new vision in which he was given a specific "commission."

The episode at the inn he evidently regarded as a separate incident, and so he did another ingredient of the Robsahm story— his "admission" into the freedom of both worlds. After the middle of April, 1745, he had, he said, "conversed with those who are in heaven the same as with my familiars here on earth, and this almost continuously," for, he reckoned, about eight months, at the time he was writing this.[37] During the succeeding four years, Swedenborg made about twenty references [38] or more to his admission into the spiritual world as having taken place in the middle of April, 1745, but in none of these does he mention either the inn episode or the Lord giving him a commission.

Since 1743, whenever he was in a state of mystic ecstasy, he had now and then been conscious of "angelic voices," and in the summer of 1744, when he was writing about the sense organs, he noted from time to time that he had been "ordered" to write this or that. (An "angel" for him was a highly evolved spirit.) At the beginning of these experiences he was still rather vague about terms, mixing up "kingdom of God," "heaven," and "the spiritual world," giving rise to inconsistencies.

"The kingdom of God," however, was usually written of in the tradition of mysticism. About the end of 1745 he writes of "the heavenly sweetnesses and felicities" of the kingdom of God having been experienced so frequently by him "during the past two years that I forbear to count the occasions," also that it has several times been shown to him "first in the quiet of sleep and afterwards in midday or time of wakefulness," [39] which makes it clear that he dates his first experience of "the kingdom of God" from 1743. That also tallies with his dream diary from this time.

Also about the end of 1745, he writes of having been admitted into the kingdom of God "by the Messiah himself," and that there he has spoken with various heavenly personages, and "with the dead who have risen again," and "this now for a period of eight months."

Here is no mention of any commission either, but he is aware of certain inconsistencies, for he adds to this the following humble note:

"As to those things that have been written concerning myself, I cannot so confirm them as to be able to testify to them before God; for I cannot know whether the several words of the description [descriptions?] are such, and this in least detail, as to coincide entirely. Therefore, if God grants, they must be amended at some other time, and this in such a way that I can then seem to myself to speak things absolutely true." [40]

Eight months or so after he was supposed to have received a divine commission to reinterpret the Bible, could he write such a confession of uncertainty as the above?

That he came to believe firmly in the commission we know, since in his old age he told Robsahm and Beyer and others about it, more or less in the same way. It is perhaps unlikely that Robsahm—the careful bank official—telescoped several different stories by Swedenborg into one story. No, Swedenborg undoubtedly did it himself, unconsciously of course. But the human memory is a great dramatist, and it loves the unities of time and place, especially when, instructed by overwhelming need, it selects the incidents to be combined.

Swedenborg needed to believe in the symbolic exegesis of the Bible and in divine authority for it, since that was the only way in which he could keep both the Bible and his reason. But what really shocked him into devoting himself to the "mission" of this interpretation was undoubtedly something that happened to him in April, 1745. It was his feeling that he had seen and spoken with "dead" acquaintances of his, "of all classes," in other words, with people he *knew*. This is what "convinced" him, as he told Robsahm, and it is too much to expect that, considering his need for belief, he should have seen the illogicality of thinking that everything he was experiencing was "real" just because he was suddenly put in the presence of people of whose identity he was able to feel sure.

He had been in and out of dreams and semidreams and visions which might have been traced by him to his own knowledge and wishes—he was subtle enough for that to have occurred to him, indeed he seems at times to have doubted everything, even the Delft vision.[41] But the experience of being with his "dead" friends and acquaintances was nothing he had apparently been either wishing for or preparing for. There was not one word in his diary preceding this experience to show that he was at all interested in proving "survival" so as to be reunited with the loved and lost. He wanted to prove by his science, and he felt he had done so, that man's body was governed by a "soul," because he thought this a necessary step in proving that there was a receptacle in man into which God could flow or with which He could unite Himself. Of course a consequence of believing in a soul was that he believed in its survival, but neither in 1742 nor in the summer of 1744 did Swedenborg touch on a description of the other world as a state with a great resemblance to this one—at least for a while. It was either heavenly felicity or else hellish damnation.

But, if Swedenborg thought that what seemed to him the stark reality of the spirit world would help to convince other people, he had a lot to learn. And he was wise enough to say nothing about his experiences when, in August, 1745, he was back at his old job in the Board of Mines. During the next two years his health was even better than usual; he was listed as absent on account of illness for a total of only eleven days.[42] To his colleagues life must have seemed to go on as before for Swedenborg—metals were tested, charcoal allotted, claims judged, mining districts inspected.

Little they knew!

CHAPTER THIRTEEN

Swedenborg's Sanity

S O far there was little in Swedenborg's published works that would have been thought anything except slightly fanciful, but even so he seems to have been careful about their circulation at home, although they were in Latin. When he heard of someone who had read *Of the Worship and Love of God,* he offered to lend him one of the physiological works, because, he said, in it "the intellectual mind and soul are here and there treated of. The copies which I have of this work are freely at the service of those who possess understanding and are interested in such subjects." [1]

But he does not seem to have depended on anyone's understanding in regard to his double life among men and "spirits." In 1746, after a year's social experience with spirits, he noted privately that, "in company with other men, I spoke just as any other man, so that no one was able to distinguish me either from myself as I had been formerly, or from any other man; and, nevertheless, in the midst of company I sometimes spoke with spirits and with those who were around me; and perhaps they might have gathered something from this circumstance. However, I do not know whether anyone noticed anything from the fact that the internal senses were sometimes withdrawn from the external, though not in any such way that anyone could make a judgment from it; for at such times they could judge no other than that I was occupied with thoughts." [2]

He added that the actual speech was not heard by anyone save himself and the spirits, although at times "the speech is as clear and distinct as the human voice, though not so high or with so rough a sound as when coming through one's lips. So much is this the case that sometimes even angels and spirits were afraid they would be heard by those who were present in the world."

Their fears seem to have been unfounded. If anyone had noticed anything it was at any rate not Swedenborg's colleagues in the Board of Mines, for they unanimously recommended him to the high position of Councilor of Mines when one of the two councilorships fell vacant in the spring of 1747.

Thirty years before, the Board of Mines had been very reluctant
to accept the young engineer as one of their members; now he had
arrived at the top. Above the two Councilors, there was only the
President of the Board, and he had to be of hereditary nobility.

But Swedenborg wrote briefly to the King that, although he had
been proposed for this office, he begged His Majesty not to appoint
him. In fact, he applied for permission to be released from public
office altogether, and this without the customary promotion in
rank. All he asked for, on the ground of his often having spent
his own money in mining researches abroad, was that he might be
pensioned on half salary, because he had to go abroad again to
finish some important work on which he was engaged.

The King of Sweden, with gracious words for the services Swedenborg had rendered the State and with earnest wishes that he
might continue to do so, did nevertheless grant the suppliant's
wishes.

In the minutes of the Board of Mines, it was duly recorded that
Assessor Swedenborg had been released from his duties, and "all
the members of the Royal College regretted losing so worthy a colleague." He was asked to remain until all his cases were finished,
which he did.

On July 17, 1747, he took leave of his colleagues amidst thanks
and good wishes; "they wished him a prosperous journey and a
happy return, after which he left." [3]

It is now two hundred years since Emanuel Swedenborg, at the
age of fifty-nine, cut loose from his established existence as an important servant of the State and fully committed himself to strange
voyages. As far as his world knew, he was only going to Amsterdam
and London for his usual work with libraries and printing presses,
but the question also has to be asked—Where was he going as to
his mind?

In brutal brevity: Was Swedenborg insane?

As mentioned before, his own definition of insanity "from the
medical point of view" was "acting contrary to accepted customs

or obstinately defending one's own opinions against acknowledged truths."

From that point of view he was not insane.

There is, however, a story (circulated later by John Wesley, who did not care for competitors) that once in London (during his crisis period) Swedenborg behaved as if delirious in the house of his second Moravian landlord. It was recorded many years later by Mathesius, a Swedish clergyman, who was averse to Swedenborg, and there is testimony that the Moravian later retracted most of what he was alleged to have said, also that Swedenborg had left the house because the man meddled with his papers. The story of Swedenborg's fit of madness could have been told in revenge for Swedenborg's removal to lodge with the wigmaker Shearsmith.[4]

The truth probably is that although this, like Andersen's story of the feather blown up to five hens, had little foundation, yet there had at least been a feather. Perhaps under the double impact of a fever which he is reported to have had and his puzzling new "spirit" experiences, Swedenborg had appeared to be delirious at least once. A later reference in his diary shows he was aware that at one time his behavior could have been interpreted as insane (see page 247), but there is nothing in his previous or subsequent life that hints at any overt oddity of behavior, barring of course the considerable oddity which remains to be discussed—his claim to familiarity with "spirits." But as far as social behavior went, his polite correctness was often praised by people who knew him, as well as by casual acquaintances.

But he might have suffered from a subtler unbalance. His continued intellectual interests after 1745 (he wrote his clearest book at the age of eighty-two) would not prove to a psychoanalyst that his visions and his ideas were not the result of unresolved complexes. But from that point of view Luther, George Fox, John Wesley himself, and many other of mankind's religious teachers, both in the East and the West, would be considered unbalanced. They had "visions" and heard voices ordering them to do this or that, which they usually obeyed. As has been said before, it comes down to whether it is believed that such "projected" religious experience is always due to a neurosis.

Some of the psychoanalysts who believe this—religiously—have attempted to deal with Swedenborg *in absentia* mainly by the aid of excerpts from his so-called dream diary and "spiritual" diary. They do not seem to have been well acquainted with his scientific work, nor do they seem to have studied history with a view to finding out whether Swedenborg could not at the time have held certain ideas without differing much from his contemporaries.

Nowadays certainly a man who claimed to communicate with spirits *and* to have received a divine commission to reinterpret the Bible might legitimately be committed for observation if that served any useful purpose. But, hard as it is to remember with the often so amazingly modern Swedenborg, he did live and these things did take place over two hundred years ago, when the mental climate was different.

What Professor C. D. Broad of Oxford in our day has called the "antecedent improbability" [5] that renders belief in even the best-attested psychic phenomena so hard, was then not so improbable, both for people in general and for Swedenborg in particular.

As for his specifically religious ideas, they were far from unrelated to those of his time and that immediately preceding it. Among the pietist Protestant sects, and especially with those who had a tinge of mysticism, there was a strong belief that the "visible church" had lost authority after the death of the last of the Apostles, and that a new, world-wide "invisible church" would come. This was particularly true of the "Collegiants" in Holland. One of their leaders, Cornheert, had pleaded for people to wait—wait "for the coming of new and divinely commissioned apostles, who would really reform apostate churches and unite all divided sects and gather the world in a true Church of Christ." He also wrote a great deal about the "Inner Word of God," and about symbols and ceremonies as nothing in themselves but as pointing to spiritual realities.

The same ideas were held by the so-called "Seekers" in England. Both Holland and England pullulated with books expressing such views.[6] They often literally coincided with those of Swedenborg, as in the case of Castellio's. (See page 151.)

Mitigating circumstances, however, do not prove sanity. In our day, Professor Martin Lamm of Stockholm has exonerated Swedenborg from insanity on the ground that his visions and voices were only pseudohallucinatory, and that only once or twice did he "place" them as outside of himself. In his brilliant book on the origin of Swedenborg's ideas [7] Professor Lamm, in effect, says that Swedenborg was not insane; he was a poet with a vivid imagination.

Before Professor Lamm another champion of Swedenborg's sanity was Ethan Allen Hitchcock, the scholar (and incidentally soldier) who was called to be President Lincoln's and Secretary Stanton's adviser during the Civil War. Hitchcock wrote a clear and well-documented book,[8] in which he noted the similarity of many of Swedenborg's ideas and expressions with those of the "hermeneutical" writers—the very ones whom Swedenborg once had stigmatized as "occult"—writers who in all ages out of the Kabbalah, nature mysticism, and various kinds of Neoplatonism had constructed "secret" systems, sometimes crudely "magical," sometimes of elevated religious philosophy, disguised from heresy-hunters by "occult" terms.

The General was right, but the similarity may have been due to the same sources having been tapped by Swedenborg and the hermeneutical writers. But Hitchcock concluded that Swedenborg had not meant what he said, except in the same symbolic sense that some of the hermeneutics meant their allegories. "It is also possible for me to talk with Luther," Hitchcock exclaimed in effect, "by reading his books!" And he thought that by saying he was "in the spirit" Swedenborg meant that he communicated with the living hermeneutical brethren, a secret and world-wide fraternity.

Hitchcock was well-intentioned but he was too rational. Swedenborg most assuredly meant it when he said he was in communication with the spirit world. His accounts of it, he asserted more than once, were based on "things heard, seen and felt."

But here also, it cannot be too often repeated, Swedenborg had spent many years in lessening the antecedent improbability of this, as far as he was concerned.

First, his extensive study of physics had, as we know, made him believe that matter was ultimately motion and hence essentially immaterial. He conceived of the universe as consisting of matter in different states of energy (the *Principia*), and the "soul" as being of the same energy substance as that element or state which he called the "magnetic." Then his study of physiology, especially of the embryo, made him believe that the immaterial force which he called the soul directed the material atoms in forming the body. He decided that the place where the soul continued to influence the body and to cognize sensations was in the cortical cells of the brain. He regarded it as possible that other entities (spirits) or forces from the immaterial universe could influence the cortical cells (neurons) and induce "sensations" besides the force of a man's own soul.

All his further studies of psychology and physiology led him to feel certain that the external senses of the body were merely the mechanical reporters or carriers of stimuli which did not become conscious sensations until they became "known" by the "internal senses" which he regarded as belonging to the subtle body of the immaterial soul, the governor of the material body. He thought that the soul with its "internal senses" (or psychic properties) could exist separately from the material body, and that hence it could survive apparent death. Swedenborg believed he had proved this, not by either accepting or receiving "revelation," but by means of all the scientific knowledge his time afforded, plus his own power of synthesis, of putting things together.

What he did not claim to have any idea of, before April, 1745, was under what form man would survive. This, he said, would be a case of the caterpillar trying to guess the appearance of the butterfly.[9] But even earlier, in 1741, he was sure that space and time as we know them would not obtain in the world of the dematerialized; he even then supposed that there thought could be directly communicated.

From the convictions Swedenborg had arrived at there was no antecedent improbability in his being aware of discarnate spirits, especially as he now felt he could use his "internal senses" at will. He need not have considered and did not consider himself insane because of this. Of nothing was he more stubbornly certain than that he did have communication with the souls of the dead.

A Swedish scholar is reported to have said that either Swedenborg was insane, which he was not; or Swedenborg was dishonest, which he was not; but if he were neither we should have to change all our ideas.

That scholar seems to have forgotten psychoanalysts. But they have not neglected Swedenborg.

If the object of the present study were to try to account in full for the remote origin of Swedenborg's visionary life, it might be necessary to give a thorough presentation of psychoanalytical opinion on the matter; but that is not the object.

William James, in dealing with the tendency to class the religious impulse as pathological, says that two kinds of inquiry are often confused. One is, How did it [anything] come about, what is its origin? The other is, What is its significance or value, now that it is here? [10]

Both lines of inquiry are surely necessary, but it is chiefly with the latter aspect that the present study attempts to deal. What were Swedenborg's ideas, after he had turned his gaze from the material to the immaterial, and what interest and meaning can they have in themselves for us?

This does not mean that any study of Swedenborg can fail to profit by the discoveries of the ways in which the unconscious functions, made by students of the mind from Flournoy,[11] Myers,[12] and Freud on. Such tricks as projection, identification, etc., were played also by Swedenborg's unconscious mind, one might say visibly.

But, apart from the religious side of his experience, the question *why* his particular unconscious behaved as it did—that is, the question as to the origins of the alleged "complexes," is too occult for the lay person, especially after two hundred years have passed. Yet it may be of interest to give a few samples of what the intrepid professionals believe they have discovered by studying Swedenborg's dreams and what they consider his behavior.

In a paper by R. Lagerborg,[13] of Finland, Mr. Lagerborg quotes from E. Hitschmann, a German colleague, that Swedenborg's disease is paranoia, and that it is undoubtedly a regression to the infantile. "As a boy Swedenborg wanted to surpass his father [no evidence adduced] to be a Nazir, an instrument of God." He also suffered from "narcissism." "With his illness, the underside turns up, a more primitive psyche appears, and when he becomes like a child again the childish dreams of greatness return. The Lord's words to him 'eat not so much' contain reminiscence of paternal admonition. Father and God-the-Father coalesce, and what his parents said about angels speaking through him becomes a reality for the insane man."

Hitschmann also said there were homosexual components in Swedenborg's love of God, while Lagerborg considers his references to innocence and childhood in heaven as proof of the regression theory. Lagerborg, however, is also willing to consider it a case of Jungian regression, to primitive man's mythomania. Physically, Lagerborg says, one must remember that Swedenborg was oversexed [no evidence for this] and that fear of impotence caused the tension of the crisis, the ecstasy, the hallucinations, the desire for self-improvement and "erotomania."

Lagerborg's final dictum is that "*all* mysticism regresses to mankind's irrational attempts. A mental disease starts this off, and we return to the crutches of our ancestors."

Von Winterstein, another psychoanalyst, confirms and elaborates Hitschmann's diagnosis.[14] According to Von Winterstein, Swedenborg had an unsolved inverted Œdipus complex. Instead of hating his father for being the husband of his mother (as he apparently "normally" should) he had, mainly owing to the early death of his mother, a repressed and unconscious homosexual attachment for his father. The evidence for this, as Von Winterstein sees it, is, for one thing, that Swedenborg quarreled with his father about money (presumably to dissemble his love), but chiefly that Swedenborg emphasized the significance of "God," which is a "father-symbol," both before and after his "conversion."

Swedenborg, according to Von Winterstein, in changing from science to religion, "accepted the purport of his homosexual attachment, and developed paranoia as a kind of psychological penalty for his perversity. The turning to God is merely a symbol for accepting and condoning, at least in a disguised form, the implied relation to the father."

Evidently it is not for the uninitiated to try to penetrate such clever disguises.

In regard to Swedenborg, as has been stated, the present study is not meant to be an attempt to explain in psychoanalytical terms of *how* Swedenborg came to have those experiences which seemed to him to come from another world than this. Whether such an interpretation would leave any more room for Swedenborg as an experiencer of spiritual truths than Freud's study of Da Vinci leaves for the great painter is a question that really seems to have been answered by the psychoanalysts cited above.

In Swedenborg's diaries material can certainly be found which shows that he "projected" many of his fears and wishes into "visions" of both good and evil, things that nagged and haunted him apparently from outside of himself. We can see that fairly easily now when those realms have been more or less charted. But if such material is all that is used for a picture of him there would indeed be little difference between it and that of some poor wretch in an insane asylum. From this point of view it would be impossible to fit in his contributions to ethics and his deep and subtle religious experiences. He would be just another case history, pegged out on the conventional pattern.

But the religious impulse has its geniuses as well as its idiots. The cause of truth is not served by classing the former with the latter just because the case history of every religious genius, if it were as well known as Swedenborg's, would be found to contain false sense perceptions, conflicts, terrors, and even beatitudes which could be pigeonholed under the same labels as those of the idiots.

It is not meant to imply that such is the constant practice of all modern soul doctors whether they call themselves psycho-this or psycho-that. Many, especially of the followers of Jung, "admit" the "religious drive" (as has been mentioned) as something not pathological. Others, even if they apply pathologic labels, do so with the same breadth of understanding that made Ibsen in *The Wild Duck* plead for the preservation of the "vital illusion."

A good example of this in the Swedenborg case is the treatment of it by Dr. Karl Jaspers (doctor of medicine and professor of philosophy at Heidelberg), who wrote, in 1926, a psychiatric study of Strindberg, Van Gogh, Swedenborg and Hölderlin.[15] Dr. Jaspers is not concerned with tracing the origin of all emotion to infantile perversions,[16] he is busy fitting four different personalities into a grandly elastic frame of schizophrenia. Dr. Jaspers proves to his own satisfaction—again apparently on the sole basis of Swedenborg's notes of dreams and visions—that all four of his subjects were schizophrenes (suffering from split mind and consequent delusional thinking), yet the Swedenborg conjured up by him seems as weirdly unlike the *whole* man as that of the various psychoanalysts quoted.

Nor is it possible to find any real likeness between Swedenborg and the three others considered by Dr. Jaspers. After all, Strindberg's mania went so far as to make him assert publicly that "all women" were out to slay him and poor Van Gogh cut off his own ear in a fit of depression.

What similarity is there between the Swedenborg of Dr. Jaspers and the man of whom Count Höpken, the wise Swedish statesman, wrote (as cited previously), "He possessed a sound judgment on all occasions; he saw everything clearly and expressed himself well on every subject. The most solid memorials on finance and the best penned at the Diet of 1761 were presented by him"? And, Höpken said, Swedenborg "was a true philosopher and he lived like one." Could such tributes have been paid to Strindberg?

Either Dr. Jaspers was not going by all the data or he did not have them. But he is also a professor of philosophy, and he can look beyond psychiatry. It is conceivable, he says, that something subjectively spiritual exists, and that this Spirit (Geist) is timeless, but may reveal itself in time through "emotions." It is as if, he says, this demonic force under control in the healthy can break through at the beginning of the schizophrenic process. Not, Dr. Jaspers explains, that *it* is either sick or healthy, "but the morbid process gives a chance and a condition for this breaking-through, though it may be only for a short while. It is as though the soul were unlocked," and made creative, if it has native talent.

These creative schizophrenes do us good, Dr. Jaspers continues, "when we experience the appeal of their being, their inward questioning orientation, and when we find in their works, as in all that is genuine, that gaze into the Absolute, which, always hidden, only becomes visible for us in its final form."

With a certain amount of German indefinition, this amounts to saying that even the insane, if they have native talent, can be peekholes for the Absolute, which, in Swedenborg's case, was called God.

It is most curious to consider that if Swedenborg, like many a mystic of every religion, had limited himself to reporting the visions and intercourse with whatever forms of the Godhead his religion called for, he would probably not have been thought different from them. All of them insist that man has a soul and that it somehow survives the death of the body, so even that belief need not have disqualified him from respectful attention. Oddly enough it comes down to this: Swedenborg is blamed not so much for saying that the soul survives the death of the body as for insisting that he became capable of talking with such souls, or spirits. It is as if at the word "spirit" such fears of superstition arise in modern man (because he is still so close to it) that all power of objective judgment departs from him, and the label that means "insane" to him is hunted out and affixed to the sinner who said "spirits."

It might be possible for us, instead of giving way to panic, to try to find out whether Swedenborg could not have believed in "spirits," given his background and experience, without having been "psychotic." (Many people nowadays cherish, one might almost say, a pet psychosis, convinced it can do no harm provided they know its name.)

Or again, it might be worth while, if it is true that Swedenborg had a "split" mind, to investigate whether that very fact could not have helped to produce phenomena for him of the kind that some scientists of today call "psychic," such as telepathic phenomena. Dr. Jaspers suggests that a split mind is almost essential for attaining the creative glimpse of the Absolute, either in art or in religion. If, in other words, the common-sense mind is in full control all the time, feeding and protecting the body, few if any magic casements will be opened on this or any other possible world.

Suppose we translate the "split" of the schizophrenic into the "dissociation" which may tend to produce either "inspiration" or psychical phenomena.

For, it can never be shouted too much, in the matter of understanding mental events "not by one road alone is so great a goal reached."

Arthur Koestler in *Arrival and Departure* speaks of a childhood puzzle that looked like a tangle of red and blue lines. But if you put a blue tracing paper over it a clown emerged. And if you put red tracing paper over it a lion emerged. You can explain man both ways, he says; "the method is correct, and the picture is complete in itself. But beware of the arrogant error of believing that it is the only one."

Swedenborg may have had an "inverted Œdipus complex." He may also have been of at least a schizoid type. But he may equally well have had psychic experiences of the kind that modern experimental psychical research makes part of its object of study.

Whatever one may decide as to what were the "spirits" of whom Swedenborg spoke, he soon realized that he had to be dissociated from the external world in order to "converse with them."

On March 4, 1748, he noted that for thirty-three months he had been able to talk with "them," yet had also been able to be "like another man in the society of men," but, "when however I intensely adhered to worldly things in thought, as when I had care concerning necessary expenses, about which I this day wrote a letter, so that my mind was for some time detained therewith, I fell as it were into a corporeal state, so that spirits could not converse with me . . . whence I am able to know that spirits cannot speak with a man who is much devoted to worldly and corporeal cares; for bodily concerns draw down the ideas of the mind and immerse them in corporeal things." [17]

Instead of shying from this, like a horse from a piece of white paper in the dark, let us try to see how far modern psychical research can go in making Swedenborg's belief in "spirits" intelligible, even if not credible. That may belong to another department! Do not be put off by the fact, if it is a fact, that psychical research is not "generally accepted"; what science ever was so, in its beginning —certainly not psychoanalysis!

Try the new piece of tracing paper, even if the only picture which emerges from under it is one which you feel you must classify under "imagination." The only question then is whether Swedenborg's experiences, imaginative or not, have value in themselves as pieces of thinking that can send us off to reflect for ourselves on fundamental issues. This highly intelligent man, as by common testimony he continued to be till his death—how did the possible future of man out of the body present itself to him? With what religion did he finally content himself? His experiences and opinions on these subjects may have been all in his imagination, but they were still experiences.

CHAPTER FOURTEEN

Psychical Research

SWEDENBORG once sighed over the kind of people "who deny everything and yet refuse to apply their minds to anything."

To understand him it is unfortunately necessary to ask the reader to do a little work, since the only practical clue to a comprehension of the last third of his life is to be found in the science of psychical research. That is not primarily a feast of ghosts and haunted houses. It is a feast of statistics based on the results of experimental methods seemingly as careful as scientific ingenuity can make them. These results are so upsetting to the old mechanistic conceptions of the laws of nature that they have been fiercely questioned by statisticians—only to be validated by as good or better statisticians.[1]

The Society for Psychical Research was founded in England in 1882 by a group of scholars, largely from Cambridge University. Among its presidents (not all English) have been such men as the American psychologist William James (who helped to found the American Society for Psychical Research); the physicists Sir William Crookes, Sir William Barrett, Sir Oliver Lodge; the French philosopher Henri Bergson; Gilbert Murray; the psychologist William McDougall; the biology professor Hans Driesch; professor of logic at Cambridge, C. D. Broad; Professor H. H. Price, Oxford; Dr. Robert Thouless, head of the Department of Education, Cambridge University; while among the Society's membership, past and present, have been a number of well-known scholars such as Sir J. J. Thomson, Julian Huxley, and others.

In 1885, the American Society for Psychical Research was founded, Professor Simon Newcomb being its first President. Among its other officers have been Professor G. Stanley Hall, Professor E. C. Pickering, William James, while, in our day, research is being done under the direction of the psychologist Professor Gardner Murphy.

These men, and women such as Mrs. Henry Sidgwick, so far

from being credulous, were rather specialists in incredulity. A
great deal of the work of the Societies consisted in, and still consists in, unmasking fraud or tracking down self-deception. Some of
their members even learned professional "conjuring" in order to
find out if certain alleged mediumistic phenomena, such as slate-
writing, could not be duplicated by normal means. This negative
part of their work [2] has been so effective that the positive contributions are perhaps not equally well known.

Yet precisely because these researchers had studied fraud and
self-deception, they have been able to work out methods that seem
to prove the existence of telepathy and kindred "psychic" abilities,
and to prove it by strictly scientific experimentalism.

No one can or should be convinced by mere assertions of this
kind, but neither should anyone air his opinion on the matter without having studied the large technical literature now existing.[3]

Of the facts that seem to have been established by this kind of
research, two are especially relevant to an understanding of Swedenborg—telepathy, or, more broadly speaking "extrasensory perception," and precognition, defined as "a noninferential knowledge of the future."

So far the studies made of Swedenborg (aside from those made
by members of the sect started in England after his death) appear
to take it for granted that the stories of his telepathy and precognition are either false reports or else signs of his supposed madness.
Things would look different if any one of them could have been
true. There is no doubt that Swedenborg began very early to puzzle
over such phenomena. In 1733 or 1734 he was interested in precognitive dreams, and, as previously mentioned, he later made a
list of passages he found in the classics concerning prophetic
dreams. In his dream diary of 1744 he says, without giving details,
that in a dream he had warning of two mortal dangers which enabled him to escape them. In another dream he says he saw the
Moravian church in London and the curious way in which the
congregation was dressed three months before he actually saw
them. His very casualness in noting this makes one fancy he must
have had similar dreams before.

Precognition seems to have played a part only in the early period
of his supernormal experiences; after that they consisted mainly

of telepathy and/or clairvoyance. Now, these were things which he felt he could verify. Is it not extremely likely that when, mixed with these, he experienced the unverifiable, such as visions and apparent "other-world" phenomena, he concluded that they also were "real," since, as will be seen, he felt he had other reasons for thinking so?

Let the psychical research color be put over this puzzle, and something new may emerge.

To find out if extrasensory perception and precognition must at least provisionally be considered facts, it is necessary, as has been said, to make a careful study of the technical literature. Here only brief hints can be given of a couple of the objective methods which have been worked out by individuals or by groups, some working at colleges and universities.[4]

G. N. M. Tyrrell [5] had five small boxes made, completely light-proof, and fitted with tiny electric lamps. A mechanical device selected at random which of the boxes was to be lit up when Mr. Tyrrell (the experimenter) from behind a screen pressed a noiseless key. At a given signal the subject of the experiment, or "sensitive," opened the lid of the box which she guessed to be the one lit up, another device automatically recording her choice and whether it was or was not correct. About seventy trials a minute were made. By another mechanism, which the experimenter could use without the knowledge of the subject, the lamp of the box opened by the subject was not actually lit until she lifted the cover.

The Tyrrell experiments were in fact safeguarded and tested in far greater detail than sketched here. Results achieved were far beyond chance, whether the lamp was lit before the cover was lifted, or simultaneously with the lifting. In a series of 7,809 trials, made with mechanically selected numbers, the odds against the results being due to chance were many millions to one.[6] And, in a series of trials testing precognition by the subject of which box was going to be lit up, the odds against chance were likewise many million to one.

In the Soal and Goldney experiments [7] carried on in England from 1941 to 1943, a specially gifted subject was tested for "precognitive telepathy" under the most elaborate precautions. In one room the subject, under observation by one experimenter, wrote his guess of what the card was which an "agent" in another room was looking at. The agent was also under observation by an experimenter, the number of the card he was to look at being chosen by the experimenter's drawing counters of various colors from a bag.

The results showed that the subject had a marked tendency to guess not the target card but the one following it; that is, he knew what the card was going to be two and a half seconds before it was turned up and looked at by the "agent." Tests showed that there were "good agents" and poor ones, successful procedures and unsuccessful ones, but, pooling all conditions, good and bad, the results could not have been due to chance more than once in 10^{35} times.[8] Independent and eminent witnesses were frequently present at the experiments.

The experiments in "extrasensory perception" at Duke University by Dr. J. B. Rhine and his students (such as the Pratt-Woodruff experiments) are by now so well known as hardly to need description; while the University of Colorado study by Martin and Stribic, the University of Groningen (Holland) study [9] and many others show that by the same or similar objective techniques similar results can be arrived at.

As relevant to Swedenborg, however, Whately Carington's distance experiments in telepathy [10] are most interesting, as are Carington's theories to account for these phenomena.

Here the experimenter looks at a picture, say a hedgehog, and draws it at 8 P.M. of a certain day; a fixed time later he draws another picture, and so on. The persons to be tested, who may be seas or continents away, try to draw the picture they think it is at the same time (previously arranged) and, before midnight, they must put their guesses in the mail for the experimenter. The postal date on the envelope is a check.

Instead of a few cards the whole pictorial universe is now the target of guessing, so far as the person tested knows, but correct guesses, some fantastically above chance, have even so been made. The results are conscientiously tabulated. For example, in one of Mr. Carington's experiments the drawing of a bow-tie was "sent," and in the answers there were a number of hourglasses (very similar in shape), but they were rejected.

It is usually a picture that is transmitted. A hedgehog appears before one's mind, or inner sight, but the word may also appear, either visually or as if "heard." Yet, generally speaking, telepathy is in a picture language. Many complex questions are raised in regard to the manner in which the faculty of extrasensory perception (also called the "psi" ability) functions, or doesn't, but innumerable tests scrupulously made and analyzed prove that it exists.

Swedenborg knew the fact if not the name, and he had his own theories to account for it, but before examining these it is best to consult modern experimental psychical research.

Telepathy, so the experts agree, is not "something like radio." It differs in fundamental respects. The distance between the experimenter and the subject or percipient makes no difference in the quality of the reception, as it does in radiative phenomena. A radio has to have at least a condenser and an inductance coil.[11] Such instruments have not been found in the human body, dissected as it now is down to its last millimeter.

Even more important, researchers have pointed out, is the question of code—acoustic disturbances, dots, dashes, etc.

"Are we to suppose that the ever-industrious 'subconscious' . . . translates into Morse (say) at one end and interprets at the other, without anyone being aware of the process or knowing what code is used?"

Whately Carington, who asks the question, prefers to suppose that telepathy can take place because mankind possesses a common subconscious. He does not claim this as an original idea (Jung's collective unconscious links into it, for instance), but he asks a searching question. Why if Mr. Smith thinks of Cat and draws a cat, sending it per telepathy to Mr. B, should the latter tend to think of Cat and not of Dog or Razor-blade or Pyramid?

His answer is that if minds have "underground" access to each other, making them in certain respects one mind, then the same psychological laws must apply to "it" as apply to the individual mind. With the individual mind, should two ideas be presented to it at the same time, there is a consequence when one of these ideas is presented to the mind again; the other is apt to accompany it. In a series of brilliant experiments, Mr. Carington has demonstrated that this "law of the association of ideas" with its sublaws, applies also to telepathy between minds.

Go back to the experimenter drawing a picture and to the sub-ject or percipient waiting to guess what it is. Both have the idea of this experiment in common. Therefore if one of them thinks of Cat and draws Cat, the experiment-idea is, as it were, drawing the cat-idea to it in the mind of the other person. Instead of trying to guess one object out of all creation, it comes to him by force of the ordinary process of association, barring of course emotional in-hibitions that might prevent it.

Any idea which is shared by two or more people can, if it is asso-ciated with another idea in one of these minds, cause the latter idea to rise into the consciousness of the others. This linking idea Mr. Carington calls the "K" idea, for brevity (key idea).

But what is an "idea"? And what is a "mind"? Is it a box which holds things? Swedenborg pondered the same problems; distant as all this discussion may seem from him, it is really bringing us closer to him, as will appear eventually.

Mr. Carington adds to his association theory of telepathy his "psychon" theory of mind. (These curious terms are a legitimate attempt to get away from words that are shabby with too much use.)

Like Swedenborg, psychical researchers are interested in what a sense impression "really" is. It is a common fallacy, Swedenborg often lamented, when people think that the organ of the eye sees, or that the organ of the ear hears. Knock out the optic area of the brain and the most perfect eye can't see. Without the brain cells in whose company the sense impressions are changed into conscious-ness of them, the sense organ is nothing.

But neither can you depend on what the mind tells you about the sense reports. For instance, Swedenborg said, the sun, stars, and planets are not little molecules, the earth is not at rest, the anti-podeans do not fall off into space, etc.; "if we have faith in our senses only we shall be more like animals than rational beings." [12]

Mr. Carington would largely agree, yet he insists that these sense reports are all that one can *know* directly in perception. Your phys-ical sight presents a white patch to you; then something takes place in the right brain cells, and you say, It is an egg!

But it may not be an egg. All you really *know* is the sense report that there is a white patch. How that is changed into the idea of an egg is still a mystery.

Swedenborg calls this a "material idea" and says, as does of course Mr. Carington, that memory helps to classify the sense report. "There is as much memory as there is experience of the senses," [13] Swedenborg said, not the whole story by far according to him; he meant the kind of memory he called "external," but this is what Mr. Carington comes to write about when he develops his "psychon" theory of mind.

All ideas, sense reports, and images he proposes to call "psychons." The mind, for him, *is* a system of these units or psychons, held together by associative links, as a material system of particles may be held together by the force of gravitation. And, for him, "consciousness" *is* that system of forces which unites the psychons, and it is no more a "stuff" than is gravitation. For him there is no "ego" or its equivalent, no boxlike container, which is conscious of them.

The "self" is the semipermanent mass or nucleus of psychons which has its origin in sense reports, plus the images and ideas which have gathered round them, plus "events of our earlier life." Our "self" is our psychon-system. "Wherever there are two or more associated psychons there will be some sort or degree of 'consciousness' between them."

These may be strange words and stranger ideas to many people, yet it is absolutely necessary to think a little about what a mind is or is not before beginning the attempt to understand the extraordinary mind of Emanuel Swedenborg, and, if only as a hypothesis, one must try to think in the terms that have proved useful for the elucidation of psychic phenomena.

Now, if, in Mr. Carington's words, there can be some degree of consciousness among associated psychons in the same mind (or psychon-system) it follows that there can be subsystems within it —moods, sentiments, repressed complexes, "full-blown secondary personality." But, not only that, the individual psychon-system is capable of "entering as a component into super-systems."

The common subconscious of mankind would be such a super-system, in which, according to Mr. Carington, the individual would really only be a kind of condensation, but some individuals—about one in five—would have greater ability to connect with the super-system than others. These have "true" dreams, or see visions or apparitions, sometimes acquiring correct information in this way, which they could not otherwise have received.

The reason for this as Carington would explain it would be that in their individual psychonsystem a subsystem can be split off and take the control away, temporarily, from the central system whose job it is to keep the organism alive in the struggle for existence. If this subsystem is in almost complete control, the condition of the person is said to be that of "trance," more or less deep, in which the subsystem sometimes announces itself to be another person-ality (see studies in multiple personality) [14] or even declares it is a spirit "control," a declaration which it is sometimes hard to dis-prove.

Within the individual psychon-system such a subsystem may communicate telepathically with the central system or with other subsystems, in which case the "normal" consciousness may be aware of symbolic visions or hear voices, usually much to its distress. They would usually be a demonstration by frustrated emotion psychons, or they might be an attempt to convey an extrasensory perception. That would have to be tested. Some Jungian psychiatrists are begin-ning to do so.[15]

Continuing for a little while longer to use the psychon terms, it can be said that there seems to be a subsystem which is capable of manufacturing "real" sense impressions. Take dreams. As Sweden-borg had noted, one can have "sensations" in dreams with an extraordinary "reality" about them, with details so vivid that one could never supply them from the best memory while awake.

The ordinary theory is, of course, that it is from "memory traces" that such dreams are built up. But a good hypnotist can persuade a good subject that the lemon he is holding is a sweet pear and the subject will eat it with every sign of sweet-pear enjoyment. He may even be persuaded that a pear is there when it is not, or he may be told that he feels no pain when a pin is stuck into him, and he will feel no pain. Or, as Pierre Janet proved, the hypnotist can taste, say, salt, out of sight of the hypnotized subject, and the latter also "tastes" it.[15a]

There is evidently something in the "mind" which fabricates these "real" sensations, or which inhibits them, and this something has been especially studied by G. N. M. Tyrrell.[16] For the understanding of Swedenborg it is important to try to follow Mr. Tyrrell.

The latter's theories dovetail nicely with those of Mr. Carington. Mr. Tyrrell, however, deals with more advanced combinations of the psychon-systems that may exist within the individual mind. To the subsystem that is able to fabricate sense impressions so real that they are called hallucinations he gives the name of the "producer," and to the subsystem which provides the producer with an infinite richness of (often symbolic) data he gives the name of the stage-carpenter.

Mr. Tyrrell's point is that there are hallucinations and hallucinations. Those which interest the psychical researcher are the ones which can be proved to have contained correct information that could not have been obtained by any other means—the others he leaves to the psychiatrist, generally speaking.

These "veridical" hallucinations—or "spontaneous cases"—most often have to do with news of danger or of death. There is a great abundance of verified cases of this kind in which "apparitions" have brought such news to people who could not normally have known or inferred it. Such people sometimes have made a note of the event before it was verified. Mr. Tyrrell tells of such a case:

A lady opens her eyes, still half awake, yet she sees on the pillow a slip of paper on which she reads the words: "Elsie was dying last night." Rousing herself fully, she sees that there is no slip, it was an hallucination. But—"Elsie" had died last night, as she later found out.

In Mr. Tyrrell's opinion, this and many similar cases are also telepathic in nature, but coöperative. That is, the agent, "Elsie," consciously or subconsciously thinks of the lady whom she wants to know of her plight. Some link exists between them ("K" idea) which makes it possible for the news to come to the attention of the "producer" in the lady's mind (psychon-system), and the news comes in dramatized form during that half-awake morning period known to favor hallucinations, because the central government is not yet entirely in control.

The producer has rigged up the device of the slip on the pillow, but this is rather unusually polite. More often it would be a tele-pathized apparition of Elsie herself, perhaps with an added auditory hallucination "I am dying," or "Good-by," or with a sad expression, or with dripping clothes, if the death were by drowning. If it were not possible to manage this as an externalized hallucination, it might appear as an extraordinarily vivid dream.

In the many cases where bits of the circumstances are shown (such as a part of the ship or building where the accident or whatever happened), circumstances which the percipient could not have known, it must be supposed that the two producers have pooled their information through the intercommunicating subconscious.

We are still, however, dealing only with what goes on in one person's mind. There are cases of several normal, fully awake people having the same hallucination. Mr. Tyrrell deals with this significant "collective percipience of apparitions," of which a number of attested cases exist.

They may be telepathic "infection" from one to the other per-cipient, but in some of the cases quoted by Mr. Tyrrell where several people have seen the same "apparition," they have seen it as it would have looked from their different points of viewing it if it had been "real"; that is, the person in back of the apparition sees its back, the one at the side sees the side, etc., though it also happens that one or two of the persons present either see nothing at all or else get only a confused perception. Or, if the apparition "speaks," they may hear and not see it, or vice versa.

Mr. Tyrrell's theory, backed by much evidence, is that the "producer" levels of the different personalities, who are necessary for the "reality" of the apparition, are all acted upon by the agent and perhaps by the chief percipient. According to the capacity of each, all the producer levels then get to work and produce in each the view of the apparition which that person in fact would have seen if something physically "real" had been there. (Incidentally, Mr. Tyrrell asks, how, if the various aspects of the same apparition seen simultaneously by several people are caused by physical traces in the brain, do the brain traces in the various brains get into a state of exact correlation with each other?)

The cases collected by the English Society over a long period of time (more than sixty years) and from many different localities, so

Mr. Tyrrell points out, all agree on certain features that apparitions have in common and on certain features that they never have, usually those dear to fiction-writers. "Ghosts" do not perform physical actions. The one thing, according to Mr. Tyrrell, which the perfect apparition is *not*—be it of the living, dying, or alleged dead —is physical. Literally "nothing" is there, even if you should feel the touch of a hand, for a sensation of touch can be hallucinated by the producer as well as any other sensation. You might even, he says, feel the hand of an apparition, while your own passed right through it.

Mr. Tyrrell catalogues the nineteen points of the Perfect Apparition with the conscientiousness of a judge at a fox-terrier show, and he convinces us that nearly all the apparitions of fiction show how "their authors have not even dimly conceived the idea of a visible, audible, and tangible, yet non-physical ghost."

But, "I have seen, I have heard, I have felt," Swedenborg said in solemnly asserting that his experiences in and of "the other world" were real. No well-meaning friend could budge him from that attitude.

Here it is extremely pertinent to ask what he meant by "real." In his diary he notes a "dream," which, however, was like a "wakeful persuasion of being awake," and in this state he saw a being "who appeared in all respects as a man," yet Swedenborg proved to him that he, the man, was a spirit, "by the fact that when he would touch me with his hand and arms, he actually passed through my body, though subsequently the experiment was made with a different result, as he did not pass through, and the sensation of touch was felt just as in the waking state." [17]

Throughout his nearly thirty years of familiarity with "spirits," Swedenborg constantly insists that although "newly arrived" spirits only think they have physical bodies, still as long as they think it they have the same sensations as if they were actually in the flesh. In fact, according to Swedenborg, he spent much of his time in that world doing a kind of missionary work by explaining to its denizens something very similar to the modern theories of sense data. He tried to make them understand that, although they did feel the same old sensations, this did not mean that they weren't "dead," only that they had been wrong in supposing that their perception of sense data had been exclusively linked to their grosser physical mechanisms.

He did not always succeed in convincing them. Skeptics seemed to be numerous even "there," and determined ones, for Swedenborg also noted in his diary that one day when he wanted to "represent" a microscope in order to aid an argument, "the spirits resisted, and did not wish to allow it, saying they do not wish to admit those things which convince, for they fear to be convinced." [18]

Absorbing from any point of view as is his account of that spirit world in and out of which he dropped with such ease, there is so far no way of proving that it was not entirely a subjective hallucination put on by a producer-level-of-genius in his personality, leaving him, as some worthy people of his time thought, brilliantly sane except in this respect.

There may never be any way of proving what his experience really was, but it is relevantly interesting to try to find out whether he had any of the abilities of the "gifted subjects" with whom psychical researchers get their star results; whether there is any evidence that he showed extrasensory perception in spontaneous cases; and whether he had the kind of "splittable" psychic constitution known to facilitate such states.

The last question would seem to bring us into the territory reserved, apparently, for psychiatry. Part of the object of this study is to show that in reality it also belongs to another and a different province, that of psychical research. The two may be contiguous, but they are not the same. For instance, a question that never could be asked of psychiatry can be asked of modern psychical research: How far can it bear out Swedenborg's stubborn claim that man survives the death of the body?

CHAPTER FIFTEEN

Swedenborg's Clairvoyance

IN Swedenborg's work on the nervous system (*The Fibre*) there is evidence that he had not neglected the study of abnormal mental states. While he was writing this book, in 1741, he had a chance to apply his knowledge, since he was given charge of a case that came before the Board of Mines. It was that of Duseen, a copyist clerk, accused of drunkenness and violence. Many witnesses testified that Duseen was good, but weakminded. Many others swore he was the worst of drunkards. Swedenborg with remarkable breadth of mind for his time saw that he had to find out, as he told his fellow Assessors, whether the man was weakminded because of intoxication, or intoxicated because of being weakminded. He decided for the latter, after having most ably sifted all the evidence. But he urged caution in dismissing him, bad servant of the State though he was. "His negligence comes from his sickness, and such a course would put him in a miserable condition as to both body and soul." Duseen was allowed to retire on a pension.[1]

Two years later Swedenborg was going through his religious crisis, but in spite of the deep emotions that almost swept him away from his faith in rationality, he did study his own case, as is evident in the dream diary of 1743–44. He interpreted his dreams not according to their manifest content (or what they seemed superficially to mean) but as symbolic of the ambitions that were preoccupying him so intensely—his scientific work and his longing to be a wholly "spiritual" man, to be regenerated.[2]

He noticed a real split in his personality and very much wondered at it. "It was strange that I could be of two minds, quite separate at the same time . . . I did not know whither to flee, for I bore it within me." The two minds, the "double thoughts," as he literally called them, he saw of course as the carnal man striving with the spiritual man, but there was more than symbolism in it for him. He noted that he felt the "inner man" as "another than myself," and that he seemed to speak to himself as if to another.[3]

During this period he also noted that he had unusual physical symptoms, such as sleeping for ten or twelve hours at a stretch, and unaccountable sweats and tremblings. He practiced, as we have seen, self-invented breathing exercises (of a yogic kind) involving holding his breath, as a help toward "controlling" his thoughts. Whether because of such practices or not, he experienced "a swoon such as I had in Amsterdam six or seven years ago." [4]

He was aware that most of his strange experiences seemed to come after he had just awaked in the morning, but one whole night, "I was neither asleep nor awake, but in a strange coma; I was aware of all my dreams; I kept control of my thoughts, which made me sweat now and then; I cannot describe that kind of sleep, through which my double thoughts were separated or were torn asunder." [5]

It is evident that he distinguished between this conscious but trancelike state, characterized by inner strife, and his other states of mystic ecstasy, in which he felt as if he might be wholly dissolved in "the real joy of life." [6] Those he associated with "the only blissful Christ spirit." But at the end of the so-called dream diary he notes that he had discovered there are spirits of all kinds, and this is the first mention he makes of "spirits." These other spirits, he says, "take the form of our desires [amores]," which would make it seem as if he were trying to picture one set of his "double thoughts" as a kind of infernal crew symbolizing temptations. It must be remembered that Swedenborg to a high degree thought in images. Even in his strictly physiological works he is always illustrating his point with some very concrete simile as previously cited —"the grate-work" of the ribs, "the pipes, ovens and little bladders" of the body, etc. Everything was always like something else, something visual and specific.

But through this period he does not seem to have had, or at least recorded, more than one real auditory hallucination—one, that is, as coming from outside of himself. This occurred on an occasion just before he went to sleep. He says he was thinking hard about his current work (it was *The Worship and Love of God*) when "it was said to me 'shut your mouth, or I'll hit you!' " He says he was frightened. But he drew the conclusion he shouldn't work so late at night.[7]

Such threats from an ebullient sub-psychon-system, either trying to become more or resenting becoming less, are not uncommon in periods of spiritual adjustment.

Ever since childhood Swedenborg had tended to disregard his introspective life, enthralled as he was by experimental science. Busy as science kept him, he may also have kept down his emotional life, or not given it enough practice, while at the same time he yearned for the release of feeling that abandonment of self which he described as the real essence of love.

In the language of Dr. Jung, it could be said that Swedenborg was an introvert type who flung himself into an extrovert career. But his real bent kept pulling him toward psychological and religious interests, culminating in the religious crisis when the introvert philosopher conquered the extrovert scientist in a battle that took the form of spiritual versus worldly ambition.

What was subjective and what was objective was certainly not so subtly disentangled in Swedenborg's day as it is now. At that time it was not strange that he should have been "aware" of, or have "seen," as dark forces outside of himself, the things in himself with which he was struggling.

This, in modern terms, is called projecting a dissociated fragment of yourself. Jung calls it an integral part of the mechanism of the unconscious, and says it stands wholly outside the conscious will.[8]

In Jungian psychology the battle in Swedenborg would not necessarily be ascribed to unbalanced sexuality or to unbalanced desire for power, as it would with Freud or Adler. Jung recognizes other "drives"; he recognizes, in his own words, "before and above all that which belongs to man alone—the spiritual and religious need inborn in the psyche." [9]

Turning from Swedenborg the mystic, however, back to the Swedenborg whose consciousness was being "torn asunder," he was certainly "dissociated," or, in Mr. Carington's terms, a sub-system of his general psychon-system was leading a dark life of its own, or perhaps several of them were doing so. Does this prove that he was capable of extrasensory perception—of getting impressions, later discovered to have been true, without the aid of the senses?

Certainly not.

"Dissociation," or a split personality, does not need to mean that its owner will dream true dreams, receive correct objective information from "apparitions," etc.—far from it. As Gardner Murphy has pointed out,[10] before the latter kind of dissociation can take place, there is usually a deep need for paranormal contact in the individual. And this deep need may even be the cause of the cleavage.

Swedenborg had noted this. He wrote in *The Fibre* that what we should now call hallucinations (he called it "fanatical imagination") were apt to come from "a most intense application and ardor of the mind . . . especially in the case of those who ardently desire to contemplate the state of the soul after the fate of the body . . ."[11]

Whether he was writing here with himself in mind or not, there can be little doubt but that he had deep need for paranormal contact.

Did it result in his obtaining it, in the sense of his having "veridical hallucinations," and thus procuring information apparently unobtainable by ordinary sensory means?

The three chief stories on which his reputation for clairvoyance rests are his having perceived a fire in Stockholm while he was in Gothenburg three hundred miles away; his having guessed a secret known only to the Queen of Sweden and her dead brother, and his having obtained knowledge of the whereabouts of a lost receipt, its location being "known" only to the dead Dutch ambassador Marteville.

That he himself admitted the truth of these stories has been recorded by a number of witnesses, and since there is overwhelming testimony to Swedenborg's own truthfulness, the case might be considered closed if it were not also a fact that even the most truthful can be self-deceived.

To analyze the evidence for Swedenborg's "psychic" experiences after two hundred years is not so difficult, however, as it might seem—if we make the present come to the aid of the past. Through modern experimental methods, as has been mentioned, strong evidence exists in favor of the reality of telepathy. But what about the so-called "spontaneous" cases, where, for instance, a person has a "vision" of a distant event, later proved to have occurred in the way and at the time the percipient was aware of it?

A questionnaire regarding the frequency of veridical hallucinations of this kind was sent out by the English Society for Psychical Research. The results were statistically analyzed and showed that for a certain number of people the chance expectation of such a coincidence would be 1, whereas the census showed 24. As the questionnaire dealt only with impressions of the death of a distant person and the attendant circumstances, when there had been no reason to apprehend a fatality, the results could be dealt with statistically.[12]

In such a case as that of the Stockholm fire perceived by Swedenborg, the modern research officer of a Society for Psychical Research would have wanted to get the testimony of all concerned as soon as possible after the event. Failing that, he would want the testimony of a trustworthy person who had gone to interview the persons present at Swedenborg's description of the fire, if he could not himself get it through interview or letters. He would of course also inquire about other ways in which the news could have come to Gothenburg and about the normal frequency of fires in Stockholm, etc. In short, he must be a specialist in incredulity, and, indeed, he usually is.

Modern cases of telepathy and/or clairvoyance similar to the case of the Stockholm fire have passed unscathed through the fire of such searching inquiries, so that by analogy and in view of Swedenborg's truthfulness, one might—with a little goodwill—consider true the stories which go to show his clairvoyance.

That is not necessary, however.

In the cases of the Stockholm fire and the Queen's secret and the lost receipt a contemporary research officer did get on the job, and though it was not till some eight or nine years later, the fact that his name was Immanuel Kant should have some weight.

Kant put his information in a letter to a friend [13] who had asked him about Swedenborg's alleged psychic gifts, excusing himself for his delay in so doing, but he had wished first to inform himself thoroughly. He then reminded her that no one had ever perceived in him "an inclination to the marvellous, or a weakness tending to credulity." So it was with him, he continued, till he heard from a friend and student of his that the latter had been present when a letter was read by an Austrian ambassador from a Mecklenburg ambassador who had been with the Queen of Sweden when Swedenborg told her the secret.

This impressed Kant. "For it can scarcely be believed that one ambassador should communicate to another for public use a piece of information, which related to the Queen of the court where he resided, and which he himself together with a distinguished company had the opportunity of witnessing, if it were not true."

He resolved to investigate further, communicating again with his friend and persuading him to interview the Austrian ambassador once more on the subject, with the result that the event was again confirmed. "Professor Schlegel also had declared to him that it could by no means be doubted."

Kant wrote to Swedenborg himself, who promised to answer, but either he did not or the letter did not arrive. Kant did not give up, but when a friend of his was going to Stockholm he commissioned him to investigate these matters, especially, it would seem, the Stockholm fire. (The Queen would presumably not be easy to interview in those days.)

This friend was the English merchant Green, of whom Kant thought so highly that a biographer of the latter writes, "Kant discovered in Green a man possessed of much knowledge and of so clear an understanding that he often avowed to me that he never penned a sentence in his 'Critique of Pure Reason' without reading it to Green, and subjecting it to his unbiassed understanding unfettered to any system."

Green, according to Kant, not only saw Swedenborg, whom he found "a reasonable, polite and open-hearted man," and also a man of learning, but he "examined all, not only in Stockholm but also, about two months ago, in Gothenburg where he is well acquainted with the most respectable houses, and where he could obtain the most authentic and complete information, for, as only a very short time has elapsed since 1759 most of the inhabitants are still alive who were eye-witnesses of the occurrence."

The occurrence was the Stockholm fire, and the story given to Kant by Mr. Green is the fullest account extant of it.

Kant writes: "The following occurrence appears to me to have the greatest weight of proof, and to place the assertion respecting Swedenborg's extraordinary gift beyond all possibility of doubt. [In the year 1759 toward the end of July [14]] on Saturday at four o'clock, P.M. Swedenborg arrived at Gothenburg from England, when Mr. William Castel invited him to his house together with a party of fifteen persons. About six o'clock, Swedenborg went out, and returned to the company quite pale and alarmed. He said that a dangerous fire had just broken out in Stockholm, on Södermalm (where his house was), and that it was spreading very fast. [Stockholm had great fires in 1723, 1751, 1759, 1768, and 1769.[15]] He was restless and went out often. He said that the house of one of his friends, whom he named, was already in ashes, and that his own was in danger. At eight o'clock, after he had been out again, he joyfully exclaimed, 'Thank God! the fire is extinguished, the third door from my house.' This news occasioned great commotion throughout the whole city, but particularly amongst the company in which he was. It was announced to the Governor the same evening. On Sunday morning, Swedenborg was summoned to the Governor who questioned him concerning the disaster. Swedenborg described the fire precisely, how it had begun, and in what manner it had ceased, and how long it had continued. On the same day the news spread through the city, and as the Governor had thought it worthy of attention the consternation was considerably increased; because many were in trouble on account of their friends and property, which might have been involved in the disaster. On Monday evening a messenger arrived at Gothenburg, who was despatched by the Board of Trade during the time of the fire. In the letters brought by him the fire was described precisely in the manner stated by Swedenborg. On Tuesday morning the royal courier arrived at the Governor's, with the melancholy intelligence of the fire, of the loss which it had occasioned, and of the houses it had damaged and ruined, not in the least differing from that which Swedenborg had given at the very time when it happened, for the fire was extinguished at eight o'clock."

Another instance of Swedenborg's apparent gift of clairvoyance was told by the granddaughter of Mr. Bolander to Dr. Im. Tafel, the collector of the Swedenborg documents. The gist of it is as follows:

At a dinner given in his honor in Gothenburg about 1770, Swedenborg suddenly turned to Mr. Bolander and said to him sharply, "Sir, you had better go to your mills!" Mr. Bolander was the owner of large cloth mills, and although he disliked Swedenborg's tone he did leave the table and go to his mills. "On arriving there he found that a large piece of cloth had fallen down near the furnace and had commenced burning. If he had delayed but a little longer he would have found his property in ashes. After removing the danger Mr. Bolander returned to the company and expressed his thanks to Swedenborg, telling him what had happened. Swedenborg smiled, and said that he had seen the danger, and also that there was no time to be lost, wherefore he had addressed him thus abruptly." [16]

Jung–Stilling, a German doctor who was acquainted with all the persons present at the scene of the following event, reports that one of them, a universally trusted man, told the company: "In 1762, on the very day when Emperor Peter III of Russia died, Swedenborg was present with me at a party in Amsterdam. In the middle of the conversation, his physiognomy became changed, and it was evident that his soul was no longer present in him, and that something was taking place within him. As soon as he recovered he was asked what had happened. At first he would not speak out, but after being repeatedly urged, he said, 'Now, at this very hour the Emperor Peter has died in prison,' explaining the nature of his death. 'Gentlemen, will you please to make a note of this day, in order that you may compare it with the announcement of his death which will appear in the newspapers.' The papers soon after announced the death of the Emperor which had taken place on the very same day." [17]

The most likely theory of the above cases of "far-seeing" is that they were impressions gathered telepathically from some person present at the event (some moron may have been present as the cloth burned); a theory which the experimental work on the transmission of images goes to support. Mr. Whately Carington and Dr. Hettinger especially have done important work in this field. [18]

Why should the roll of burning cloth or the death by strangulation of Emperor Peter III have reached Swedenborg? We do not know, but an experiment conducted by Usher and Burt [19] seems to indicate that events or images may "broadcast" themselves at large, and may be perceived by the appropriate kind of human apparatus. In this case A, who was several hundred miles away from B, had arranged that at 8:30 on a certain evening he was to try to "transmit" telepathically a certain drawing to B. The day before the experiment B (of course without telling A) told a friend, C, that she might take part in it, and try to guess what the drawing was.

The evening of the experiment A dined in a restaurant, playing chess after dinner. Near him three men were talking loudly; they ate roast capon with bread sauce. The room had green hangings. Someone was playing a piano. At 8:25 A remembered he had to transmit the drawing and withdrew to concentrate on it at 8:30. It was a diagram.

But the impression received by the friend C (of whose participation A did not know) was "roast capon, bread sauce, three men, much talk, green hangings, somebody strumming." With it was a crisscross pattern resembling a chessboard. C, however, as is often the case, did not receive this impression at the conscious level, it came via automatic writing.

There are well-attested cases of "spontaneous" clairvoyance (if that is what it is) in the files of research societies, but, as the experimental work previously cited covers such phenomena fairly well, some other questions must be asked in regard to Swedenborg.

Was Swedenborg a "medium"? It seems clear that he was capable of extrasensory perception, but did he go into "trance," do automatic writing, and claim that in these states, or even in his normal state, he was able to transmit messages from the dead to living people?

The answer is that though he did not know the names of those dissociated states he did feel he experienced them and he did claim to have knowledge obtained from the deceased.

It is easy for us *now* to say: "Why did he not conduct proper experiments, have them properly recorded and controlled by trust-worthy witnesses?" Why, in short, did he not behave as if he lived in the twentieth century and was a member of the Psychical Research Society in Tavistock Square, London, or at 40 East 34th St., New York!

The mental climate has to be considered. On the one hand were the few Voltairean intellectuals who would have greeted such experimenting as ridiculous. Few of them were as liberal as the eighteenth-century Danish playwright Ludvig Holberg (rightly called the Danish Molière), a most learned and acute man, who, being asked if he believed in "ghosts," said that although no doubt most of such stories were due to a superheated imagination he would not altogether deny them, chiefly because "many credible people testify that they have both heard and seen things which they by no means can explain naturally," and also, he said, because he himself together with another person once had an experience which completely convinced him of the reality of such experience.[20]

Such an attitude was rare, especially in a man like Holberg whose genius was entirely at the service of rationality. But, besides the rationalists who then kept their opinions more or less to themselves, there were the orthodox Christians, like Count Tessin, who thanked God that their "faith" was so strong they could not believe in Swedenborg's alleged intercourse with spirits. And then there was the semi-medieval mass of the people and the still-powerful church.

In Sweden right into the eighteenth century people were brought into court for witchcraft, if they showed "psychic" or even unusual mental powers, and sometimes condemned to death.[21] Late in the seventeenth century, in Swedenborg's own lifetime, the witchcraft hysteria in the country took on terrific proportions, and while most of it was "superheated imagination" it was also mentioned at a trial that some of the "possessed" could describe things that were going on in a different part of the city of Stockholm at the same time. It was of course all ascribed to the Devil, and sentences of decapitation and burning at the stake were frequent.

It did not conduce to much public appraisal of clairvoyance or kindred abilities. Perhaps it was for this reason that hardly any of the testimonies to Swedenborg's psychic powers were put on paper until long after his death, a fact which has induced some scrupulous researchers to rule them out.

On this score, however, some testimonies cannot be ruled out— even if for some of the cases one must, as previously mentioned, fall back on Swedenborg's truthfulness, the analogy of modern cases, and experimental work. J. C. Cuno (see pp. 339–340) seems to have recorded his stories of Swedenborg's alleged clairvoyance at the time he heard them from him and approximately at the time that they occurred, but we have one contemporary recorder at least in that very Count Tessin who at first felt so skeptical.

He recorded the story which first had drawn Kant's attention to Swedenborg's supposed powers, that of the Queen of Sweden's secret. Kant, it will be remembered, paid attention to it because it had been reported by an ambassador, and in his letter to his friend about Swedenborg he affirmed that through his own "special investigations" (through the Englishman Green) he had found out that the ambassador's account was correct.[22]

The story, only published in our own day, which Count Tessin put in his private diary involved Queen Louisa Ulrica of Sweden, sister of Frederick the Great of Prussia, and herself a woman of strong intelligence. (Kant said of her that she was "a princess whose great understanding and penetration ought to have made an attempt at imposition almost impossible.") She herself said haughtily that she was "hard to fool," when someone hinted that she might have been fooled in this matter of Swedenborg.

Count Tessin wrote in his diary for November 18, 1761:[23] "A remarkable report is being circulated which has caused me to ask Assessor Swedenborg himself about the connection of the matter. This is his own account: About three weeks ago he was engaged in a long conversation with their Majesties at the Palace, on which occasion he also requested gracious permission to present copies of his published books; during the conversation he related many things which are not particularly in place here except as confirming his system of angels and heavens, etc. Her Majesty ended by requesting him, in case he saw her brother, the Prince of Prussia, to tell her something from him.

"Three days ago, which was last Sunday, he again presented himself, and, after having delivered his various books, requested an audience with the Queen, and he then told Her Majesty something privately, which he was bound to keep secret from everyone else. The Queen thereupon turned pale and took a few steps backwards as if she were about to faint, but shortly afterward she exclaimed excitedly, 'That is something which no one else could have told except my brother!'

"The assessor expressed regrets at having gone so far, when he noticed Her Majesty's intense consternation.

"On his way out he met Councilor von Dalin in the antichamber and requested him to tell Her Majesty that he would follow up the matter still further, so that she would be comforted thereby.

" 'But I shall not venture to do so,' he added to me [Count Tessin] 'until after some ten or twelve days; for if I did it before it would have the same terrifying effect, and perhaps still more intensely upon Her Majesty's mind.'

"However remarkable this may appear," Tessin wrote, strictly for himself, "as well as other things which he said to me during an hour and a half, I nevertheless feel all the more safe in putting it down as Her Majesty's obvious consternation is unanimously testified to by all those who were in the room, and among others by Councilor Baron Carl Scheffer. [In another account, which Swedenborg gave to General Tuxen of the same affair (see p. 192) Tuxen asked if anyone else heard what the Queen said, and Swedenborg answered that at least the King and Baron Scheffer were near enough to hear her.]

"The Queen also tells it in very nearly the same way, adding that she was still in doubt as to what to believe, but that she has put Assessor Swedenborg to a new proof, if he managed in this she would be convinced he knew more than others.

"Perhaps this was what he referred to when mentioning his intention to say more in ten or twelve days.

"For all that we can see," was Tessin's conclusion, "this statement is so clear and confirmed by so many testimonials, that it must needs be regarded as reliable."

There is no record, apparently, of Swedenborg's having been a second time to see the Queen about this matter. However, when in later days she was asked whether it was true that he had told her something which no one knew except her and her dead brother, she either said that it was true, or else changed the subject.

After her death Count A. J. von Höpken wrote an account [24] of the incident which explains the Queen's occasional reticence about it; he said that as the Queen had been carrying on a secret correspondence with her brother while Sweden and Prussia were at war she did not want to touch on these matters with everyone.

In Höpken's own words: "Swedenborg was one day at a Court reception. Her Majesty asked him about different things in the other life, and lastly whether he had seen or had talked with her brother, the Prince Royal of Prussia. He answered No. Her Majesty then requested him to ask for him and to give him her greeting, which Swedenborg promised to do. I doubt whether the Queen meant anything serious by it. At the next reception, Swedenborg again appeared at Court; and while the Queen was in the so-called white room, surrounded by her ladies of honor, he came boldly in and approached her Majesty, who no longer remembered the commission she had given him a week before. Swedenborg not only greeted her from her brother, but also gave her his apologies for not having answered her last letter; he also wished to do so now through Swedenborg, which he accordingly did. The Queen was greatly overcome, and said 'No one except God knows this secret.'"

There are other, and distorted, versions of this story, but it is corroborated by Major-General Tuxen,[25] a Dane who came to know Swedenborg and himself asked him whether the story were true. Swedenborg said, "Tell me what you have heard and I will tell you what part is true." Tuxen told him the story as he had had it from Count Höpken's brother, agreeing in essentials with the Count's own narrative. Swedenborg affirmed its truth.

An interesting detail from Tuxen's testimony is that the Queen asked Swedenborg, "Can you, then, speak with every one deceased or only with certain persons?" Swedenborg answered, "I cannot converse with all, but with such as I have known in this world; with all royal and princely persons, with all renowned heroes, or great and learned men, whom I have known either personally or from their actions or writings; consequently of all of whom I could form an idea; for it may be supposed that a person whom I never knew or of whom I could form no idea I neither could nor would wish to speak with."

In Mr. Whately Carington's terminology, Swedenborg needed an association or "K" idea in order to get in touch with the psychon-system, if such survived, of the deceased.

However, since the Queen herself knew about her secret correspondence with her brother, there is no way of proving that Swedenborg on the "producer" level of his personality had not got hold of the secret from the Queen's mind and dressed it up for his conscious mind as a communication from her brother.

But there is a story involving a secret which seems not to have been known to any living person, the story of the Marteville receipt.

Green's account to Kant of the case of the lost receipt was as follows: ". . . the widow of the Dutch ambassador in Stockholm, some time after the death of her husband was called upon by Croon, a goldsmith, to pay for a silver service which her husband had purchased from him. The widow was convinced her late husband had been much too precise and orderly not to have paid this debt, yet she was unable to find the receipt. In her sorrow, and because the amount was considerable, she requested Mr. Swedenborg to call at her house. After apologizing to him for troubling him, she said, that, if as all people say he possessed the extraordinary gift of conversing with the souls of the departed he would perhaps have the kindness to ask her husband how it was about the silver service. Swedenborg did not at all object to comply with her request. Three days afterwards the said lady had company at her house for coffee. Swedenborg called and in his cool way informed her that he had conversed with her husband. The debt had been paid seven months before his decease, and the receipt was in a bureau upstairs. The lady replied that the bureau had been quite cleared out, and that the receipt was not found among all the papers. Swedenborg said that her husband had described to him how after pulling out the left-hand drawer a board would appear which required to be drawn out, when a secret compartment would be disclosed containing his private Dutch correspondence as well as the receipt. Upon hearing this description the whole company arose and accompanied the lady into the room upstairs. The bureau was opened; they did as they were directed; the compartment was found, of which no one had ever known before; and to the great astonishment of all, the papers were discovered there, in accordance with his description." [26]

In other versions of the same story Swedenborg is said to have had his conversation with the departed ambassador in a dream, during which he was told of the whereabouts of the receipt. Since a similar modern case is on record, it seems relevant to tell it here.

This is the Chaffin will case,[27] in which a will, unknown to any living person, was discovered through the seeming agency of the testator in a dream. The apparent facts in this case were convincing enough to the Superior Court of Davie County, North Carolina, to admit the new will to probate in December, 1925, canceling the will previously admitted to probate.

As investigated both by the Court and by a lawyer deputizing for the Psychical Research Society, the facts seemed to be that Mr. James L. Chaffin made a will in 1905 leaving his farm to the third of his four sons, Marshall Chaffin. In 1921 he died, Marshall inheriting the property. The widow and three other sons did not protest as they knew of no valid reason for doing so.

In June, 1925, the second son dreamed several times that his father appeared to him wearing a certain overcoat which the son knew and, pointing to a pocket in it, said that his will was there. The overcoat was at last found, and sewn into the lining was not the will but a slip of paper in Mr. Chaffin's handwriting saying, "Read the 27th chapter of Genesis in my daddie's old Bible."

This Bible was in the house of Mr. Chaffin's widow, but the second son got two neighbors to go with him before he undertook the search for it. At last it was found, and, according to the sworn statements of the five witnesses present on the occasion, the will was found in the twenty-seventh chapter of Genesis—a will dated 1919. It was unattested, but as ten people swore to its being in the testator's handwriting it was legal in North Carolina. In it Mr. Chaffin willed his property to all four children. The beneficiaries under the first will were prepared to contest the second until they saw it and were perfectly convinced of its genuineness.

In another modern case where knowledge was obtained that seemingly could only have been gained from a "discarnate" mind, an Englishwoman, Mrs. Dawson Smith,[28] had a "sitting" with the well-known English medium Mrs. Leonard. Her son, killed in 1920, purportedly communicated to his mother that she must search a certain place of the box-room for an old purse with a tiny paper in it, a counterfoil. He stressed its importance without saying why. She found it; it was the counterfoil of a money order. This was in 1921. In 1924 she had a letter from "The Enemy Debt Clearing Office" which demanded payment of a sum of money said to be owing by her son to a Hamburg firm, a debt said to have been incurred in July, 1914, before the war.

Mrs. Dawson Smith knew that her boy had paid it, but the Hamburg people insisted they had not received the money. She then remembered her boy's "message," looked at the old counterfoil, "and found it the identical paper needed to prove the account had been paid." The Government acknowledged that she was right. The existence of the counterfoil, and the correspondence with the Enemy Debt Clearing Office were verified by two members of the Society for Psychical Research, Sir Oliver Lodge and Mrs. Henry Sidgwick.

Such cases, and there are a number of them, seem difficult to explain except in terms of survival of some sort. How do they look in terms of Mr. Carington's theories?

Telepathy has proved, Mr. Carington feels, that "psychons" (ideas, images, sensa) can act independently of the body. They are "real." That combination of them which we call a human mind is real. The question for him is chiefly this: if you believe that Jones survives death, "what part do you consider survives, and where?" [29]

According to the association theory of telepathy and the psychon theory of mind, the answer is that Jones's mind survives, his mind being the psychons which have been organized in the course of his life, including those which have been brought to him by his sense organs, and those which he may have acquired by telepathic interaction with other minds. As to *where* Jones's mind survives, "that ceases to have any ordinary meaning, because psychons and psychon-systems are not spatially located in the physical sense; and there is no difficulty about continuity, because the psychons surviving immediately after death are identically the same as those which formed Jones's mind immediately before it."

A Swedish innkeeper in London who kept the inn King Charles

XII asked Swedenborg what Charles the Twelfth was like in the other world. "No different from what he was in this," was Swedenborg's answer, and his stand was consistently that for some time after the death of the body the "spirit" remained the same kind of man.

Neither he nor Mr. Carington, however, believes that this condition can last. The psychon-system, getting no more fresh impressions via the physical body, might well disintegrate. You might, as Mr. Carington says, survive shipwreck on a desert island, but die of starvation after you got there.

According to Swedenborg, that would depend on whether your mind were a mere pattern of reactions to physical stimuli or whether you had developed your "understanding."

Mr. Carington can well imagine that certain psychons in a "surviving" psychon-system might, via the law of association of ideas, link up with certain psychons in a "medium." A "medium" may be said to be the kind of person whose psychon-system is more easily dissociated than that of a normal person, for one reason or another, perhaps because of a neurosis. A fairly permanent subsystem of psychons may be formed in such a person, may even develop into something resembling a separate personality, able to dissociate itself so completely from the normal personality that the latter becomes unconscious or goes into what is called "trance." In this condition, which closely resembles the deeper hypnotic sleep, the subsystem personality may take "control" of the body and speak as a separate personality, referring to the normal person as "she" or "the instrument" or the "subject" and to itself as a departed spirit who "controls" or uses the body for the purpose of communicating messages from the spirit world.

This phenomenon would belong to the province of psychiatry if it were not that the medium's "control" so often produces knowledge that cannot possibly have been known to the medium, sometimes not even to the sitter, and not even to any living person.

Mr. Carington therefore is willing to suppose that the "surviving" psychon-system of Jones, say, is able to associate part of itself with the medium's dissociated system, the result being a sort of Jones-plus-Medium which has some of the characteristics and knowledge we identify as his, and some others that puzzle us. The latter, usually rather vapid, may be elements from the medium's subconscious, or, not impossibly, also from Jones's subconscious.

A kind of composite personality would thus be formed, which might, Mr. Carington says, harden into a stereotyped pattern, and that might account for the "horrid banality" of so many "communications."

It is an error, however, which Mr. Carington certainly does not share, to suppose that all "spirit communications" are horribly banal. Like attracts like in the psychon kind of world, and if really intelligent "sitters," working with an honest medium (of whom there are some), try to get "in touch" with really intelligent and interested discarnate entities some remarkable results may be obtained.

At Duke University a female medium was isolated in a room and a person unknown to her was put in another. The medium went into "trance," and her "control" was asked to tell all "he" could about the unknown near-by person. "He" responded by telling about deceased relatives. The experimenter made a list of the alleged facts and had the sitter check them, true or false. He also tried the experiment of giving a list of facts communicated by the medium to a person for whom they were not intended. This was tried often enough to show that the number of chance hits thus obtained was far less than the hits obtained with the person for whom the communication was intended.[30]

Nevertheless, the wondrously elastic association theory of telepathy could account for such communications. But there are others in which it seems to snap, unless one is willing to include in the "common subconscious" the psychon-systems of those who are no longer in the material body, or whatever euphemism one prefers for "dead."

Those are the "cross-correspondence" cases.[31] After certain leaders of the English Society for Psychical Research died, messages began to come to various sensitives, some of them thousands of miles apart. One was a trance medium in the United States, professional, but one who had never been caught in any fraud. (Incidentally, "fraud" may also be unconscious or subconscious. Given the theatrical abilities of the "producer" level of the personality, which is probably the one which becomes dissociated as a "control," an alleged communicator may be manufactured either in part or altogether.) The others in the cross-correspondences were private individuals, one in India, several in England. They practiced "automatic" writing. This is an important form of dissociation in which the sensitive, who may or may not be in trance, writes without consciously moving her own hand or at least without seeming to know where the words come from. Sometimes a word or two ahead is known, sometimes not till the word is written, then the writer promptly forgets it.

Generally one finds out something about what is going on in one's subconscious, indeed some psycho-analysts [32] use automatic writing as a method of investigation, but paranormal knowledge has also been obtained in this way. In the celebrated cross-correspondence cases, the automatic "scripts" were sent to the Secretary of the Society for Psychical Research, who, on comparing them, found that they contained evidences of classical scholarship, not at all comprehensible to the writers, but quite comprehensible as communications from the deceased F. W. H. Myers, who purported to be sending them. The references were not alike, nor were they telepathic echoes of each other. "Myers" in fact stated that he expressly guarded against that. But they were "parts of an integrated message," and, later on, when the classical scholar Dr. A. W. Verrall died, messages began to come of an even greater complexity, purporting to be the result of Dr. Verrall's coöperation with Professor Henry Butcher, also deceased. They came through one very remarkable automatist, known as Mrs. Willett (since for private reasons she did not want her identity known), but they contained material completely unknown to her, and, until the clue was given by the alleged communicators, no one else, scholars though they were, could put the puzzle together correctly.

Professor Gardner Murphy's brilliant résumés of the best arguments for and against survival can only be briefly touched on. His general conclusion is that in asking, "Does personality survive bodily death or not?" we are asking the wrong kind of question. In his paper on "Field Theory and Survival," [33] he points to the fact that "paranormal events appear to depend . . . on powers set free by the *relations between persons:* they are interpersonal."

(While he has most enthusiastically greeted Mr. Carington's theories he prefers "interpersonal" to the term "associational" linkage, as of ideas.) The individual is "far indeed from the sharply defined and autonomous little capsule of energy which he is likely to imagine himself to be." He is a part of an "interpersonal psychic field," and "if, on independent grounds, there is reason to believe that the discarnate exist and are capable of contact with the living, there is no theoretical difficulty involved in their participating jointly with the living in an interpersonal psychical field."

Most modern psychical researchers believe that there is strong evidence for some form of survival but no actual proof. What would constitute proof? More complete evidence of the kind that suggests the people "on the other side" had thought up a test that could only have originated with them and not with anyone living here.

Professor Murphy's cautious verdict is: "There is some reason to believe that personality continues after death to be, as it is now, an aspect of an interpersonal reality, and to doubt whether it could survive as an encapsulated entity."

Previously he has called attention to the fact that from infancy to old age the "field properties" of personality change profoundly (the field theory being the treatment of a thing as a whole and not as the mere sum of its parts). Now, "with the change called death, there is every reason to believe that in so far as psychical operations continue, they [the personality characteristics] must, as aspects of larger fields, take on new qualities, new structural relationships," which yet would only be an extension of the interpersonal relationships in which they existed while in the flesh.[34]

There is no possible way of deciding now, Gardner Murphy says, how far such "surviving organized impressions" (or such discarnate psychon-systems) would resemble us.

There is no way of deciding this, and it is as yet hardly possible to speculate on such questions, without being put down as either fool or charlatan. It is as if so much fear still remained from the days when the church caused men of science to be burnt at the stake that license to speculate on conceivable other-wordly realms were only issued to poets. Many people of course are utterly unable to entertain hypotheses; they must either believe or not believe, but there is more in the avoidance of such topics than this. There is the primitive fear of letting the mind dwell on the thought of death. Or the equally primitive fear of ridicule.

For the unafraid, however, there is a vast realm of ideas necessarily connected with Swedenborg's beliefs regarding disembodied states. No intellect so mature as his, so well trained, with such an amount of scientific knowledge, has ever reported "from experience" what it was like to be "as a spirit among spirits, while still a man among men."

To the modern reader it may still remain a matter of speculation, but he has to note a good deal of similarity between these reports made by Swedenborg on "the new structural relationships" and the more recent findings of psychical research as to how these relationships ought to be *if they were*.

It is no use denying that any such modern reader is up against discouraging handicaps in studying Swedenborg for this purpose. If he follows him beyond 1745 he will be richly rewarded, but patience and understanding are needed. Time and again he will hold his head or wring his hands and ask: How could an extremely intelligent and scholarly man like Swedenborg mix up his subtle psychological observations with these fantastic interpretations of the Bible, and with ideas of the cosmos that seem to belong to the Kabbalah and other books which he used to disdain as "occult"?

No questions are more legitimate. Nor are they easily disposed of. Perhaps they never can be. But any approach to an answer must start with a consideration of what were the special reasons which led Swedenborg to believe he received his information from some source outside of himself, which he could not disregard, even though he knew with awful certainty what the "learned" would think of him.

CHAPTER SIXTEEN

Automatic Writing

THE "thousands of stories" about Swedenborg's commerce with the other world that so astonished some of his acquaintances, such as Baron Tilas, did not start circulating till after about 1760, when Swedenborg was seventy-two. For the demonstration of his supernormal powers interested him very little. What is known about them is mainly through the testimony of his contemporaries. Although he was willing to confirm some of the stories, branding others as obvious nonsense, he always insisted that such things were unimportant in comparison with what he felt was his real mission.

One cannot help pausing to reflect what a misfortune it was for the science of psychical research, as well as for a lofty ethical view of religion, that Emanuel Swedenborg happened to become entangled with an unscientific method of interpreting the Bible. In spite of the chaotic character of his last "worldly" book, *Of the Worship and Love of God,* it has passages of brilliant clarity about the very physics of the body-mind relationship; passages stimulating and suggestive on ethics, psychology, and religion; passages of great beauty, half symbolism, half "real," in that they suggest he is merely veiling actual psychic experiences under the form of allegories. If any book was ever written under the direct pressure of "inspiration" this one was, and one thinks with regret of what might have been written once Swedenborg had calmed down and begun to sort out and relate his impressions. All that can be done now, and it is not little, is to try to sift those from as objective a point of view as possible, given that no one ever can be objective.

The man who returned from London to Stockholm in August, 1745, was careful to keep his "mission" to himself. He worked hard when he rejoined the Board of Mines, and he must have worked well, or the offer of promotion would not have come to him. One wonders if it would have come had the members of the Board known what was occupying their affable, cosmopolitan colleague nights and early mornings in the house set in a large garden which he bought soon after his return.

He lived on Södermalm, a rocky island, part of that water-gleaming tracery of sea and lake and inhabited cliffs that make up the silvery splendor of Stockholm. If he walked a short distance to the edge of the rocks he could see the grand panorama almost in its entirety, nor had he very far to walk or drive to get to the stately center of the town, passing along quays where shipping from all the world furled its sails, restless in the bright living waters, for Stockholm is no stagnant Venice.

It was the first home Swedenborg had had of his own, and it was to be a permanent one, to which he returned after his many journeys. Judging by the many times he praised the ideal marriage in which there was no domination of either partner by the other, but perfect abandonment of self, he must have hoped to settle into just such a home with that ideal wife. But he was now fifty-seven, and instead of the wife he settled into his house with his mission.

The great work on the brain was not to see light until the twentieth century. The third part of *Of the Worship and Love of God* was not published by him either. He deprecated it, feeling that now he had more important work in hand. He was cool and methodical, however, in laying the foundation of his new work. While he was still in London he began the first of his several gigantic indexes to Biblical passages. One ran to eight hundred passages. Swedenborg as early as when he was thirty-two wrote to Eric Benzelius that "my head does not well recall things from memory"; [1] and indeed he always scorned "memory-knowledge." His indexes were his memory, besides which he numbered almost every paragraph he ever wrote, so that he could refer and cross-refer. He already was familiar with Greek and now he refreshed his Hebrew. But even before he could depend on the latter he began to interpret the Bible by the aid of carefully compared Latin versions.

Was it his own, this tumultuous spate of words that runs into eight big volumes as now published? [2] He said that what he was writing here was not his own, not one least word of it. It was inspired.

No doubt he felt freer to write this in a house of his own, belted by a large garden. Having to work at odd hours and in odd states, it was of importance to him to be free from interruption and from street noises—heavy carriages on cobble stones—the cries of vendors.

In his new work, which he provisionally called a "spiritual exposition" of the Bible, there was a strand of the same Christian Neoplatonism as had preoccupied him for so long, bar the crisis period; and there was a beginning thread of "psychic" experiences; but the dominant strand was the Bible exegesis. It was that which he particularly felt was inspired.

A good many authors feel so about what they write, while they are in the fervor of composition, when thoughts rise up from the stores of the subconscious, almost seeming to come from an outside source. That is a common-sense interpretation of Swedenborg's large claim, and probably partly justified. On this view one could well say that, confronted by the vast gap between much of the Old Testament and what he knew to be true in science and ethics, he explained the gap by saying, in effect: These things that offend your reason and your heart are true (they had to be true, even literally, being the Bible) in so far that they do give us a history of the Jews, but this history was so contrived by the Almighty that their innermost truth is symbolic of spiritual matters and prophetic of the Messiah that is to come. They are moral and spiritual allegories, in every detail, as well as history.

Castellio, whose work he knew, believed this, but it must be remembered that Swedenborg had read a great many other books, enough to have forgotten some of them. (It was not till he was fifty-six that he thought he was "forbidden" to read theological books.[3]) As already stated, he knew Philo Judæus, who interpreted the Old Testament allegorically in the same way, minus the Messiah, Philo being a Jew. Swedenborg had read most of the Church fathers, among them Origen. In Origen's Alexandria of the third century enough of the skeptical spirit of Greece was still alive to make an educated Christian work hard at reinterpreting the Bible. Origen concluded—and he was not the first or the only one of that time to do so—that Scripture had three kinds of sense, one moral, one historical, and one spiritual,[4] corresponding fairly well to Swedenborg's divisions.

Origen said that those who would insist on the letter alone were like the Philistines who filled up with earth the wells which the servants of Abraham digged; the spiritual interpreter was, like Isaac, to open up the wells.[5]

Swedenborg used the same interpretation. And, according to Origen, Jacob did not wrestle with an angel, it was an evil spirit. Swedenborg said the same.[6] There were other similarities, and the principles of the "interpretation" were the same.

"On this method," it has been said of Origen, and could equally well be said of Swedenborg in this respect, "the sacred writings are regarded as an inexhaustible mine of philosophical and dogmatic wisdom; in reality the exegete reads his own ideas into any passage he chooses. The commentaries are of course intolerably diffuse and tedious; a great deal of them is now quite unreadable . . ." [7]

Nothing could be truer! There probably never has been anything written so overpoweringly alien to normal interest as these Biblical commentaries by Swedenborg, nor anything more foreign to the results of modern Biblical research. Neither has anything served so much to conceal the true greatness of the man. No one who chances to meet him first in these earnest crossword puzzles can be blamed for turning quickly away.

For instance, in the verse referred to above, the "inner" meaning is said to be that by Abraham is to be understood the Messiah. And by the Philistines are to be understood the crew of the Devil who stopped up the fountains of the Divine Word, etc.[8] In some other places Abraham represents something else, not so flattering, and so on.

Of course Swedenborg did not sit down and copy Origen or anyone else, consciously. But it might be maintained that when he so desperately needed a new kind of understanding of the Bible, in order to retain "faith," up from his subconscious rose these interpretations, mingled with other elements from the same great creative realm—and, one might concede, perhaps reaching even into other "psychon-systems" of similar beliefs, now passed into the world subconscious.

Even so it is discouraging to try to puzzle out how a man who was capable of such clear, incisive thought, a worshiper of experimental science, could so uncritically accept these symbolisms. Only a few years before, he had noted that ideas contained in words are "confused images which are disclosed as to their quality by nearer approach, by sedulous examination and by touch; meanwhile they are vague conjectures, vain and empty." [9]

How could he now commit his life to such unexamined emptiness!

Some great novelist said that the most important things to examine in one's manuscripts are the transitions. They must be rightly understood and fully expressed.

Luckily Swedenborg left us the document of his transition period in the first draft of his first series of Bible commentaries, *The Word Explained,* as it came to be called. He wrote these notes so soon after he began having his other-world experiences that he had not yet arranged, trimmed, or dressed them up to suit his theories; he had not yet fully rationalized them. They contain the key to the puzzle.

He took most of what he wrote of Bible commentary as divine revelation, and therefore to be believed uncritically, because it came to him in a very special way, at least much of it; in a way nothing seems to have come to him before.

This began as far back as the winter of 1745, after he had settled into the quiet of his garden home.[10] There something happened to him so startling that its influence can almost be compared to that of his Delft vision. It brought the same sense of utter conviction, the same sense of an external force.

His hand moved of itself!

And it wrote things which, he said, were "arcana"—secrets never known to anyone before, some of them almost repellent to him, yet at least others fitted into the whole background of his thoughts as it had formed itself for years. Twice convincing—to him.

There can be no doubt that it was through so-called "automatic" writing that Swedenborg obtained the bulk of his Bible commentaries, and much that to us seems inconsistent with his real self.

Automatic writing,[11] it has been explained (see p. 198) is one of the forms in which alleged spirit communication comes to those individuals who are known as sensitives or mediums, capable of such dissociation.

From Swedenborg's own testimony it is clear that he was a medium, though far from an ordinary one, because he was an extraordinary man.

Of course he cannot be called an "automatist" just because he says that the words he writes are not his own; that they are inspired by the Lord, either directly or through various angels. That could be a manner of speaking. But he explicitly says of the ten pages which he has just written: "These words . . . were said to me verbally and almost enunciated, and this by infants who were then with me and who also spake by my mouth and moreover directed my very hand." [12] That is clear enough, yet there is much more supporting evidence.

In this form of automatic writing, he hears the words with his "inner ear," seeming to get either a few words or a sentence at a time from a dictation that appears to him to come from an external source (elsewhere he speaks of getting the text only "piecemeal"), but he passed into other, more advanced kinds of dissociation.

"Nay I have written entire pages, and the spirits did not dictate the words, but absolutely guided my hand, so that it was they who were doing the writing." [13]

Here he apparently still knew what was being written as it came word for word on the paper, but, once in a while, not only "was the finger led to the writing by a superior force so that if it wished to write something else it could never do so," but it was done even without his knowing what he had written, "so that I did not know the series of things until after it had been written; but this was extremely rare, and was merely for the sake of information that revelations have been made in this way also." [14]

This sounds as if he had been in that state of extreme dissociation from consciousness known as trance, but, as he says, it was very rare with him. Usually he seems to have remembered everything that took place, which trance mediums do not, any more than people who have been in deep hypnosis.

These notes of his have another characteristic of automatic scripts, their repetitiousness; and still another, which is the frequent reference to whether it be "permitted" [15] to reveal this or that. "I do not know if it be allowed to publish this," [16] and he also says he must "consult" before he can find out what something means.

Consult whom?

In automatic writings the "writer" often announces himself to be a spirit, "controlling" the medium, or at least controlling the medium's hand. Swedenborg mentions that "infants" not only guided his hand but spoke through his mouth. Several modern mediums claim to have child "controls." This, if one likes, is the infantile form taken by the dissociated element of their personality, that subsystem of the psychon-system, which, according to Mr. Carington, one could imagine as forming a sort of stereotyped combination with elements from a discarnate psychon-system, viz., a "spirit."

But whatever tried to control Swedenborg did not stereotype in infant form. The messengers from his subconscious, or from the world-subconscious, took different forms in this transition period (indeed during the rest of his life), at first puzzling him considerably.

"These words," he notes in one place, "were written by my hand, and dictated by Isaac, the father of the Jews . . ." [17] Abraham too, he affirms, used his hand as an instrument, but "they were dictated of the Messiah himself through Abraham . . ."

In another place he wrote (and crossed out) "this was written by my hand as an instrument; indeed it was even said it was by Jacob himself, who is somewhat indignant that I should write such things concerning him." [18]

What he had been writing was that Jacob was inferior to Esau, who "represented" (was symbolic of) the Messiah, but Jacob then "said" he was now in a better frame of mind, to which Swedenborg added, "whether this is true I cannot myself confirm, but I write what is said by him, because it is permitted him, or someone in his place, to insert these words." [19]

In a marginal note to these paragraphs, which have been crossed off, he writes that they are by no means to be inserted here. Indicating the draft character of the notes, he also says that he does not know if they may be included for printing later on; this "cannot as yet be clear to me, I being merely an organ, as also is Jacob himself. If they proceed from the latter, such as he has been described, then a conclusion can be formed as to what faith is to be put in them." [20]

He early began to lose faith in the declared identity of the spirits, and it is evident that he was worried by their claim that they were doing the dictating. What then became of divine authority for it? He tried to retain this by saying that although he talked with these spirits "concerning these matters both before and after the writing . . . it was not allowed me to tell anything here of what was dictated to me orally by any one of them. When this was done, and it happened at times, the writing had to be obliterated [this may account for some of the crossed-out lines]; it being allowed to tell only such things as flowed in from God Messiah alone, both mediately through them, and also immediately—which yet was manifest to me." [21]

He does not explain in what way it was manifest; indeed he often complains that meanings are yet obscure to him, nor does he always know whether the spirit is good or evil.

In a more cautious passage, meant for publication as it were, he says, "For with me it has many times so happened that when I was writing my hand was directed by a superior power into the very words, and this even to the point of sensation . . . Wherefore I then said that those words were not written by me, but by someone outside me. Sometimes it was also granted me to know by what angel of God Messiah they were thus written." [22]

Here, as early as 1746, the foundation was laid for the statement he stuck to in later life, that he never had instruction from anyone except from the Lord himself, or, as he sometimes put it, from the Lord in the Word—that is, through reading the Bible.

He was of course perfectly honest about this assertion, and yet it was a bit of a quibble. Since essentially he was a monist, believing that all creation was a manifestation of the One Life, that of God, naturally he felt he could say it was really God who spoke through these spirits that called themselves by various names—so long, that is, as they spoke things not too contradictory to his ideas of religion.

His idea of religion and of God was again the same in 1746 as it had been in the *Economy of the Animal Kingdom* and as it continued to his death, becoming more and more dominant and purified. "Love therefore is the very essence of man," he wrote in 1746, "for man is man from understanding, and the understanding is from love. That which is holy is love, for to love God above all things, and the neighbor as oneself is a holy thing, inasmuch as holiness then comes from God Messiah." [23]

The gist of Swedenborg's belief then and later was that the essence of divine life, therefore of all life, was love. Men, whether in or out of the material body, were mere dead forms unless animated by love. They might appear alive if animated by selfishness, but they were in a state of spiritual death.

Such crystal statements are the heart of "Perennial Philosophy," and they appear fairly frequently in the automatic scripts of *The Word Explained*. When they do, it is as if Swedenborg himself were speaking, or at least those parts of his psychon-system of which he still had control. But much of the matter in the Notes is so strange, so unlike anything one knows of his background and way of thinking, that one is almost forced to fantastic speculations.

He had certainly long been occupied in studying the Bible, and as late as 1744 he had written *A Hieroglyphic Key,* and *Correspondences and Representations,* in which he foreshadowed an allegorical method of interpreting the Bible. In that it can be seen that he had already studied theories, such as Origen's, that claimed the Old Testament as essentially a prophecy of the New. But nowhere is there any trace of the curious sectarian ferocity dominant in much of the script "dictated" to Swedenborg.

Things foreign to him, dogmas he did not at all approve of, stick up like thistles, such as a very literal idea of the Trinity, of the Devil, of the Blood-Atonement, and, strangest of all, a violent barrage of anti-Judaic propaganda.

Swedenborg cannot be classed as an anti-Semite. One of his friends in Amsterdam has mentioned with a shade of reproach that Swedenborg went to the houses of all kinds of people, he even "associated with Jews and Portuguese." He was certainly not a "racist." According to him Africans were better liked in "heaven" than anybody else.

Yet here in these notes, or in long sections of them, it seems necessary to trample on and discredit the pillars of Judaism— Abraham, Isaac, Jacob, and more especially Moses, the chief pillar.[24] He is shown as a bad character entirely, and so are David and Solomon. The only exception is when these figures can be made to "represent" or symbolize something in the New Testament.

It is as if one had been hurled back into the early centuries and were surrounded by zealous disputants belonging to the various Gentile Christian or Judaeo-Christian churches, all feeling it vitally important to shout down the Jewish religion. "God-Messiah," used almost exclusively in these scripts by Swedenborg, is a Judaeo-Christian term; so is God-Jehovah, also used by him. So is the emphasis on the atonement. It is as though Marcionites and Ebionites were going at it, hammer and tongs; glimpses of a Gnostic can be had, or a Manichean flits by. The seething unsettled theologies of the second century seem to swirl around us.[25]

The style is different from Swedenborg's. The tone is extremely argumentative, at times addressing itself as if to a present Judaic adversary. "Give now some other interpretation!" In a part of which Swedenborg says specifically that it was written by his hand, not by his mind, the "speaker" rants against "the descendants of Jacob," calling them "backsliders from their benefactor, nay, their Savior . . . and now let each one of you say whatever he can." [26]

Swedenborg did not like to write some of it. At times he even expressed his objection. When Jacob was declared to be the very serpent who was going to bruise the heel of "God Messiah," he dissented from "so sinister a meaning," and he added that "for myself it is abhorrent to say this, to write these words. Therefore they must be said by those who are permitted thus to bring them in." [27]

There is nothing traceable in his previous writings or in what he is known to have read which would seem to account for this. At times one is tempted to use the license offered by Mr. Carington and imagine that Swedenborg's psychon-system, so long preoccupied with Biblical exegesis, had, by the power of association of ideas, attracted out of the world of discarnate psychon-systems little whirls, still stuck in the second century, but very lively, and carrying with them whole landscapes of ideas and large casts of persons. For at times Swedenborg seems to himself surrounded by Jews, but Jews seen inimically.

Before these scripts he had a high opinion of David and Solomon, for instance. In 1744 he wrote that the psalms of David and Solomon "contain veriest wisdom in simple form" and that he doubted whether all of Seneca contained as much wisdom as a single one of those psalms.[28]

Now Solomon was shown to him (as he was supposed to be after death) "that he had no knowledge of spiritual things." [29] And doubt was thrown on David's financial statistics, if not his probity. The Bible said that David had collected a hundred thousand talents of gold for the temple, but the script said "this everyone is apt to doubt who knows the value of a single talent of gold." Not a fifth nor a tenth part of it could have been expended on the temple, so the "speaker" asserted.[30]

This *furor theologicus* does not resemble Swedenborg. Much more like him was the other stream of discourse, the one on man as matter molded by spirit, and on love and wisdom, truth and good. Different from putting Moses in the dock were little tranquil sayings such as, "the sole object of understanding is truth; not however for the sake of truth, but in order that from truth it may see what is good." [31]

One might almost imagine that some calm Neoplatonist took turns with the hair-shirt monk in using the "instrument" of Emanuel Swedenborg's hand.

Now in automatic scripts the handwriting is likely not only to vary from the subject's normal writing, but also to vary in accordance with the different "spirits" who claim they are moving the hand or dictating the topics.

Obviously it occurred to the writer of this book that one did not have to be a handwriting expert to detect differences in Swedenborg's manuscript between the pages allegedly dictated by spirits and the ones in which he seemed to be his normal self. Therefore when she was in Stockholm, tracing other Swedenborgiana, she applied for permission to study Swedenborg's original manuscripts, most of which are in the custody of the Library of the Royal Academy of Sciences, among them the manuscript of *The Word Explained,* the work just discussed.[32] Permission was granted by the kind Librarian, and it was an odd sensation to sit down with these firsthand records before one, brown ink on the good heavy paper of those days, to inquire whether the pages in which Swedenborg claimed to be guided by the controversialists, seemingly from the second century, should be markedly different from his normal hand.

Such proved to be the case. A good deal of the *furor theologicus* script is in an angular, slashing, obscure style, rather typical of certain automatic scripts.

Illustration A. (The Original is 7″ wide.)

Contrast the above with a sample of Swedenborg's best normal writing, from a page of the manuscript of a book on the mind-body relationship, written throughout in the same rounded, harmonious way.[33] It was written about four or five years previous to *The Word Explained,* but the same kind of writing can be found in his personal letters even many years later, and even in other pages of *The Word Explained,*[34] those in which Swedenborg asserts that he is being told these things by heavenly beings, the ideas however, being very close to his own Neoplatonic sentiments.

Illustration B. (The Original is 6½″ wide.)

The Librarian having generously given permission for several photostats to be made from the manuscripts, it seemed interesting to the writer to find out if a professional handwriting expert would detect any significant difference in the pages from which the samples are here given. Accordingly she marked one A and the other B, and submitted them to an expert, merely asking for an opinion on the enclosed specimens, naturally giving no information as to what or whose they were, nor even who was sending them.

The expert,[35] an Oxford B.Sc., and an associate member of the British Psychological Society, discovered such marked differences that she reported they were by different writers of opposite character. The author of the script which has been characterized here as "automatic" (Illustration A) was said to be the type of man "who is liable to project his own inner problem into the outer world, and fight it out visibly," also the type "who may agitate with great intolerance for the cause of tolerance, or with great ruthlessness for the cause of kindness and love. His humbleness is deep-seated, but the impatience of his temperament makes him act as a fanatic." Quite suitable for the *furor theologicus!*

The writer of the script here called "normal" (Illustration B) was said to be the kind of man who "seeks to give expression to his visionary and intuitive experiences. He tries to be precise and rational for he wishes to bring into harmony rational thinking and irrational feeling." The expert further mentioned this man's fine sensibility, remarkable integrity of character, tender soul and warm heart, and also "a certain inner vanity," which, "he shares with most of those who consciously and conscientiously strive after perfection."

However one may feel about judging psychology by means of handwriting (though the above is fairly striking in its insight, considering that the expert had no means of knowing who was in question) the fact remains that the two specimens were held to be so different as to be thought by different men.

These differences in style were not lost on Swedenborg himself. A couple of years later he noted in the diary he kept of his "psychic experiences" (as we should say), "That my style of writing is varied according to the spirit associated with me." He added, "This is evident to me from many things in past years as also from those of the present time that my style is varied and that from merely the style of the writing I could know how things cohere." [36]

This would explain, if nothing else did, the interesting fact that in the so-called *Spiritual Diary,* mainly kept during 1747 and 1748, he often has five or six entries for the same day, each of them dated and paragraphed separately. On examining the manuscript it is found that these entries often vary startlingly in the handwriting,[37] as they do in the topics. Swedenborg kept a travel diary in 1739,[38] often putting a week's entries on a single page in a hurried but normal style. Comparing this with a page of the *Spiritual Diary,* there are often far greater variations in style noticeable between the entries of a single day (or night) in it than there are in the entries for the days of a whole week in the travel diary.

One observes further that when the *Spiritual Diary* notes are in the same or similar violent "automatic" type of script as passages in *The Word Explained,* they are usually of the same character— attacks on the Jews, interpretation of the Old Testament in terms of the New, or else accounts of what might be called his "automatic" cast of characters—such as, among others, one "Mahomet" and a "Dragon."

A graphologist could live a long and thrilling life with Swedenborg's handwritings alone, but here let it be noted only that these different "styles" offer a good guide at least to knowing whether Swedenborg was in a normal or in a specially dissociated state of mind when he used them. The violent automatic is used in most of those strange accounts that have puzzled his readers—the visits to the realms of spirits of other planets, and the report of the Last Judgment.[39] There are other good reasons for believing that he was in trance or semitrance when he wrote these passages, but the handwriting is convincing, being about the same as in the passages which he says were written by "spirits" through his hand. (He says elsewhere that in regard to "visions" he was in the spirit when he saw them and returned into the body to write the account of them, presumably still exalted.[40])

To return to his first script, *The Word Explained.* Besides the Neoplatonism and the physiology that managed to creep in here and there, and the dominating Bible exegesis, there was yet another visible strand. He indicated its separateness from the rest by indenting the paragraphs. This seemed to be himself speaking as himself

—his own comments on what he was experiencing. Sometimes he voiced his bewilderment in shaky and half-entranced writing; sometimes he made remarks as if the observing scientist asserted himself again—not to doubt the reality of his new life in the other

From *The Spiritual Diary*. (Original 5¼″ wide.)

world, but to study it and make an attempt at explaining the laws that governed phenomena there. It was these remarks that grew and grew, until in 1747, after he had left his job and gone to Holland, he put them into the separate journal, variously known as *The Spiritual Diary* or, his own word for it, *Memorabilia*.[41]

But even before then, while he was still at home, he wrote, "These words are written in the presence of Jews who are around me, nor do I doubt but that Abraham is also present." He said they were still intent on turning everything into "phantasies," meaning they threw doubt on the reality of his experiences.[42]

The word "phantasy" (which he used for "hallucination") apparently bothered him. "Yet it is not in the least degree phantasy, but a continuous speech as of one man with another . . . and this now for fifteen months . . . that it is no phantasy can be clearly known by those in Sweden, with whom I have conversed in the meantime." [43]

He had mentioned several times before that he was able to have inward conversation with spirits and to be with people in the flesh at the same time without the latter noticing anything.

But he finally looked to the future to prove that it had not been "phantasy." "It can also be evident from an historical account of my life, if opportunity be afforded for describing this." [44]

Emanuel Swedenborg never tried to justify or explain himself by writing such an account, but perhaps he could not do more than he did do—put down his experiences as they came to him as honestly as he could, and venture on such explanations as he had available.

The year 1746 was long before the subconscious and extrasensory powers of the mind had been charted as much as they are now, little though that is, for it is still true what Swedenborg said early in his first script, wondering at the new vistas before him:

"There are marvellous things occurring in the human mind, so marvellous indeed that they cannot be expressed. In number they are infinitely more than all the things contained in the human body, in the three Kingdoms of Nature and in the universal world, visible and invisible. The sciences have drawn out only a few of them, and these are mere rivulets emanating from an ocean." [45]

CHAPTER SEVENTEEN

"What Is a Spirit?"

SWEDENBORG continued devoutly to take down, as it were, the scriptural explanations that came to him, but he could not help also turning his attention to the new powers of mind which he was discovering. His curiosity asserted itself. Not content to be a "hand," he seemed to become aware that he need not be tied to the secretarial duty; he could (as Mrs. Willett did) get up and look around. He could "see" more and more as well as hear; he could, and did, interview the inhabitants and argue with them. "I inquired" became a common phrase in his diary, which swelled enormously. And wholesome doubt returned. About a year after his talks with alleged Old Testament characters and a couple of Apostles he wrote that during the several weeks while he was in conversation with them he could believe no otherwise than that it was so, but afterwards, "being taught by experience," he said he could perceive they had been spirits pretending to be those persons, perhaps authorized as spokesmen for the authentic characters, perhaps not. He cautiously added (November 29, 1747), "These things came today into my thought, but whether the matter be so with them as stated I do not yet certainly know." [1]

The names of Abraham, Moses, *et al.,* slipped into the background though they remained part of the cast, and increasingly his acquaintance widened. Much more important for his sense of reality, so did his reacquaintance. He never was a man to put in names of actual persons (except toward the end of the diary a little), but he did note on a certain day that now he had talked to thirty people who had been known to him in life, and, a few months later, he added to the same entry that the number was now sixty. [2]

But before trying to follow Swedenborg in his extremely crowded and far more than merely double life, it might be well to consider what methods he evolved for putting himself into a state of dissociation or trance for the purpose of having such experiences.

Reference has been made (Chapter II, p. 129) to the fact that he seems to have accidentally stumbled on something similar to the old yoga technique of breath-control as a means of inducing such states, although at the time he was not conscious of doing so.

As early as 1744, however, in his so-called dream diary, he notes that he can produce certain effects by holding his breath, or varying the rhythm, and soon he was deliberately resorting to such practices. He says in his *Spiritual Diary,* "My respiration was so formed by the Lord that I could respire inwardly for a considerable time, without the aid of external air . . . in order that I may be with spirits and speak with them." [3]

Reviewing the matter, he explained that this "tacit," or partly inhibited, breathing was not a new thing with him. "I was first accustomed thus to respire in my early childhood, when saying my morning and evening prayers, and occasionally afterwards, when exploring the harmonies of the lungs and heart, and especially when deeply engaged in writing the works that have been published [his *Economy of the Animal Kingdom,* etc.] . . .

"I was thus during many years from the period of childhood introduced into such respirations, especially by means of absorbing speculations in which the breathing seems to become quiescent, as otherwise the intense study of truth is scarcely possible. Afterwards, when heaven was opened to me, and I was enabled to converse with spirits, I sometimes scarcely breathed by inspiration at all for the space of a short hour, and merely drew in enough air to keep up the process of thinking . . .

"I have also again and again observed that when I was passing away into a state of sleep [here he undoubtedly means trance] my respiration was almost taken away, so that I would awake and catch my breath. When I observe nothing of the kind, I continue to write and think, and am not aware of my respiration being arrested, unless I reflect upon it. This I may say has happened in instances innumerable. Nor was I at such times able to observe the various changes because I did not reflect upon them." [4]

This seems to be a description of the lightly entranced state of consciousness he was in while doing his automatic writing, which is borne out by what follows: "The design of all this was that every kind of state, every kind of sphere, and every kind of society [of spirits], particularly the more interior, might find in my own a fit respiration, which should come into play without any reflection on my part, and that thus a medium of intercourse might be afforded with spirits and angels." [5]

But at times of course he did reflect on the various changes in the rhythms of his breathing and heart-beats. Once when the "more interior" spirits of "heaven," as he called them, were "operating" on his body, he said he noted a fourfold effect. One into the left temple, one into his lungs, one into his heart, and one, but obscurely, into his loins. He was clearly aware, however, of the effect on the systole and diastole of his heart which he particularly watched. The beats were "gentler and softer than at other times," indeed, so "soft and regular" were the pulsations, he said, that he could "count them one by one." And he noted particularly the coincidence of breathing and heart-beats. "The terminations of the heart's times closed in the pulmonic beats." [6]

Elsewhere he observed that "when I wished the times of respiration to agree with those of the heart . . . then the understanding began almost to fade away . . ." [7]

Now and then he mentions that the respiration is to his normal respiration as three to one, quick and shallow; it seems to be a preparatory stage for an almost entire withdrawal of breath. The entry is not very clear, but apparently this shallow breathing happened before the slowing down of his heart. [8]

Listening to the heart sounds is one way of reaching that condition of ecstasy which the Hindu yogins call samadhi, according to students of the subject; [9] in fact, measurements of such phenomena taken with the most modern recording instruments reveal in black and white the reduction of the voltage of the heart, as well as the shallow breathing preceding it. [10]

Whether one consults Hindu lore or electrocardiograms made of the yogins in samadhi, there seems to be some similarity between Swedenborg's more or less conscious technique for entrancing himself, and that of the East.

But of course when he said that the understanding began to vanish when he engaged in these practices, he meant that his awareness of sense impressions from the external world vanished, as he often made clear. He believed firmly that he entered into awareness of other worlds, other levels of consciousness. We have no means of knowing what they "really" were, but he has left descriptions in his diary of his several kinds of "visions" and the corresponding states.

(Incidentally, one of his entries mentions that some "spirits" from the "Indies" taught him a kind of breathing.[11])

Early in 1748 he was trying to distinguish between different kinds of "spiritual sight." He said there were four kinds. "The sight of sleep" was the first, by which he must have meant of the same clarity as the peculiar phenomena called "veridical dreams," for he adds that this "is as vivid as sight by day; so that in such sleep I should say if that be sleep wakefulness could also be sleep."

Psychologists might call the second kind "eidetic imagery"; it sounds like a very light trance. Swedenborg continues: "It is vision with the eyes closed, which is as vivid as with the eyes open, and similar objects, and even more beautiful and agreeable, are represented to view; the same kind of vision can also exist with open eyes, which I have experienced twice or three times." [12]

In another reference he notes that he has sometimes, while thinking he was wide awake, though being in conversation with spirits, walked through city streets and country roads and yet been "in vision, seeing groves, rivers, palaces, houses, men and many other things. But after I had thus walked for hours, suddenly I was in the sight of the body, and became aware that I was in another place." [13]

This corresponds to the so-called hallucinations of the sane, known to psychic research records, but Swedenborg was well aware that it was not objectively real as he considered other visions to be, for he expressly notes that this kind of vision is not the same as "the things I have habitually 'seen' . . . these are not visions but things seen in the highest wakefulness of the body, and this for several years." [14]

The third kind of "spiritual sight" clearly implied awareness of what he considered the objective spirit world, without actual participation in it. "It is a state when the eyes are open, when those things which are in heaven, such as spirits and other objects, are represented. This is a representative vision which has been made most familiar to me, but it is rather obscure; it differs entirely from the common imagination of men." [15]

Possibly this was the state in which the Danish General Tuxen found him many years later when Tuxen happened to enter unannounced in Swedenborg's cabin on board ship off Elsinore. "I found the Assessor seated in undress, his elbows on the table, his hands supporting his face, which was turned towards the door, his eyes open and much elevated. I was so imprudent as immediately to address him, expressing my happiness at seeing and speaking with him. At this he recovered himself (for he had really been in trance or ecstasy as his posture evinced), and, rising with some confusion, advanced a few steps from the table in singular and visible uncertainty, expressed by his countenance and hands, from which, however, he soon recovered." [16]

(It is worth noting that in *Of the Worship and Love of God* Swedenborg makes one of his characters come out of a state of ecstasy in this way: "She briskly wiped her eyes with her finger, that her mind might recover its former ken." [17])

Swedenborg's description of the third kind of spiritual sight is as if he considered himself a stationary spectator (as indeed he always considered his physical body stationary in trance experience) with other-world visions being induced (or telepathized) to his brain, or, as he also put it, with mental images being represented to him. He was sometimes hard put to it to decide whether they were of symbolic significance or not, but he often says that his "conversation" with the more evolved spirits was by means of mental images.

All the other states he definitely distinguished from the one he called the fourth kind: "that in which a man is when separated from the body and in the spirit. In such a state a man cannot know otherwise than that he is in wakefulness, and in the enjoyment of all his senses, as touch, sight, hearing, and I cannot doubt respecting the other senses. The sight is more exquisite than in a state of wakefulness, nor does man perceive it any otherwise than such, except by this that a man [who is in such a state] relapses into the wakefulness of the body." [18]

By this he clearly means that he comes out of the deep trance condition into normal physical wakefulness after having been, so it seems to him, actually in the other world in his psychic organism, "as a spirit among spirits," as he so often says elsewhere. But at that time (February 6, 1748), he added that he had only experienced this fourth kind three or four times "with much delight." In this connection it may be noted that in later years one of his London landladies and both his servants in Stockholm testified that Swedenborg would sometimes go to bed for three or four days and ask only for a basin of water to be placed by his bed, giving orders he was on no account to be disturbed. And, according to his friend Robsahm, they said he came out of these seclusions hale and hearty.

During the first year or two after he began automatic writing, Swedenborg was overwhelmed by the oddity of his experiences, but the diaries from 1747–49 are also full of evidence that he was increasingly trying to sift and weigh the happenings. In one entry, August 23, 1748, he seems to be trying to say that some of these scripts are obscure, and to be convincing himself of their origin. The latter, of course, was for the reason that he believed he was thus getting his interpretation of the Bible. He says: "It is to be held in general that all things which I have written in this book are written wholly from living experience, from conversation with spirits and angels, from thought, like tacit speech communicated (to me); also when I wrote of the things insinuated by them who were then together they experienced them to the fullest degree; and under their direction as to thoughts, writings, hand, so that everything which in these three books [*The Word Explained*] and elsewhere is written, though occasionally incoherent, still pertains to experience, and everything in its manner from spirits and angels; this is likewise directed by spirits next my head, for I have, as often, perceived their presence." [19]

Swedenborg often expresses his despair of accounting for it; of getting people to believe him. Very early he said, "If I should bring forth my experience in these matters, besides being abundant, it would also be incredible . . ." [20]

And elsewhere, also early, "I am well aware that many will say that no one can possibly speak with spirits and angels as long as he lives in the body, and many will say that it is all fancy, others that I relate such things in order to gain credence [presumably for his theology], and other will make other objections. But by all this I am not deterred, for I have seen, I have heard, I have felt." [21]

Emanuel Swedenborg was a brave man. Charles XII, the warrior king, was no braver. But Swedenborg might have flinched from publishing his other-world observations had he known that they would generally be taken as of things he had seen, heard, and felt materially. Even a psychic researcher has been heard to say, "Why, Swedenborg, he believed that there were actually palaces and gardens and food and drink and so on in the other world!"

Swedenborg claimed that before his "sight was opened" the idea he cherished concerning the other life "differed but little from that of others"; he thought it must be immaterial, and, being so, that either "no idea of it could be grasped, or it was nothing." Either incomprehensible or nonexistent. "And yet," he said, "the fact is just the reverse, for unless spirits were organized, and unless angels were organized substances, they could neither speak, nor see, nor think." [22]

He did not say or believe that the organized substance was material in any sense we know. He said it had "extension," not materiality. He had long ago convinced himself on scientific grounds that something could exist such as a magnetic field which had extension, although immaterial, and he had also made up his mind that "the animal spirits" constituted a subtle kind of organism used by the rational mind after withdrawal from the body. He scorned the idea of spirits having fleshly body and organs, but he insisted strenuously that they were capable of sensations, since it was the spirit in the body of the living man and not the body that was "having" the sensation. (That "psychic factors" or detached thoughts could drift around without either being part of a thinking subject or originating from one, he specifically rejected.[23])

In a passage that fits nicely into the idea that the psychon-system carries its sense impressions with it for a while after "death," he wrote: "Certain [spirits] greatly wondered that spirits had the sense of touch, and, indeed an exquisite one, when yet they were spirits, and it was contrary to all their opinion in the life of the body that spirits can have touch." Luckily Emanuel was around to enlighten them. As he modestly puts it, "It was given to tell them that this should by no means be wonderful, since man during life does not have the sense of touch, and the other senses, from the body, but from the spirit that is in the body from which the body has its life . . . Wherefore, after the death of the body a similar principle remains; for the spirit supposes itself to be certainly in the body, *which opinion at last ceases. This is the reason of the corporeal touches, which only exist with them, who come recently from the life of the body into the other life.* Subtler senses succeed, all of which must still be referred to the sense of touch, in order that they may be senses." [24] (Author's italics.)

He never tires of saying that "the life of the body does not belong to the body" but only appears to do so. "Spirits take that life with them, because they have become accustomed to corporeals. . . ." But life is "formed in the body according to its organs," so, because spirits are accustomed to this, the old body-senses seem for a while to remain with them.[25]

One is not surprised that he had vivid personal arguments on this topic. Inconsistency he soon discovered was no peculiarity only of the material world. "I conversed with those who in the life of the body believed that spirit was not extended," people who had such rooted phantasies (false ideas) on the subject "that they would not even admit the use of a term implying the idea of extension. Upon being aware of the fact, I inquired of one who was deeply rooted in this persuasion what he now thought respecting the soul or spirit, whether it was extended or not, reminding him that he saw, heard, smelled, touched and had appetite just as if he was actually in the body . . . He confessed that during life he had been of the opinion that the soul or spirit was not extended . . . He was then held a while in the idea in which he was when he thought thus in the world, and he then said that spirit was thought. But I answered him as if he were still living in the world by inquiring whether sight could exist without an organ of sight . . . [or] whether he could conceive of thought . . . apart from organs . . . He then acknowledged that he had during the life of the body indulged the phantasy of supposing that spirit was only thought, devoid of everything organic or extended." The phrase "or extended" was added by Swedenborg when he was commenting on this interview, and he also said that "this shows very clearly that the learned have no other conception of the soul or spirit than that it is mere thought, and so cannot but believe that it will vanish when they die." [26]

Apart from the ghosts of the learned professions, however, Swedenborg usually had the opposite opinion to combat, of which the following is a little example:

"A certain novitiate spirit, on hearing me speak about the spirit, asked, 'What is a spirit?' supposing himself to be a man. And when I told him that there is a spirit in every man, and that in respect to his life a man is a spirit, that the body is merely to enable a man to live on the earth, and that the flesh and bones, that is, the body, does not live or think at all; seeing that he was at a loss, I asked him whether he had ever heard of the soul. 'What is a soul?' he replied, 'I do not know what a soul is.' I was then permitted to tell him that he himself was now a soul, or spirit, as he might know from the fact that he was over my head, and was not standing on the earth. I asked him whether he could not perceive this, and then he fled away in terror, crying out, 'I am a spirit! I am a spirit!' " [27]

It must be admitted that when Swedenborg spoke of spirits and angels as being organized "substances," he laid himself open to misinterpretation. We find it hard to think of a substance as immaterial. What did he mean by the "form" of the spirit? Later he was to say that it constitutes the "cutaneous covering of the spiritual body which spirits and angels have. By means of such covering which is taken from the natural world, their spiritual bodies maintain existence; for the natural is the utmost containant; consequently there is no spirit or angel who was not born a man." [28] (There are no wings on Swedenborg's angels.)

An angel, he came to believe, was a human spirit who had developed far enough to be admitted into a higher spiritual sphere (various kinds of "heaven"). As for the cutaneous covering taken from the "natural" world, here a backward glance must be taken at the conclusions he had arrived at in *The Economy of the Animal Kingdom* and in a lesser, unpublished, work, *The Animal Spirit*.

He had decided that the development of the embryo was determined by "a certain most fluid matter," which he also spoke of as "this substance or force." This was "the spirituous fluid" (or the "animal spirits") in which and by means of which the soul carried the pattern of a human being into materiality. It was "natural," or matter in its finest manifestation, that of force or energy; therefore it could create and govern the body; it was "spiritual" in that matter of this immaterial kind could be acted on by the still subtler energy of higher states of being or soul. *It was the link between soul and body.*

Swedenborg believed that when the outward material body died the "animal spirits" withdrew from it in the form of the human being which they had brought to it. This form served as the "organ of the soul," both in and out of the body.[29] But with men who had not cultivated their intellectual or spiritual capacities, or who had not done it in the right way, the spirit-body was hardly more than a body; it was still "natural," still obsessed by its corporeal experience—only a psychon-system, as Carington would say, a mere assortment of sense impressions, held together by consciousness.

After Swedenborg's "sight was opened," he was rather careful not to commit himself too definitely, partly, he said, because it was not "for various reasons" given to know "of what quality are the forms of spirits," but mostly because "natural terms cannot suffice to express them . . ."[30]

In any case, though their substance might be organized and still resemble a human body, the fact that this substance was now more obviously a kind of energy gave it a great many advantages and disadvantages from the material state. Swedenborg was industrious in recording his observations of these. The chief point noted by him, and indeed the key point for an understanding of everything he wrote on the subject, was what we now should call the almost fatal facility of telepathy.

Very early he discovered, he said, that "Thoughts are nothing but activities, and they become perceptible when the door is opened to heaven, this also has come clearly out in my own experience."[31]

The chief trouble of the psychic organism in its new environment, according to Swedenborg, might be summed up in saying that it has to learn to tell the real from the unreal, imagination from fact. To use our terms again, the something in the human mind which can create persons and events in dreams, which can project hallucinations as if they were external, which can also succumb to suggestion by a hypnotist so that he can induce "sensations" on it—that something, called by Tyrrell "the stage-manager," becomes a main factor in the "world" observed by Swedenborg. Indeed it becomes a good servant or a bad master according to the spiritual state, one might say, of the "novitiate spirit."

In modern experimental telepathy, as has been mentioned, images of drawings have been transferred between "incarnate" minds without the aid of the usual sense mechanisms. Among dis-carnate minds, according to Swedenborg, something similar takes place; indeed, it is exactly the same but, being unhampered by the material body, it takes place on a grand scale. Here telepathy is an immense aid to communication. Really only newcomers use any-thing so clumsy as speech (and even then it is not what they think it is; Swedenborg took pains to explain to a spirit that the lips with which the spirit thought he spoke were not "real"). The more advanced inhabitants communicate by means of "representations"; that is, by mental images. But there is nothing vague about these, they can be made to appear as if they were "there."

"I also spoke with spirits by ideas alone, without words, and they understood as well as with words, by my merely representing from internal sight, as was the case when I ate," so Swedenborg entered in his diary June 8, 1748. "I represented merely from the internal sight what I ate without words, and they clearly comprehended; and if also at the same time [were represented] these things, viz., whatever a man has on his table or whatever is worn on the same occasion, or whatsoever it might be which was displayed to the sight, they were immediately understood and seen by the spirits by the discourse of ideas without words." [32]

Other sensations of his, he said, could be transmitted to the spirits; "thought" was not only visible, but "perceptible," he could (as a hypnotist can) transmit the taste of what he ate, etc., but he made careful note of the fact that unless he "reflected"—that is, gave his attention to—what he was perceiving, the spirits did not perceive it. When some of his new acquaintances had discovered, he said, that through Swedenborg they could reëxperience bodily sensations (their psychon-systems by now apparently having forgotten) they would sometimes pester him—such as the spirit "so goaded by a longing for a linen under-garment, that he said he could scarcely live if I did not put one upon him." The spirit showed nice psychological distinction, however. "I asked him whether he had a sensation together with mine, when I touched the linen for which he so much longed," Swedenborg noted, and "He said that he had no sensation himself, but he perceived that I had." [33]

Much more elaborate conversations were held, however, for small talk about physical sensations did not interest Swedenborg, and he rather disapproved of the spirits who would not move on to higher things. But that ideas could be made visible greatly interested him. In one entry he said that the spirits told him that his ideas "appeared before them as if alive . . . so that when peoples, camps, and the like were displayed representatively, they appeared before spirits just as if they saw them . . ." Here it is not clear whether he saw them himself, but he said, "In like manner representations of spirits very frequently have appeared to me, when my eyes were closed, entirely as alive, as if in the highest light." [34]

The more advanced spirits, or angels as he called them, were especially expert in this kind of communication, in fact he sometimes called it "angelic speech."

Connected with what might be termed the telepathic facility of the psychic organism was its extreme responsiveness to suggestion, or what Swedenborg spoke of as "induced phantasies." They could be good and they could be bad, they could be heaven and they could be hell. It was a case not of "seeing is believing" but very much of "believing is seeing."

He tells of one newcomer—a good soul—who "knew not at first where he was, supposing himself to be in the world altogether as if living in the body, for of this impression are all souls recent from the life of the body, inasmuch as they are not then gifted with reflection upon place, time, the objects of the senses and the like," but when he discovered how it was with him he began to feel "a certain anxiety," "not knowing whither he should betake himself, where he should dwell, etc."

Good spirits and angels came to his rescue, and by means of this suggestibility of his new form, they gave him "whatever he was prompted to wish and long for in his thoughts," "for they can give whatever is desired, inasmuch as such things can be represented, and thus can be made to appear to the person altogether as if he possessed them in the world," for, Swedenborg said subtly, "the possession of goods in the world is nothing else than imaginary, and when the imagination enjoys them to the full and has them in its eye, then it possesses them as in the world, and is delighted with them." [35]

Collective hallucinations were also formed. For those good spirits who still had the "phantasy" that heaven consisted in being in "paradise," paradises were arranged. They told Swedenborg concerning heavenly happiness; "and as I was ignorant about it, it was said that they have distinct houses, where those who are conjoined can live together and form societies; and from the still remaining phantasy or imagination heavenly pleasantnesses and delights appeared to them to be formed in which heavenly peace reigns. If they also desire it, paradises appear to be formed, with every variety of trees and shrubs; and likewise cities and palaces, and similar things . . ." [36]

He added a counsel of prudence to this entry in his journal: "but these things are not to be so written, or described to the world, lest they should seek heavenly things in such phantasies."

Induced hallucinations also accounted for the bodily punishments of the evil by the evil. "They can represent their associates by phantasy alone as being changed into various species of animals, as into serpents of various kinds; their companions being thus represented cannot deliver themselves from that phantasy . . ." [37]

But although phantasy, their sufferings were real.

Swedenborg looked around in this world of ecstatic or of dreadful make-believe, and he decided to describe it, since, as he said, "Man knows nothing more than simply, that there is a hell and a heaven; that in hell there is fire and torment and in heaven felicity, but in what these things consist he is profoundly ignorant . . . It is as though a man knew nothing more than the earth exists, without knowing anything of its kingdoms, governments and societies . . ." [38]

CHAPTER EIGHTEEN

"*Arcana Celestia*"

MEANWHILE, as to that "earthy loan," his body, Swedenborg had moved about a bit. In the summer of 1747, after he had finished all the work connected with the Board of Mines, he went to Amsterdam. At the end of September, 1748, he went to London, and about September, 1749, he returned to Holland.[1] Perhaps the house in Stockholm had not been secluded enough after all, but in any case he intended to begin publishing some of his new writing, and that could only be done abroad.

The interpretation of the Bible, his mission, was of course his chief interest. He settled down to this about the end of 1748 in lodgings in London, "at six shillings a week for half a year," with a reduction should he stay a whole year. The new interpretation (of Genesis and Exodus) was called *Arcana Celestia* ("Heavenly Secrets"). It was published in London during the years 1749–56, without the name of the author, which was not disclosed till 1768. The work ran to eight large quarto volumes. It received almost no public attention, and this despite the fact that his publisher, John Lewis of Paternoster Row, declared the author to have a "depth, which if once fathomed (and it is not unfathomable) will yield the noblest repast to a pious mind." To ward off low suspicion he added, "But if anyone imagines that I say this to puff a book, in the sale of which my interest is so nearly concerned, any gentleman is welcome to peruse it at my shop, and to purchase it or not, as his own judgment shall direct him." [2]

John Lewis was plainly overcome by Swedenborg's personality; especially by his insistence that the books must be sold cheaply, though printed in so "grand and pompous a manner." The first volume cost the author, so the printer tells us, two hundred pounds, and he had advanced as much for the second, yet any profit was to go to the "propagation of the gospel." Quite understandably the publisher found this author modest, benign, and generous, but he had no hope of the immediate success of the work, comforting himself however with the knowledge that it took years for Locke's *Human Understanding* and Milton's *Paradise Lost* to make their way.

Lewis's insistence that this was a book-bargain beyond all book-bargains was not incorrect. But not till our day, really, with its non-sectarian interest in religion and ethics, new light on the subconscious workings of the mind, and great development of psychical research, can this rather chaotic mass of "heavenly secrets" be seen for the treasure trove it indubitably is, from several points of view.

The Bible interpretation had been freed from the cruder aspects of *The Word Explained,* which comprised Swedenborg's first, almost unchanged, automatic writings. A comparison: in the latter the "Philistines" (Genesis 26:15) are said to mean "the gentiles who do not profess the true faith and also the Jews who are not yet converted, and who thus are separated from the members who have entered into Christ's church," and in the "inmost" sense as being "the crew of the devil," or the devil's intermediaries.[3] But in the *Arcana* the "Philistines" are interpreted as meaning the kind of people who "applied themselves little to life but much to doctrine," the kind who "being without good cannot understand truth and are not even willing to know it." [4]

The first interpretation savors of those bellicose opinions, cited previously, belonging to the second century's strife between converted and unconverted Jews, but the second is purely ethical and universal. In general, although the *Arcana* continued, most tediously, to explain the Old Testament as referring symbolically to the New, the stress throughout was laid on the spiritual regeneration of man, with marvelous twistings of the text to suit the interpretation.

Swedenborg claimed for the *Arcana,* as indeed he did for all his theological works, that they were not his own, in the sense that they had been celestially "dictated" to him. That raises the question of the "authority" of these writings. It was one that preoccupied him considerably at the beginning. In the latter part of his life he always stated as an absolute fact that the Lord, or the Lord "in the Word," was his sole source of information, but at the beginning of his intercourse with the other world, when he so often quotes this or that entity, he felt he had some explanation to make. In a diary entry he insisted that he did not accept any "representation, vision or discourse" from spirit or angel without reflecting on them "as to what thence was useful and good, thus what I might learn therefrom." Now as he believed that all truth and good were from the Lord, he could reassure himself that he had been instructed "by no spirit nor by any angel but by the Lord alone from Whom is all truth and good . . ." [5]

"God-Messiah," a Judæo-Christian expression, disappeared from his writings in January, 1748,[6] and "the Lord" took His place, since in Swedenborg's developed theology, as with other Protestant mystics before him, there was only one God who had taken the form of Jesus Christ in order to divinize humanity, not by any "Atonement," but by ethical example.[7]

In the diary passage quoted above, Swedenborg explains the not unessential point as to how he knew whether what the spirits said was true and good and thus from the Lord; it was by "an interior and intimate persuasion."

For those who consider this authority enough, Swedenborg's Bible exegesis may have the value of "revelation"—there are many such revelations in the history of sects—but others find it hard to understand how so intelligent a man could so uncritically have accepted interpretations devoid of scholarship.

And the only explanation is of course that he was startled into belief because they came to him and continued coming to him either by way of automatic writing, or, as was probably the case later, by way of auditory hallucinations, or clairaudience, depending on the point of view taken of his experiences.

Were those experiences furnished by his unconscious mind or were they at least in part from some discarnate mind or minds? The "interpretations" furnished by much of the automatic writing in *The Word Explained,* those seemingly from the second century, are so unlike his known reading and interests that adherents of "spirit" hypotheses could be tempted to imagine them as coming from discarnate minds attracted to their favorite sport of Bible exegesis with which to slam their opponents, the "unconverted" Jews who still clung to Moses.

But we do not know everything read by Swedenborg.[7a] In regard to the interpretations in the *Arcana* we know that many of the ideas are the same as those of Neoplatonist-influenced writers whom he might have read, but it is certain that he accepted them as "revelations" because they too came to him when he was more or less entranced, as we now should say. (He was to call it "a suspension of bodily sensations" during which man could receive "angelic wisdom" "by influx from above into the spiritual parts of his mind." [8])

Certainly it could be said that while in this state his unconscious mind produced ideas for him that seemed visible or audible, but which might have their origin in his past reading. For those who favor the "spirit" theory it could of course be maintained that as he recovered from the surprised shock of having his hand move of his own accord, he stopped accepting the more primitive "spirits" which were doing the writing and, reverting to his own enlightened beliefs, became connected, through the power of the association of ideas, with "spirits" sympathetic to those beliefs, who then took control either of his hand or of his attention.

It is clear from the handwriting of the first draft of the *Arcana* that he was not in a normal state when writing most of the work. Although it varies from the violent script to the almost normal, it is certainly written under stress.

But it is not the Bible exegesis of these volumes which is likely to be of interest now, nor even the frequent sublimity of the spiritual perceptions. They could be matched from the writings of other mystics. What cannot be matched are his reports from "the other world," "from things heard and seen"—they could not have been predicted from what we know of his reading or his experience. Quite the contrary. In the work on *The Soul* he asserted that once free of the body the soul would live a life pure beyond imagination. But after he had had, as he claimed, experience of the world of spirits, he said they had hardly changed a bit from this world, that, in fact, the Christians were the worst of all.[9] He said, in effect, it is very different from the way you think it is, and merely dying is no admission to either heaven or hell.

Had he come to his new experiences with settled opinions and fixed ideas as to what the other world was to be like, one would expect that a consistent account would soon emerge, but it did not. Time and again he eagerly tried to construct the whole from some little bone of supposed fact, only to have to confess later that he had been wrong. His assertions in regard to memory, for instance, had often to be modified—in other words, his behavior was like that of a scientist coming into an entirely new field armed with an inadequate working hypothesis, and having to yield to first-hand observation of the phenomena.

He was right in having said that popular notions of heaven and hell were simply that there was felicity in the one and torment in the other, but he must have known that there had been people before him, even in Europe, who had progressed farther. Many of Jacob Boehme's sayings [10] about self-will being the cause of torment in hell and abandonment of self being the cause of "heaven" even here on earth, could have been said (and often were) by Swedenborg.

Indeed the ethical, mystical and religious speculations of Boehme bear so much resemblance to Swedenborg's that later on he was constantly being asked if he had read Boehme.

This he constantly denied, but he could easily have found the same ideas in other books to which he had access. J. G. Gichtel,[11] who lived forty years in Holland and who wrote a book whose doctrine of the Grand Man much resembles Swedenborg's, was a disciple of Boehme's, while others of the "occult" fraternities entertained many of the ideas of the Beyond which Swedenborg seemed to regard as "arcana" revealed to him alone.

And, on the spirit hypothesis, perhaps they were, as far as he knew.

But where others had described heaven and hell as immaterial states of mind in exalted but vague language (though often surprisingly similar) Swedenborg was as specific as when he had been sent out by the Board of Mines to report on the supplies of charcoal and metal in Sweden. His contribution was not so much toward a new understanding of those ultimate conditions of joy or sorrow as toward a factual survey, more especially of the in-between state, which he called the world of spirits. It was, he said, beyond our space and time, yet with local or psychological space and time, into which human beings consciously arrived soon after the departure of the spirit from the material body. Unconsciously, he maintained, their spirits while still in the body could commune with this region or state, and he believed that in his own case he was able to visit it consciously when he "suspended bodily sensations."

While, as has been said, he at first incorporated these experiences in *The Word Explained,* he soon put them into separate diaries, which are most valuable source material for a study of a "medium" or "sensitive," as these supposed links between two worlds are now usually called.

From the point of view of psychical research a "medium" is defined (by G. N. M. Tyrrell) as "a person who manifests paranormal phenomena, usually in a state of trance," and a "sensitive" as "one who possesses the special faculty of experiencing paranormal phenomena, especially of the extra-sensory type." [12]

Psychical research notes but does not underwrite the medium's customary assertion that while he or she is in a state of trance (usually unconscious) "spirits" speak through the entranced body, sometimes giving veridical information. The sensitive may or may not believe in spirits, but he or she claims to be capable of acquiring correct information by other than normal means, such as clairvoyance, etc., or, sometimes, by automatic writing.

Swedenborg was a most unusual combination of the two, except that his mediumship differed from the customary form by his being conscious of his experiences.

For a long period he noted them in his diary as they came to him day by day. Between December, 1747, and November, 1748, he wrote about fifty folio pages a month.[13] He also wrote a detailed index of what he "saw, heard and felt," in order to use his observations in a sort of guidebook.

This guidebook he combined with the Bible commentaries of the *Arcana Celestia* in a way reminiscent of modern magazine-wile when advertising is sandwiched into a story. Before a chapter of exegesis he put an account of life in the spirit world, ending it by saying that the continuation would be found at the close of the chapter.

Sometimes he copied his diary entries literally; sometimes he trimmed and arranged them. Still the descriptions in the *Arcana* are often nearer his unedited and unrationalized impressions than what he was to write in his later theological books. The latter did gain in clarity, but lost very much in that Swedenborg often omitted or only referred in passing to what he meant by saying that the "objects" in the "other world" were "appearances" only. This may have been prudence on his part—orthodox churches still had power—for although his books were anonymous their authorship did leak out eventually; but he may also have become tired of for-ever having to explain his theory that matter was energy and psychic organisms still finer energy, and thought something still subtler which could be visibly projected by the psychic organism.

It may have been something like the weariness that overcomes the writer on psychical research, who has to say for the nth time something like "the dissociated fragment of the medium's per-sonality and/or the alleged communicating spirit," and who finally lapses into saying "the spirit" or "Jones," slipping in an "alleged" now and then to pacify his conscience.

In any case, Swedenborg thought that he had cited particular cases enough in the *Arcana Celestia* (eight volumes of which peo-ple could go and buy if they wanted to, and if they could read Latin). In *Heaven and Hell* (1758) he went in more for general principles, giving a partial survey of the world he felt he had visited without putting in very much of his theory about its "reality" and without quoting many of the specific experiences on which the survey was based.

It is convenient to take a look at this map [14] before going into his absorbing account of what he felt was the symbiosis, the close "living-together," of men and spirits, especially Swedenborg's own case.

To read the map, his ideas must be reviewed once again. Sweden-borg brought to his experiences the belief that man had several "natures," one dependent on the other, and yet, in subtle ways, each distinct and capable of taking dominion over the rest, because of a certain amount of free will. He also believed, as firmly as the most convinced worshiper of Brahman, that no "real" life existed except God's. The spirit or soul of man was created to be a recep-tacle of the divine life, whose essence was love and wisdom. With this indwelling capacity, the soul made for itself a physical body, vivifying it in every cell by means of "the animal spirits." This was itself a psychic organism, in between the material and the spiritual. It had its own kind of instinctive sensual mind which received the sense impressions from the organs and passed them on to the intellectual mind. This, also called the rational mind, had, it will be remembered, an upper and a lower division, and enough free will to choose whether life was to be lived on the terms of indulging the senses at the expense of the soul or of using the sense impressions in order to advance in goodness and wisdom.

In the latter case, communications were kept open with the spiritual mind, or with that in man which was capable of letting the Divine enter and rule all the rest of his natures.

Swedenborg kept changing the names of these natures, but generally speaking he called them external and internal. He insisted that even if the gross material body were sloughed off, a considerable part of the external man remained—his sensual psychic organism with its instinctive desires, and the lower half of the intellectual mind, the part which dealt with impressions from the outer world. This it usually had learned to do with such competence and gusto that it seemed to itself to be the better half or even the whole man. The inner self, capable of receiving divine wisdom in its understanding and divine love in its spiritual mind, could atrophy or be perverted because of the gross dominance of the outer.

This aged, and ageless, conception of the inner and outer natures of man has been put into modern psychological terms by Dr. Jung. He calls the "external man" the "Persona," or the mask, which he defines as "a compromise between the individual and society, based on that which one appears to be." [15]

The destruction of that compromise Swedenborg "saw" as taking place in the other world, in the "world of spirits," as he called it. This was the limitless region, or rather state of mind, between the ultimate states of heaven and hell into which nearly all men come after death.

In this region, about which Swedenborg was much more articulate than about either of the others, "there are three states of life through which a man passes before he enters either heaven or hell." The first state is that of his outer mind.

"There is an inner region and an outer region of every man's spirit. In the outer region reside those powers by which in the world he adapts his body, especially his face, speech and demeanor to the society in which he moves, but the inner region of the spirit is the seat of his own will and thought." These he rarely exhibits, if they are selfish. "For man is accustomed from childhood to make a show of friendship, benevolence and sincerity, and to conceal the thoughts springing from his will. He has consequently acquired the habit of living a moral and civil life outwardly, whatever he may be inwardly; and the effect of this habit is that man scarcely knows or thinks anything about his inner mind."

"The first state of man after death is like his state in the world, because his life is still external. He has therefore a similar face, speech and disposition, thus a similar moral and civil life; so that he thinks he is still in the world, unless he pays close attention to the experiences he meets with . . ."

He does not usually pay close attention. Swedenborg has explained that immediately after death there has been a little interlude in which angels try to do their best for the new arrival, but he generally leaves them as quickly as he can and forgets about them.

And he meets his friends and acquaintances from this world; they know each other because, all being in the first or external stage, they still look the same. "When anyone in the other life thinks of another, he thinks of his face, and at the same time of many of the facts connected with his life, and when he does this the other enters his presence as if he had been summoned. This is so in the spiritual world, because thoughts are there diffused around, and there is no space such as exists in the natural world."

But these and other little oddities soon become familiar to the new arrivals, and they cease to notice them, because, as Swedenborg says, they are from the order of things in the other life, and "that which happens according to order is like a familiar thing, which is not thought about." [16]

There are many reunions in this stage, at least temporarily. "I have frequently," Swedenborg says, "heard those who have come from the world rejoicing at seeing their friends again . . . Very often a husband and wife meet and congratulate each other, and also remain together for a longer or shorter time, according to the delight they had felt in living together in the world. If true marriage love, which is a union of minds brought about by heavenly love, has not joined them together, they are separated after a while.

But if their minds have been discordant and inwardly opposed to each other, they burst forth into open enmity, and sometimes in actual fighting; not withstanding this, they are not separated until they enter the second state . . ."

The length of the stay of a spirit in the first state differs, from a few days to about a year; it depends on "the agreement or disagreement of his inner with his outer mind." Even in the other world it seems to take time to ferret out hypocrites, but gradually they show their true colors until they are in the second state, where every spirit is obliged both to be and appear as his real self. This is his "ruling love" or his will, the desire of his thoughts when he is unrestrained by any social bonds.

"Thought means everything by which man confirms himself in his affection or his love; for thought is nothing but the form of the will, or the means whereby the desires of the will may be made manifest."

Any external morality the wicked may have flaunted drops away from them, even if it has become as it were second nature to them, before they are irresistibly attracted toward hell, "because no one there is permitted to have a divided mind, that is, to think and speak one thing and will another."

But before a spirit is thus integrated downward, a good many punishments may have to be administered. Many of the evil ones cling to their shreds of moral respectability, and it takes force to make them drop it. "In the world of spirits there are many kinds of punishment, and no respect is shown to persons; it matters not whether the offender has been a king or a slave in this world." And then, like the most orthodox Buddhist, Swedenborg asserts that: "Every evil brings its own punishment with it. They are inseparably connected . . ." The punishment seems to be that being evil gives evil its power over one. Like natures are attracted to each other with the force of gravitation. In the first state after death the good and the bad and the indifferent still are mixed with each other, only the more advanced spirits being able to pierce the various moral disguises; but in the second state the inner mind is disclosed for all to see, even in the new face of the spirit, fair or foul, according to character.

Infernal spirits, candidates for hell, roam about in a region of the

World of Spirits which Swedenborg calls "the lower earth," and when a spirit in the second stage does "evil from an evil heart" he "discards all protection from the Lord," and the infernal crew falls on him, induces him to believe he has a real physical body, and then they mangle or change it in various startling ways. Hieronymus Bosch would be needed to paint the somber horrors that Swedenborg relates in his cool way.

Good spirits also, or ordinary human mixtures, have their troubles in this second stage, which has aspects of purgatory. They are not, Swedenborg insists, punished for any evil they have done out of a badness of heart inherited from their parents. But those who are not altogether good, with blots on their character due to "falsities," are not immune to attacks by evil spirits—the latter seeming to be like moths that go for the grease spot on the garment. They "infest" those who have falsities to get rid of before they can leave the second stage; and sometimes they "vastate" them —a specifically Swedenborgian expression which might be translated "purify" or "purge." He sometimes speaks of the evil being vastated of all pretense of good in them, and the good of their "falsities."

When the good have shed their worse selves they enter the third stage, that of preparation for heaven. This, Swedenborg says, is a period of instruction. Angels from the heavenly societies, for which the good souls have begun to qualify by their life in the world, come to instruct them about their new state; "those [souls] that have been brought up from childhood in heaven, not having imbibed falsities from the falsities of religion or defiled their spiritual life with the dregs pertaining to honors and riches in the world, receive instruction from the angels of the interior heavens"; those who have died adult "mainly from angels of the lowest heaven."

For the evil souls who have been made to give up the pretense that they had better selves, there is no third stage. They are as it were magnetically attracted to the societies of infernal spirits, from which no instruction is needed to proceed into hell, the reservoir of rampant egoism.

As Swedenborg describes the process of evolution in the other world, it seems to be a succession of states in each of which the "person" who is in it finds it hard to imagine or to believe that there is another state. He fears "death." In a diary entry Swedenborg describes a discussion he had with spirits "of a middle character" on this subject. He told them (in the best Upsala University style) that "the better kind of spirits live a more interior life than souls recently deceased; the angels of the exterior heaven after having laid down the former life lead a still more interior life; and the angels of the interior heaven when they have laid down the former exterior life lead a still more interior life, of which the exterior angels can have no conception, but all the superior angels can." [17]

The middle-character spirits tried to deny this, and Swedenborg could understand their attitude, for, he said in effect, if they were to lose the life they had at the time and come prematurely into another more advanced state, "they would not know what life it was." When he then asked them in plain language if they did not wish to become angels, they said yes they did want to become angels, but they did not want to lose their life. "When I replied that they would then receive a better life, they could not understand it."

"Heaven" consists of innumerable varieties of selflessness, as "hell" consists of the opposite. There is no personal "Devil." No schematic presentation of Swedenborg's ideas, however, is fair to him. What charms and astonishes the reader is the wealth of vivid detail "from experience" with which the stark generalities bloom. These are in all his books, though most frequent in the diaries, but none can be rightly appreciated unless his fundamental conceptions are studied with whatever light one can bring to them.

There is first of all that unit of the "new structural relationships" in the other world—the "society." This is the outcome of the great law Swedenborg sees as reigning throughout creation: like ultimately attracts like. Through its force evil punishes itself and goodness is truly its own reward. In "heaven" "those who are in spiritual relationships know each other at first sight, exactly as if they had been kinsfolk and relatives on earth. They are like intimates, although they have never seen each other before." [18] Elsewhere Swedenborg speaks of coming into his own society, where he observed that they were like acquaintances and friends of long standing. Man, he says, "after death receives many companions, friends and brothers, as if they had been known to him from infancy." [19] This is due to "similitude of soul," and the society is so likeminded that it seems like "a composite person."

Many of Swedenborg's observations concerning the nature of "societies" bear a resemblance to the modern "field" theory of psychic phenomena, as presented by Professor Gardner Murphy.[20] It is not a contradiction of Whately Carington's law of the association of ideas applied to telepathy, but, as has been said, it stresses another aspect: the "interpersonal" nature of the phenomena. In other words, better results have been obtained in experimental work if two or three persons are working together. Gardner Murphy makes it part of his hypothesis that "such interpersonal powers are much richer and more complex than any possessed by the individual when isolated from his fellows."

They make a "field . . . a distribution of energy in time and space . . . a unitary, structural whole."

(This might be said to be a part of that great underlying field of deep-level psychic activities which has been supposed to be the common subconscious of mankind.)

Human beings may, as Gardner Murphy has suggested, be mere aspects of that interpersonal field, not so separate as our physical uniqueness implies, and, if psychic activity does continue after death, Gardner Murphy supposes that it would be knit still more closely into the "complex structural whole of which it is an aspect," without therefore necessarily giving up conscious individuality.

It would still be a weak or a vigorous part of the whole. And that whole might include both the quick and the dead. "If," Professor Murphy continues, "on independent grounds there is reason to believe that the discarnate exist and are capable of contact with the living, there is no theoretical difficulty involved in their participating jointly with the living in an interpersonal field."

With hundreds of examples drawn from what he called "experience," Swedenborg maintains practically the same theory. But he calls the "interpersonal psychic field" a "society."

In the spirit world especially, Swedenborg saw the "society" as of such importance that he ascribed the state of confusion of the newly arrived soul to his not having had spirits "adjoined" to him yet. In his diary he says: "The souls of the dead, whether a short or a long time after the death of the body, are very dull and know almost nothing before they are consociated with spirits . . . But as soon as they are associated with their like in a certain way . . . they are much more acute than when in the life of the body." [21]

He mentioned specifically a man whom he had known who couldn't remember who he was (about five months after his death) until "spirits were adjoined," when he came into "full understanding and remembrance." And he was then able to recognize himself from having "his own image when alive" presented to him in Swedenborg's imagination.[22]

Swedenborg had indeed, he said, been spoken to by "separate spirits," but they were, whether they knew it or not, what he called "subjects"—or spirits whose job it was to "receive the reasonings of others and thus express the general sense of the genus to which they belong, and collect their thoughts and thus converse with me. When these spirits had departed from me, they were seen to unite again with their own species, that they might lead a life in harmony with them." [23]

Such spokesmen were a feature of the other world. While his acquaintance was still mainly limited to the in-between state or "world of spirits," Swedenborg said he could only communicate with "the interior heaven . . . through an intermediate angel, who told me that he was then made a medium by which a conversation could be established between them and me." [24]

These angels were aware of their being mouthpieces of their societies and rejoiced in the greatly increased happiness they derived from the "communication of delight" that being "consociated" gave them, but spirits were not usually pleased with the idea, even if they could be made to believe it through Swedenborg's arguments.

"It can never happen," he wrote, "that any spirit can be absolutely alone; he must be in a certain association with spirits who speak together; certain spirits, however, think that they are alone and that they speak from themselves, and when they are told that it is not so, they are wont to be indignant . . ." [25]

Swedenborg confessed that he himself was indignant at first

when "all the others who are near" would understand and perceive what he was thinking about, but he soon asserted that all men in the body were aspects, as we should say, of interpersonal fields, made up of both the living and the dead, the incarnate and the discarnate. He said:

"All men whatever are kept through the medium of subjects in some society of spirits—apart from which one could not live—and that too in a society suited to the nature of each; so that if we suppose a thousand men at once, each of them is kept in his society." [26]

"There was a certain spirit who believed that his thought was independent of all else, neither diffusing itself beyond himself nor communicating with other societies. To convince him of his error, all communication with the societies nearest to him was cut off, whereupon he was not only deprived of thought, but fell down as if lifeless, except that he threw his arms around like a new-born infant." [27]

Each society was itself a facet of still larger aggregations in the spirit world, and, through these, man was even linked with the societies of hell and heaven, those states into which he would be irresistibly attracted by the law of affinity. Some time after death he was to step into his ultimate society as naturally as an absentee member into a club to which he had long paid dues. Whether he would like the members was another matter, but it was one which he had a chance to provide for by his good or bad behavior in the earthly body. "For in the life of the body they (men) are much more left to themselves than after the life of the body . . ." [28]

Swedenborg maintained that man could by the right kind of mental effort cultivate the right kind of emotions, and the importance of this was that good or evil feelings "conjoined" man with similar spirits. Ordinarily neither party was aware of this. It did not usually imply obsession of man's body by spirits. As Swedenborg generally explains this, it resembles an association of feelings as well as ideas (both "psychons," of course!) between minds. He speaks of the many changes of understanding and affection in the mind of man, so many as to vary every moment, and "into whatever state a man passes or comes, spirits with whom a like passion was dominant in their lifetime correspond and cooperate . . ." [29]

These spirits, by adding their passions to that of the man, make a double battery of emotions, good or bad, according to circumstances. Mostly bad, of course. They tend to enforce man's evil passions; "they smell them out as dogs smell wild beasts in the forest." Around every living being, alive or "dead," Swedenborg, like the ancient Hindus, claimed he saw a kind of "sphere" or "aura" indicating the predominant thoughts and affections, and "such as the sphere is, such are the spirits, whence it appears what kind of spirits are with those who think of nothing else and are affected by nothing else than cupidities, hatreds and revenges. Where the carcass is, there the ravens are." [30]

As an example of how spirits confirm men in their desires or fears, Swedenborg mentions in his diary (while he was still abroad in 1748) that as soon as he thought of his garden, "of him who had charge of it, of my being called home, of money matters, of the state of mind of those who were known to me, of the state or character of those in my house, of the things that I was to write and the probability that they would not be understood, of new garments that were to be obtained, and various other things of this kind . . ." then, he said, the spirits would immediately add their "inconvenient, troublesome and evil suggestions" and thus fan his worries. But, he philosophized, "when I had not been in the thought of such things for months or years, I had no care of them, still less did they give trouble." [31]

He also warned (as we should say) against getting a compulsion neurosis. He said it was bad to make up one's mind that something had to come to pass in a certain way, if it were only a trivial matter, because spirits might seize on the idea and add to it and induce the thought that it absolutely must be so, blowing it up into undue importance, and in that way man lost his liberty. This, he said, he knew also from experience. [32]

So overcome was Swedenborg at times by his sense of the interpersonal field in which man lived, this shower of discarnate influences affecting him continually, that he could sometimes say man had nothing at all from himself—all his thought was in a sense thought transference. But at other times he maintained that spirits also had many of their thoughts from men. In fact kindred spirits often associated themselves with men's thoughts and mem-

ory to such an extent that they believed them to be their own, especially since, generally speaking, they were wholly unaware of their
[telepathic] association with men. Swedenborg said this was due
to a kind provision of the Lord's, for if evil spirits knew they were
with human beings they would set out to destroy them directly, so
great was their hatred and cupidity.

But in Swedenborg's case he claimed he could live consciously in
both worlds. He could so change his plane of awareness that he
knew of the presence of his motley companions, and they of his.
His faith in the Lord kept him from being hurt by them, he said,
though he often lamented their attempts to hurt him.

His life was not always "double." One morning he noted some
facts about that in his diary. He said that this morning he was in
his former familiar state, before he began to converse with spirits;
that is, he was vividly thinking about some subject, "so that I spoke,
as it were, with myself." He was like this too, he said [not aware of
spirits] when he was talking with his friends, or at table, or writing
letters. In short, while his attention was directed closely to the business at hand.

But then, he said, his state changed, he became aware of spirits,
and was told by them about the state in which *they* were when he
was, as he thought, alone with himself. They thought they were he,
thinking his thoughts. This illusion depended, however, on the
"nearness" of the spirit—that is, Swedenborg explained, on the
spirit's degree of affinity with the subject on which he was meditating. And, he added, with people who think abstractly there are
many spirits present, but with men who are only led by the senses
of the body and who cannot keep their minds on any one thing
there are only a few spirits associated.[33]

Corresponding to the encyclopedic range of his interests and
knowledge, Swedenborg felt conscious of almost the entire hier-
archy of discarnate beings. At the beginning especially, he studied
the ways in which they affected his life in the world. He was evidently not a little preoccupied by whether a spirit could enter into
and possess or obsess a man's body, and one catches glimpses of his
crisis period in London in 1745. Among the gossip collected by his
enemy Mathesius in later years from a former landlord was some
to the effect that Swedenborg had once run out into the street in his

shirt, had been delirious and spoken strange things about angels, had spent an undue length of time washing his feet, and in general behaved very queerly.[34]

Exaggerated as this undoubtedly was, some of it had a basis in fact, as can be seen from what Swedenborg wrote in an aside of *The Word Explained* about the spirits having persuaded him to wash his feet "when I was in that state." [35] And in his diary he speaks of hypocrites in the world who can be very persuasive, as "when they persuade others that I was insane." [36] Did he think he had been? No, but he was apparently aware that he might have been thought so. He said he had chanced several times to have spirits "act out their insanities" through him, but "it was granted me to know that it proceeded from spirits and not from me," and he was "told" that a man who had "faith" might sometimes "appear to men not like another," or that he might be "insane in the body but not in mind or thought." [37]

"It is wonderful," he comes right out and says, "that I have been obsessed, and yet nothing has ever injured me—further, I could enjoy my rational mind, just as if they were not present." [38]

Although in the above entries, from 1748, he speaks as if that state of occasional obsession no more occurred, he continues to note that certain spirits who cannot get used to the new existence try to get a kind of bodily satisfaction through his senses. One in particular was told by Swedenborg that he should desire to be free of physical desires, but the spirit said that he was a young man and wished to return into the world. Swedenborg did not oblige him, as he said he was a wicked young man, but elsewhere he complains that spirits wanting bodily experience try to make him eat greedily, seeking to make him take up his "almonds, cakes, pears and pigeons" [39] with his hands and shove them into his mouth, or to make him buy or steal something they covet. But by this he usually means that they excite his desires.

He often repeated that spirits could not "see" the objects around him unless he directed his attention to the objects, thus forming an image in his mind which then became visible to them. In fact, he said, even if he were only thinking of certain persons or places the spirits would be sure that he really was with those people or in those places.

Of so-called "physical phenomena," that is, the alleged influence of mind or of "spirits" on actual material things, Swedenborg has not much to say, but he does make references to them. In a diary entry he says that the inhabitants of the world of spirits have "peculiar skill in these things" which have an "effect on material and corporeal objects." He calls them "magical arts" and says they could easily "induce the minds of men to believe they were miracles." [40]

From his personal experience he mentions that "spirits have produced on my body effects entirely perceptible to sense . . . have scattered disagreeable and sweet odors often enough," and "they have maltreated my body with grievous pain . . . have most manifestly induced cold and heat, and cold more frequently; have as it were driven along blasts of wind; I have felt the wind plainly, yea so as to cause the flame of the candle to flicker," and papers too have been moved, he says. [41]

From these phenomena, familiar to the modern investigator, especially the sensation of cold, Swedenborg deduced that although spirits were not "material," yet they were "real substances" and not "mere thought," and such "substances in man are conjoined to the material body."

Other semiphysical "mediumistic" phenomena mentioned by him are for instance that he sometimes felt lifted up by spirits when passing over steep places. [42] (Levitation.) He tells furthermore that sometimes when he looked into a mirror and at the same time spoke with spirits his actual physical face would be changed so as to resemble the faces of those he spoke with. "Nevertheless my face remained, but the changes seemed to belong to theirs . . ." This happened several times, he says, "sometimes to their indignation, sometimes to their delight. They perfectly recognized themselves." [43]

It is clear that Swedenborg conceived of the role now played by mediums. He says (January 26, 1748): "I have already said and shown that spirits, who are the souls of those who are dead as to the body, whilst they are with man stand at his back thinking they are altogether men, and if they were permitted they could through the man who speaks with them, but not through others, be as though they were entirely in the world, and indeed in a manner so manifest that they could communicate their thoughts by words through another man, and even by letters, for they have sometimes and indeed often directed my hand when writing as though it were entirely their own, so that they thought that it was they themselves who were writing—which is so true that I can declare it with certainty, and if they were permitted they could write in their own peculiar style, which I know from some little experience, but this is not permitted." [44]

He tells himself why he disliked to function as a medium. After mentioning that he had seen and spoken with many of his friends, he says: "They have desired me to tell their friends that they are alive and to write and tell them what their condition is, even as I had related to themselves many things about that of their friends here. But I replied that were I to tell their friends such things . . . they would not believe but would call them delusions, would scoff at them, and would ask for signs and miracles before they would believe, and I should merely expose myself to their derision. For at heart men deny the existence of spirits, and even those who do not deny it are unwilling to hear that anyone can speak with spirits." [45]

So he continued for a long time at least to keep his strange new experiences as his private field of study. But as he had a correct idea of how the "learned" would regard these studies, he did not bother much with what is now called "evidential" material. He noted his own mental and physical states when he seemed to himself to be in communication with the other world, and he considered its chief features and in what it differed from our world. He gave especial care to the study of time and space, a great deal to memory and "speech," and some to "spheres" or "auras"; and if he had not unfailingly insisted that he was making these observations on another plane than ours, their keenness and suggestiveness would have attained recognition even here.

It is no loss of time to follow Swedenborg's probing excursions into these unorthodox fields.

CHAPTER NINETEEN

Space, Time, and Memory

IF a man who has followed the sea settles down on land in an office, he will continue just the same to sniff the air and notice the wind and the stars, as he goes to and from his cave; and so Swedenborg, with the best will in the world, could not become entirely theological; he kept casting side-glances at his previous interests, often dragging them by the ear into the most incongruous exegetical surroundings, where he could retain them only by the unfettered use of symbolism. But he loyally let them remain side-interests, and one has to dig them out piecemeal, mostly from his diaries, because there he did not always try to make them work to prove his theological points.

It was in his talks with what seemed to him spirits that his old interests of physics, physiology, and psychology mostly got a chance, and there is something convincing even in their fragmentary character. On the whole, as his other-world experiences continued, the fragments really turned out to fit together well enough to make a fairly consistent picture of the various phenomena which interested him. Of these the interlocking questions of time and space preoccupied him a good deal.

When he said that the spirits who were "near" him perceived his thoughts, he made it clear that the use of such a spatial word was only a makeshift. For in that world, he insisted, "change of place and distance is only an appearance, according to each one's state and its change." [1] If he were thinking of a certain topic, the spirits with whose mental or emotional state it had some relation would be "near" him; in fact their thoughts might be so closely linked to his that they would believe they were doing the meditating.

Space in their world, in other words, was "psychological"; something which, Swedenborg said, the angels or advanced spirits understood, but which was difficult to explain to newcomers, since to their view it really looked as if they were still in place and space. Swedenborg tried to make them understand that this was a kind of illusion, although it was a real enough expression of their mental and emotional states. As he said: "I have frequently conversed with spirits concerning the idea of place and distance among them—that it is not anything real, but appears as if it were, being nothing but their states of thought and affection which are thus varied, and are in this manner presented to view in the world of spirits . . . the spirits to whom bodily and earthly ideas adhere do not apprehend this, for they suppose that the case is exactly as they see it to be. Such spirits can hardly be brought to believe otherwise than that they are living in the body, and are not willing to be persuaded they are spirits and thus scarcely that there is any appearance or any fallacy in relation to the matter, for they desire to live in fallacies." [2]

He told them that "it is thought which conjoins, for to thought there is neither place nor distance . . ." and, elsewhere, he wrote that the case was the very same with men in the flesh. Men's souls were "constantly bound to some society of spirits and of angels . . . it matters not that they are distant from one another on earth . . . still they can be together in the same society—those who live in charity in an angelic society, and those who live in hatreds and such evils in an infernal society. In like manner it matters not that there be many together on earth in one place, for still they are all distinct in accordance with the nature of their life and of their states, and each one may be in a different society." [3]

In the same paragraph, he touched on apparitions. "Men, who are distant from one another some hundreds or thousands of miles, may when they appear to the internal sense, be so near each other that some of them may touch, according to their situation." And a kind of two-way telepathy: "Thus if there were a number of people on earth whose spiritual sight was opened, they might be together and converse together, though one was in India and another in Europe, and this also has been shown me."

Swedenborg did not think that this would necessarily be by means of their "spirit-bodies" or psychic organisms. "I have been informed," he said, "both by conversation with angels and by living experience, that spirits as spirits, in regard to the organic forms which constitute their bodies, are not [always?] in the place where they are seen, but may be far away and yet appear there." [4]

In other language, spirits whether in or out of the flesh could project mental images of themselves. This indeed fits in with Tyrrell's theory of apparitions, that they are not "real," but conceivably projected "idea-patterns," made up by coöperating intelligences (in or out of the flesh) with all the paraphernalia of apparent reality, including spots of three-dimensional space, as anybody can create for himself in a dream.[5]

But did the "organic form" of the spirit—that little tight condensation or field of suggestible energy-stuff—have a "situation"?

Yes, Swedenborg said, and even if it is only an appearance it is real because it is the same as the ruling general state of the spirit both as to mind and as to character—the state which draws him into his own "society." From that state there are many variations and excursions, but into it the spirit always returns. It cannot be more than apparently "placed"; there is no up and down in the nonspatial world; but these changes of state "appear in the world of spirits as changes of place." [6]

Tyrrell, in discussing the "reality" of collective hallucinations, says that even if one could imagine a group of living people so collectively hallucinated that they seemed to themselves to be living in whatever environment the "idea-pattern" had impressed on them, they could still test it by comparison with the physical world. They could, for instance, pass through the wall of a hallucinatory house.

"But if we take the further step" (Tyrrell takes it), "and suppose these persons to have shed their physical bodies, without having otherwise changed their personalities, then this impressed, hallucinatory world would have no competitor. Everything in it would behave *as if* all were physically occupied; and there would be no test by which they could tell whether their world were physical or hallucinatory." [7]

That was precisely the trouble which Swedenborg said he had with those spirits who wouldn't believe anything to be true that they did not see with their eyes, "even if this were mere fallacy." He stuck to it, nevertheless, that their "walkings and removal" and "their advancements which are frequently seen are nothing but changes of state; that is to say, they appear in the world of spirits as changes of place, but in heaven as changes of state."

Swedenborg realized that "thinking makes it so." He also could conceive that a three-dimensional space might be interimagined by a group who would then seem to themselves to live in it. But, as Tyrrell says, "If problems about space are mooted, people turn at once to geometry. It seems that it may be more enlightening to turn to the observer. These suppositional spaces provide a universe with plenty of room in it." That is, every like-minded group, or even individual, could have its own hallucinated three-dimensional space, which "they no doubt would call 'physical' space, and this would be spatially unrelated to what *we* call physical space." Yet it would not be entirely subjective, but the question of "where" such spaces could be "simply disappears and becomes meaningless." [8]

Swedenborg, despairing of "natural terms" with which to explain these subtleties, did not think the hallucinatory space was entirely subjective either. Again and again he repeated that the *reality* of the apparent change of place was due to a real change of state—mental or emotional. Later on he tried to sum it up:

"Approaches are likenesses of the state of the interiors, and separations are unlikenesses; and for this reason those are near each other who are in like states, and those are at a distance who are in unlike states; and spaces in heaven are simply the external conditions corresponding to internal states. For the same reason the heavens are distinct from each other, so are the societies of each heaven and the individuals in each society; and furthermore the hells are entirely separated from the heavens, because they are in a contrary state.[9]

"For the same reason, again, anyone in the spiritual world who intensely desires the presence of another comes into his presence, for he thereby sees him in thought, and puts himself in his state; and conversely one is separated from another so far as he is averse to him . . . whenever in that world several are together in one place they are visible so long as they agree, but vanish as soon as they disagree." [10]

Presumably they seem to themselves to walk away. Swedenborg said, "Walking, going and departure are nothing else but changes of state of the interiors; but still before the eyes of the spirits and angels they appear exactly like walking, going and departure . . ." [11]

"That this is so can be confirmed by much experience in the other life, for I have walked there in spirit with them, and among them through many of their abodes, and this though in body I remained in the same place." [12]

Innumerable times Swedenborg stressed that his physical body stayed in the one spot and only his mind roamed, and this not in our space but through "changes of state." When he went on those odd excursions which he termed visits to the spirit realms of other planets, he maintained that it took two days for all the necessary changes of state to occur in him.

Well aware as Swedenborg was that time can also be psychological—a good companion shortens time, a dreary one lengthens it—he was prepared when he came to converse with "angels" who had forgotten what calendar and clock time was. They had been so long dead to that kind of time, they had forgotten the alternation of night and day due to the earth's rotation about the sun, and Swedenborg had to explain all that to them. But though they had no notion of our kind of time they knew well enough, he said, "that relatively to the duration of state there is time, just as much as in the world" [13]—a kind of local time, just as the appearance of three-dimensional space was local. Even angels had their ups and downs emotionally, he noted elsewhere; even for them there were states of greater and lesser joy and even some sadness—for otherwise than by contrast it is hard to seize those states.

However, he said, even the idea of time, any kind of time, perished with those who were of the innermost heaven, "because with them the natural [self] which is in the notion of time is put to sleep." [14]

The aspect of time which most fascinated Swedenborg was memory—man's precarious hold on time. As early as in his first published writings on physiology he had maintained that memory was a change of state in the little "brains" (cells) of the cortex, not tablets stored in little boxes in the brain.[15] Nobody surely believes that any more, he said about this theory, and he would have been surprised at its persistence. In the summer of 1744, in his draft of the book on the five senses, he sketched out what he meant to say about memory—for instance that the memory was the "field" (campus) "which the external senses establish, as also the internal." [16]

What he thought changed was "the cortical substance," but by that he usually meant the energy-stuff of the psychic organism, in this case its brain, from which the physical brain derived, not the other way around. "That all thoughts are changes of state is confirmed by all philosophers, but that such changes really exist, and indeed in an eminent organism, has not yet been demonstrated, nor can it be demonstrated until the brain shall have been scanned . . ." [17] and the connection between superior and inferior forms made clear, or the mind-body relationship again. This is what he meant to do in his future brain studies, but as it happened he completed his study of memory, so it seemed to him, in the other world, where he had the vast advantage of being "taught by conversation with souls and spirits on this subject," and indeed of actually seeing the field of memory in operation.

In brief, he would have agreed with Bergson that "memory is something other than a function of the brain, and there is not only a difference of degree, but a difference in the nature of perception and remembrance." [18]

Not unlike Bergson either, Swedenborg had decided that there were different levels of consciousness and subconsciousness in man, and "memories" corresponding to each.

First of all, Swedenborg maintained, there was the external or corporeal memory of "material" ideas, by which he meant those images which man had acquired as a result of the physical "affection" (stimulus) of his sense organs, and which was "useful for man inasmuch as it is suitable to those things which his life in the body and the world require." [19]

This external memory, dependent on sense reports or their associated ideas, is the one, according to Swedenborg, which seems to die or to become at least passive immediately on the death of the body.[20] But after a brief period of stupor, the recollection of physical sensation is still so strong that the recently arrived souls continue to think of or to remember themselves as they were in the body, with clothes, possessions, appetites, etc., and thus in a sense they re-create themselves as they were. Out of these memories they scaffold "the phantasies which they love," which he also now and then describes as a kind of dream world. When they are in "these physical phantasies," he says, they are really asleep and dreaming.[21]

They cannot, however, remember at will details from their life on earth, which often seems to make them indignant. ("Indignation and restlessness," Swedenborg says elsewhere, are characteristics of the less evolved spirits.) He tried to soothe a certain morose spirit by telling him that he ought to be grateful that he was now gifted with a much subtler understanding and not mind being unable to remember everything, but the spirit seems to have been no more grateful than the elderly in the body are when their memory fails to function.[22] But, as with them, so the memory of spirits can be excited into action by giving it a clue (Carington's "K" idea).

"Souls in the other life seem indeed to themselves to have lost the memory of particulars, or the corporeal memory in which merely material ideas inhere, because they are unable to excite anything from that memory, though they still have the full faculty of perceiving and speaking as in the body. . . . Still, that memory remains, not however as active but as passive [subconscious?], and it can be excited by others, for whatever men may have done, seen or heard in their lifetime, when these things are spoken of to them with a like idea, then they at once recognize them and know that they have said, seen or heard such things, which has been evinced to me by such abundant proofs that I could, in confirmation, fill many pages with them." [23]

Swedenborg asserts that in the first bewildered period following the death-shock, spirits do not always know even who they are, as when he mentions a spirit who first recognized himself from seeing his own image in Swedenborg's mind.[24] In another case, "A certain one whom I had not previously known, and who seemed to have but recently died, was with me today, and when it was permitted to inquire whence he came he was led by my memory through various cities which he did not know, but when he was conducted through his own city then he recognized the streets and everything connected; and if I had known the situation of the houses I could also have found the house where he had lived." [25]

He concluded that the reason spirits were not "allowed," generally speaking, to remember more details from their earth life was that the Lord meant them to lead a more "interior" life now, but he often sorrowfully mentions that spirits do not at all relish this wise provision or even realize it. "Souls are not at all aware but that they speak from their own memory, and do in fact sometimes thus speak, as I have heard, but then it is from the interior memory, through which the things in their corporeal memory are excited." [26]

Here Swedenborg touches on what he considered the relationship between the different levels of memory or "memories."

Swedenborg defines the corporeal or external memory as that which is useful and necessary for life in the body, saying moreover that this memory only retains those things on which man has consciously "reflected"—his word for "attended to." "Although the human sight is diffused into thousands and thousands of objects," he says, "yet out of those the external memory retains only those which it has reflected on." [27]

This is not too dissimilar to Bergson's saying that "perception" is essentially dependent on what is useful to the body, so that only the object is selected, and therefore perceived and remembered, which serves that "centre of action," the body. Bergson also supposes "a plane of pure memory where our spirit preserves in every detail the picture of our past life," and, according to him, it is from this enlarged plane that consciousness selects the recollections that are to stimulate the apparatus of the physical brain into present perception. [28]

According to Swedenborg, the interior memory "is as it were the interior faculty of taking forth and viewing the particulars of the corporeal memory." [29]

And the "plane of pure memory" of Bergson corresponds exactly to the "interior memory" of Swedenborg in its all-registering capacity, even of things to which the attention has not been consciously directed, "so that," as Swedenborg says, "there is not even the least thing whatever that has reached the sight of the body and whatever has reached the internal sense but is most accurately impressed . . ." [30]

It is no news to students of modern psychology that the subconscious has a photographic memory. Strong evidence for this comes from studies in multiple personality,[31] where some segment of the personality can remember things under hypnotism which the conscious mind cannot possibly recall. Hans Driesch puts it this way: "The enormous extension of simple memory in hypnosis allows us to establish the hypothesis that, at the very bottom, the soul is able to retain *everything* that has ever been experienced during the whole mental life . . ."[32]

Swedenborg distinguishes between the interior photographic memory and another "more interior," which includes all of experience. That the latter has a resemblance to modern views of the subconscious is shown by his assertion that in it man's experience is arranged in such a way that *emotions* constitute "the nucleus," and "scientifics" (facts) occupy the "surface."[33] For him it was indeed the very nature of a man, and he said that this memory-disposition was actually visible to the higher beings of the spiritual world.

"Man cannot ever think anything which does not come into clear light after death, yea, into so clear a light that nothing at all is hid of the least of all that he has thought; it is inscribed on his disposition, and, if it may be credited, this is what is understood by everyone's book of life."[34]

People who had succeeded in concealing their evil deeds in this life, and who persisted in denying the charges in the other, were confounded by having their actions represented before them visibly (as if seeing a modern film). Swedenborg cites several such cases, which, he said, he had witnessed. It was also a kind of punishment.

Apart from having been told about the all-recording memory by his friends in the other world, Swedenborg believed that mankind possessed it because of dreams. While dreaming, he said, such portraits were made as the waking mind could not produce. "For in a dream a man is wont to appear as the very same with all his lineaments, together with every condition of his body, his speech, his gait and many other particulars, which one never could know from the memory of material things, nor is man able to describe any such faculty."[35]

The ability of his interior memory to retain everything about people who had been known to Swedenborg caused him, he says, a certain amount of trouble. For some, though not all, of the spirits around him, had access to this memory and could fish out of it the details necessary to give a perfect impersonation of a man he had known, "as though it were his very self." He sometimes refused to believe in somebody's alleged identity, because "all things, even the minutest particulars, can be so counterfeited as to confirm the illusion." Only "the interior angels" could know the difference, and he warned "anyone with whom spirits converse that similar personations are most frequent in the world of spirits." [36]

It disquieted him, this accessibility of his memory. "They are able to read the deeper things which are with me in my memory, whilst I am unaware of it . . ." [37]

He saw the spirits, in other words, as having access to both the conscious and subconscious parts of his memory, insisting that they could speak from it "with variety." In fact he said that this was all which most of the spirits *could* speak from, *his* memory. But not as if they merely repeated what he thought; it was rather as if the topics in his mind were so many keys on a piano which they picked out into tunes of their own, according to their own character, or lack of it.

For, as Swedenborg often stressed, although the corporeal memory was usually in abeyance so that the spirits could not at will remember their experiences in the body, yet the result of those experiences remained—that is, their nature, disposition, personality.

"The two lives which remain after death," Swedenborg said, "are the lives of persuasion and of cupidity," [38] or—as we might say— of opinions and emotions. It was evident to him that though persuasion might subdue cupidity, yet it was usually the other way around, "for that which is loved perniciously is confirmed on many grounds, even until the man is persuaded."

Spirits were especially prone to the life of unbalanced opinions, being without the common-sense checks of the physical world; and Swedenborg often complains of their self-confidence and arrogance, no matter how mistaken they were. He says they did not know whether the things they picked from his memory were true or not, but believed them equally and often supposed them to be from

their own superb memories. "Consequently, if I demonstrated anything falsely, they would be persuaded concerning that also, for in
respect to material things, they cannot judge from themselves,
though they still suppose that the knowledges which are in my
memory are in theirs." [39]

The ease with which spirits had access to Swedenborg's conscious
and subconscious memories was greatly aided, he explains, by the
fact of ideas being visible in the other world. "In the spirit world,"
he explained, thoughts can be seen "as when one sees in a picture
everything simultaneously represented to him . . . a single obscure
idea [to man in the body] is made clear by means of many representative and intelligible ideas that are set forth by spirits. Angelic
spirits employ comparatively still more illustrations, for as is a man
compared to spirits, so is a spirit compared to angelic spirits, and
so are angelic spirits compared to angels." [40]

In a manner of speaking, Swedenborg seems to have considered
that his "memories" were complete pictorial archives available at a
glance, or a presentational field, from which clusters of information could be fished with the hook of a single fact. "I had no need
to do more than think about a person with the idea of his qualities
and at the same time of his position, dignity and other circumstances, without any idea of his face, body, and of such things as a
man is described by in human speech—still less his name—and they
at once discerned and knew who it was, and of what quality he was
in my thought. In like manner respecting kingdoms, cities and
similar things." [41]

These "idea-patterns" (in Tyrrell's language) seem to remain
constant. Swedenborg says specifically that whatsoever is connected
with the idea of a person remains connected, "whatsoever one has
heard concerning him, has seen in connection with him, has observed while he spoke with him, whatever he has thought about
him, both well and ill—all remain; and many more things than he
was ever aware of . . . all these ideas remain and are presented
simultaneously in the other life, when anything is thought about
anyone . . . also ideas of places are presented at the same time; and
with these all things that happened there. Whatever happened
there adheres to the memory of the place and is presented at the
same time with it, thus thousands of things simultaneously." [42]

The same was the case even for science ". . . whatever one has learned and thought concerning that matter is simultaneously presented, thus more fully when he has thought much about such a thing."

These idea-pictures, available with the speed of thought, were not only to be got from the minds of the incarnate, however; Swedenborg admitted that at times spirits could gather facts from each other's memories and in this way unlock them. "I heard a certain spirit speak with another. I was acquainted with both in the life of the body. He described the genius and character of the other, and what opinion he had of him, and then recited a letter which he had written, and many other things in a series. The other acknowledged the whole, and was silent." [43]

When Swedenborg spoke of "spirits" he usually meant the ordinary run of what he called "middle-character" deceased, neither good nor bad, hardly changed from their uninstructed life on earth, and hardly as yet aware of their change of condition. Most of them could not grasp what he persisted in trying to tell them, that though they had apparently lost their "corporeal memory" they now had access to another and better mental apparatus.

For if they really learned to make use of their interior memory and their inmost memory they would be able to think "much more subtly and distinctly," since the interior memory was part of the faculty of rational understanding, and the inmost memory enabled one to judge of what was "true and good." [44]

The mere verbal knowledge of philosophy and religion Swedenborg considered part of the corporeal memory. It was "the understanding of these things which belongs to the interior memory"; [45] therefore when the merely book-learned arrived in the other world they often appeared quite idiotic.

CHAPTER TWENTY

Speech, Odors, Auras

THE different kinds of memory levels described by Swedenborg could roughly be said to resemble a pyramid in shape. This would then have the corporeal memory at the thin top and the others progressively spreading wider and going deeper, not only in accumulation of impressions but in understanding and in sympathy. They tend to correspond to the different levels of consciousness, with which psychic research is familiar. It will be remembered that in order to account for the facts of so-called "psi" phenomena, the supposition has been made that some deeper level (or levels) of the mind can enter into communication with other minds either directly without the aid of the senses or through a common subconscious of mankind.

The cross-correspondence cases (see page 197) seemed to furnish evidence that there could be interaction between the minds and memories of men and those of "spirits," at any rate they furnished the "subconscious" with powers akin to the miraculous. "Mrs. Willett" was one of the principals in this experiment, and Lord Balfour's report on her mediumship [1] contains interesting parallels with some of Swedenborg's descriptions.

Like Swedenborg this lady did not ordinarily go into complete trance; no "control" alleged that it took possession of her faculties. Like Swedenborg she remained fairly well in control herself, more or less conscious of the voices she heard and at whose dictation she felt she wrote.

Of especial value are the explanations given by her "communicators" of the process by which they telepathized the information to the mind of the automatist.

They admitted that remembering was difficult. "Wonderfully similar is our condition in regard to knowledge of reaching back, as yours of reaching up . . ." [2]

The quotations which were used by the "communicators" to hint at the information to be conveyed were such as were known to the normal self of Mrs. Willett, even though she had no idea what the "communicator" was driving at—just as Swedenborg said that his memory was tapped by the "spirits" who then used the topics for their own purposes.

But the process described by the Willett "communicators" was also said to be one of mutual selection. The "communicator" said he selected from the contents of both the "conscious and unconscious self" of the sensitive, and insisted that the sensitive selected "from such part of the mind of the communicating spirit as she can have access to."

Putting it briefly, the partially entranced Mrs. Willett is "shown" a number of ideas in visual form by the communicating "spirit" ("representations," as Swedenborg would say), and, say, ten of those stick in her subconscious memory. Telepathically the "communicator" then selects two of those and "pushes them up" to where they will be "grasped and externalized" by automatic writing or speaking. Incidentally, they say, the risk is run that some of the sensitive's own ideas will accompany the ones that have been planted in her telepathically, so to speak, hence the difficulty in disentangling such messages.

There was also the difficulty of language. Mrs. Willett became quite indignant when she had to repeat a long and abstract word with which she was unfamiliar, and even more worried if a Greek and Latin phrase had to be conveyed. "I can see the thoughts," she said once, "but it is so difficult to get the words."

Swedenborg would have diagnosed the trouble as consisting in the fact that the Latin or Greek verbal form of the thought was not already a part of the vocabulary in her memory. He believed that you can have thought without words; that thoughts are really images, mostly visual; and that this was how conversation was possible in the spirit world between people of different languages.

It should by now be clear that Swedenborg in relation to what he considered the spirit world did not sit with bated breath and his attention like a wide-open funnel ready to receive without objection whatever "spirits" told him about matters which he had studied for years.

As to speech, for instance, he stressed that in the spirit world it

was only apparent. It was really transmission of ideas; obviously
spirits had no "real" vocal apparatus and no real air to set in motion. He had no hesitation at all about setting them right on this
point. Not without a certain satisfaction he tells that "When a
certain spirit who had been known to me in the life of the body
conversed with me he appeared to be as though he moved his lips
and as though he spoke with his lips; which, when I mentioned it
to him, he said that so he did speak with his lips to me; but when
I told him in reply that spirits have no lips and that consequently
he could not speak with them, he nevertheless persisted, until he
was instructed by a lively demonstration . . ." [3]

Swedenborg does not explain how—but one has a faint feeling
that it was perhaps the spirit of one of those members of the Board
of Mines who kept him so long from becoming a full Assessor.

Perhaps he very soon explained to the said spirit that, if the deceased is "utterly unconscious" that his sensations are not physically
"real," then, in spite of the absence of "any organ or member of
sense" they are real.

When "spirits" spoke with him, however, he noted they did have
a reason for believing their speech to be one of real sound—that is,
of pronounced words. Among themselves, he soon found out (being as curious as when he first went to England) they had a universal way of communicating by means of ideas, or clusters of
images, and in using this they attended only to "the sense of the
words"—not reflecting, he said, on "the words or articulations"
any more than a man does when he speaks. But, Swedenborg maintained, when a spirit turned to him and transmitted its image-ideas,
then "their ideas fall with me into words, and thus they suppose
that the words and tone of voice are from them." [4]

That is to say (using the Willett report terms) the "spirit" tele-
pathizes its message in image form to that layer of Swedenborg's
mind which is receptive to it and which can retransmit it to the
conscious part either as an image or by using the vocabulary in his
memory, and the machinery of his physical brain for writing or
for hearing.

Swedenborg's reply presumably seemed to him to return in the
same way, while the "spirit" heard and understood the words as if

they were in its own language, although he might be speaking another language.

Swedenborg had many arguments with spirits on this ticklish point, proving to them they were wrong "from this single fact that they speak to me in my vernacular as well as though born to it, although they were born thousands of years previously or in quite another region . . ." [5] Nor, except in a few cases, did they speak to him, he noted, in languages that he did not know. If they tried Latin or Greek, he pointed out ruthlessly that it was again a case of picking his memory, translating their idea-thought into his speech-thought.

He tried to show that man, being a spirit in a body, also possesses this universal language of spirits, though he is usually not aware of it. It has its origin in the interior memory—that all-recording reservoir—and the speech is "pictorial"; it is formed, he said, "from the visible objects in the world." [6] The pictorial ideas of the interior memory are the very origin of language, Swedenborg insisted, and when man wants to speak these ideas fall into the language he has acquired. Then, when spirits speak with a man, that picture-speech falls into the words of the man's language, just as his own "interior ideas fall into the speech of his words." [7]

The light so to speak was the same, but the globes gave it different colors.

Among themselves, he said, the more developed spirits who knew what was what did not of course try to spell thought out into words, and Swedenborg despaired of expressing the rapidity of this mode of communication. The thought of man, he said, is infinitely quicker than his attempt to put it into speech or writing; the speech of spirits infinitely quicker than that of man; and the angels can think infinitely more quickly than spirits, seeing all the branching implications of an idea in all its complexity at one and the same time.

It is understandable that Swedenborg thought spirit "speech" a very rapid one as he considered that man's "interior memory" (or subconscious) was made up of clusters of associated ideas any one of which could be simultaneously presented in the other world in a visible form.

All things whatsoever that a man or spirit has known about a subject, he said, appear as if in the middle of a sphere and in the light, and the rest is around at a distance from the middle, in the shade. Those at the circumference of the subject, he said, are "like objects of sight . . . when the sight is strained to a certain object." [8]

Then, as if searching for the useful word "telepathy," Swedenborg said that this common speech of spirits "is in every man whatsoever, and would become of the same character, if one man should enter into the thought of another with his own thought . . . thus he can bring forth more in a moment than by his words during half an hour."

It was so, he maintained, in the other world, one spirit entered into the thoughts and affections of another "and then knows what he had not known, just as if he knew it of himself." But there were exceptions since the "full communication" could only take place if the participants were "in like truths and in like affection from truths"; since all spirits were not equally endowed with receptivity; and since—mercifully, one would suppose—all one's ideas were not necessarily visible. A spirit could, Swedenborg said, "think in silence" when with other spirits of a similar quality.[9]

Many notes in Swedenborg's diaries are concerned with ways of communicating in the other world. These notes are not always consistent. It is not as if he had sat down and been "inspired" to write a systematic account that always fitted in with his own previous ideas. In this case, as in the case of most of his descriptions in that strange realm, it is more as if a traveler in a foreign country had listened to many of the inhabitants and put down some of what each had told him, contradictory though it might sometimes be, interpreting it in the light of his own preconceptions where he had no other light. Like Marco Polo, one might almost be tempted to say; a man whose observations were good enough, but whose interpretations were colored.

As he divided the denizens into spirits (of several kinds), spiritual angels, and celestial angels, so he distinguished between their ways of conveying thought. What spirits were able to say to man was only a small part of what they knew, "for it does not fall into the words, neither into the sensual ideas of the thought which is with man in the body." [10] Nor could spirits understand the greater part of the language of the spiritual angels, and these again could not always grasp the infinitely wise and loving speech of the celestials. One has a slight shock when Swedenborg mentions that the editor of the London *Spectator* (identified as Addison) had doubts whether there really was such wisdom in celestial speech that he couldn't grasp it. As all reasonable wishes are granted, he was "let into the company of the celestials, and then he perceived those things which they spoke; but when he went back to his fellows who were spiritual, he was not able to express anything, not even by ideas of thought. He said that the things spoken were most replete with wisdom." [11]

Swedenborg noted that in changing from one spiritual realm to another the language of one's own state is forgotten, nor is it always possible to remember what was heard and understood in the superior state—something to which many rapt but inarticulate mystics bear witness.[12]

Angelic thought when visible, he said, was like a transparent wave or a surrounding sphere in which all things were seen in order.[13]

He frequently despairs when he tries to give an inkling of angelic language, because angels have the power, he says, of expressing myriads of things either by visible representation or in a few words made eloquent by the inflection of the voice. He cites the case of a certain hard-hearted spirit who wept when an angel spoke to him, saying he had never wept before, but this was love speaking.[14] The innermost angels can tell a person's whole life from the sound of his voice in a few words, since in it they hear his ruling passion and hence know the details of his life. Yes, Swedenborg said, they can even tell all about a person from a single sigh, "because a sigh is a thought of the heart." [15]

Just as in this world, Swedenborg observed, there are other ways of perceiving what a man is like than by what he says. "There is a sphere, as it were, of spiritual effluvia, which exhale and produce a perception of the life of one's mind. This sphere I recollect myself to have perceived and it has rarely if ever deceived me. Nor need this appear wonderful, when a shrewd and intelligent man is aware from the face, speech and actions of another, of what quality he is, whether stimulated or sincere, and many other things which are manifest to a man's internal sense."[16] (Swedenborg had used this sense of his in spotting a dishonest servant.)

This power was, he said, much more perfect with spirits, with whom the quality of another spirit could be at once revealed "even from his mute presence." He explained this by saying that the "interiors" of either man or spirit "are in a kind of unconscious activity" and that this forms a kind of sphere which "not only extends itself to a distance but that sometimes also, when the Lord permits, is in various ways made perceptible to the senses."[17]

As spirits, worse luck, generally have an exquisite sense of odor (according to Swedenborg), they were very sensitive to those spheres of other spirits which manifested themselves through smell. There was a definite smell-register. When the sphere of hypocrites was "turned into an odor" there was "a stench of vomit." "When the sphere of those who have studied eloquence in order that everything may redound to self-admiration, is made odoriferous, it is like the odor of burnt bread."[18] (One of the heavenly odors, he said, was like good bread freshly baked.) Mere pleasure hunters who had neither believed in nor loved anything had a sphere as of excrement in odor; that of the adulterous was even worse. If the sphere of the revengeful and cruel were offered to the nose, the stench was cadaverous. The sordidly avaricious smelled like mice, and those who persecute the innocent like lice.[19]

The stench of a certain woman who though fair was evil was perceived as "deadly" he said, yet she knew nothing of it. Certain spirits were sometimes surprised when others fled at their approach; their circumambient perfume was unknown to them.

Swedenborg developed a whole doctrine of odors. The societies of the other world had their own general spheres which also could manifest as odors. The "infernals" love stenches; they cannot bear the heavenly odors of fruit and bread and flowers and frankincense. In fact it makes them sick. "Once I saw," Swedenborg tells, "an astute devil like a leopard ascending a high mountain where there were celestial angels encompassed by a hedge of olive trees; after he had drawn in a full breath of that odor, he was seized with spasms, became stiffened in all his joints, writhed like a snake, and was cast down headlong. Afterwards he was lifted up by his associates, and taken into a den and into his own odor, where he revived." [20]

That poor devil was better off, however, than another (here one suspects humor) whom Swedenborg said he saw scourged by his associates in hell, because he (though without meaning to and because he had a cold in his head and couldn't smell) "had approached such as were in a heavenly odor and had brought back some of their perfume in his garments," [21] which seems unjust but what can you expect of devils!

But life in the spirit world did not all smell like London in the eighteenth century. Swedenborg perceived a pleasant vinous odor and was informed "that it came from those who compliment one another from friendship and rightful love, so that there is also truth in the compliments. This odor exists with much variety, and comes from the sphere of fine manners."

The spheres of "charity and faith," or, as he sometimes called them, of love and wisdom, when they were perceived as odors smelled of "flowers, lilies and spices" of infinite variety.

"Moreover, the spheres of angels are sometimes made visible as atmospheres or auras, which are so beautiful, so pleasant and so various, that they cannot possibly be described." He did, however, sometimes try to describe the visible spheres or auras, not only of angels but of men, animals, plants, and minerals, for he saw them all as having their own sphere around them, "even the minutest particle." Man in the body he saw as "solid" as to his "terrestrial parts" inside his spiritual sphere, and both men and spirits he sometimes saw as surrounded by spheres of various colors, having spiritual significance, the darker colors pertaining to selfishness, the lighter to better qualities. They could be muddy; they could be rainbowlike.[22]

How those spheres were acquired which could sometimes be represented visually or via the spiritual equivalent of smell Swedenborg also tells. "Take as an example," he said, "one who has formed a high opinion of himself and of his own pre-eminent excellence. He at last becomes imbued with such a habit, and . . . wherever he goes, though he looks at others and speaks with them, he keeps himself in view; and this at first manifestly but afterwards not so manifestly so that he is not aware of it, but still it is regnant . . . . . . Men can see this in others. And this is the kind of thing that in the other life makes a sphere . . . as it were the man's image extended outside of himself, the image in fact of all things that are in him." [23]

Swedenborg mentions that he had known a man in the world who appeared in the spirit world with such a sphere of high opinion of himself that all other spirits fled away and he was left alone. Another person known to him had "contracted a sphere of supereminence and authority" surrounding him like a mist that crept over the other spirits, so that they wanted to go away. But those who had been born to a sphere of high authority and who were also good soon strove to put it off.

As among men so among spirits there were spheres tranquil and pleasant, others disturbing and depressing. Each soul, so to speak, carried its own climate with it favorable or unfavorable to those near it. Worst of all Swedenborg found those spirits in the nearness of whose spheres it was almost impossible even for him to believe in the good and the true; under whose influence in fact evil seemed good and false seemed true; spheres they had carried with them from their life on earth. But he was not undefended. Once, he says, when he was surrounded by such spirits, "an angel came, and I saw that the spirits could not endure his presence; for as he came nearer, they fell back more and more." They could not "endure the sphere of mutual love." [24]

CHAPTER TWENTY-ONE

Gardener, Statesman, Author

IN following Swedenborg into the next world, it is easy to forget that he had by no means retired from this one. From 1747 to about 1751 he was abroad in various countries, busy putting down his new interpretation of the Bible or trying to fathom the psychology of spirits, but he also took pains to see his friends and he was concerned about his garden in Stockholm. He ordered seeds and bulbs for it, in 1750, from his good friend, the Swedish merchant Wretman in Amsterdam, and received useful advice from the latter about putting the tulip, hyacinth, and other bulbs into the ground in the autumn before the frost began.[1]

He was back in Sweden in 1751 and deep in gardening, on the rocky islet of Södermalm where his house stood. He owned a piece of land 336 by 156 feet, enclosed by a wooden fence. About two thirds of it were used for orchard and garden, the rest for his house and outhouses. The house was about 57 by 48 feet, and the upper story had an "orangery," or greenhouse, lit by six windows in the roof.[2]

There Swedenborg had his seedlings in spring. In his almanac for 1752 he notes not only what copy for the *Arcana Celestia* he had sent to John Lewis the printer in London, but also what he had planted and when. In February he had "in the first box crown artichokes; second box, lemons, in the centre *mallium,* after that cypresses; third box gilliflowers of three kinds, with white ones in the middle."

The garden was divided by linden avenues into four parts, and in the 1752 almanac he also noted where he had planted lemon seeds, cypress seeds, and carnations, next to them sweet peas, and next to them parsley-roots and beets. But he had a proper flower section with "Adonis roses, scarlet beans, larkspur, violet-roses and plants with white and yellow bordered leaves," and elsewhere violets, bleeding hearts, sweet william, a bed of spinach and another of parsley, and then large sweet white roses, flax, scabiosa and wild roses. (He wrote somewhere that in working with flowers, trees, and vegetables he was often aware of what their heavenly origin was; for to him a rose was not just a rose, it was the earthly expression of some celestial emotion.)

As he had inherited the garden from another owner, he of course did not always know what was going to come up in it, and he noted that "by the currant bush there were old roses, marsh mallows and gilliflowers of a curious kind," and elsewhere there were other flowers and vegetables, not on his program, such as African roses and velvet roses and beside them lilies, rose-mallows and sun-flowers.[3]

It may have been during the discovery of and communion with these frail messengers from other people and times that he became aware, so he said, of spirits in the garden who greatly resisted the idea of a new owner who introduced changes; but he pacified them,[4] and introduced "singular Dutch figures of animals cut in box-tree" and little garden pavilions like some he had seen in his travels. In the middle there was one copied from an English model; another had curious mirror effects, another was a volière for birds with wide netting, and at the end of the garden he finally built himself a summerhouse, containing his library, where he liked to work, being apparently like every other man who gets a house of his own, anxious to have a little house still more his own.

Near this there was a "labyrinth," or, as his friend Robsahm[5] wrote, "a maze of boards, entirely for the amusement of the good people that would come and visit him in his garden, and especially for their children; and there he would receive them with a cheerful countenance and enjoy their delight at his contrivances."

The little house with the mirrors, Robsahm said, was arranged so that when the visitor opened a door, he faced another door with a window that seemed to look into another garden, but it was a mirror which reflected "a green hedge where a beautiful bird-cage was placed . . . the effect was most charming and surprising. Swedenborg derived much sport from this arrangement, especially when inquisitive and curious young ladies came into his garden."

Swedenborg was no recluse—but neither was he merely an amiable and sociable man of independent means, secretly devoted to "occult" studies, and publicly devoted to pottering in his garden.

He kept the same keen eye on the doings of the Swedish legislature that he had done before he seemed to himself to have crossed the boundaries of the physical world. In his code, attention to civic duties ranked high, and, as Robsahm says, "in acting with a party he was never a party-man, but loved truth and honesty in all he did."

As head of the Swedenborg family he was a member of the House of Nobles, and he had already presented useful memorials to the Diet while he was in the Board of Mines. In 1734 he was very much against declaring war on Russia. "The greatest honor seems to consist in our acquiring a position of respect by wise economy . . ." [6]

His next memorial to the Diet was in 1755, while he was in the midst of writing the *Arcana Celestia*. There was nothing occult about his advice to the legislators. He viewed with alarm that the excess of imports over exports amounted to three to four million of silver *daler*. He scored the evils of inflation. People were allowed to raise money on their property but it was paper currency with no backing. He wanted such banknotes to be called in and payment in coin to be resumed. [7]

The Swedish immoderate use of hard liquor he saw as a great drawback to industry. He wanted the right of private distilling taken away from people and given to the highest bidder in each district so as to raise revenue for the state, "that is, if the consumption of brandy cannot be done away with altogether, which would be more desirable for the country's welfare and morality than all the income which could be realized from so pernicious a drink."

Granted however that it had to be sold, he recommended, much as the present Swedish liquor control has it, "that all public houses in town should be like bakers' shops, with an opening in the window, through which those who desired might purchase whisky and brandy without being allowed to enter the house and lounge about in the tap-room." [8]

But Swedenborg was no total abstainer; he liked an occasional glass of wine which he probably also offered to his friends either in the garden or in his living room, "neat and genteel but plain," where stood the inlaid marble table he had brought from Italy. Robsahm says that "Swedenborg was not only a learned man but also a polished gentleman; for a man of such extensive learning, who by his books, his travels, and his knowledge of languages had acquired distinction both at home and abroad could not fail to possess the manners and everything else which, in these so-called serious and sober times, caused a man to be honored and made him agreeable in society."

The times were serious. No doubt the disastrous state of Swedish finances continued to be discussed by him, for late in 1760 he presented two memorials to the Diet, in which he dealt again with the cause of the bad rate of foreign exchange, the consequent debasement of the currency, and the terrible results for everybody. His language was simple and clear; even those ignorant of financial problems could understand his explanation and the remedies he suggested. Swedenborg knew about metals; he knew them, so to speak, from their cradle in the mine to their obituary in paper currency.[9]

These memorials were the ones characterized by Count von Höpken as the most solid and best penned of that Diet. Höpken said, "In one of these he refuted a large work in quarto on the same subject, quoted all the corresponding passages of it, and all this in less than one sheet."

This was a reference to a book by one Nordencrantz, in which the form of government of Sweden, at least partly representative, was attacked through the assertion that government by many led to the formation of cliques and to corrupt practices. It was really a plea for the restoration of absolute monarchy, and it did not deceive Emanuel Swedenborg. "One absolute monarch," he wrote, "is able to do more mischief in one year than a clique or combination of many at a session of the Diet could accomplish in a hundred years. . . . Corrupt practices in free governments are like small ripples, compared with large waves in absolute monarchies;" in the latter, he said, "favorites and the favorites of favorites, yea the unlimited monarch himself, are corrupted by men who study and appeal to their passions . . ." He threw in a timely reminder about Baron Görtz and Charles XII.

He admitted faults in representative governments; still there was freedom. "Should I undertake to make known all the mistakes of which I have heard and which I know from my own experience have happened in England and Holland to the detriment of justice and the public good, I believe I might fill a whole book with lamentations, when nevertheless those governments together with our own in Sweden are the very best in Europe, as every inhabitant, notwithstanding all the shortcomings which take place there, is safe in his life and property, and no one is a slave but they are all free men."

Considering that by this time, 1761, it had become known that he claimed to communicate with the other world, he was rather bold to continue as follows: "The honorable Houses of the Diet will allow me to go still higher: If there in this world should exist a heavenly government, consisting of men who had an angelic disposition, there would nevertheless be in it faults caused by weakness, together with other shortcomings; and if these were ferreted out, reported and exaggerated, this government too might be undermined by calumny and thereby gradually a desire might be raised among the well-disposed to change and destroy it." [10]

The terse and cogent arguments for better government which the vigorous man of seventy-two expressed in his memorials grew out of a social philosophy which he had acquired in his long service of the state, and in which he had been confirmed by what he considered his observations in the other world. He had seen during his tenure of office men with petty souls and big voices who even while they claimed to be working for the common good were in reality working for their own profit, power, or renown. So to every action he applied one test: What is the end the man has in view? Did he desire the welfare of others for the sake of the common good, or was it for the sake of himself? [11]

In Swedenborg's life there had been an overwhelming example of a man, perhaps self-deceived, whose loud trumpetings about his own piety, humility, and unselfishness were in reality blasts from as theatrical an ego as ever posed in a pulpit—his father, Bishop Swedberg. In his writings, Swedenborg often came back to the subject of how detested hypocrites were in the other world, not only the crude sort, but those who performed pious and useful actions. "If anyone should convert the whole world to Christianity, and the end be self-glory, self-reward and the like, he then obtains no reward therefor in the other life . . ." [12] He remarked that spirits did not like to hear this, because they commonly held the belief that, "If anyone had bestowed anything for the doctrine of faith in the life of the body he wishes to be rewarded therefor no matter what the end is." [13]

To attribute merit to yourself, even real merit, Swedenborg saw as the beginning of danger, the beginning of the black knot of the ego. "The more anyone thinks he merits heaven through such things . . . the more he puts himself away from heaven . . ."

The cardinal point in his ethics was that the Lord was Goodness and Truth, and Goodness and Truth were the Lord. All that man could do "as of himself" was by an effort of will to open his mind and heart to this Goodness and Truth and let that divine union flow in and act through him. "Suffer yourself to be an instrument!" [14] to be employed by this Goodness, he often exclaimed. Shut your mind and heart to the evil promptings of evil spirits, who also want to use you.

Could feelings be compelled into "good" channels? No, Swedenborg emphatically said, but thoughts can yield to reason. That kind of self-compulsion is freedom. He assumed that ethical truths were known; the Bible was there. Hence man could think even if he could not feel that something was wrong or unjust and against divine will. "Man can enter this state freely, for who is not free so to think?" Then, if that became a mental habit, the "inner man" would open and really be able to see what was unjust and wrong, and "to the degree in which he sees this it is dispersed, for nothing can be canceled out until it is seen."

Incidentally, Swedenborg saw evil spirits as serving the above useful purpose: by their smelling a man's evil inclinations, reinforcing them and dragging them to the surface, the man would know that he had such inclinations and could do something about them. And, if he had once really seen himself as he was he would not be left to himself. "The Lord will cause the man not only to see the evil but not to will it and finally to detest it."

The motive of an action was the true test of it. A thousand men could do what seemed like the same deed, yet they would all be as different as the different motives for it, "for the deed is as the will."

But the will was not the same as the deed. "To think and to will without doing, if there is opportunity, is like a flame in a vessel which dies, or a seed thrown on sand, which is lost without its germinating power." [15]

Like a Buddhist he proclaimed that man is the sum of his willed deeds. "Man's spiritual body is none other than his deeds done out of his will." But "the road to heaven is not away from but in the world." [16]

Swedenborg saw those who gave up the world as often burning with a desire for "merit" which defeated itself, for, he said, in heaven it was impossible for the self-torturers to be with the angels, who do what they do out of joy. Lest, therefore, the ascetic "sphere" should disturb the heavenly harmony, such grim candidates for sainthood were put off in a department by themselves. [17]

In human society Swedenborg did not want either the individual or society to dominate; he sought interdependence, not slavery. The "general good" he saw as having its origin in the useful work of individuals, and this work he saw as being nourished and continued from the established fund of general food—a beneficent circle. He had no use for drones. But "he who performs uses for himself alone is also useless though not called so." [18]

Instead of setting up as prophet, saint, or "revelator" demanding a following, Swedenborg most definitely continued to act as a good Swedish citizen, although he was of course convinced that he was performing the most useful of all functions in passing on the information he had received about the true interpretation of the Bible and the real conditions in the other world where he felt he had actually seen the working out of spiritual laws. The books were anonymous, until 1768, and not published in Sweden, but still, as we know, about the end of 1760, Baron Tilas was writing to a friend the startling news about Swedenborg's alleged commerce with the other world.

Carl Robsahm testifies that, after the secret was out, Swedenborg "at first used to talk freely about his visions and his explanations of scripture," although "he never tried to make proselytes or to force his explanations on anyone." But when the Swedish clergy began to be ruffled by his heresies, "he resolved to be more sparing of his communications in company." Robsahm found him "even in his old age cheerful, sprightly and agreeable in company, yet at the same time his countenance presented those uncommon features which are only seen in men of great genius."

"It was difficult for him to talk quickly, for he then stuttered, especially when he was obliged to talk in a foreign tongue . . . He spoke slowly, and it was always a pleasure to be with him at table, for whenever Swedenborg spoke, all other talk was hushed, and the slowness with which he spoke had the effect of restraining the frivolous remarks of the curious in the assembly."

Those who could not read his writings (as they were in Latin) were likely to be among the frivolous, according to Robsahm, but those who could read them judged him quite differently. "And what is remarkable, most of those who do read his books become in a greater or less degree his adherents . . . ," he said, though noting that they were shy about admitting it. Their judgment, as evidently that of Robsahm himself, cautious banker that he was, seems to have been that there was much that was good in Swedenborg's writings, except for the other-world visions and conversations.

Even those might have been accepted in a sense, if only Swedenborg had not insisted that they were really "from things heard and seen." Cultivated people in the eighteenth century were well used to having opinions presented in various disguises. Montesquieu had written *Lettres Persanes,* for one instance; still further back there was Sir Thomas More's *Utopia;* and of religious allegories there were Bunyan's *Pilgrim's Progress* and Milton's *Paradise Lost.*

And now here was Swedenborg's *Heaven and Hell.* It had been published in London in 1758, being extracts from the eight volumes of the *Arcana Celestia,* which again were mainly from the spiritual diaries, as far as conditions in the Beyond were described. *Heaven and Hell* began to trickle into Sweden about 1760, and if it had only been presented by its author as symbolic of spiritual truths it would have charmed the readers by its imaginative insight, poetic fables, shrewd psychology, and lofty ethics, as indeed it did charm a man like Höpken, who thought that Swedenborg's works "sparkled with genius."

What delightful ideas, one can imagine his friends saying, in this book with the inclusive title, supposing of course that they are not put forward seriously. Innumerable "societies" of angels in heaven, and yet no man's heaven and no man's hell like another's. The angels shiver at the thought of monotonous conformity; their unity is a harmony of units, not a similarity. If the reader smiled at the similarity of some of the angelic environments to those of earth, he could not of course realize that these were what Swedenborg termed "appearances," though they seemed actual to those whose states of mind they expressed. These angels and angelic spirits lived in houses and Swedenborg said he had been in them. They were much finer than earthly ones, with every kind of room and court. There were gardens, flower beds, fields. Palaces shone with gleams of gold and precious stones and architecture was in its flower, because, Swedenborg said, that art was itself from heaven. There were towns with streets, roads, and marketplaces. There were temples, because angels, having reason and affection, were capable of having them infinitely perfected; and there was government and administration because though all were equally good not all were equally wise; and each member of the community had many duties which, however, were joys, as a mother who loves her children "does not think about merit like a hired nurse, but grieves if she is deprived of that useful function and is willing to give all she has only to be allowed to possess her joy."

The functions of the angels were innumerable, both such as they were conscious of and such as they were not. Some instructed new arrivals, some were with men and reinforced any good impulse, some protected others, some gently awoke the dead.

They talked with each other about every kind of question pertaining to much the same things that men discuss. Swedenborg said he had often heard them. Some lived in communities, some lived in separate abodes, and they were "the best of angels." One thing they never argued about was faith." "They say, 'What is faith? I feel and see that this is so.' As if someone showed another a garden and said, 'You ought to believe that this is there,' when he sees it before his eyes."

Heavenly pleasure could not be understood, Swedenborg said, by those who did not know what spiritual joy was. Nor could those who put their joy in honor and profit and carnal pleasure believe that there can be inexpressible joys having nothing to do with these, any more than thick and pungent dust was comparable to a pure and gentle breeze. The greatest joy was to wish to share it with others. Swedenborg tried to say how all the inward being seemed to open and to be dissolved, spreading the blessedness to every single fiber. He had felt this sense of order in the joy himself, and how greatly it increased when he shared it with another.

Angelic love was to love one's neighbor *more* than oneself, something that could be seen, he said, in true marriage love, in maternal love, and in true friendship.

He was happiest in heaven who knew that he was nothing of himself or in himself, but, ever watchful against the crafty ego, Swedenborg warned that a man who sought to be "nothing" in order to be happy would seek in vain.

Perhaps it was because of the opportunities for hypocrisy offered by official Christianity that Swedenborg was so distrustful of it. He often said that heathens may live better lives than Christians. Certain Chinese spirits showed distrust when he mentioned Christ to them, because they knew that Christians were worse than they, but he said they liked to hear about the Lord. The Church of the Lord, according to Swedenborg, is with all who admit divinity and live in love of their neighbor, and it is wherever people live in charity, according to their religion.

Swedenborg said that those heathens or others who had worshiped human beings or images in the world were for some time let believe that they encounter those deities in heaven, and in this way were gradually weaned from their fancies.

The *Tibetan Book of the Dead*,[18a] certainly not known to Swedenborg, contains observations similar to his, such as the different visions seen by men of different faiths; the belief of the "dead" that they are still in their physical bodies; the hallucinatory experiences; even the "clear light" seen at first is common to both the Tibetan after-world and that of Swedenborg.

From his diary he took a little incident, relating how once when he was reading the Old Testament about Micah, from whom the sons of Dan took away his graven image, there was a certain spirit present, so aware of what Swedenborg was reading that he identified himself with Micah and grieved innocently at his loss. He was from India and in his life had worshiped a graven image. But Swedenborg observed that his adoration was much more holy than that of any Christian. There was pity in him, and because this spirit could feel such pity he could be with the angels, and, when he had forgotten his graven image, he could worship the true Lord, "differently from very many Christians." [19]

Yet, though Swedenborg believed in one true Lord, he could imagine Him as manifesting in different ways. Not unlike the Saiva saying, "O Thou Who dost take the shapes imagined by Thy worshippers," is Swedenborg's saying that the Lord reveals himself differently in each community of heaven, according to the kind of goodness in each.

Of children in heaven Swedenborg said that no matter what the creeds may say, all children go to heaven when they die, and are brought up there. If caught early enough they can become angels, not having any positive evil in them as yet. They are given to motherly angels who had greatly loved children when on earth, and taught to speak, first by "sounds of affection." Later they are taught (in the best Montessori manner), without having their wills broken, through "representations" scaled to their understanding, and when educated enough they become angels and look grown-up.

As to whether the rich could get into heaven, Swedenborg said that man can obtain heaven even if he has lived well and merrily on earth, if he had not made rich living the object of his life. Those who do not use their riches for others are like moist soil without the light of day, he said, they rot. But the poor have plenty of vices too. As for traders, it is on the whole easier for them to reach heaven than for officials; the latter are apt to take to themselves the merit belonging to their office and they become arrogant.

Beauty in heaven corresponds to inner development; there is something, he said, dim and unillumined about the less developed. Love illumines and shapes faces and forms until those who see such a form are astounded, and that is why persons who have inherited an ugly body may be transformed into the greatest beauty in heaven. Hence Swedenborg's report that he saw a former teacher of his, Moræus, so transformed.

In hell love also rules, but it is love of self. At first the new arrivals are received quite well, while the demons investigate how crafty they may be, but as in hell everyone wants to command (while in heaven all want to serve) trouble soon arises. Incidentally Swedenborg remarks that the pangs of conscience are not the pangs of hell, for those who are capable of pangs of conscience are not spiritually dead, therefore not in hell.

With a lightning phrase Swedenborg says that the forms of those in hell are "those of contempt for others." Some are reduced to a bundle of ugly teeth. "In general, evil spirits are forms of contempt for others, or forms of hatreds and revenge. They are full of menaces for those who do not pay them respect . . . but if worshiped they can look pleased for a while. Each looks as his ruling passion is."

Swedenborg wondered at the monstrous forms of the love of self, for, he said, in the world the haughty love of self is regarded as a kind of noble and necessary spur to action, the fire of life itself, honor and glory.

In Swedenborg's view love of self was to do good only for one's own sake, or for one's children and grandchildren who really, he said, are part of the man himself and called his own.

Imagine a community, Swedenborg said, of such as love only themselves and others only as they seem part of them, and you will see that their love is only as that among robbers, who kiss and call each other friends as long as they act in common, but who wish to slay and destroy the others if they protest their dominion. They laugh at everything which is divine.

Of such is hell. The worst are the deceitful egoists, he said, since deceit presses deeply into thought and purpose and poisons them and disturbs all spiritual life. But with many the evil in their souls has been so wrapped up in outer honesty and decency that they hardly know themselves what devils they are. It takes death to reveal them to themselves.

Eternal slander, quarreling, hate, and unfriendliness fill the horrid little towns in hell, or rather in the hells, since each inhabitant in a sense creates his own, but enough are like-minded to have similar districts. In the milder departments are huts that sometimes are arranged as if in streets; from those huts come the noise of brawls and fights. Some are like ruined cities after fire. Others are full of dirty brothels where lust feeds itself forever joylessly. There are also dark forests, sandy deserts, scraggy cliffs, black mines and caves. There seems to be fire, both smoky and flaming, but it is not such as can be felt by the inhabitants, Swedenborg says. It is correspondence with their self-love.

His eighteenth-century reader would probably have been as much troubled by "correspondence," one of Swedenborg's favorite words, as is his twentieth-century reader. It was correspondence that evil, false, haughty, tricky spirits lived in caves and darkness and filthy places. It was correspondence that those who had lived "in heavenly love out of affection for truth" spent their spirit-life in bright light on beautiful mountains in spring; that they saw "represented" before them meadows and fields of corn and vineyards and olive groves; that their rooms gleamed as if with precious stones; that they looked through windows as if through purest crystal.

It was likewise correspondence that those who had loved science and used it to develop their reason with, and to acknowledge the divine, now lived in symmetric gardens with artfully trimmed trees, where trees and flowers daily went through beautiful changes. It was for the same reason that those who had given the divine all credit and who had regarded nature by itself as comparatively dead now lived in the light of a heaven where, all things being as if transparent for them, they saw infinite changes and gradations of heavenly radiance. In their houses shone a diamond light, their walls seemed of transparent crystal in which they saw an ever-changing flow of beautiful things.

Swedenborg's friends must have shaken their heads over this mysterious "correspondence" that turned up everywhere in what he now wrote, both about the other world and about the Bible. Nor puzzled only by that. There were many strange allusions to the "Grand Man," and to visits to other planets, or casual mention of the Last Judgment having taken place in Swedenborg's observant presence. But especially "correspondence" gleamed and darkened everywhere. It seemed to be a world-principle, so ubiquitous and bewildering that it had to be confronted if one would understand Swedenborg.

And that was difficult, not to say impossible, on the basis of the published books, in which he neither bothered to explain its many meanings, nor said how the idea had developed for him. Nor could he tell, possibly, why some of his strange ideas seemed to him factual; he was not aware that some of them, at least, had risen from his unconscious mind via automatic writing. The ideas had a history, however.

Interworld "Correspondence"

IF Swedenborg had only been willing to be considered allegorical in his other-world reports, there would have been no
great difficulty about understanding those likenesses between
spirits and their environments, which he set forth so vividly. No
more difficulty than in understanding that a gloomy-tempered man
makes a gloomy house or garden for himself, or that a gay person
prefers gay colors. In a sense a house expresses a man; indeed it
"corresponds" to him. Swedenborg would have agreed, to be sure;
he felt that his own symmetrical garden with the artfully trimmed
box trees "corresponded" to one who loved science.

But Swedenborg went much farther; he made a system of it,
being a born system-maker. He believed of course that everything
which takes place in the mind, even if still in the body, really takes
place in the spiritual world, which is not in our kind of space. All
psychological processes were immaterial events which could have
an effect in the material world. And these effects were often "correspondences"; they expressed either directly or in symbolic form
their spiritual cause. Smiles and scowls might be direct material
expressions of spiritual events.

If the soul had left the physical envelope, it entered, according to
Swedenborg, into a world where its states of mind and mood had
vastly greater scope than merely throwing a cup of coffee on the
floor if it were angry. That world had a kind of malleable atmosphere, or immaterial substance, which the feelings of the spirit
could affect in various startling ways. Not only could it "project"
its own sane or mad fancies on it so that they actually became visible
to other spirits, even seeming real to both the projector and witnesses, but a luridly wicked mind involuntarily gave off effects that
looked like smoke and flame, because that "corresponded" to its
nature.

They were not, however, "real," nor were the dark caves, the
dirty brothels, or the sandy deserts real—they were self-created by

those to whose willfully acquired natures they corresponded. But, if they had not so totally deprived themselves of all good that there was no redemption for them out of their private hells, then they were in "the lower earth," as Swedenborg called it, or nether world of spirits, where they might through their suffering be "vastated" of their evil, and perhaps develop latent goodness into better natures which in turn would create pleasanter environments for them, perhaps even advancing to "paradises."

In the paradises too everything "corresponded" to the natures of the denizens—the varied bright colors of the garments of the lower angels, the luminous white of the higher realms, and the utter nakedness, corresponding to innocence, of the innermost, celestial angels.

Swedenborg could still have kept respectably within the allegorical fold if he had limited his doctrine of correspondences to such things, but he went much farther, applying it to everything in the world.

He was not being original in this, as indeed he often said himself, pointing out that the "ancients" believed the same. So many of them did. Persian, Platonic, and Neoplatonic mystics and their many descendants thought that all here below was in some sense caused by events in the spiritual realms of heaven and hell.

But Swedenborg was not satisfied to dismiss nettles and gnats, for instance, as originating in diabolical hatreds; he did try in some respects to link up "correspondence" with his studies of physiology. From embryology he felt he had reason to believe that something apparently immaterial could have effects on the material level, and in his work on the nervous system (*The Fibre*) he said it was well known that a mind foiled of its desires could trouble the body, causing an overflow of bile.[1] Then in his later period he simply added on spirits who reinforced the noxious emotions, which in their turn caused physical diseases.

Yet beyond this now quite respectable psychosomatic theory, he came to accept wholly the old doctrine that the material world in every aspect is entirely created by the spiritual. Life, for him, was a force emanating from the Divine. Self-willed man, whether in or out of the body, was free to receive this force and turn it into good or into evil. The furniture and scenery of hell, its animals and plants, were "appearances," or "mere correspondences of lusts that swarm out of their evil loves and present themselves in such forms before others." [2] Yet he believed, or came to believe, that these temporary, soul-stuff "phantasies" could become materialized— appear in solid earth-stuff—if they "which in themselves are spiritual meet with homogeneous or corresponding things in the earths for then are present both the spiritual that furnishes a soul and the material that furnishes a body." [3] Or, as he also put it, if those forms become filled with matters from the earth they become fixed or enduring. Luckily for man and for the growing of roses, the emotions of heaven could also be in this way materialized on earth.

Swedenborg worked this out in much dry detail, but to illustrate the doctrine he gave an incident "from experience," as he said, and undoubtedly meant. With the astounding casualness that often startles the reader into nearly believing that he really did loiter behind a heavenly huckleberry bush and overhear the inhabitants, he begins:

"I heard two presidents of the English Royal Society, Sir Hans Sloane and Martin Folkes, conversing together in the spiritual world about the existence of seeds and eggs, and about production from them in the earths."

(Note that Swedenborg was well acquainted with the Royal Society and had undoubtedly seen both of these gentlemen and may have known them personally.)

Sir Hans Sloane contended that nature by itself produced seeds and eggs by means of the sun's heat, but Mr. Folkes (his real name was Ffoulkes) said that the force for this came into nature unceasingly from God, the Creator.

"To settle the discussion, a beautiful bird appeared to Sir Hans Sloane, and he was asked to examine it to see whether it differed in the smallest particle from a similar bird on earth. He held it in his hand, examined it, and declared that there was no difference. He knew indeed that it was nothing but an affection of some angel represented outside the angel as a bird, and that it would vanish or cease with its affection. And this came to pass."

"By this experience," Swedenborg says, "Sir Hans Sloane was convinced that nature contributes nothing whatever to the production of plants and animals, that they are produced solely by what flows into the natural world out of the spiritual world. If that bird, he said, were to be infilled in its minutest parts, with corresponding matters from the earth, and thus fixed, it would be a lasting bird, like the birds on earth, and that it is the same with such things as are from hell." [4]

Putting it a little differently one might say that Sir Hans acknowledged that the induced hallucination of a bird was perfect, lacking only "the matters from the earth" to be eaten with bread-sauce in London. As it vanished, that test could not be made, and perhaps the learned gentlemen were in a sphere where enjoyments were on a higher level.

Swedenborg explained that of course once these forms had been started on earth they continued in the natural way of propagation by egg or seed. But the origin of species apparently was in the spiritual world where "affections or lusts" could take on visible form.

Once he was fully started on this train of thought it quite naturally followed that he returned to the belief of many "occult" writers who thought that nature was one big picture-book symbolical of the spiritual world. Indeed, as early as in the *Animal Kingdom* he had written that "you would swear that the physical world is merely symbolic of the spiritual world, and so much so that if you express in physical terms . . . any natural truth whatever, and merely convert those terms into the corresponding spiritual terms then . . . will come forth a spiritual truth or a theological dogma . . ." [5]

Still at that time he also warned that comparison illustrates but does not explain, a piece of common sense which he forgot later when much of what he called "correspondence" was not causal in character at all, but either analogy or simple association of ideas. In this way he could manage to interpret "the internal sense" of everything, especially of the Bible, to suit himself, and what came to suit him was to interpret the Bible so that everything in certain books of it had some relation to truth and good, those twin poles of the world for him, as well as to Jewish history and prophecy of the Messiah.

He made up a kind of dictionary. For instance, since "bread" can be taken to mean all food in general, it "corresponds to" or means "in the internal sense" all celestial food, which is spiritual good.

Similarly gentle animals "correspond to gentle affections; fierce animals to fierce passions; light to truth; heat to love," etc.[6]

Of course he did not believe that this key to the Bible was entirely self-made, but that the theory had been confirmed by the angels who dictated to him or who even moved his hands to write the words. Here, as wherever in Swedenborg's later period he stubbornly maintained theories that seem completely at variance with the level-headed author of financial memorials, the explanation of the mystery can be found in that other mystery of automatic writing. It could not, at that time, seem an uprush from his needs and from the stores of reading in his unconscious mind; it joined forces with other inexplicable things that had happened to him, seeming to become a communication from higher powers and therefore to be believed.

Nowhere is this so apparent as when he extends the "doctrine of correspondence" to that great stumbling block to an understanding of Swedenborg—the "Grand Man" (Maximus Homo).

On March 3, 1748, he noted in his diary, writing at least semi-automatically, that heaven had the form of a Grand Man. He had been having a little discussion with angels about various things in the human body "and they wonder that they do not fall into the understanding of everyone, as they now dictate, for they guide my thoughts to write these things. Moreover, the states of spirits and angels, together with all their varieties, can in no wise be understood without a knowledge of the human body; for the Lord's Kingdom is like a man; and without such a kingdom, which is like a true man (for the Lord is the only Man, and his Kingdom resembles him) no man could possibly live, since all things in heaven conspire to the conservation of the minutest things in the body, as may be manifestly demonstrated, and if thou art willing thou shalt hear still greater arcana." [7]

Here it seems, we get the "angel's" very words, and we can even make a guess as to the "society" for which he was spokesman, for although Swedenborg seemed now to believe that the doctrine of the Grand Man was an "arcanum," a secret, it was one which had been freely passed around for many centuries among those pseudo-scientific occultists whom Swedenborg used to denounce. It was a popular doctrine of the Kabbalists, vigorous during the Renaissance and even later. Swedenborg was acquainted with their writings, and even with the fountain itself, the Kabbalah, itself at least partly derivative from older occultisms.[8]

According to these doctrines, when God, the Unmanifest, manifested himself, he flowed or emanated into the form of a giant man, this becoming the shape of the universe, and when man was created each member of his body "corresponded" to a part of the universe. The world was the macrocosm and man the microcosm, and the two interacted.[9]

Swedenborg, through what he was "told," took what he liked of these interweaving symbolisms, and what he especially liked— what took root most speedily and deeply in his background of experience and preference—was the physiological symbolism. As it solved many problems for him, especially those of "location," very soon he saw it as real.

As he tells it in *Arcana Celestia,* it is heaven that has the form of the Grand Man, and "man is so formed as to correspond to heaven in regard to each and all things in him."

Now, if there was anything which Emanuel Swedenborg felt certain he knew about it was nearly each and everything in the human body—where it was, and what was its function, its "character." So when he was "told" that a certain society of angelic spirits was located in "the province of the kidneys" [10] of the Grand Man, he was not surprised to learn that the function of these spirits was to separate the false from the true; in a manner of speaking that is what he knew the kidneys did in the physical body of man.

Another instance: certain "interior angels" (the best kind) belonged "in the province of the eye." This, he said, was because the eye "is in the face and proceeds from the brain," evidently the noblest part of the Grand Man. Whereas those who are in "the province of the mouth" were less esteemed, because the mouth was indeed in the face but it was an entrance to the stomach.[11]

This Grand Man whose body was heaven was no small affair. No angel of Swedenborg's acquaintance had ever seen Him, though some claimed to have seen one society in Him, which though itself made up of innumerable individuals also had the general shape of a man. Not only our little earth contributed. "Unless there were innumerable worlds or earths, which together constitute such a

Man, the souls coming from one world or earth would by no means suffice, because there must be infinite varieties, and in every part innumerable spirits to confirm or establish it," so the angels dictated to Swedenborg on March 3, 1748.[12]

Who was in the Grand Man? The angelic societies. Who was outside it? The hells or infernal societies. The qualities of the angelic societies could be known from their position in His body, "in the plane of the head, breast, shoulders, feet," etc., and the qualities of the infernal societies could also be known from their situation "under the soles" or "under the buttocks" of the Grand Man, "in planes in every direction."

Living men too, Swedenborg said, "have a situation either in the Grand Man [that is in heaven] or outside of it in hell. During his life in this world man is not aware of this, but still he is there and is thereby directed." [13]

Through variations in the quality of their feelings spirits might seem to change place, but their ruling love determined the location in or out of the Grand Man to which they inevitably returned. Swedenborg admitted, however, that novitiate spirits wandered about for some time before their characters were sufficiently clear-cut to give them their final abode, or home in the appropriate "province." [14]

This physiological symbolism was carried very far by Swedenborg. He determined the "genera and species" of any spirit by the place in which it seemed to appear or manifest itself in relation to his own body, either inside or outside it. (So and so appeared near the left temple, etc.) "When it is known where spirits are, relatively to the body, it may be known who they are and of what quality." He explained that the spirit was not really "there," of course; it was only an "appearance," to express the situation of that spirit in the Grand Man.[15]

Bad spirits also had their situation which they usually seemed to announce by giving Swedenborg a pain in that part of his body which "corresponded" to their province; and if he had had all the pains in real earnest which he said the spirits gave him he would never have lived to be a hale eighty-four!

(Modern mediums, it may be noted here, often complain of specific pains in their own bodies, which, they say, are really the pains suffered by the communicating spirit just before its passing from this world. Incidentally, Swedenborg says elsewhere that the dead at first relive those things which happened at "the extremity" of their life.)

But Swedenborg's physiological symbolism was also useful to him in providing a mass of similes for the kind of people he had met, whether in or out of the body. Certain ones, he said, were like the "external ligaments" that connect the organs of the body; "they are such as in the life of the body loved to perceive what others thought, or to appear to themselves to perceive it, and when they hear anything they cannot rest, but are carried away by a certain cupidity or passion of the mind for making it known to others with whom they associate, and who, on that account, retain them in their society . . . they [these gossips] think themselves loved, but they are only loved as means for the attainment of ends." [16]

There were also spirits, and men, Swedenborg said, who "correspond" to the nasal mucus. They are those "who make it a rule to cause dissensions . . . divide in order to rule . . . like many politicians . . ." He explained it was because the nasal mucus may obstruct natural breathing and thus could correspond to the breaking of communication between inner and outer things.[17]

"Cuticular spirits" were unduly particular about the care of the skin, and they hated all useful work; they were "adjoined" to similar human beings.[18]

But those who belonged to the province of the colon, "were such as are devoid of mercy, and who without conscience desire to destroy, slay and plunder . . . whether they be men who resist, or boys or women or infants . . . of so ferocious a disposition are they—even as for the most part soldiers and their commanders are." Swedenborg said he had talked about these with other spirits and said they were worse than wild beasts, "which do not in this manner rush on the destruction of their own species."

He said that a "representation" (mental image) of what he was saying reached the celestial angels, and they "were struck with horror that the human race on this earth should be of such a nature, for without seeing the like spectacle it would have appeared incredible to them." "And I also conversed with them [the angels] asking could such souls ever be admitted into heaven where love, mercy and peace prevail?" He also informed the angels that "when such spirits see masses of the slain scattered about, to the number of several thousands, and when they hear the miserable lamentations of the wounded and behold streams of blood covering their bodies, and also themselves and their own swords dipped in human blood, then they are rejoiced at heart and are proud in spirit, boasting and imagining themselves to be heroes; yea, at such a time they sing their Te Deums and nevertheless call themselves Christians."

He excepted from censure men "who defend themselves from their enemies, and wild animals who kill others for necessary food," but for those spirits, in or out of the body, whom he saw as belonging to the province of the colon, he had a few final lines of scorn in this diary entry:

"Men abhor executioners, whose office it is to punish criminals and those sentenced to death; but such as are described above, who are far worse than executioners—since they slay, burn and plunder the innocent without mercy and conscience—are praised, esteemed and raised to honor and dignities." [19]

By this strange way of symbolism did Swedenborg return to his most dearly loved science, physiology, often in the greatest anatomical detail. He applied it also, as had other Kabbalah-influenced men before him, to his Bible exegesis, via this doctrine of the Grand Man, to whose cosmic body he tried to show that numerous references in Genesis and Exodus "corresponded."

It was part of the "occult" lore of the Grand Man that in his all-containing body the spirits from other planets also had their place. As early as in 1748, Swedenborg, the one-time student of astronomy, sought "permission" from the Lord to know "what kind of men they are who live in other planets." [20] He first made the acquaintance of the spirits from "Jupiter." Many entries in his diary, in his abnormal handwriting, are taken up by his descriptions of the appearance, customs, habits, etc. of the spirits from the different planets, as he claimed he observed them on his different visits. He makes it clear he did not believe he flitted bodily around the universe; his body stayed in his bed, he said, while his spirit went through several "changes of state" which enabled him to "travel" into the kind of state in which he could communicate with spirits not of earth, who nevertheless "corresponded" to various universal ideas and feelings.

Swedenborg said that the spirits of Jupiter "represent rational ideas," those of Venus and the earth "corporeal appetites," etc.[21]— the lore had little to do with astronomy, and a good deal to do with astrology, though Swedenborg never admitted that the "stars" could influence human lives. But, if one peers around to see where he could have found the patterns for interpreting these experiences of his, one finds that he had read [22] and greatly admired the so-called *Theology of Aristoteles,* a late Neoplatonic work, filtered through the Arabic into Latin. In that, for instance, "Jupiter souls" were spoken of and a book referred to, which he may also have read, in which it was alleged that "to every people and clime pertain a group of spirits," and in which the regions of the different spirits were mapped out according to planets and zodiac.

It is not possible to trace all the different strands that manifested themselves to Swedenborg as these planetary visits. Some of the "spirits" recall descriptions of primitive tribes. It is at least worth remembering that his cousin Andreas Hesselius had brought back descriptions of American Indians, for a drawing that Swedenborg made of one of the spirit dwellings resembles just the kind of "Quonset" hut which other early travelers had drawn of Indian wigwams.[23] But at any rate, his experiences, whatever they were, he set down in his diary in the "dissociated" handwriting just as they came, at different times, less neatly put together than when he published them separately in 1758.

Another little book that Swedenborg published in 1758 in London had likewise been drawn from the diaries, after having been, like the visits to the planets, filtered through the *Arcana Celestia.* This was the one which had upset Baron Tilas, Swedenborg's account of what he called *The Last Judgment.*

Going back to the diaries, one finds that very early in his otherworld experiences Swedenborg had mentioned that spirits told him the world was in such a bad way, both here and yonder, that some sort of housecleaning, so to speak, was due. It was hinted that this would take place in the world of spirits, the in-between place, because too many evil spirits had banded together and were upsetting not only their own but *our* world, and it seemed as if the time had come when there was no more "charity." Therefore Swedenborg, putting this together with his interpretations of the Apocalypse, believed that the time had come not when the visible world would be destroyed but when the "constructs," so to speak, of evil spirits in the other world would be thrown down.

Furthermore, he needed the Last Judgment. Too many people believed that the dead would not "rise again" until after the Judgment; how was he to convince them unless he could report that it had taken place? Not that Swedenborg for a moment would have consciously deceived anybody even for the most pious of motives, but he was a man who in the most literal sense seems to have been able to see what he wanted to. That is what makes it so extremely difficult to evaluate his experiences.

If the spirit of man can survive the death of the body—and modern psychical research offers some evidence which tends in that direction—then many of Swedenborg's reported experiences may have a basis in objective fact, but even so there may be others of his reports which have a basis only in his "phantasy" for various psychological reasons. The strange thing is that he was so fully aware of this trickery of the unconscious—in others, and those others he said were "spirits."

Again and again he cited cases where he had noticed spirits projecting their thoughts and fancies and seeing them, even suffering from them, as if they were real. A fine example is in a diary entry where he mentions seeing a man he had known, now a companion of Charles XII in the spirit world. This man, Swedenborg said, saw many things which he insisted were magnificent "when, nevertheless, there was not anything; for whatever occurs to his thought, this he sees as if it were real."

That this kind of fantasy could take place on a continued and large scale Swedenborg also admitted, for he said, in the same entry: "Afterwards Charles XII became like this; and he said that he sees all thoughts in forms, at one time armies and battles, at another other marvellous things, exactly according to the thought of his spirit; and that he took delight in them, just as he delighted in his thoughts, even filthy ones. It was also stated that others near him did not see anything." [24]

It is to be doubted—unless Swedenborg had "helpers" in the other world—whether his visions of the downfall of "Babylon," etc., were seen by anyone else. He explained very reasonably that by Babylon he meant all those who desire to dominate by means of religion, and some of his descriptions of priest-ridden communities on high mountains being toppled over into chaos have a curious atom-bomb reality, but one is grateful that he seems to have ceased having those visions. At any rate they also served the purpose of being sufficiently startling to draw attention to his seemingly more objective reports of the other world, which he sandwiched in the little book of *The Last Judgment.*

Swedenborg repeated his accounts of the other world in all the theological and semi-theological books he wrote, under whatever name they appeared, with, on the whole, enough consistency and not too much. But it is in the day-by-day entries in his diaries of other-world experiences that his "reports" have the most factual air, blended though many of them are with obvious projections from his unconscious and with sheer dream-stuff, which he did not bother always to label dream-stuff. But he did not publish it.

In the later diaries names of actual personages appear. The one who appears most frequently was the King whom he had met in his youth, the man who had had his fate in his hands, King Charles XII. In the 1730's, Swedenborg had written a public appreciation [25] of the King's keen mind, his encouragement of and love for science —from which no one would guess how Swedenborg saw the King in the other world!

Pithily commenting on the King's nature, as it seemed revealed, Swedenborg said that Charles "made royalty consist in obstinacy even to death," and that the spirits who aided him in such an attitude were from another universe, "for such obstinacy does not exist within the limits of this planet." Charles, he said, had been "pitiless and cruel, caring nothing for human life." And though he had lost his country believing this to be for its glory, "he ought to be considered insane." [26]

Swedenborg acknowledged Charles's ability to take in a hundred things at a single glance, and to draw correct deductions, "in relation to his end which was dominion"; he acknowledged that Charles thought himself a good man, but, after about a year in the other world, he was stripped of his self-deceit and appeared as he really was—a devil.

Twelve hours after the execution of the Swedish noble Eric Brahe for conspiracy, Swedenborg says he spoke with this acquaintance of his. Eric Brahe had made a most edifying end, professing saving faith, but, "after two days he began to return to his former state of life, which was to love worldly things, and after three days he became just as he previously was in the world." [27]

Polhem, Swedenborg's old teacher, died on a Monday. "He spoke with me on Thursday," Swedenborg notes, when he was at Polhem's funeral. Polhem saw "his coffin and those who were there and the whole procession, and also when his body was laid in the grave; and in the meanwhile he spoke with me, asking me why they buried him when he was still alive . . . besides many other things." It is to be hoped for the sake of the other attendants that Swedenborg did not answer out loud, for he said himself in his diary that sometimes when he was in conversation with spirits he forgot that he was in the body because his attention was not centered on the body. [28]

Newton he said he had a very pleasant chat with, very happy that Newton was "among his own and is beloved." [29]

And in 1759, on the thirteenth day of September, near the eighth hour, Swedenborg had a rare experience in the spirit world, an experience which undoubtedly would also there be labeled "dabbling in the occult." Swedenborg saw a spirit, he said, go into a sleep, or trance, in order to visit a man in this world. The spirit, by means of showing Swedenborg a "representation" of Versailles and other things, conveyed that he was King Louis XIV of France, then he fell into this kind of sleep. When he awakened he told Swedenborg that he had shown himself in a vision to King Louis XV, who was in bed, and exhorted him to desist from applying the papal bull "Unigenitus" against the Jansenists, telling him he must entirely abandon it, or misfortune would befall him. [30]

Louis XV had, so it seems, been eagerly supporting the Jesuits against the Jansenists and therefore the Bull "Unigenitus," making it the law of the land since 1756, and enforcing it through the year 1759. After that he stopped enforcing it, and expelled the Jesuits, his former favorites from France. [31]

In the diary notes as in the books, Swedenborg maintained that out of the knowledge and experience man obtained here on earth he could literally build his own heaven and hell. Thoughts were substantial things, in a sense. All the books a man had read, all the sights he had seen, all his sense impressions indeed, were still his, and under certain circumstances could again, at least for a while, become his consciously in the forms, or even better, under which he had enjoyed them. If people had enough memories in common, cities appeared. He noted libraries, public and private, which, naturally, Swedenborg visited. "There was a vast number who studied the books, and some of them become learned, many intelligent, and others wise." [32]

Every kind of activity of human beings could be found in the other world, only they were subject to the law of "correspondence." Not man's mere wish decided what he was to experience in that world, but his character. Houses, garments, gardens, all might change or disappear, if the spirit yielded to evil thoughts, and these again created their own dire punishments.

Both charming and fantastic vignettes can be culled from Swedenborg's diaries—subjects for artists of imagination. Once he said he saw a little girl of five or six, beautifully clothed, walking on a path in a garden full of leafy arches, and when she entered, "the most exquisite garlands of flowers sprung forth over the entrance and shone with splendor as she approached." New garments according to her perfection were given her, and although these things were not of course "real," Swedenborg said, "for spirits cannot either possess or walk on gravelled paths," yet "it is sufficient that they perceive them as vividly, yea more vividly than men perceive similar things in gardens in this world, as I have also perceived them when I was in the spirit . . ." [33]

Idle rich women, he said, those who suffer themselves to be served like queens by a retinue of servants, "having no concern about any use . . . but living in luxury and idleness, lolling on sofas, adorning themselves, presiding at entertainments and thus spending their lives—the punishment of such women in the other life is dreadful." According to the law that like attracts like, they are put with women of the same kind. This works well for a while, they keep up appearances, but "they soon begin to strike, to bruise and to tear each other in the most miserable manner, plucking each other by the hair of the head in a manner so dreadful that one cannot endure the sight." [34]

Swedenborg said he had conversed with comedians in the other world—he was fond of the theatre—and he had found that because they "could simulate everything or seize upon and represent it in such a dextrous manner that it could scarcely be distinguished from the original," they were used by their respective "societies" as "mediums of lively representation"—meaning that they were experts at making thoughts and images visible. As to their character he remarked, "They were not evil nor were they easily excited to anger. When anyone inveighed against them, they seemed to take no notice of it at the time though they spoke about it afterwards. They can be led both by the evil and the good . . . Although they speak tolerably well, yet they have but little life of their own." [35]

Courtesy in others was noticed by Swedenborg (his own was often mentioned by people who knew him) and he spoke with delight of certain societies in the spirit world which he called civil, or polite, societies.

"Living in their own agreeable and pleasant sphere, they fear no one, and when any spirit not good approaches, they speak civilly to him as one who is too good to say or do aught that is amiss; such a spirit is then himself also reduced into a civil state"; apparently he then either behaves himself or else departs.

Swedenborg admits that the charming spirits perform civil offices to everyone, not perhaps so truly from the heart as from the mouth; they may say to a guest that his coming is grateful and acceptable, when they really have other business in hand and wish for his departure. But still, he says, they do not falsify from any desire to deceive or do evil; they were brought up so in the life of the body, and "they are a good kind of spirits." [36]

Music, Swedenborg often noted, had great power; even the restless and angry spirits of the lower societies could be soothed into a mild doze by it, during which they might even catch a glimpse of one of the heavens, because their egos would be temporarily lulled into abeyance. [37]

Of the higher heavens Swedenborg said little except to hint that he had had glimpses of their inexpressible felicities, their unimaginable light. There even the necessity for hallucinating oneself a body seems to have vanished, though blissful consciousness remained; but in the lowest realms of the spirit world the inhabitants attempt to carry out "the lowest functions of the body."

In the societies of the lower heavens, he often said, the spirits, although they may reproduce seeming earth conditions, experience a flow and a change in themselves and their environments according to their ethical state. Their houses, gardens, clothes, even faces, vary. If evil or insincerity had crept into their minds "when they go out, the garden products seem to have either vanished or changed as regards varieties, or beauty or brightness." Then they begin to think about what they may have thought or done, and if they repent, "the former loveliness returns. Spots on their clothes call for another examination of conscience, before the garments are again lustrous, white or roseate," and "maidens are also admonished through changes of beauty in the face." [38]

Swedenborg said he "wondered exceedingly" that spirits and angels noticed these curious aspects of their life so little, but he concluded it was because they did not "reflect" on them, or, as we might say, no externally acquired knowledge from material things reminded them that once life was not in such a flux.

Modern psychical researchers sometimes stop measuring "quantitative phenomena" and speculate on what life apart from the body might be like. Whately Carington thinks that

It seems reasonable to suppose that after death the mind, no longer held up against the physical world by the incoming stimuli, will be much more free to indulge its own sequence of thought and fantasy, as in reverie, only more so; but that interaction with other minds will later take the place of the previously body-mediated relation to the physical world. In other words, what I might term mental or psychical objects, conforming to psychical laws, will take the place of the material objects conforming to physical laws which make up the mundane environment.

Mr. Carington had not read Swedenborg.[39] Indeed, Swedenborg's convictions as to the illusory reality of the other world he only wrote about explicitly in his private notebooks, no doubt because, as he said, "to write about more than men can receive is to sow in water."

The last date on the last page of his so-called *Spiritual Diary* is April 29, 1765. After that he put his other-world experiences into his published books under the name of "memorable relations." He did not bother much to explain them in such terms that people would clearly understand they were not supposed to deal with material heavens and hells. These little stories are more like mosaics of what he considered facts than they are like "factual" reports. They evidently are written to support his pleas for men to live not only according to civic and moral laws but according to the spiritual laws which Swedenborg considered he had seen in irresistible action in both worlds.

CHAPTER TWENTY-THREE

Stories from Beyond

BY 1765, seventy-seven years old, Swedenborg was well under way with the formulation of that body of spiritual laws which is also known as a religion—no more original with him than with other mystics, but stamped of course with his personality and the circumstances that had formed him. This was to be the religion of the New Church or the New Jerusalem, not at all another dissenting sect but a set of "doctrines" or teachings that were meant to be cleansing and revivifying to all "churches"—all condensations of man's spiritual endeavors, which Swedenborg sometimes simply called "the church."

As he saw it, whenever "the church" became corrupt, it was largely because of overwhelmingly bad influences from the spirit world, and men's giving in to them. Then there had to be a "judgment" in the spirit world, not necessarily the last, though it was so called. There had been several such, Swedenborg said. After the one he insists he observed in 1757, he believed that man was much freer to think spiritually (he had after all seen the eighteenth century burst many orthodox bonds), and Swedenborg used the new freedom to come out openly against what now seemed to him the wicked doctrine of the vicarious atonement and the bewildering, faith-choking doctrine of the Trinity. He also attacked the Lutheran doctrine, as he saw it, of "faith" as sufficient for salvation. (If he called the Roman Catholics "Babylon" for what he considered their lust of dominion over men's souls, he called the Protestants "Philistia" for their "faith without works" and general self-righteousness, as well as other striking names.)

The English reception of the five books which Swedenborg had published in London in 1758, those drawn from the *Arcana Celestia,* had been discouraging. When he had his new books nearly ready for the press he went with them to Amsterdam, in 1762, left them with the printer, returned to Stockholm the same year, and went again to Amsterdam with more copy in 1763,[1] having, in the meantime, sent a paper on the process of inlaying marble tables to the Swedish Academy of Sciences, of which he was a member.

In 1763 and 1764 his new theological works, the Four Doctrines, appeared in Amsterdam, but in the same years he published two books of "angelic wisdom" (meaning that "angels" had dictated them to him), one called *The Divine Providence* and another *Divine Love and Wisdom*.[2] These two are perhaps the most beautiful of his works, not too tangled up with Bible exigesis. In them he showed himself to be a worthy descendant of Plato, through Plotinus and the Areopagite. And, indeed, with very few changes, the "Lord" of Swedenborg in these books could be the Brahman of the Upanishads or the Nirmanakaya of the Sutras or the Krishna of the Bhagavad-Gita.

But, in *The Apocalypse Revealed,* published in Amsterdam in 1766, he returned to his special explanation of the Bible by means of "internal sense" and "correspondences." It was not his first boring into the Apocalypse; he had already treated of it in an unfinished manuscript of vast proportions, *The Apocalypse Explained*. One was enlivened with "memorable relations." In the same year he sent an old love of his to press again; it was his *New Method of Finding the Longitude of Places on Land and at Sea*.[3]

Swedenborg, in his late seventies and with the travel conditions of that time, spared himself no trouble. As censorship prevented his getting his works published in Sweden (or even importing them, except with difficulty) he went back and forth. After returning to Amsterdam in 1763, he went over to England, hopefully delivering the printed books to the Royal Society, then he returned to Sweden over Denmark in 1764. In 1765 he took the *Apocalypse* to Holland, visited England from there in 1766, and returned to Stockholm the same year.[4]

Great traveler as he was, even on this earth, it is mainly from his diary observations on what he felt he saw in the other world that we learn what he thought of various nations. For, according to him, especially just before the "Last Judgment," the spirits had clustered together in nations and in cities, following their inveterate habits.

The Dutch, whom he loved with a kind of exasperated affection, he saw as still concerned with business and wealth; very crafty and taciturn in their designs, most incredulous as to things of the spirit, but also most constant to them if the truth had once dawned on them. Yet, tenacious, stubborn, secretive people was his opinion of them.

In spite of the fact that the English had been anything but welcoming of his freely distributed books, he seems to have liked them best of any. Why, he asked, have they such a capacity for seeing and for following truth? He thought it was free speech. There was liberty in England, he said, to speak both about civil and church matters, but no liberty at all to cheat, murder, or rob. In Italy, on the other hand, there was almost entire liberty to cheat and kill "on account of there being so many sanctuaries," but no freedom at all to speak and write about the matters so openly discussed by Englishmen. Hence the fire of evil smoldered inwardly in the Italians, whereas with the English it flared up and burnt out "because it is conceded to them to speak and write freely." [5]

Swedenborg regarded the English as the best and the most sincere of the Christians. Alas, in his opinion, the same could not be said about the Swedes. He blamed them for being only externally sincere, for being envious and revengeful, and he attributed this to the fact that, not being a wealthy nation, they sought eminence by way of public office, seeking to govern others, either for honor or for profit.[6] And "in the love of governing there dwells contempt, enmity, envy, hatred, revenge, ferocity, cruelty."

He visited cities too in the other world. Incidentally there was one "on the edge of Gehenna," which with its cloud-capped buildings with many windows, square blocks, and dark streets sounded not too unlike New York[7] (after all, time is not a factor in the other world!). In London, this time the best people were in the East End.

But he also came into Stockholm. Being escorted by an angel through Stora Nygatan, he was told that if the inhabitants of the houses were spiritually dead no lighted windows would appear there, but only dark holes. So it was. The angels shuddered and said they could go no farther, all in that street were dead. At the market place scarcely anyone was living, except in one house at the corner, nor in many other streets. Yet all the houses were full of people, he was told, and if evil spirits had been there they would have seen lighted windows and people at them.[8]

Swedenborg was also told about the citizens of Stockholm that "they care for nothing except to hear what happens in the city, and outside the city, as for instance, who was with me . . ."

"Who was with me . . ." This was written about the time when Stockholm had recently discovered that Assessor Swedenborg had, as Baron Tilas put it, conversations with the dead whenever he chooses, and the word went around that now the dead Senator Ehrenpreuss had been with him, now Count Gyllenborg, now Baron Horlemann, and now, forsooth, he claimed he had talked with Luther![9]

It is understandable that Stockholm wanted to know who was with him. By 1764 Gjörwell, the librarian of the Royal Library, was so curious that, although he did not know Swedenborg, he called on him, putting down the impressions he received the same day.

Gjörwell found Swedenborg in his garden, simply dressed and tending to his plants. He offered to show the librarian the garden before he knew who he was or what was his purpose. Gjörwell's ostensible purpose was to procure Swedenborg's books for the Royal Library, which the latter readily agreed to. "My purpose," he said, "in publishing them has been to make them known and to place them in the hands of intelligent people."

Then he showed his visitor the garden and as they walked among the lindens and roses, box and carnations, Gjörwell drew from Swedenborg by "polite questions" and by not being too challenging, some statements in regard to his system of theology. As Gjörwell reported them, Swedenborg said "that faith alone is a pernicious doctrine, and that good works are the proper means for becoming better in time and for leading a blessed life in eternity. That in order to acquire the ability or power to do good works prayer to the only God is required and that man also must labor with himself, because God does not use compulsion with us; nor does he work any miracles for our conversion." Man must live temperately and piously. "He also said that Doctor Luther was at the present time in a state of suffering in the other world; simply on account of having introduced the doctrine of faith alone; although he is not among the damned."

Gjörwell noted other things, among them that Swedenborg did not mention the doctrine of the atonement, which shows that Swedenborg was not telling everything he believed to a stranger, hesitating to express his horror at what he considered an immoral slander on God.

He said that "when a man dies his soul does not divest itself of its peculiarities," on which, Gjörwell reports, he could not refrain from asking with what Professor D. Nils Wallerius now busied himself. "He still goes about," Swedenborg said, "and holds disputations."

He also told Gjörwell that he enjoyed supernatural sight and hearing and could speak with the departed and with angels. Also ' that God had revealed Himself to him in May, 1744, in London (this might be what is called a memory displacement for the Delft vision of April that year), and that since this time God had been preparing him for the reception of a new revelation. This "light" which it was his mission to reveal consisted in this, that "a New Jerusalem is to be established on earth; the meaning of which is, that a New Church is at hand, about the nature of which and the way to enter it his writings really treat."

Swedenborg said nothing to Gjörwell about a reinterpretation of the Bible as his mission; clearly this had sunk into being a secondary task, the chief task as he saw it being the introduction of a more ethical system of religion, for which the vision had now become the supreme authority.

He also told Gjörwell that since the vision he had been in constant communication with God "whom he sees before his eyes like a sun" (a reference no doubt to Swedenborg's belief that the "sun" which he saw in heaven was in reality the "sphere" that emanated from the Lord).

"About all this," Gjörwell recorded, "he spoke with a perfect conviction, laying particular stress on these words: 'All this I see and know without becoming the subject of any visions and without being a fanatic; but when I am alone my soul is as it were out of the body and in the other world; in all respects I am in a visible man-

ner there as I am here. But when I think of what I am about to
write, and while I am in the act of writing, I enjoy a perfect inspiration; for otherwise it would be my own; but now I know for
certain that what I write is the living truth of God." [10]

Into such certainty Swedenborg's experience that tremulous night
in Delft had now crystallized. He was unshakable on two points:
that God had entrusted him with a mission, and that he had his
"memorable relations" from first-hand observations in the other
world.

After Swedenborg's death, his friend Count A. J. von Höpken
said about these memorable relations: "I could wish the happy
deceased had left them out as they may prevent infidelity from
approaching his doctrines. I represented to him these inconve-
niences, but he said he was commanded to declare what he had
seen in the other world; and he related it as a proof that he did
not reveal his own thoughts, but that they came from above." [11]
In other words, understandably though illogically, Swedenborg
continued to feel, as he had in 1745, that the "reality" of his other-
world experiences—seeing people he knew—guaranteed the reality
of his religious visions.

At any rate, when a new book came from Swedenborg, *Conjugial Love,* published in Amsterdam, 1768, he yielded not a fraction of his claims, let his friends deplore it or not.

The very first lines were: "I am aware that many who read the
following pages and the memorable relations annexed to the chapters will believe that they are fictions of the imagination; but I
solemnly declare that they are not fictions but were truly done or
seen; and that I saw them not in any state of the mind asleep, but
in a state of perfect wakefulness . . ."

After which he again claimed that he had a mission from the
Lord to teach about a New Church, and he reaffirmed that he had
been able to be in the spiritual world with angels and at the same
time in the natural world with men, "and this now for twenty-five
years."

Then he plunged into a memorable relation, so long as to be
almost a short novel. It was so brilliantly suited to jolting the com-
placence of his fellow-Christians that only his truthfulness prevents
one from thinking it a conscious "fiction of the imagination."

Höpken was right, these "memorabilia" do present a stumbling block. They are too well suited to their expressed purpose to have just happened as Swedenborg perambulated the heavens. In fact he expressly says of one of them that it was "written against Dr. Ernesti," a German theologian who had attacked him.[12] But he also describes just how it took place in the spirit world, Dr. Ernesti being represented by one of the spirits "adjoined" to him. In this particular case the easier way out is to suppose that Swedenborg did what he so often said the spirits did; he saw and heard what he wanted to see and hear, by means of "phantasy." Likewise when he described how he heard discussions in the spirit world between disciples of Aristotle, Descartes and Leibnitz,[13] and so forth. Vivid and circumstantial though these accounts are, they prove too obviously what Swedenborg wants them to prove.

Of course this could be said of all his other-world experiences. But there is a vast difference between the hesitating, fragmentary, feeling-his-way notations of the diary, mixed as they are with stuff evidently from his unconscious, and the posed recitals of the later books. Yet many of these recitals contain elements that one recognizes from his diary notes, so that Swedenborg might feel he was in his right to say the stories were true, since he had made them up out of actual observations. (Many a good reporter has made up a nice, connected story out of events that happened, but not at the same time and place as represented.)

Swedenborg was in the spirit world one day, so the story at the beginning of *Conjugial Love* starts, when he saw an angel who told him the other members of his society could not believe that among the Christians in the spirit world such crass ignorance prevailed as to the real nature of the joys of heaven. They said to the angel messenger that he must go to the spirit world and collect newly arrived spirits, find out what were their ideas of heavenly happiness and then give it to them, for "You know that everyone that has desired heaven . . . is introduced after death into those particular joys which he had imagined . . ."

Six companies of spirits were selected "among the wisest," and they were brought to their "heavens," where were "those who in the former world had had the same conception of the joys of heaven."

The first company thought that heavenly joy consisted solely of "most delightful companionship and most agreeable conversation." They were brought to a spacious house with more than fifty rooms. "In some of the rooms they were talking about such things as they had seen and heard in public places and in the streets; in some they talked of the various loveliness of the fair sex; intermingled with pleasantries, which increased until the countenances of all in the company expanded with smiles of merriment; in other rooms they talked of news of the court, about the ministries, state polity, various matters which had become known from privy councils; together with reasonings and conjectures respecting the events; in others they talked of business; in others on literary subjects; in others of such things as pertain to civil prudence and to moral life; in others about ecclesiastical affairs and the sects, and so on."

Swedenborg says that it was given him to look into that house, and he noted that among those running from room to room there were three kinds: some panting to speak; some longing to make inquiries, and others eager to learn. But then he said he noticed that many left the rooms and made for the exits. There he found them sitting in sadness and he asked why. "They answered, 'the doors of this house are kept closed to those who wish to go out, and it is now the third day since we entered and we have lived the life of our desire for company and conversation, and are utterly wearied with continual talking, insomuch that we can scarcely bear to hear the murmur of their sound.'" But they had been told that they must stay and enjoy the delights of heaven. "'From which answer we infer that we must continue here to eternity. This is the cause of the sadness that has entered our minds; and now our hearts begin to be oppressed and anxiety rises!'"

Then the relieving angel came and told them that heavenly joy "is the delight of doing something that is useful to ourselves and to others; . . . there are most joyous companionships in the heavens which gladden the minds of angels, amuse their spirits, fill their bosoms with delight and revive their bodies; but they enjoy these delights when they have performed the uses of their employments and occupations. From these are the soul and life in all their joys and pleasures; but if you take away this soul or life the accessory joys successively become no joys, but become at first indifferent, then as if frivolous, and finally bring sadness and anxiety."

After these words of the angel, Swedenborg says, "the door was opened and those sitting near sprang out and fled to their homes, every one to his employment and to his occupation, and revived."

The second company of spirits had the idea that heaven consisted in feasting with Abraham, Isaac, and Jacob and with the Apostles. On being introduced into their heaven, they thought they met these venerable personages, with their wives, and were delighted that they were going to feast with each one in turn, and that after the feasting, as they had also expected and wanted, there would be "sports and public shows" and then feasting again, and so on.

Hardly necessary to say that after a few days the aspirants said "Food has become inspid to us, we have lost relish for it; our stomachs loathe it; we cannot bear to taste it." "We have dragged on some days and nights in this luxury and beg earnestly that we may be permitted to go away." And then "they with rapid pace and panting breath fled to their homes."

Not, however, without first receiving a little homily by the angel, who told them that in heaven there were feastings, and music and song, and sport but that there was only happiness in those joys because of work well done.

The desires of the third company of spirits was to have the promise of the Bible literally carried out that they should reign with Christ forever. They expected to be kings and princes.

So they were introduced to their thrones and scepters and had crowns for their heads, and young men who seemed to be angels from heaven flew to them to wait on them. And they sat and they sat, until a voice from heaven cried out to them some timely warnings about their folly in preferring to be idols rather than men.

Emanuel Swedenborg may not have been thinking of his father's autobiography, but certainly Bishop Swedberg had stated in it that he knew when he got to heaven his guardian angel would have his throne and his crown ready for him, there to sit forever.

And the fourth company were very sure that heaven ought to be a wonderful garden, a paradise. They found it, a place in which as they expected "there is entire rest from labor, and that this rest

is nothing else than . . . walking upon roses, gladdened with the
most delicious juice of grapes and celebrating festive banquets . . .
[they saw] a vast multitude . . . sitting three by three and ten by
ten upon beds of roses, weaving garlands," adorning each other,
"or plucking fruit or smelling flowers, or singing or playing with
fountains, or dancing . . ."

Of course the result was the same. The angel found the weary
ones weeping among "an abundance of olives, grapes, oranges and
lemons" which made them sick.

There was the fifth company—they had supposed heaven to be
perpetual glorious worship of God, and they were led to a "sacred
city," where they were to listen to sermons and worship God in
the temple, and then, after three days of this, to continue the same
in each of the buildings and in communion "pray, shout and recite
sermons."

The finish of that experiment was "Our ears are stunned. End
your preaching, we no longer hear a word and are beginning to
loathe the sound." They had stood it for two days. And angels from
heaven spoke to the ministers who had preached for so long, telling them that they fed their sheep "even to insanity. You do not
know what is meant by the glorification of God. It means to bring
forth the fruits of love; that is faithfully, sincerely and diligently to
do the work of one's employment—for this is of love to God and
of love to the neighbor. And this is the bond of society and its good.
By this God is glorified and then by worship at stated times."

The sixth company had believed that they would by divine grace
be admitted into heaven where they would be surrounded by "an
aura of felicities." They told how they tried to ascend to heaven.
Each had a different experience. One got as far as inside a heaven
when he heard the angels say, "What is this monster? How came
this bird of night here?" and he was quickly ushered out, saying
that he felt he had been changed in appearance although to himself he still looked a man.

Others who had tried to force an entry found that instead of joy
they were tortured by heavenly light and heat, or were like animals
in a vacuum or fish on land. Now they only wanted "common life
with their like, wherever they are."

Upon which the angel delivered a lecture on heaven not being a

fixed environment or program of events, but a state that "corresponded" or was really created by the spiritual state of the inhabitants. Naturally those who did not correspond were unhappy, even
suffered torture, by "the violence of activity of opposite against
opposite."

Nevertheless the angel received orders from his society that by
the Lord's permission ten persons out of the whole assembly were
to be chosen, and they would be enabled to visit a real community
of a real heaven for three days.

Swedenborg enjoyed describing that visit. The gardens and the
gorgeousness and the stately processions and the superb palaces and
entertainment—it was all there, but as the Prince of the Society said
to his guests—they were reclining at his table at a banquet—"You
have seen now that all your joys are joys of heaven also, and are
more exquisite than ever you could have thought; and yet these do
not affect our minds interiorly." For they were governed, he said,
by a strand of three that flowed in from the Lord: Love, Wisdom
and Use. The two first did not really appear except as they were
together "in bodily act and work," and this, as had indeed by this
time been sufficiently emphasized, was what kept the angels from
becoming bored with joy.

Sight-seeing later in the heavenly community, the visitors noticed that "at the sides in the outlying parts of the city are various
games for boys and youths; there are games of running; games of
ball; games with balls driven back and forth called tennis," and
debates, and "many other games for calling forth the latent abilities of boys." And there were theaters too, that gave moral performances. The public orchestras had male and female singers as
well as instruments, indeed the main diversion of the girls seemed
to be song. But they also got married. Only once, however, for in
heaven first their spirits were united with their bridegrooms and
then their bodies. The visitors attended a wedding, but the six
virgins present would not speak with them. Being questioned by
the angel guide as to why they so suddenly withdrew, they said,
"We do not know. But we perceived something that repelled us and
drove us back. They must excuse us."

The angel returned to the visitors and said, "I surmise that you
have not a chaste love of the sex. In heaven we love virgins for their

beauty and loveliness of manner, and we love them exceedingly but chastely."

The visitors smiled at this, and said, "You have guessed rightly. Who is able to behold such beauty near and feel no desire?"

The three days were up, and the visitors were escorted back to their society in the spirit world, where they presumably told their wives about the members of this "Society of the Eagle," whose very clothes they could have described. For, Swedenborg says, "The prince was clad in a long purple robe, embroidered with stars the color of silver; under the robe he wore a tunic of shining silk of a violet color. This was open at the breast, where the front part of a kind of belt was seen, bearing the badge of his society. The badge was an eagle on the top of a tree, brooding over her young. This was of shining gold in a circle of diamonds. The chief counselors were not very differently attired, but without the badge in place of which were graven sapphires pendent from the neck by a chain of gold. The courtiers were in togas of chestnut brown into which were woven flowers encircling young eagles. The tunics under them were of opaline silk, as were also their breeches and stockings. Such was their apparel."

But if the account of the visit to heaven finished with a marriage it was because the new book was at least ostensibly about marriage.

CHAPTER TWENTY-FOUR

Marriages in Heaven

THE new book had a long but promising title: *The Delights of Wisdom pertaining to Conjugial Love, after which follow The Pleasures of Insanity pertaining to Scortatory Love,* and it was signed by Emanuel Swedenborg, A Swede, the first of his books since his scientific publications that he had signed. (In plain English "scortatory" means whorish.)

But the book was also about his religious ideas and about his observations in the other world. When Dr. Beyer wrote to him, asking him about certain attributes of God, Swedenborg answered that he would write further about these when he was dealing with angelic wisdom concerning conjugial love. He was fully aware that too many abstractions were not readable by most people, for as he said to Beyer, "To write a separate treatise on these Divine attributes without the assistance of something to support them would cause too great an elevation of the thoughts, wherefore these subjects have been treated in a series with other things which fall within the understanding." [1]

These other things in the present book were certainly if not within the understanding at least very much within the interests of everybody, for here Swedenborg frankly gave his views on love and sex, and love versus sex, in and out of marriage, on earth and in the other world.

As Baron Tilas had written, gossip in Stockholm mentioned that Swedenborg claimed there was marriage in heaven, and gossip was right. Tilas was "all in a flutter" for fear his deceased wife might have remarried, and he might well be. According to Swedenborg if the Baroness had not been united with him in "conjugial" love (the word "conjugial" is peculiar to Swedenborg) the chances were that she either had or would eventually find not only a mate for her soul but one who would be a mate of her body as well, when she had advanced so far as one of the heavens.

Except for certain forms of Hinduism or Tantric Buddhism, it is doubtful if in any advanced form of religion so much stress has been laid on the symbolic significance of sex. In Swedenborg's philosophy "good and truth" (or love and wisdom) are united, or married, so as to form "one" in the Lord, or, as he sometimes says, good and truth *are* the Lord. Therefore, he says, "a universal conjugial sphere proceeds from the Lord and pervades the universe from its first things to its last, thus from angels even to worms." [2] It is the same, he says, as the "sphere of propagation." But as it is the sphere of propagation, "it follows that from this comes the love of the sex." It flows differently into all the different forms of the universe. In man "as he increases in wisdom his form is perfected; and this form receives, not the love of the sex, but the love of one of the sex," and that enables him to be united with heaven. If "the form of his mind" doesn't progress toward intelligence and from intelligence to wisdom, he can receive the influx of the universal sphere of sex "no otherwise than as the lower subjects of the animal kingdom." [3]

Swedenborg's marriage mysticism, which he elaborates in great detail and works into his theology, may have stemmed partly from his own longing for an ideal marriage or it may have been another one of the topics that he received via automatic writing—there are conversations on the subject with angels recorded in the diary—or it may have been both. (The great modern Hebrew scholar Gershom G. Scholem has pointed out that certain Kabbalists used sexual imagery to describe the union of God and His "Shekhinah" —the feminine element in God—and saw this union as "the central fact in the whole chain of divine manifestations in the hidden world.") [39]

At any rate the long new book with the alluring title contained a great deal of shrewd wisdom about the relations of men and women, whether in or out of this world. Swedenborg was not afraid of "the flesh." When asked in the other world as to whether marriages were not "doings of the flesh," he said, "Are they not also deeds of the spirit? And what the flesh does from the spirit is it not spiritual?" [4]

That, in brief, was his philosophy of sex.

"I once saw three spirits recently deceased," he told in this book, "who were wandering about in the world of spirits, examining whatever came their way and inquiring concerning it. They were all amazement to find that men lived altogether as before. . . they by turns viewed and touched themselves and others, and felt the surrounding objects, and by a thousand proofs convinced themselves that they were now men as in the former world; besides which they saw each other in a brighter light . . ."

Two angelic spirits talked with them and the newcomers were curious to hear about heaven. "As two of the three newcomers were youths there darted from their eyes a sparkling fire of lust for the sex," and the angelic spirit said, "Possibly you have seen some women?" They admitted it, and asked if there were any in heaven. The angelic spirits said there were youths and maidens in heaven. Was the human form, the newcomers inquired, altogether similar to that in the natural world? Nothing was wanting, they were told, either in the man or the woman. "Retire, if you please," they said to the youths, "and examine whether you are not a complete man as before."

"Is there then the love of the sex there?"

"Not your love of the sex," they were told, "in heaven we have the angelic love of the sex, which is chaste and devoid of libidinous allurement."

"If there be a love of the sex devoid of all allurement," the youths observed, "what in such case is the love of the sex?" And they sighed, and said, "Oh how dry and insipid is the joy of heaven! What young man if this be the case can possibly wish for heaven?"

The angelic spirits smiled and explained that it was a kind of exchange of pure celestial sweets, tone of voice, eyes, gestures, speech, but the newcomers declared, "What is a chaste love of the sex but a love deprived of the essence of its life . . . we are not stocks and stones . . ."

They were told by the angelic spirits that angelic chastity common to each sex prevented their chaste love from descending below the heart. Yet it was an indescribably joyous and abundant delight, and they possessed it because they had conjugial love only, which was a love of the spirit and thence of the body, not a love infesting the spirit.

The two young men grasped at the straw. "There still exists in heaven a love of the sex—what else is conjugial love?"

"That," they heard, "is not love of the sex, but love of one of the sex." It went from the soul to the mind, to the body, "and thus becomes love in its fullness." The angelic spirits added, "In heaven they are in total ignorance of what whoredom is . . . with the male all the nerves lose their proper tension at the sight of a harlot, and recover it again at the sight of a wife."

The newcomers, now all attention, asked, "Does a similar love exist between married partners in the heavens as in the earths?"

Altogether similar, the angelic spirits said, even to "the ultimate delights," but it was "much more blessed because angelic perception and sensation is much more exquisite than human . . ." Furthermore, the only offspring was an increase in both partners of love and wisdom, ". . . hence it is that angels after such delights do not experience sadness as some do on earth, but are cheerful . . ." also because their powers continually refreshed themselves, "for all who come into heaven return into their vernal youth and into the vigor of that age . . ."

The three newcomers, Swedenborg says, were "made glad by this intelligence," and fired with a—new-found—desire for heaven and with the hope of heavenly nuptials, they declared they meant to lead a chaste life, "that we may realize the enjoyment of our wishes." [5]

The hope of reward, needless to say, was not Swedenborg's idea of the right reason for morality, but here he was speaking to the kindergarten.

Like a primer too, with answers to many questions from people he knew, is the account he gives of what he saw as happening to earth-marriages after death. Explaining that for some time in the world of spirits, man behaves outwardly as he always did, he says that married partners come together again and live together until their real inclinations manifest themselves, "and if it be in mutual agreement and sympathy they continue to live together a conjugial life, but if it be in disagreement and antipathy their marriage is dissolved."

In cases where a man had been married several times he lives with his wives in the same order that he did on earth, but only while he is still in the "external" state. When he has been induced into sincerity, "He either adopts one or leaves them all." The same with women, but, "It is to be observed that husbands rarely know their wives, but that wives well know their husbands, women having an interior perception of love and men only an exterior."

Separations take place after death, because so many marriages in the natural world are made for geographic reasons or for ambition or purely of the body, "when yet it is the conjunction of souls which constitutes a real marriage."

"All those married partners who are merely natural are separated after death." (Here as nearly always Swedenborg means by "natural" those who are without any real love.) "Married partners of whom one is spiritual and the other natural are also separated after death; and to the spiritual is given a suitable married partner; whereas the natural one is sent to the resorts of the lascivious among his like." [6]

Those celibates who "have altogether alienated their minds from marriage" remain single if spiritual, but if natural they become "whoremongers" in the lower world. As to monks and nuns, they are given their choice. If they really prefer celibacy, "they are conveyed to those who live in celibacy on the side of heaven." This, Swedenborg says (with perhaps the greatest compliment a bachelor ever paid to marriage) is because the sphere of perpetual celibacy disturbs that of conjugial love, "which is the very essential sphere of heaven."

Blessed marriages are provided, he says, for those who in their single state have desired marriage, if they are spiritual, "but not until they come into heaven."

In one passage Swedenborg hints that the heavenly marriage of the celibates or the mismarried may take place on the basis of a union of souls which has already taken place on earth, "as happens with those who from an early age have loved, have desired, and have asked of the Lord an honorable and holy connection with one of the sex, shunning and abominating the impulses of a loose and wandering lust." [7]

Whether he was speaking of himself here, one can only guess.

Even in his most private diary Swedenborg hardly ever put down names, only feelings.

According to his theories there was nothing to prevent his having met an unattained love in the world of spirits even before either of their deaths. In a charming passage,[8] he describes how once, when he was "in the spirit" and yet now and then concerned with worldly matters, he was asked by a teacher-spirit what it meant that he kept appearing and disappearing from their sight, was he really of their world? Swedenborg explained that he was of both worlds. Since to him man's real self was his spiritual self, he believed that when man was in such deep abstract thought that his soul was unaware of the body, or when he was asleep, his spiritual self, or soul, might become visible in the spirit world. Such thinkers are sometimes seen there, he asserted, deep in thought, visible to the inhabitants, but not aware of them, except in cases such as Swedenborg's, amphibious as he was. In this way too, he had seen, he said, and even conversed, with people still alive, whose spirit was set free in sleep.

But it is guesswork as to whether he felt he had formed a kind of precelestial marriage with the Countess Gyllenborg while they were both alive. He had rented an apartment in their house in Stockholm, calling them his friends, as early as 1733. The Count had borrowed money from Swedenborg. After the Count's death, Swedenborg noted in the diary that Gyllenborg became one of the worst of spirits; one, moreover, who was always trying to injure Swedenborg. The Countess died in 1769. It was after that date that Swedenborg is said to have spoken of a Countess Gyllenborg as his future mate to the English Member of Parliament, C. A. Tulk.

In any case, while in the book *Heaven and Hell,* published in 1758, he had spoken of marriage in heaven as purely of minds, in *Conjugial Love,* published ten years later (but which he had planned at least as early as 1759),[9] he had concluded that heavenly marriage included the same physical sensations as a successful marriage on earth. It was logical for him that he did so, because of his belief that sensation was a power of the soul rather than of the body, a power the soul continued to possess after "death," to such an extent that it could hallucinate itself a spiritual body with more exquisite sensations than it had before.

When Swedenborg condemned merely "natural" marriage, he was not therefore condemning sexual feeling—far from it—but for him "natural" meant selfish, hence something that was bound to fail. And when such marriages failed, as they often did in his day, he said that one or other of the partners was likely to turn to adultery."

Just as "conjugial love" was haloed with celestial radiance for Swedenborg, so the word "adultery" flickers with sulphureous fire through his writings and in his diary. They are the important symbols in his marriage mysticism, equivalent to heaven and hell, since, he said, adultery "signifies" the marriage of falsity and evil. But the meaning of adultery is peculiarly his own. He published a long and liberal list of reasons why a married man could, without committing adultery, have a concubine, though he must not then live maritally with his wife at the same time. The list included many diseases of body and mind, but also "antipathy," or that the wife had "a passion for divulging the secrets of the house," or that she was given to "wrangling." [10]

What Swedenborg most often means by adultery is self-regarding lust; whether it is in or out of legal marriage, and by conjugial love he means a union of minds, hearts and bodies, which symbolizes heaven itself.

"Love truly conjugial," however, "at this day is so rare that it is not known what is its quality and scarcely that it exists." It was of infinite variety, "it being in no two persons exactly similar," yet everyone who married from love of one alone of the sex had a glimpse of this love, and he described how it grew from before the marriage ceremony and some time after. At such times, he asked, who would not agree "that this love is the foundation of all loves, and into it are collected all joys and delights from firsts to lasts?"

But, after "this season of ardor," the enjoyment lessens by degrees, until at last it is scarcely felt; and then if asked whether this love is not all delights in one it will not only be denied but even qualified as "nonsense." Only with those who are joined in common interests of soul, mind, and heart will the first heavenly mirage advance by degrees into eternal reality. "But such instances are rare," he adds, and, it would appear from his many talks on the subject in the spirit world, incredible to any but the denizens of the higher heavens.

In language much more rainbow-colored and with much more detail than is usual with him, Swedenborg in this book described visions of his, such as that of a married pair from heaven who descended to him that he might see two angels that yet were spoken of as one angel, because they utterly complemented each other.[11]

It must be confessed that many of the discussions Swedenborg said he had in the spirit world, especially with women about the nature of love, have a flavor not of the eighteenth century but of the salons of the seventeenth. A little less emphasis on the other world, and one might be in the salon of the Marquise de Rambouillet, discussing the points of the *Carte du Tendre*.

But he had a reason for it. In a garden called, in other-world language, "Adramandoni," among laurel and palm, olive trees and flowers, he said he saw near a fountain husbands and wives, youths and maidens, seated on the grass and listening to two angels, clad in purple and scarlet, telling them about marriage and its delights. "This being the subject of their discourse, the attention was eager and the reception full," Swedenborg says, and one suspects he knew what he was doing when he chose these wrappings for his messages about ethics, religion, and the other world. The angels told the eager listeners that conjugial love was divine because it consisted of divine love, divine wisdom, and divine use. Without wisdom love was a mere infatuation; without use even love and wisdom were but a transitory emotion. "Love cannot rest unless it is at work, for love is the essential active power of life," the angels declared, "and to work is use." [12]

The specific "use" of earthly marriage, as Swedenborg saw it, was of course the procreation of children, for otherwise the communities of heaven might lack new citizens, but his "doctrine of use" became one of the foundation pillars of his teachings. Swedenborg was nothing if not practical; he had had too many of his good memorials dustily filed not to want theory carried out into practice.

Having established the high ancestry of sexual psychophysical pleasure, Swedenborg also discussed with the spirits many of its problems, with amazing knowledge and shrewdness for a bachelor. He wrote of marital "coldness" as matter-of-factly as any modern doctor, tracing its origins to mental and emotional factors. He favored neither sex against the other; in that wonderful table of weights, so to speak, in which he assesses the gravity of various kinds of adulteries, he blames equally a "crafty wife" who inflames a man and a man who "by powerful enticements" leaves a woman no longer mistress of herself "by reason of the fire kindled in her will." [13]

With his idea of adultery as self-regarding lust it was natural that he saw the place in hell for those who delight in adultery as also "the place for those who delight in cruelty . . . they think nothing can be more pleasant." This kind of pleasure, he adds, "is today so common as to extend even to infants." [14]

In a series of deeply etched pictures from hell, he gave his report on the fate of those who sinned even more grievously against love. Those whose lust it had been to deflower maidens, among whom there were many of the rich and noble, he said he had seen in hell where they inquired after virgins and were shown harlots who assumed a florid beauty, but who turned into monstrous shapes when the bargain was clinched. Nevertheless the Casanovas had to remain with them. Among themselves, Swedenborg said, these men might indeed still look like men, but to the eye of others who were allowed to see them "instead of their former agreeable and courteous expression of countenance they appear like apes with faces stern and bestial, walking with their bodies bent forward, and they emit a disagreeable smell. They loathe females, and turn away from those they see, for they have no desire for them." [15]

In similar plight Swedenborg saw those who had lusted for variety, wanting "all the women in the world, and wishing for whole troops and a fresh one every day." They, he said, think of "the whole female sex as a common harlot, and of marriage as common harlotry . . ." In hell they are rationed to a harlot a day, but they lose their potency and on this account, he says, they loathe the sex.[16]

Still viler are those who need to be stimulated by resistance and thus become violators. Fighting cats, they look like, when at "their theatrical venery" in hell, and Swedenborg gives an extremely vivid description of such a "brothel-contest." [17]

But lust, for Swedenborg, was an aspect only of that state of love of self with its desire for profit and dominion which he saw as being hell. The book *Conjugial Love* contains some of his best vignettes from that realm.

There were the judges who warped justice in favor of their friends, being acclaimed with "O, how just!" by their clients, but shown by the angel who was with him to Swedenborg as they looked in the sight of one of the celestials: "Their faces appeared as of polished steel, their bodies from the neck to the loins as graven images of stone, clothed with leopard skins, and their feet as snakes; the law books too, which they had arranged in order on the table were changed into packs of cards" and, instead of judging, they were given the job of mixing up paint "to bedaub the faces of harlots." [18]

Another time, while Swedenborg was pondering on the love of dominion grounded in self-love, he saw "a devil ascending from hell, with a square cap on his head, let down over his forehead even to his eyes; his face was full of pimples as of a burning fever, his eyes fierce and fiery, his breast swelling immensely; from his mouth he belched smoke like a furnace, his loins seemed all in a blaze, instead of feet he had bony ankles without flesh, and from his body exhaled a stinking and filthy heat."

On seeing this personage, Swedenborg admits that he was alarmed, crying to him, "Approach no nearer; tell me, whence are you?"

He replied in a hoarse tone of voice, "I am from below, where I am with two hundred in the most super-eminent of all societies. We are all emperors of emperors, kings of kings, dukes of dukes and princes of princes . . . we sit on thrones of thrones and des-patch mandates through the whole world and beyond it."

Swedenborg suggested that he was insane, to which the devil replied, "How can you say so when we absolutely seem to ourselves, and also are acknowledged by each other, to have such distinc-tion?" [19]

By linking up his discussions of sexual joys and problems with his doctrines and his other-world experiences, Swedenborg had not hurt the circulation of his new book. Published when he was eighty, it became one of his most popular. In April, 1769, a year after it was out, he wrote to a friend, "The book is very much in demand in Paris, and in many places in Germany." And the Dutch reviewed it favorably. Copies even trickled into Sweden.

The fact was that since it became known about 1760 that Swedenborg claimed to have communication with the other world, people of all classes, high, middle and low, flocked to him to consult him about such things—especially, of course, those who had lost their spouses, and who hoped to regain—or lose—them in the other world.

CHAPTER TWENTY-FIVE

Swedenborg in Daily Life

EMANUEL SWEDENBORG no longer cared whether he should be thought insane if he told people about their friends and relatives in the other world. "I have related a thousand particulars respecting departed spirits, informing certain persons that are now alive concerning the state of their deceased brethren, their married partners and their friends." [1] But he did not tell everybody. His friend Robsahm, for instance, reports how Swedenborg "with great firmness" refused to have anything to do with the great ruck of the curious, people who thought "that he was a fortune-teller and could reveal wonderful secrets, thefts, etc." Nor did he receive all the disconsolate widows who wanted to know the state of their husbands. He was careful to have one of his servants in the room when he gave other-world information, for, as he said, "it is well known that such people misrepresent, because they do not properly understand what they hear." [2]

However, such misrepresentation of course overtook the true stories about him as they flew from mouth to mouth. He often complained of this, characterizing some stories as only partly true, others as wholly untrue. Foremost was, of course, the story of the Queen of Sweden and the secret known only to her and her dead brother. Besides that story, the one of finding the receipt for the Dutch ambassador's widow and the one about the Stockholm fire perceived by him clairvoyantly in Gothenburg were those he was most often asked about, and which he always confirmed. But first the questioner was asked to tell Swedenborg what he had heard and Swedenborg would tell him if it were true.

Of the many people who came and went in his large garden and in his simple house, one or two have left their recollections. Robsahm, the aforementioned treasurer of the Bank of Stockholm, writing his memoirs of Swedenborg in much the same neat cursive hand [3] that Swedenborg used in the manuscript of the *Principia*, said that the latter "worked without much regard to the distinction

of day and night." " 'When I am sleepy,' he said, 'I go to bed.' "
He asked his servant, the wife of his gardener, to make his bed and
to put a large jug of water in his anteroom, all the attendance he
required. He made his own coffee in his study, where the fire was
never allowed to go out. He drank a great deal of coffee with a lot
of sugar in it. (In experimental psychic research it has been found
that coffee helps the "psi" ability.) When he was not invited out,
his dinner consisted of nothing but a roll soaked in boiled milk,
but in company he would eat freely and indulge moderately in a
merry glass.

His dress in winter was a fur coat of reindeer skin, and in summer
it was a dressing-gown, both well worn, but his outdoor clothes
were neat though simple. "Still, it happened sometimes that, when
he prepared to go out, and his people did not call attention to it,
something would be forgotten or neglected in his dress; so that, for
instance, he would put one buckle of gems and another of silver on
his shoes." Robsahm saw this himself, he says, at his father's house
where Swedenborg was asked to dine, and the occurrence "greatly
amused several young girls."

And their amusement probably greatly amused Swedenborg, but
when less naïve persons tried to ridicule him they often found the
laugh turned on themselves. No less a dignitary than Archbishop
Troilius, who was fond of playing "tresett" (a card game needing
three people) and who had just lost one of his card partners, Erland
Broman, met Swedenborg in a large gathering and asked him
jocularly, "By the way, Assessor, tell us something about the spirit
world. How does my friend Broman spend his time there?"

Swedenborg answered instantly, "I saw him but a few hours ago
shuffling his cards in the company of the Evil One, and he was only
waiting for your worship to make up a game of tresett." [4]

Robsahm freely asked Swedenborg questions in regard to his
psychic gifts, inquiring once whether other people could come into
the same degree of spirituality. Swedenborg warned against trying,
saying it was the direct road to insanity; indeed he often said it was
nothing for ordinary people to experiment with; but he did not
maintain he was the only person who had the gift of communicating with the other world. Once friends of his wrote to him about
a boy who apparently was "psychic," could converse with spirits

and could heal people, and Swedenborg offered to place him with a good family in Stockholm where he could become educated.[5] And he often wrote that all men could and should have been able to communicate with the other world, if they had only kept the spiritual part of themselves alive and open.

One day when a public execution had taken place, Robsahm was with Swedenborg in the evening, and asked him how a man who leaves the world in this manner feels at the moment he is executed. Swedenborg said that when such a man laid his head on the block, he was already so much out of himself that after decapitation when he entered into the world of spirits he didn't realize that the execution had taken place, but was terrified of it and tried to make his escape. Then good spirits would come to him and reveal to him that he was really dead, and, if he had been purposely wicked on earth he would escape from them as quickly as possible and lead himself to his likes in hell, but if he had committed his crime without premeditation, he could repent, receive instruction, and in time become a blessed spirit.

Another of Swedenborg's friends who put down his recollections of him, though it was eighteen years after Swedenborg's death, was the Danish Major-General Tuxen.[6] Tuxen lived in Elsinore, the charming Danish town on the Sound, where sailing ships were often becalmed. Luckily for Tuxen, who was most curious to meet Swedenborg, having read some of his works, there was no breeze on a day in 1768 when Swedenborg was on board a ship off Elsinore, and Tuxen was asked to dine at the Swedish Consul's to meet the famous man.

Tuxen asked and received confirmations of the stories relating to Swedenborg's psychic powers, and he also asked for information concerning various Danish personages in the other world. He was given some interesting answers, and, without his asking, he was also informed as to the fate of the Russian Empress Elizabeth, that it was much better than might have been supposed.

Now it is only in our day that it has come out what Tuxen's job really was:[7] the King of Denmark had practically forced him to be a Danish secret agent to secure information on Russian affairs, a charge which he held from 1742 till his death in 1792. Officially he had various other posts, so that Swedenborg's detailed and unsolicited information about the Empress Elizabeth, who had died in 1762, must have considerably impressed him. At any rate Tuxen continued to seek every opportunity to meet Swedenborg that wind and weather might furnish, and in 1770 he found a good one. Swedenborg's ship was becalmed off Kullen, near Elsinore, and Tuxen boarded it. That was the time, mentioned before, when he disturbed him in trance, but Swedenborg soon recovered himself, and consented to dine with Tuxen, "pulling off his gown and slippers, putting on clean linen, and dressing himself as briskly and alertly as a young man of one and twenty" (being eighty-two).

At Tuxen's house the Major-General apologized for having only his sickly wife and her young girls to meet him, to which Swedenborg replied, "And is not this very good company? I was always partial to the company of ladies."

This made Tuxen ask if he had ever wanted to marry. No, he said. Once Charles XII wanted him to marry Polhem's daughter but she refused. Tuxen excused himself, but his guest told him to ask anything. The Dane inquired if Swedenborg while young could resist sexual temptation. "Not altogether," he said, "in my youth I had a mistress in Italy."

Mrs. Tuxen—a notoriously hysterical woman—began to tell him about her bad health, and Swedenborg assured her that the time was coming when she would again attain the same health and beauty as when she was fifteen, not specifying that it would be necessary for her to die first. The daughter sang and Swedenborg said, "Bravo, very fine!" And he persuaded the mother to sing with the daughter, paying Mrs. Tuxen many compliments. He talked on other "indifferent subjects," Tuxen wrote, such as the "favorite dogs and cats that were in the room, which caressed him and jumped on his knee, showing their little tricks."

Tuxen loved him, and continued his faithful friend, and even became one of his disciples. That they were not many we have Swedenborg's own word for, since, in a postscript to his recollections, Tuxen said that once when he asked Swedenborg how many people he knew in this world that favored his doctrines, the latter answered "that there were not many yet that he knew of, still he might compute their number at perhaps *fifty,* or thereabouts; and in proportion the same number in the world of spirits."

Not the statement of a messianic megalomaniac, certainly, and all the evidence of Swedenborg's contemporaries goes to show that he was free from such insanity.

Among his character witnesses, so to speak, there is a Swedish-American pastor by the name of Nicholas Collin, who published his recollections of Swedenborg in the *Philadelphia Gazette,* in 1801.[8]

As a young man Collin had had frequent opportunities to see Swedenborg during the years 1765–68, and he too testified that although the latter was firmly persuaded of his religious mission, "he had no desire to see it enforced by violent measures; nor did he exert himself in making proselytes except by his writings. As to Sweden he never intimated a wish to be the head of a sect; but indulged in the fond hope that the ecclesiastical establishment would by a tranquil gradual illumination assume the form of his New Church. His natural mildness, education, connections, learning and experience both in public and private life produced a warm esteem for social order inimical to fanatical turbulence."

Not that Collin thought Swedenborg lukewarm in his beliefs. The Swedish-American Lutheran pastor wrote, "All parties generally agree that he had a firm belief in all his doctrines, and all his visions in the spiritual world. I never heard any person in Sweden surmise the contrary. He withdrew, in the unimpaired possession of his talents, from a career of public life which would have led him to greater honors and emoluments; and he sacrificed the enjoyments of his favorite sciences. He could expect no pecuniary advantage from his new pursuits; and the compensation of honor was dubious. By the laws of Sweden he was not permitted to print his books at home, nor to translate them; neither could he set up as a public teacher."

Pastor Collin was full of admiration for Swedenborg's character, his "integrity and benevolence," but that it was "an extraordinary character" and a frequent subject of public discussion he also admitted. As Collin was tutor in the house of Dr. Celsius, who knew Swedenborg well, he had opportunities to make observations, since the latter not only received company in his own house but "appeared in public and mixed in private societies."

In the summer of 1766 the young tutor himself called on Swedenborg with the innocent introduction that he desired to speak with a "character so celebrated." Swedenborg received him very kindly, gave him "delicious coffee," and they talked for three hours "principally on the nature of human souls and their states in the invisible world." The young man asked if Swedenborg could procure for him an interview with his deceased brother. The old man inquired what his motives were. Collin confessed he had none but brotherly affection and "an ardent wish to explore scenes so sublime and interesting to a serious mind." Good reasons, Swedenborg said, but not sufficient; but if any important spiritual or temporal concern had been involved he would have then "solicited permission from the angels who regulate such matters."

Swedenborg had a pretty tall, erect, rather slender figure, Collin said, a fair complexion, eyes of serene brightness. "At the time of my interview with him he was seventy-seven [78] yet retained marks of beauty and appeared to have considerable vigor of mind and body."

In Collin's opinion many people believed in Swedenborg's intercourse with the invisible world, though "not a few judicious persons believed that Swedenborg might on some occasions receive information from invisible agents, and yet be a visionary as to many things; and that such a faculty was not at all a proof of doctrines unconnected with it."

The same persons carefully investigated the facts of the cases where Swedenborg had apparently acquired supernatural knowledge, such as the case of the Queen of Sweden, the Marteville receipt, etc., which Collin himself had heard frequently, always the same as to substance though differing in details, "nor was either of them disputed, so far as I knew."

Swedenborg's religious doctrines, according to Collin, were hardly known to the general public "because Swedenborg was not solicitous to communicate them, and few of his readers thought proper to do it." He never, he said, heard anyone discuss the doctrine of the unity of God, except among some of the learned.

There were, however, people who did not overlook Swedenborg's doctrines. These were clergymen of quite a different stripe from the amiable and liberal Collin, who was to become pastor of Swedes' Old Church in Philadelphia.

EMANUEL SWEDENBORG AT ABOUT
EIGHTY-ONE

Painted by the noted Swedish portrait painter PER KRAFFT, the elder, at the request of Count A. J. von Höpken. In Gripsholm Castle. (*Courtesy, Svenska porträttarkivet.*)

It must be admitted that Swedenborg was frank in saying what he thought about the kind of clergymen he didn't like. Robsahm once asked him whether a certain pastor whose pathos and eloquence had always kept his church filled were not in a blessed state. "This man," was the answer, "went straight to hell among the societies of the hypocrites; for he was only spiritually minded while in the pulpit; at other times he was proud of his talents, and of the success he had in the world; he was an inflated man. No, no," he added, "there no dissimulation and no deceitful arts are of any avail . . ."

There is a story that a young man who seems to have regarded Swedenborg as a danger to Christian society approached him and asked what was the lot of his, the young man's, father in the other world. Swedenborg told him it was pitiable, "if your father belonged to that order of which very few are saved. Your father was a clergyman, was he not?" [9] This was true.

Since Swedenborg denied the vicarious atonement and the Trinity (as a trinity of persons) and generally insisted that religion was not something to save men from the consequences of their wickedness but something to prove to them that wickedness had inevitable consequences, and that hence the Lutheran theory of saving "faith" was wrong, it is hard to see how the pastors of the Lutheran state church of Sweden could look on him with a very friendly eye. Nor did they, although for a long while his good connections and favor at Court made them shut both their eyes when they looked in his direction. It was fairly easy so long as his books printed in Latin remained abroad, but when they were introduced little by little into Sweden, and when a Swedish clergyman, Dean Beyer of Gothenburg, began openly to say that Swedenborg was right, the ecclesiastical guns were unmasked.

Swedenborg was not surprised, he told Robsahm, when the latter asked him why only Beyer had accepted his explanation of Scripture. The clergy, he said, hear their doctrine of "faith alone" daily through schools and university, and then they cannot change. The clergy of every religion is like that, he added; they cannot be made to give up the most preposterous propositions after they have confirmed themselves in the doctrines.

The attack was led by Dean Ekebom of Gothenburg, who, in the marvellous manner of his kind, declared: "I am not acquainted with the religious system of Assessor Swedenborg, nor shall I take any trouble to become acquainted with it."

Still, leaning apparently on hearsay and on angry glances at one of Swedenborg's books, he did not hesitate to declare "Swedenborgianism" *"corrupting, heretical, injurious,* and, in the highest degree, *objectionable."* [10]

Swedenborg had gone to Amsterdam with the manuscript of a new book when the full heresy hunt was on in 1769, but he fought back by letter, a letter which the orthodox clergymen involved said was "sinister." Swedenborg did in effect call them all liars, but what the clergy was most upset by was, not unnaturally, that Swedenborg in the letter came right out and said that the Doctrine of the New Church had been published to the world by the Saviour through his servant, Swedenborg.

When Swedenborg returned to Stockholm in October, 1769, he found himself well received, dined with the Crown Prince and Princess, had long talks with them, with the senators, with all but one of the bishops present, "all of whom treated me with kindness," as he wrote to Dr. Beyer. There is no doubt that the storm raged chiefly among the more provincial clergy, and in May, 1770, Swedenborg wrote a spirited letter to the King himself, reminding His Majesty how, when he had been dining with the royal family, as well as five senators, his "mission constituted the sole topic of conversation, and how he had declared it before the whole of Christendom."

No answer was sent to this letter, but the King, together with Swedenborg's powerful friends, quietly sanded up the whole matter, the only sop given to the irate Dean Ekebom being that the two men accused of being "adherents" of Swedenborg's, Drs. Beyer and Rosén, were no longer to lecture on theological matters at the gymnasium.

Swedenborg, however, did not wait in Sweden to see the end of the affair. It may be true, as Robsahm tells, that in 1769 a senator warned him that some of the clergy had plotted to have him declared insane and shut up in an asylum. In any case, feelings had run high. Before Swedenborg left for Amsterdam in 1770 he gave

Robsahm a protest to be submitted if his writings were condemned in his absence. He certainly did not leave in either 1769 or 1770 out of fear. He had the stuff of martyrs in him, but his books, his work, his "mission," sent him to his printers abroad.

As his works were being more and more widely read, he began to receive letters about them. The learned German prelate Oettinger, mentioned before, who was a reader of Jacob Boehme, was extremely enthusiastic about Swedenborg too—but not about "the internal sense" of the Bible, nor about "correspondences," only about the experiences Swedenborg reported from the other world. He told him so directly: "Your experiences command more belief than your explanations of scripture." [11]

This was decidedly not what the aged Swedenborg wanted to hear. He had not relinquished his job, science, preferment, honor, nor had he spent his life struggling with "temptations" and arguing with men and spirits in order to be what he called a "subject," a mere transmitter of spirit-messages. He often said that these experiences were unimportant in themselves; they were only of value in proving that he did have access to much higher, angelic information on the subject of the Bible than anyone else.

He could not explain the reasons for his certainty, which perhaps was not so much of a certainty after all, since he became really annoyed when it was questioned.

He had no doubt forgotten about "the marvellous powers of the human mind," especially the memory. Long ago he himself had written that "in the whole study and pursuit of psychology nothing more wonderful is met with than the memory, nor anything more difficult of disentanglement . . ." [12]

Though he knew that man's "ruling love" was what to a large extent determined his thinking, he did not seem to realize that it not only determined what a man would remember but also how and in what guise it would present itself. Memory would register indifferently a real and an imagined event, an objective and a subjective one, but the ruling love would often pick an imagined event and insert it into the series of real events [13] and the passage of years would gloss it over with the patina of belief till not its own father could tell the difference.

Swedenborg might have forgotten how his interpretations of the Bible had come to him through his hand being moved involuntarily, or how voices had dictated to him, or how he had even written without knowing what he was writing (in any case he never suspected that some of these messages might have come from his own unconscious), but he had not forgotten his Vision. It had come to him resolving his long religious crisis, it had given him the mystic's direct experience of the Godhead, and all his conscious and subconscious life after that had been focused on the interpretation of it. After seventy it had become inextricably connected in his mind with the reinterpretation of the Bible, since he had to have both the Bible and his doctrines of the New Church for that new spiritual orientation which he wanted mankind to have.

This for him was his mission. He came to believe he had been "commanded" to announce it; in the spiritual world he said he had seen his theological books with the words "the Lord's Advent" written on them.[14] Not in pride but in what he considered obedience did he announce that a man filled with the spirit of the Lord would, at the command of the Lord, receive the internal sense of Scripture in his understanding and publish it in the press. This release of the Lord in the Book was to be the real Second Coming.

But no one of any importance in Sweden, except the undeniably woolly-minded Beyer, seemed to take him seriously on this, for him, so vital point that he had a commission to elucidate the inner meaning of the Bible by means of "correspondence."

Men like Höpken were delighted with the ethical and philosophic aspects of his books; they approved, if not publicly, of his attacks on what Höpken in a letter called "the polytheism taught by the priests," but Swedenborg, not they, had had the Vision. Some of them believed that he could really talk with spirits, but the thing to which he considered his spirit-communication a testimony, his mission to interpret the "Word," fell on deaf ears, or at any rate on ears very hard of hearing.

No Stockholmer has left a detailed account of how in this matter Swedenborg struck a sensible burgher of his time, but luckily an Amsterdammer has done so. The story of Swedenborg's friendship with Johan Christian Cuno gives us not only some valuable glimpses of the seer's personality but an account of how that extraordinary personality impinged on an orthodox Christian of his time, a man who, although he had some literary interests, was really a stout human bulk of received ideas, his feet well planted on the floor of the Amsterdam Stock-Exchange.

CHAPTER TWENTY-SIX

Amsterdam Report

JOHAN CHRISTIAN CUNO (born in Berlin) also kept a diary—of four thousand folio pages, bound in four volumes in morocco. Otherwise the manuscript would scarcely have been sold to a dealer in second-hand books and eventually found its way to a learned Brussels librarian in the middle of the nineteenth century.[1] Cuno's life, though it had vivid ups and downs, since he began as a soldier and ended as a merchant and banker, would not have concerned very many people except that late in 1768 he met Emanuel Swedenborg and put that in his diary too.

Cuno was interested in theology and he had read *Conjugial Love,* which caused in him "an irresistible curiosity to make the acquaintance of the author." He confessed that the title of the book made him think the author was insane, as did the claims of the latter to have been in the other world, but "occasionally I found him uttering such thoughtful things, as I had never before heard from academical desks and pulpits, and which never before had entered my thoughts." Therefore he looked for the author and decided to give an account in his diary "of the most singular saint who has ever lived, Mr. Emanuel Swedenborg."

Cuno did not rush to know Swedenborg, however, before he had inquired "most particularly" about his character from the Swedish merchants in Amsterdam, especially from the highly respected Joachim Wretman, with whom Swedenborg dined nearly every Sunday. As the result was most favorable to Swedenborg, Cuno called on him, having first met him in a French bookshop in Amsterdam. In Swedenborg's two comfortable rooms, Cuno almost at once asked him if he had no valet to wait on him in his old age and to accompany him on his travels. "He answered that he needed no one to look after him, because his angel was ever with him . . ."

Cuno comments, "If another man had uttered these words he would have made me laugh; but I never thought of laughing when this venerable man, eighty-one years old, told me this; he looked far too innocent, and when he gazed on me with his smiling blue eyes, which he always did in conversing with me, it was as if truth itself was speaking from them."

And, as has been mentioned before, Cuno told how Swedenborg's eyes seemed to have the faculty of imposing silence on everyone, even scoffers, when he told them about the other world.

"He lived with simple burgher folk, who kept a shop in which they sold chintz, muslin, handkerchiefs, and the like, and who had quite a number of little children. I inquired of the landlady whether the old gentleman did not require very much attention. She answered 'He scarcely requires any; the servant has nothing else to do for him, except in the morning to lay the fire for him in the fire-place. Every evening he goes to bed at seven and gets up in the morning at eight. We do not trouble ourselves any more about him. During the day he keeps up the fire himself; and on going to bed takes great care lest the fire should do any damage. He dresses and undresses himself alone, and waits upon himself in every thing so that we scarcely know whether there is anyone in the house or not. I should like him to be with us during the rest of his life. My children will miss him most; for he never goes out without bringing them home some sweets; the little rogues also dote on the old gentleman so much they prefer him to their own parents. I imagine that he is very rich.' "

Cuno thought so too, because Swedenborg gave his books away so liberally. But in Amsterdam, at any rate, Swedenborg lived very simply. Chocolate and biscuits served in his room were his usual dinner, of which the people he lived with got the better part; if he were hungry he went to a restaurant near by. "He was far from being misanthropical and obstinate. Whoever invited him to his house was sure to have him."

Cuno invited Swedenborg to his own house. He should have liked, he said, to introduce him into his club, since Swedenborg said he was fond of a game of cards now and then, but there was the obstacle of the seven o'clock bedtime. So Cuno arranged for an early dinner, and Swedenborg was in very good spirits, frank and openhearted.

Cuno also brought Swedenborg to the house of a friend, Mr. Konauw. Among other guests there were the two Misses Hoog,

educated "beyond the common sphere of woman." "Mr. Swedenborg's deportment was exquisitely refined and gallant. When
dinner was announced, I offered my hand to the hostess, and
quickly our young man of eighty-one had put on his gloves and
presented his hand to Mademoiselle Hoog, in doing which he
looked uncommonly well. Whenever he was invited out, he dressed
properly and becomingly in black velvet, but ordinarily he wore a
brown coat and black trousers. I never saw him dressed otherwise
than in one of these two suits of clothes.

"Our old gentleman was seated between Madame Konauw and
the elder Demoiselle Hoog, both of whom understood thoroughly
well how to talk; but they had promised me beforehand that, at
least during dinner, they would allow the old gentleman to eat in
peace. This promise they kept faithfully, and he seemed to enjoy
very much to be so attentively served by the ladies. This time he
displayed such a good appetite that I was quite surprised. They
could not prevail on him to take more than three glasses of wine,
which were besides half filled with sugar, of which he was more
than ordinarily fond. During the dessert the talk went on very
freely, and it continued afterwards while we took tea and coffee,
and thus uninterruptedly until seven o'clock, when I had taken
care that the carriage should be ready to take us home.

"It is astonishing what a number of questions the ladies addressed to him; all of which he answered." Cuno, to our regret, did
not feel inclined to record these, except one, which certainly had
the ladies in a flutter.

"The conversation turned upon a certain distinguished personage, I think an ambassador, who had died some time ago at the
Hague. 'I know him,' exclaimed Mr. Swedenborg, 'although I
never saw him in his lifetime. As you mention here his name,
d'Abricourt, I know him and that he left a widow. But he has already married again in the spiritual world, and he has now a wife
for all eternity who is more perfectly in harmony with his disposition than the one he left behind in this world.' "

Cuno dined several times with him again at the same house, and
also at another where Swedenborg told him that a new set of teeth
was growing in his mouth. Cuno was inclined to believe it. Swedenborg was, he said, "for his years a perfect wonder of health." Al-

though he was twenty years older than Cuno the latter said, "I should be afraid to run a race with him, for he is as quick on his legs as the youngest man."

But it was of course the other-world stories which interested the Amsterdammers as it did the Stockholmers. Cuno writes that Swedenborg told him he had recently been in the spirit world where in a certain society a newcomer had appeared whom none of the other spirits could identify and about whom they were all very curious. They asked Swedenborg to accost the unknown and inquire about his name. Which Swedenborg obligingly did, and it was King Stanislaus of Poland.

Another time a young man to whom Cuno had given an introduction to Swedenborg mentioned that the King of Portugal had hanged the Bishop of Coimbra.

"It is not true," Swedenborg said, "the Bishop has not been hanged, or else I should have known it; only recently I spoke concerning him with the one lately deceased and I rallied the Pope on that case."

The young man hastened with this plum to a bookshop near the Stock-Exchange where, among others, Cuno was present. Most of them exclaimed that the hanging was only too true; they knew it, for had they not read it in the newspapers "with all the attendant circumstances." And one of them said that the old gentleman really was crazy, whereupon he gave a detailed account of Swedenborg's whereabouts and doings and sayings during a certain period—an account which Cuno then and there proved to be false in every vivid particular, finishing up by saying, "I am not at all willing to go security for the old gentleman to the extent that everything he tells in his writings should be believed; but I am willing to remain responsible for this statement that what I have just heard concerning him is an arrant and manifest falsehood."

But in a few days the papers retracted the news of the hanging of the Bishop of Coimbra, and, Cuno says, "the old gentleman was once again regarded as a prophet."

Swedenborg merely smiled when Cuno told him of the falsehoods circulating about him, and said, "How people will lie! In respect to the Bishop of Coimbra, other rational people besides myself, probably doubted the story. A bishop is not so easily hanged;

it is nevertheless true that he is a prisoner, and that I have spoken respecting him with the late pope."

Cuno did not contradict him. Cuno was not so worried by Swedenborg's stories of the other world, he said, nor even by Swedenborg's claim that he was an "entirely new teacher." What worried Cuno extremely was that the old gentleman would "teach things contrary to old truths, which, however, to my great sorrow, he frequently does."

Even from liberal Amsterdam people had been banished who came out too vigorously against the received Christian dogmas, and Cuno was cautious, as well as a true believer in the dogmas. When Swedenborg announced that he was going to publish a brief summary of the doctrines of the New Church, Cuno was thoroughly alarmed and begged him to postpone it, "or you will expose yourself to the danger of being banished from the city."

Swedenborg nevertheless published his little book, and, to Cuno's intense surprise, the clergy seemed to take no notice of it, though they had busily refuted a far less worthy antagonist, as Cuno judged him.

It does not surprise the modern reader that the clergy had nothing to say against Swedenborg's *Summary Exposition of the Doctrine of the New Church*. Perhaps it was because they regarded a spirit-seer as beneath their notice; more likely it was because Swedenborg was very difficult to refute. For the book which Cuno had so dreaded *was* a dreadful book. Both Catholics and Protestants might have risen up in horror and burned Swedenborg as Calvin did Servetus, for in this short, dry treatise he knocked all their dogmatic heads together, making them sound like empty barrels, so far as any ethical foundation for their theologies was concerned.

Out of their own words he did it; quoting from the Council of Trent in regard to the Roman Catholics, and from the Augsburg Confession and the "Formula Concordia" in regard to the Protestants. He asserted that in spite of apparent differences both sides really taught the same things: a Trinity of persons in the Godhead, original sin, the imputation of the merit of Christ and justification by faith therein—the only difference being, as he saw it, that the Catholics did insist that faith be joined with charity or good works.

Both sides were wrong, he said; if anything the Protestants a little more so, since, in order to secede thoroughly from Rome, they had given up good works, relying on being saved (justified) by the faith that the merits of Christ would be credited (imputed) to them, if they applied for them at what we might call the Bank of Grace.

This Bank of Grace existed, according to the theologians, because Jesus had sacrificed himself on the Cross to conciliate God, the Father, angry with mankind because of its original sin. Such was the doctrine of the vicarious atonement, so abhorred by Swedenborg as a calumny against Love and Wisdom. He also saw it as an invitation to humanity to go ahead and sin, and all spots could be washed out at the end by a deathbed conversion.

He, who was far from friendly to the Roman Catholic Church, said quaintly enough that its members might enter the New Church more easily than the Reformed, because although the Catholics officially still believed in being saved through Christ's merits, they did not in reality know much about it, so thoroughly had the doctrine been "removed out of sight, and withdrawn from memory, that it is like something buried in the earth, and covered over with a stone, which the monks have set a watch over, to prevent its being dug up and revived. For were it revived, the belief of their possessing a supernatural power of forgiving sins, and of thus justifying, sanctifying and bestowing salvation would cease, and therewith all their sanctity, pre-eminence and abundant gains." [2]

Swedenborg had promised that he would elaborate the doctrines of the New Church in a big book soon, but Cuno was not going to wait; he frankly confessed that he was a little anxious about his being known as a friend of the author of the *Summary,* and he wrote a long letter to refute it, circulating it among his friends, but, honorably, sent it first to Swedenborg.

It was a clever letter, evidently meant for public consumption. Cuno did not at all answer the main contentions of Swedenborg, as stated above; he left those explosive matters alone. Instead he pleaded with the author to *prove* his authority for what he said, to "adduce a Divine Testimony in Divine matters." How do we know, he said, that you yourself are not like one of those persons you mention in your writings who dwell so incessantly on religious subjects that they come to see them inwardly and to hear spirits speaking to them? You call them "visionaries and enthusiasts." "But where is that specific difference which distinguishes you from them?"

It appeared a sensible question. But it must be remembered that Cuno was not at all asking it from a modern point of view. He thought that Swedenborg was out of his head because he did not believe in all the accepted Christian dogmas. Swedenborg thought Cuno was out of his to accept them.

Cuno had, however, doubted Swedenborg's "mission." He says he waited a few days, then when no answer came, he went to see him, and for the first time he found him quite cold, "Nay, to say the truth, he appeared to me even a little angry."

Swedenborg might well have been angry because Cuno had side-stepped an answer to the charges against both Protestants and Catholics, but undoubtedly there was also another reason. As in the case of the Gothenburg clergy, his gentle tranquillity was broken when doubt was cast on his possession of "divine testimony" for the reinterpretation of the Bible.

On the contrary, if people doubted his ability to converse with spirits, there are many witnesses to the effect that this did not anger him in the least. He wrote once, "I am unable to put the state of my sight and speech into their heads, in order to convince them." [3]

But his anger with Cuno was short-lived. Soon he came to him and put a little piece of paper into his hand. It was the last paragraph of a new book he was writing. In it he stated that it was the study of natural truth (or science) which led him to study divine truth. And at the end he said that his whole theology consisted in two principles: That God is One, and that there is a conjunction of charity and faith.[4] Or, as he sometimes also put it, the union of love and wisdom is God.

In April, 1769, Swedenborg left for Paris and London, but first he came to take leave of his friend. "I shall never forget, as long as I live, the leave which he took of me in my own house," Cuno wrote. Swedenborg hoped to see Cuno once more in Amsterdam, "for I love you." Cuno said that he at least did not expect a long life, and Swedenborg replied that we were obliged to remain as long as Divine Providence and Wisdom see fit. "If anyone is con-

joined with the Lord, he has a foretaste of the eternal life in this
world; and if he has this he no longer cares so much for this transitory life. Believe me, if I knew that the Lord would call me to himself tomorrow, I would summon the musicians today, in order to
be once more really gay in this world."

Cuno noted that Swedenborg looked "so innocent and joyful
out of his eyes" as he had never seen him look before, and after a
little more talk Swedenborg embraced and kissed his Amsterdam
friend "most heartily" and departed.

CHAPTER TWENTY-SEVEN

Balm in England

THE little paper which Swedenborg slipped into Cuno's hand by way of answer to the famous letter may not have seemed a reply to the Amsterdammer, but it was part of Swedenborg's final answer to the question he had put to himself many years before: "What is the mechanism of the intercourse between the soul and the body?" In a sense he had been discussing it all through the intervening years, and the booklet he had been writing was a summary of his conclusions.

It was probably written as a result of the inquiry of one Immanuel Kant, a professor in Königsberg, Prussia, who had sent Swedenborg a letter asking if the story of the Gothenburg clairvoyance were true. No direct reply was made, but Swedenborg sent word to Kant that he was going to write a book covering every point in Kant's inquiry.[1]

However, when Swedenborg came to write the little book, which he called *The Intercourse between the Soul and the Body,* he did not go into the details that, we might say, belong to psychical research; he became absorbed in the problems of philosophy. The book, he said, was to answer the question as to whether the body acts on the soul (physical influx) or the soul acts on the body (spiritual influx), or whether the two kinds of events, mental and physical, act together, as Leibnitz had declared they did, "by pre-established harmony," using his analogy of two clocks perfectly wound up to keep the same time.

Though Swedenborg wrote with clear brevity, the book was too short to be comprehensible to those unacquainted with his work in physics and physiology and his consequent theory of "degrees" of reality, meaning that the force which is "soul" at one level inflows or manifests itself as "mind" on the next, and as body on the next again, there being subject to "natural" or "physical" laws. It was, modernly speaking, "pan-psychism." The soul, Swedenborg said, clothed itself with an organic body "as with a garment," the latter "being in itself dead and only adapted to receive the living forces flowing in through the soul from God."

So it was not, according to Swedenborg, merely a case of the soul acting on the body, though that he regarded as a true answer, but, as "there is only one life," a case of this life flowing "into forms organically adapted to its reception." Elsewhere he had made clear his belief that the soul, a fragment of divine vitality, itself created these organic forms, endowing matter (which was energy) with life—which was something more than energy.

In effect, then, Swedenborg was an interactionist of the kind who was also a monist—if one may use terms suggested by Professor Gardner Murphy,[2] with whom Swedenborg certainly would have agreed that "the mind-body problem" (which is the problem of psychical research) "need no longer be stated in terms of two irreconcilable elements, physical and mental. Rather it may be a problem of two types of psychical functioning, one defined by the spatial and temporal orders, the other lying beyond them."

"Life in successive order," Swedenborg called it in this book, and he sketched his view of the psychophysical so that one could make a diagram of it.

The origin of life was the Godhead, imagined and "seen" by Swedenborg as by other mystics in the guise of a "sun" that radiated love, wisdom, life, "soul." "Soul" created "mind" and "body." "Mind" had "two lives, one of will and one of understanding." In the mind, will was usually more powerful than the understanding, yet, Swedenborg said, "man is man in that his will is under obedience to his understanding, but a beast is a beast, because its desires impel it to do whatever it does."

The drama of man, for Swedenborg, therefore took place in the mind, as he had long ago stated in *The Economy of the Animal Kingdom*. If men could "restrain the lusts of their will by means of the understanding," *not* by blindly accepting authority in moral matters, then they could receive the "influx" of divine love into their wills and the influx of divine wisdom into their understanding, via the soul, which, being "a superior spiritual substance," could receive the divine influx directly. The human mind, being open to bodily influence as well, was of an "inferior spiritual substance" and it could also receive influx, both good and bad, through the spiritual world, which if good was, of course, originally from God. The body received its influence from God through the "natural world."

Swedenborg saw it as his duty to make known these things. He said so, in this book, with an attitude reminiscent of his position long ago in regard to trade secrets—that there ought to be none.

"Now, because I have been permitted to be in the spiritual world and in the natural world at the same time, I am obliged by my conscience to make known these things; for what is the use of knowing, unless what is known to one be also known to others?"

He said he did not mean to be spiritually avaricious, and when he left Amsterdam with the manuscript of this book it was, probably, to have it published in Paris. Perhaps he saw that Cuno was right and that the Dutch might catch on to the fact that they had a dangerous heretic in their midst.

One did not fly to Paris in those days. It must have taken the venerable man a good week to arrive there by canalboat and stagecoach. And when he arrived in the still royal city he was told by the royal censor that his book might indeed be published in Paris, but only on one condition. This was that "the title-page, as was usual, declared that the book was printed either in London or in Amsterdam." [3]

Swedenborg would not consent to this polite lie, and he packed his two suits together again and took the stagecoaches and the channel-boat for England, arriving in London early in the summer.

That summer was undoubtedly balm to him after his association with the kind but openly incredulous Cuno, for here in London he met people who made no difficulties about accepting the truth of what he said about his "mission."

He had met only silence when he sent his books to the English bishops, the House of Lords, the Royal Society, or the great universities, but now he found other Englishmen, at least he found two of them—the Reverend Thos. Hartley, and Dr. Messiter. [4]

England was not only the country of the almost openly atheistic, it was also the land of almost every shade of religious credulity. Not that Hartley and Messiter belonged to the class of ignorant fanatics, or to the simple who could be stirred by revivalists. Hartley was a clergyman of the Church of England, which has held so many scholars, and he was well thought of both as to heart and head. Dr. Messiter was reputed to be an eminent physician.

The Reverend Mr. Hartley seems to have belonged to the type who, like the believers in the Lost Tribes (British Israelites), are able to block off a vault in their minds where they house their favorite "key" to some theological problem, preferably an involved and "revealed" interpretation of the Bible. And there is no use in denying the fact that, with all Swedenborg's belief in reason, he had come to resent its application in the evaluation of his "mission" to explain "the internal sense" of Scripture, which he inexorably continued to see as necessary for proving the truth of his lofty ethical and religious philosophy.

In Hartley he found the right disciple, a man with the peculiar gift of being an intellectual who was able to suspend his intellect on the one point of accepting Swedenborg's "authority" for the Bible exegesis.

After meeting Swedenborg, apparently for the first time, in the summer of 1769, the English parson wrote a letter in which one may say that, putting it mildly, he showed himself as overwhelmed.[5]

Thanking Swedenborg for the honor of having been allowed to converse with him, Hartley said, "But your charity towards the neighbor, the heavenly benignity shining from your countenance, and your childlike simplicity, devoid of all vain show and egotism, are so great, and the treasure of wisdom possessed by you is so sweetly tempered with gentleness, that it did not inspire in me a feeling of awe, but one of love which refreshed me in my innermost heart. Believe me, o best of men, that by my intercourse with you I consider myself crowned with more than royal favor . . ."

Hartley did not stop at words alone; he offered, together with Dr. Messiter, to provide asylum for him in England in case he should be persecuted by the Swedish clergy on return to his own country, and he also begged Swedenborg to give him some biographical data, so that, if need be, they could defend him against "malignant slanderers" in England.

Swedenborg answered a little stiffly, thanking Mr. Hartley for the praises, but taking them as "love for the truths contained in my writings," and he then gave him a short autobiography and a list of his offices, honors, and his more eminent relatives. He assured

Hartley that as he had influential friends he was in no danger of persecution, nor did he need money, he had as much "of this world's wealth" as he needed.

This letter Mr. Hartley said he received "as reverently as if it had come down from heaven," congratulating Sweden (a little prematurely) on receiving the Lord in His Apostle, and begging Swedenborg to instruct, exhort, and dispose of him in any way whatever.

To begin with, Hartley translated *The Intercourse of the Soul and Body,* which Swedenborg had just published in Latin in London, and the translation was also published. Hartley made himself Swedenborg's translator and defender in England, while he and Dr. Messiter, together with a Mr. Hampe, are said to have been his most intimate friends in London. They brought others to see the old man, among them good Mr. Cookworthy, a Quaker, who also was impressed.[6] Swedenborg's circle in London does not seem ever to have been as extensive, fashionable, and gay as it was in Amsterdam, but it made up in uncritical devotion what it lacked in entertainment.

Swedenborg was not, however, one of those who, feeling "unappreciated" in their own country, avoid their compatriots abroad. He always visited and kept up with the Swedish colony wherever he went, and in London he had a special friend in Mr. Christopher Springer.[7]

Mr. Springer, when he talked about it in later years, was himself surprised that he, who was "not a learned man," should have known Swedenborg. He said that although they had been friends in Sweden he had not expected that the friendship should have become as constant as it proved to be. But perhaps he was a relief from uncritical devotion, in any case he affords another example of the width of Swedenborg's human interests. Christopher Springer was one of those unofficial and adventurous diplomats for his country which our own time was also to see. He took part, successfully, in the most secret negotiations between England, Russia, Sweden, and Prussia, and there was no doubt in *his* mind as to Swedenborg's clairvoyant power.

"All that he has told me of my deceased friends," he said, "and enemies and of the secrets I had with them is almost past belief. He even explained to me in what manner peace was concluded between Sweden and the King of Prussia; and he praised my conduct on that occasion. He even specified the three high personages whose services I made use of at that time, which was nevertheless a profound secret between us."

When Springer asked Swedenborg who had told him these things, the latter said, "Who told me about your affair with Count Claes Ekeblad? You cannot deny that what I have told you is true."

Count Ekeblad had attempted to bribe Mr. Springer with the sum of ten thousand Rix-daler, after having quarreled with him on a political matter, but they had made it up and sworn never to mention these things to anyone. But Swedenborg told Springer about both the particular sum and all the circumstances.

Swedenborg kept up his acquaintance too with Eric Bergström,[8] a Swede who kept the King's Arms (Charles XII), a tavern in Wellclose Square, where Swedenborg once had stayed for ten weeks.

When the innkeeper talked about his customer, in after years, he said he never observed anything in Swedenborg "but what was very reasonable and bespoke the gentleman." The latter had told him the various stories that proved his clairvoyance. "Some of his friends here spoke against him, and some were for him; for my own part," said the innkeeper, "I think he was a reasonable, sensible and good man; he was very kind to all and generous to me. As to his peculiar sentiments, I do not meddle with them."

Swedenborg often went to spend an evening in Poppin's Court where the partner of his publisher lived, a Mr. Hart; and he was equally friendly with Hart's son and successor, taking particular notice of the little daughter.[9] He used to distribute gingerbread to the children in the square.

In the summer of 1769 Swedenborg lived at the house of Mr. Shearsmith, the barber and wigmaker, in Great Bath Street, Coldbath fields, where he had lived before, and where his hosts greatly appreciated him, though at first Mr. Shearsmith said he was "affrighted" when Swedenborg would stand in the doorway between his two rooms and, although alone, talk "as if he was holding a conversation with some person," but as it was in a foreign language poor Mr. Shearsmith was no wiser. He said that times and seasons, days and nights, meant little to his lodger; he only rested when nature required it. When he went out he usually wore a suit of black velvet, made after an old fashion; a pair of long ruffles, a curious hilted sword and a gold-headed cane. He ate little or no animal food, except a few eels sometimes. He was fond of very sweet coffee and tea and he took a great deal of snuff.[10]

In the autumn of 1769 Swedenborg returned to Stockholm, where, besides protesting against the Dean of Gothenburg's treatment of him, he busied himself with another book, the last he was to publish, the one that was to be the compendium of the doctrines of the New Church as well as of everything he had learned and concluded about earth, hell, heaven, spirit world, and the conduct leading to each, with "memorable relations" illustrating his points. Taking a rough draft of this in hand, the eighty-two-year-old man left Stockholm again for Amsterdam in July, 1770, in order to finish it and have it printed.

This brought him once more within the orbit of that good reporter, Mynheer Johan Christian Cuno, who met him on the Stock-Exchange where Swedenborg had gone with his Swedish friend, Joachim Wretman.

Cuno was in amazement at the amount of writing Swedenborg managed to do, although he also slept some twelve hours a night, and although he continued to lead a social life. As Cuno said, "He is reserved to no one. If anyone is curious to see him, he has no great difficulty; all that is necessary for him to do is to go to his house, where he admits everyone. It can easily be seen that the numerous calls which he thus receives draw largely upon his time; and so much the less can I understand, how he, nevertheless, accomplishes his design of having printed every week two closely set up sheets, and to compose ten sheets of manuscript, without having a single line in reserve. He says," Cuno added, "that his angel dictates to him, and that he can write fast enough."

The work appeared in Amsterdam in July, 1771. Cuno was shocked that on the title page Swedenborg described himself as the servant of the Lord Jesus Christ, to which Swedenborg replied, "I have asked, and have received not only permission but express command." [11]

Hardly was the book published before he took it with him to London.

CHAPTER TWENTY-EIGHT

Swedenborg's Religion

THE title of the new work was *The True Christian Religion,* 541 quarto pages. It was truly a feat, what Swedenborg had done, but Cuno did not know about the rough draft and what writers are capable of when they have made up their minds what they are going to write. Even without angel guidance they have been known to do a chapter a day, and, though Swedenborg undoubtedly was in good faith when he said his angel dictated to him, it must be taken that both for him and for the angel it was a task made easier by the amount of repetition to be found in the new book from former works. More than half of the "memorable relations" had already appeared, and nearly all of the teachings.[1]

But still the book was an almost incredible feat, first of mere physical writing (it runs to about a thousand pages in a modern edition), and then of the system and structure which the man of eighty-two had imposed on this mass of crowded material. It was not, to our way of thinking, a rational system, except within itself, for naturally Swedenborg could not furnish a guide to the different levels of his consciousness by which or through which the book had been written. It had a good deal of the verbose repetitiousness of much automatic writing, but most of the matter was sound enough, from whatever point of view one regards it—whether as a product of Swedenborg entirely, or as at least partly due to the "angels and spirits" who, he felt, had guided his hand or whispered into his "internal" hearing or shown pictures to his inner sight of spiritual realities, ranging from the subtlest of Perennial Philosophy to rigid Bible worship by means of highly dubious personal exegesis.

As for the latter, it must not be forgotten, of course, that Swedenborg both wanted to and was required (given his times) to keep the doctrines of the New Church within the Christian framework. And that he had interpreted the Delft vision as being a manifestation of Jesus Christ to him.

Even before the new book, as well as in it, he had worked out a brief creed of five articles that sounded almost orthodox, if one did not read his explanations of what was meant by each article in it.

One was: "God is one in whom there is a divine Trinity, and the Lord God the Savior Jesus Christ is that one."

The gist of his explanations of this was that God, the invisible, unmanifest, spaceless and timeless,[2] (the Godhead of Eckhart), seeing the state into which His creatures had fallen through their injudicious use of freewill, manifested Himself in *time* by descending into a human body so that the invisible could become visible, and act materially in a world of matter, for, said the practical Swede, "no one can scale a fish without a knife or pluck a crow without fingers or descend to the bottom of a lake without a diving bell." [3]

The "Trinity" in the Man-God was his soul from the eternal and timeless *Father,* his body as the *Son* of Mary, and the *Holy Spirit* as the "operation," or action, caused by the union of that soul and body. "They make one," Swedenborg said, "as soul, body and operation make one in man." He devoted considerable skill to showing how all the polytheism had come about through the "trinity of persons" introduced by the Nicene creed.[4]

Two was: "That a saving faith is to believe in Him," something to which no heresy-hunter could object. But Swedenborg insisted that the only way by which "faith" could become "saving" was in accordance with "the laws of order." They required that unless a man regenerated himself "naturally," even God could not regenerate him "spiritually." [5] Man had to drag himself as far as he could by rational reflection and by genuine, self-examining repentance before the way would be leveled and the door open for God to come in and do His part, in accordance with His own laws of order, filling the truths acquired by man with divine light and warmth.

Salvation was coöperative. But Swedenborg had to include "redemption," or the orthodox would be after him. He said that redemption consisted in the subjugation by the Lord of the hells and the reëstablishment of order in the heavens. But he was not nearly so insistent on what redemption consisted in as on what it did *not.*

Mankind was not redeemed, he said, through the passion (or suffering) of Jesus on the cross. That passion was the completion of something that had been gradually taking place, the union of the human Jesus with the Divine from which his soul had sprung, or with his, symbolic, "Father" (or with his Real Self). As a man he had combated the temptations of men, not turning aside even from the cross, though, humanly, he had had the desire to do so. But that was his last temptation, and he conquered it.[6]

For, Swedenborg said dryly, but with much autobiographical feeling behind his words, "it is by means of temptation that conjunction is effected." Though man feels bitterly, left to himself, God is really with him in this struggle of the "internal and external" man, and therefore "when man conquers temptation he is inmostly conjoined with God."

How Swedenborg felt about the doctrine that God had to be propitiated for the sins of mankind by having His Son die horribly, and that men's "salvation" consisted in crediting them with the "merits" of Christ, he expressed, or let an "angel" express, in this book.

"Can the Christian world be so insane, and wander away from sound reason into such madnesses, and from such paradoxes draw conclusions about the fundamental dogma of salvation? Who does not see that these things are diametrically opposed to the very Divine essence, that is to God's Divine Love and Divine Wisdom, and at the same time to his omnipotence and omnipresence? No good master could so deal with his manservants and maidservants, nor even a wild beast or a bird of prey with its young. It is horrible. Is it not contrary to God's Divine essence to annul that call which has been made to the whole human race and to each individual? Is it not contrary to the Divine essence to change the order established from eternity, which is that every man is to be judged by his life?" [7]

Three was: "Evils should not be done, because they are of the devil and from the devil."

It was indeed hard to tell from article three that Swedenborg had not believed in any personal "Devil" for a great many years. He seems to have done so in the brief attack of orthodoxy he had while he was undergoing his "temptations" in the religious crisis period, but he very soon dropped the Devil. He believed, however, in *devils*—that is, in human beings who had so consistently chosen evil that everything which made them human had died. In the other world these constituted "hell" or the hells, but by choice, not because they had been "sent" there by God.

Swedenborg had thought a great deal about evil, and his reflections were much subtler than article three seemed to show. He had long maintained that evil was "sin." *Not* the other way around, that "sin" was evil. He was aware that "sin" is a terribly elastic word. It can be stretched to include the breaking of all sorts of rules, not in themselves ethical, such as food rules or attendance at ceremonies. But the Decalogue in its widest significance should, he said, leave no one unaware of what were real evils.

But why shouldn't you commit evil?

"Why shouldn't I kill my neighbor and eat him, if I'm strong enough to do it and clever enough to get away with it?" Moralists of all ages find it far too easy to answer this question, but not so that their answers convince the questioner, whose neighbor remains theoretically safe only so long as steaks from a cow are preferred to human chops.

Swedenborg had not only a negative but a positive answer to the question; not his own answers, naturally, but those he had made his own. He said first that the Ten Commandments were not only "civic and moral but also spiritual laws." "Unless evils are shunned as sins," he said, man is not leading a good life according to spiritual laws. Sin is the breaking of a spiritual law, and therefore "evil is hurtful to the soul." Swedenborg had done his best to prove to men "from experience" that he was not talking about theological niceties, but about consequences that, as inevitable as a chemical reaction, followed the "soul" into the other world.

But in the other world, he admitted, he had met with "devils" that frankly preferred the stenches of hell to the fragrances of heaven. Did he leave the question then as a matter of taste, or of taste in smell?

No. All through his works he said in effect that the best reason for not being evil was that being good opened the way to infinitely greater pleasures. He knew both. Early in his *Spiritual Diary* he had confessed that he used to feel revengeful.[8] (It might be said that some of the diary notes in which his former enemies were represented as in a sad state in the other world were projections from a not wholly sublimated layer of his subconscious.) He considered that he had been too ambitious. He knew that those states of self-occupation had been misery compared to those "ineffable felicities" he had enjoyed when he had labored with himself enough to feel he was able to be with angelic beings who were more nearly in a selfless state.

This black knot of the ego Swedenborg often referred to as man's "proprium," and he saw its annihilation as true religion. He wrote once in his diary that spirits "supposed that by losing those things which were most peculiarly their own, they would be left so entirely destitute that neither man nor spirit would be intelligently master of himself, but be like a machine, devoid of all sense and reflection . . ." but he explained that only by becoming "nothing" could one become "something." Nothing in this case meant, he said, that a man should lose all that was "his own," namely his "cupidities and so his iniquities," and then he would "come to exist as another person . . ." Other delights "in boundless variety" would then be his. As he wrote of the skeptical spirits "the sensation and perception which they thought would be extinguished are infinitely heightened when self-love ceases to be the ruling principle of their delights." [8a]

Still he knew very well that it was no use to tell someone who preferred the smell of a rotten fish to that of a rose that the rose ought to be preferred, so, on the whole, he contented himself by telling the stench-lover that his main punishment would consist in gravitating irresistibly to his like in the other world. They dealt with each other.

But—why did God "permit" evil, as Swedenborg so often said? "Evil happens by permission," as it happened often enough to him, by his own accounts of his "infestation" by evil spirits.

On this crucial question he referred his readers back to his book on *Divine Providence,* in which he had made a very fair list of the miseries of mankind, including wars.

The answer he made, on behalf of Providence, was consistent with his belief in God as Order rather than God as Omnipotence. He said: "When God is said to permit, it is not meant that He wills, but that on account of the end, which is salvation, He cannot avert." [9]

Man, he insisted, had freedom of choice in spiritual things, or "salvation" would not be possible.[10] That implied freedom to choose evil in preference to good. All the evil in the world was man-made, none of it from God.

Four, in literal translation, was: "Goods should be done because they are of God and from God."

And *Five* was: "These should be done by man as if by himself; but it should be believed that they are done by the Lord in man and through man."

Four and five were really the same. Swedenborg was confronted by the problem of "self-merit": how not to "take credit" for doing good, and thus become self-righteous, and yet leave man the amount of free choice that was necessary for salvation. He solved it quite logically by going back to the impersonal conception of God, as one might say. God was Good and Truth, but you could also say that Good and Truth were God. Therefore, naturally, if a man divided his last crust with another, or gave him the whole of it, God was acting through him. Man had in a sense done it himself, but he must never allow the "self" to boast about it, nor would he if he could continue to remember that all true good and all good truth *were* God.

There was, however, another point in article four. One might say that "humanitarians" had come up in the eighteenth century, people who from the noblest motives felt that "the good" was so good in itself it needed no "acknowledgment of the divine" to enforce it, a quite natural result of the spectacle that a power-loving church afforded. Swedenborg felt, due to his personal experience, that if the good were no longer regarded as "God," very soon it would be reduced to a level of utility. He had had a talk about that once, recorded in his diary, with an English bishop, whom he told that being good to one's neighbor for the sake of utility was Machiavellianism.[11] And utility was also a word, like "sin," which could be stretched to cover a great many different things.

Swedenborg said, in effect, to orthodox Christians: By subjecting the understanding to "faith," you have destroyed true religion. He said to the atheist: By denying the divine, by putting the good into the same class as the useful, you've opened the way to the breaking of spiritual laws. There *are* spiritual laws. I have seen them in operation.

Long before the melancholy Kierkegaard, Swedenborg propounded "existentialism," if that rubbery word be taken to mean that you can't know until you try.

Swedenborg was visiting, he reported, one of the lower societies in the spirit world where excessively learned men were arguing about religion. He asked: "What kind of religion is necessary for the salvation of mankind?" They answered: "We will divide this question into several; and until these are decided we can give no reply. The investigation will proceed as follows: (1) Is religion anything? (2) Is there such a thing as salvation or not? (3) Is one religion more efficacious than another? (4) Is there a heaven and a hell? (5) Is there an eternal life after death? besides other questions."

They admitted that it would take at least a hundred years to decide the first point, and, Swedenborg said, "Meanwhile you are without religion." He reproached them for doing nothing but *argue* "whether a thing is so or not so." That, he said, "is to reason about the fit of a cap or shoe without ever trying it on . . . have a care for yourselves, lest your minds, while standing outside the door of judgment, grow hard within and become like pillars of salt."

Then they threw stones at him.[12]

One might say that Swedenborg in his unremittent emphasis on practical, do-something-about-it, religion was Western and Christian. But he was also, probably without knowing it, and via the Platonists, not far from Hinduism in his worship of God in His Avatar, and he was at one with Buddhism in his insistence on the reality of spiritual law, or Karma. With Buddhism too he believed in the power of the understanding to change wrong feeling to right feeling, so that man would keep the commandments because he "desires to do so," like a free man and not like a slave. Nor was he far from the Dhamma, the Good Law, of Buddha, when he declared in *The True Christian Religion:* "The Christian world does not yet know that there is an order, and it knows still less what this order is which God introduced into the world at the same time that He created it, and that God cannot act contrary to it, for if he did that, he would be in conflict with himself, for God is that very Order."

CHAPTER TWENTY-NINE

A Happy End

ABOUT Christmas, 1771, Swedenborg was touched by paralysis in one side. Up till then he had been working on additions to his *True Christian Religion;* [1] now he had to stop. The Shearsmiths and their maid took care of him. He lay in a lethargic state for over three weeks, during which time he ate nothing, except that he had a little tea without milk, cold water, and once "about two teaspoonfuls of red currant jelly." At the end of that time he recovered a little, though he was still partly paralyzed and remained in bed.[2] He was then eighty-four years old.

Dr. Messiter attended him, and Mr. Hartley came to see him, though not so often as Mr. Hartley wished. The local Swedish pastor, a good man by the name of Arvid Ferelius, visited him frequently. In a letter to a friend he reported that, although Swedenborg used to talk with great energy to invisible listeners, he was not "eccentric and whimsical; but the very reverse was the case. He was very easy and pleasant in company, talked on every subject that came up, accommodating himself to the ideas of the company; and he never spoke on his own views, unless he was asked about them."

It did worry Ferelius that Swedenborg would mention various celebrated spirits as having just been in the room, but when the pastor asked why no one else enjoyed such revelations and spirit intercourse, Swedenborg said that everyone might, "the real hindrance is that men at the present time are so carnally minded."

Pastor Ferelius asked Swedenborg several times if he felt this was going to be his death, and each time the latter said Yes. The last time this happened, the clergyman declared to Swedenborg that "as quite a number of people thought that his sole purpose in promulgating his new theological system had been to make himself a name, or to acquire celebrity, which object, indeed, he had thereby attained, if such had been the case, he ought now to do the world the justice to retract it either in whole or part, especially as he could not expect to derive any additional advantage from this world, which he would soon leave. He thereupon half rose in his bed, and laying his sound hand upon his breast said with some manifestation of zeal: 'As true as you see me before your eyes, so true is everything that I have written; and I could have said more, had it been permitted. When you enter eternity, you will see everything, and then you and I shall have much to talk about.' " [3]

Pastor Ferelius then gave him the last sacrament, which Swedenborg took, in his own words, "with thankfulness." He could: the traditional vessels of the old religion he had filled with a wine of his own.

He did not die till about three weeks later, but some days before his death he told the date of it to Elizabeth Reynolds, the maid at the Shearsmiths', and, she reported, "He was pleased, as if he was going to have a holiday, to go on some merry-making." [4]

This did not mean that Swedenborg thought life had been a sojourn in a vale of tears. Once he wrote in his *Spiritual Diary:* "Some think that they who are in the faith should remove from themselves all the delights of life, and all the pleasures of the body; but this I can assert, that delights and pleasures have never been denied to me; for I have been permitted to enjoy not only the pleasures of the body and the senses, like those who live in the world, but I have also been permitted to enjoy such delights and felicities of life as I believe no persons in the whole world ever before enjoyed, which were greater and more exquisite than any person could imagine and believe." [5]

He had felt and continued to feel the peace in comparison with which, as he had said, gladness and tranquillity were as nothing. It shone from his face, and he wanted to share it with others. Let us rise, he had said, above our senses and into a loftier sphere of understanding; if we do this "the more we become neighbors to a higher, spiritual, divine power; the more we become men, the vicarious divinities of the earth." [6]

Swedenborg had noticed that when he gave dolls to children he could see that they thought of them and treated them as if they were alive.

He too had that gift. Before his eyes, as before that of the angels of the inmost heaven, all things seemed "to laugh, to play and to live."

He could see the sky covered with dark red roses. If he had seen the ape-men and the leopard-men, he had also seen the angel-men.

Swedenborg enjoyed "a sound mind, memory and understanding to the last hour of his life," so Elizabeth Reynolds and Richard Shearsmith reported, swearing it before the Mayor of London at the Guildhall, on November 24, 1775, because tongues had wagged, saying that Swedenborg had retracted everything just before he died.

In that document, so elegantly lettered by the Guildhall clerk, to which Elizabeth had set her mark and Shearsmith his signature, it was also set forth that they never did, either directly or indirectly, hear Swedenborg express or imply such an idea as that of retraction, nor did any person or persons visit him either the day before or the day on which he died, which was the twenty-ninth of March, 1772.

By his bedside, the document said, were Mrs. Shearsmith (who died soon after) and Elizabeth. The wife of the barber, and the maid: two simple East End Londoners, of those people whom he had described as the best of the Christians.

About five o'clock of that Sunday, Swedenborg asked the two women what time it was. They told him, and he thanked them, saying it was good. "In about ten minutes after, he heaved a gentle sigh and expired in the most tranquil manner."

From every human life, cast into the pool of time, waves circle out, big or little, even after that life has disappeared from time. No one knows how far they reach. The life of Emanuel Swedenborg continued to touch many lives, even after his body, that "outworn garment," had been laid in a triple coffin in the Swedish church in London.

One day the wigmaker and barber Shearsmith was visited by a stranger who begged to see Swedenborg's rooms and asked to be shown where Swedenborg used to stand. The wigmaker told him

that in the doorway between the rooms he had often seen Swedenborg talking with his invisible friends. The stranger made sure
it was the very spot, then he went and stood there. He left, after
handsomely rewarding Shearsmith, nor was anything ever known
of him than what he said of himself, that he was from the far West
Indian island of St. Croix.[7]

Another day, in 1908, nearly a century and a half later, the Royal
Swedish battleship, the *Fylgja* (not inaptly named, as that was
what the old Scandinavians called the good spirit believed to be
every man's double and companion), sailed for London, with one
mission only: to bring back to his country, at last mindful of a
great son, the body of Emanuel Swedenborg—scientist and mystic.

GENERAL SOURCES

The letters, diaries, and books of Swedenborg are, of course, the main sources for his biography. Next come the three-volume *Documents Concerning the Life and Character of Emanuel Swedenborg,* collected, translated, and annotated by R. L. Tafel (London, Swedenborg Society, Inc., 1875, 1877), and the *Chronological List of Swedenborg Documents* (in manuscript) (Bryn Athyn, Pa.), collected by Alfred H. Stroh and Sigrid O. Sigstedt (S. C. Odhner). The translations of Swedenborg's letters by Alfred Acton, published in *The New Philosophy,* have been used as far as possible in preference to Tafel's translations, and indebtedness should be acknowledged to Dr. Acton's excellent introductions and annotations to those of Swedenborg's works which he has translated. Many articles in the Swedenborgian magazines *New Church Life* and *New Philosophy,* published at Bryn Athyn, Pa., have been enlightening.

ABBREVIATIONS USED
IN NOTES AND REFERENCES

Journal A.S.P.R., for *The Journal of the American Society for Psychical Research* (New York, 40 E. 34 St.)

N.C.L., for *New Church Life,* published at Bryn Athyn, Pa.

N.P., for *The New Philosophy,* published by The Swedenborg Scientific Association, Bryn Athyn, Pa.

Proceedings S.P.R., for *The Proceedings of the Society for Psychical Research* (London, 31, Tavistock Sq.)

Tafel, for the work cited above.

The titles of some of Swedenborg's works have been abbreviated as follows:

A.C., for *Arcana Celestia*

A.K., for *The Animal Kingdom*

C.L., for *Conjugial Love*

D.D., for *Dream Diary (Swedenborgs Drömmar)*

D.L.W., for *Divine Love and Wisdom*

E.A.K., for *The Economy of the Animal Kingdom*

H.H., for *Heaven and Hell*

Sp.D., for *The Spiritual Diary* (also known as *Memorabilia*)

T.C.R., for *The True Christian Religion*

W.E., for *The Word Explained*

W.L.G., for *Of the Worship and Love of God*

NOTES AND REFERENCES

(Unless prefaced by "p" for page, a number after the title of one of Swedenborg's books refers to the paragraph number.)

CHAPTER ONE: WHY SWEDENBORG

1. Erik Nordensköld, *History of Biology* (New York, Tudor Press, 1936).
2. *Transactions of the International Swedenborg Congress* (London, 1910).
3. Swedenborg, *E.A.K.,* tr. by A. Clissold (2d ed. New York, New Church Press), Vol. I, 18.
4. *Idem,* 19.
5. Cited by Professor Herbert Dingle in *Swedenborg as a Physical Scientist* (London, Swedenborg Society), p. 11.
6. William James, *Varieties of Religious Experience* (New York, The Modern Library), p. 19.
7. F. W. H. Myers, *Human Personality and Its Survival of Bodily Death.*
8. *Tafel,* doc. 252, p. 409.

CHAPTER TWO: STOCKHOLM SHOCKED

1. *Tafel,* doc. 249.
2. *Tafel,* doc. 6, p. 65 n.
3. *Tafel,* doc. 250 A.
4. Geyer, cited by *Tafel,* Vol. I, p. 631 nn.
5. *Tafel,* Vol. I, p. 633.
6. *Tafel,* doc. 252 A.
7. *Tafel,* doc. 252 F.
8. Nicholas Collin, "A New Document Concerning Swedenborg," ed. by Sigrid Odhner Sigstedt, *N.C.L.,* January, 1914, pp. 51 ff.
9. *Tafel,* doc. 255, par. 24.

CHAPTER THREE: PARENT EXTRAORDINARY

1. Blaise Pascal, *Pensées.*
2. *Tafel,* doc. 6, p. 59 n.
3. *Jesper Swedbergs lefwernes beskrifning,* ed. by Gunnar Wetterberg (Lund, Gleerup, 1941). This work is the source of what follows in this chapter concerning Jesper Swedberg and his family.
4. *Tafel,* doc. 9 B.
5. Swedenborg, *A.K.,* 65.
6. See "Pietism" *Enc. Brit.,* 13th ed.
7. Ehrenborg documents, *Chronological List of Swedenborg Documents* (Bryn Athyn, Pa., Library, Academy of the New Church), p. 3.
8. *Tafel,* doc. 2.
9. Swedenborg, *C.L.,* 395.

CHAPTER FOUR: UNDERGRADUATE AT UPSALA

1. *Chronological List,* Bryn Athyn Library, doc. 2 b; *Tafel,* Vol. I, p. 672; see also Arvid Hj. Uggla, *Ett läkarebibliothek från början af 1700-talet* (Upsala, 1945).
2. *Tafel,* Vol. I, p. 672.

3. Swedenborg, *Sp.D.*, 4717.
4. Swedenborg, *The Infinite and the Final Cause of Creation*, tr. by J. J. Garth Wilkinson (London, 1908), p. 3.
5. A. H. Stroh, *The Cartesian Controversy at Uppsala*, etc. (Heidelberg, Sonderabdrück aus den Verhandlungen des III internationale Kongresses für Philosophie, 1908).
6. John Veitch, *The Philosophy of Descartes* (New York, Tudor).
7. Stroh, *op. cit.*
8. For Swedenborg and student life, see *Constitutiones Nationis Dalekarlo-Vestmannicae*, Jämte någre anteckningar om Emanuel Swedenborgs studentertid i Uppsala, 1699–1709 (Uppsala, 1910, utgifna af Vestmanlandsdala Nation).
9. *Ibid.*
10. Book at Library, Bryn Athyn, with his name and the date written on it by Swedenborg.
11. See translations and annotations by Professor Enoch Price in *N.P.* from October, 1931, to January, 1935 (Bryn Athyn, Pa.).
12. Nordensköld, *History of Biology.*
13. Mrs. Alfred H. Stroh, widow of the fine Swedenborgian scholar, possesses this painting. It is anonymous, both as to painter and subject, but Stroh was convinced that the tradition was correct which said the painting represented Swedenborg, and if it is compared with the Bernigroth engraving and with the Per Krafft d.ä. painting at Gripsholm one cannot but agree.
14. See Frans Bengtsson, *Karl XII*, a brilliant study of the king, while for the period's general history see C. Grimberg, *Svenska folkets underbara öden*, Vols. IV, V, VI Stockholm, Norstedt).
15. *Disputatio Academica Emanuelis Swedbergii.* Photostat original ed. (Stockholm).
16. *C.L.*
17. Bengtsson, *op. cit.*
18. For the letters of Swedenborg, beginning with the one written July 13, 1709, the excellent translations, with notes, by Dr. Alfred Acton have been made use of. They are published in the issues of *N.P.* from January, 1938, and still continuing. The current issue (January, 1947) brings the translations up to 1745.

CHAPTER FIVE: DISCOVERY OF ENGLAND

1. Wilmarth S. Lewis, *Three Tours through London* (New Haven, Yale University Press, 1941).
2. John Gay, cited by Walter Besant, *London in the 18th Century.*
3. Lewis, *op. cit.*
4. *Swedenborgs Drömmar.*
5. Suggested by E. A. G. Kleen in his *Swedenborg* (Stockholm, 1917, 1920).
6. Alfred Acton, *op. cit.*
7. Dr. C. P. Oliver, Director of the Flower Observatory.
8. *Chronological List,* Bryn Athyn Library, no. 4.
9. "Minor Poems of Swedenborg," tr. by Frank Sewall, *N.P.*, April, 1916.
10. Tr. by Alfred Acton, *N.P.*, January, 1940. See also for illustrated descriptions: *The Mechanical Inventions of Emanuel Swedenborg*, tr. and ed. by Acton (Philadelphia, Swedenborg Scientific Assoc., 1939).

CHAPTER SIX: ENGINEER AND MINING EXPERT

1. Bengtsson, *Karl XII.*
2. *N.P.*, January,, 1940, p. 266.
3. *N.P.*, April, 1940, p. 299.
4. *N.P.*, July, 1940, p. 347.
5. "Assessor Swedenborg," by S. C. Odhner, *N.C.L.*, p. 228.

6. *N.P.*, April, 1941, p. 38.
7. *N.P.*, October, 1941, pp. 122 ff.
8. Professor A. G. Nathorst, Superintendent of the Geological Dept., Royal Swedish Academy of Sciences, cited by A. H. Stroh in *Några vittnesbörd om vetenskapsmannen Swedenborg* (Stockholm, 1909).
9. "Assessor Swedenborg," by S. C. Odhner, *N.C.L.* April, 1927, p. 225.
10. *Idem*, p. 230.
11. See *N.P.*, July, October, 1943; all of 1944; April, July, October, 1945.
12. Introduction to *Psychological Transactions*, tr. Alfred Acton.
13. *Resebeskrifningar af Emanuel Swedenborg*, under åren 1710–1739 (Uppsala, Kungl. Vetenskapsakademiet, 1910).

CHAPTER SEVEN: PHYSICIST AND PHYSIOLOGIST

1. Swedenborg *Summary of Principia*, tr. by A. H. Stroh (Bryn Athyn, Pa., Swedenborg Scientific Assoc., 1904).
2. Svante Arrhenius, *Emanuel Swedenborg as a Cosmologist* (Stockholm, 1908).
3. For a modern appraisal, see *Swedenborg as a Physical Scientist*, by Professor Herbert Dingle, D.Sc., A.R.C.S., Professor of Natural Philosophy, Imperial College of Science and Technology, South Kensington, London. (Professor Dingle is an astronomer and physicist.) Trans. 4 (London, Swedenborg Society, Inc., 1938).
4. *Idem*, quotation from Swedenborg's *Principia*.
5. Heyl, *New Frontiers of Physics*, p. 113.
6. Harold Gardiner, M.S., F.R.C.S., *Swedenborg and Modern Ideas of the Universe*, Trans. 1 (London, Swedenborg Society, Inc.).
7. *Ibid.*
8. Sir James Jeans, *Physics and Philosophy*, p. 175.
9. *Tafel*, doc. 26.
10. *Jesper Swedbergs lefwernes beskrifning*, p. 591.
11. *Enc. Brit.* (13th ed.), Vol. I, p. 934.
12. *Tafel*, doc. 121.
13. *N.P.* January, 1934, pp. 276 ff.; October, 1934, pp. 361 ff.
14. Preface, *Opera Philosophica et Mineralic*, Vol. II.
15. *Tafel*, doc. 5, sec. 54.
16. E. A. G. Kleen, *Swedenborg* (Stockholm, 1917, 1920), p. 378.
17. *Tafel*, Vol. I, p. 699.

CHAPTER EIGHT: DISSECTING ROOMS ABROAD

1. See "Penn, William," *Enc. Brit.*, 13th ed.
2. *Sp.D.*, 2821.
3. *Summary of Principia*, p. 11.
4. *Idem*, p. 10, chap. i, summarized by A. H. Stroh.
5. Swedenborg, *Of the Infinite . . .* , p. 100.
6. Rufus M. Jones, *Spiritual Reformers of the Sixteenth and Seventeenth Centuries* (London, Macmillan & Co.).
7. *Ibid.*
8. *Of the Infinite . . .* , p. 111.
9. *Idem*, p. 112.
10. *Idem*, p. 229.
11. *Idem*, p. 181.
12. *Idem*, p. 230.
13. *Ibid.*
14. *On Tremulations*, tr. by C. Th. Odhner (Boston), p. 5.

15. *Idem*, p. 6.
16. Nordensköld, *History of Biology*, pp. 177 ff.
17. *Psychologica Empirica*, Latin-English, tr. by Alfred Acton.
18. *Resebeskrifningar af Emanuel Swedenborg*.
19. *C.L.*, 537.
20. *The Way to a Knowledge of the Soul*, p. 46.
21. *Idem*, p. 47.
22. *A.K.*, Vol. II, p. 608.
23. See "Anatomy," *Enc. Brit.*, 13th ed.

CHAPTER NINE: ANATOMY OF MIND AND BODY

1. Emerson, "Swedenborg," in *Representative Men* (Boston, Houghton, Osgood & Co., 1879), p. 88.
2. *E.A.K.*, Vol. II, 652.
3. *Ibid.*
4. *E.A.K.*, Vol. II, 214.
5. Haggard, Howard W., M.D., Professor and Director, Laboratory of Applied Physiology, Yale University, *Swedenborg as a Physiologist* (Hawthorne, N. J., Swedenborg Publishing Society).
6. *Några vittnesbörd om vetenskapsmannen Swedenborg*, samlade af A. H. Stroh (Stockholm, 1909).
7. *Ibid.;* see also L. Tafel, in *N.P.*, July, 1942, p. 213.
8. *British Medical Journal*, October 15, 1910.
9. F. T. Lewis, in *Science*. Reprinted in *N.P.*, October, 1942.
10. *Ibid.* (At this period Swedenborg believed he sometimes received instruction in dreams.)
11. M. F. Ashley Montagu, Hahnemann Medical College, Philadelphia, in *Isis*, pub. by History of Science Society; cited in *N.P.*, January, 1942, p. 146.
12. Gardner Murphy, "Psychical Research and the Mind-body Relation," *Journal A.S.P.R.*, October, 1946.
13. *E.A.K.*, Vol. II, 283.
14. *E.A.K.*, Vol. II, 217.
15. *E.A.K.*, Vol. I, 214.
16. *E.A.K.*, Vol. I, 199.
17. *E.A.K.*, Vol. I, 64.
18. *E.A.K.*, Vol. I, 253.
19. *E.A.K.*, Vol. II, 275.
20. *E.A.K.*, Vol. I, 247, 248.
21. *Ibid.*
22. *E.A.K.*, Vol. I, 255.
23. *E.A.K.*, Vol. II, 235.
24. *E.A.K.*, Vol. II, 236.
25. See Erwin Schrödinger, *What Is Life?* (New York, The Macmillan Company, 1945).
26. *Idem*, par. 6.
27. *Idem*, par. 64.
28. *Idem*, Epilogue, p. 87.
29. *E.A.K.*, Vol. II, 168.
30. *E.A.K.*, Vol. II, 304.
31. *E.A.K.*, Vol. II, 303.
32. *E.A.K.*, Vol. II, 311.
33. *Ibid.*
34. *Ibid.*
35. *Ibid.*

36. Gustaf Strömberg, *The Soul of the Universe* (Philadelphia, McKay, 1940).
37. *Idem*, p. 49.
38. *Idem*, p. 87.
39. *Idem*, p. 97.
40. See *E.A.K.*, "On the Formation of the Chick, etc.," Vol. I, 168, 247 ff.; also "The Animal Spirit," in *Psychological Transactions*, tr. by Alfred Acton.
41. *Psychologica Empirica*, Latin-English.
42. Arthur Koestler, *The Yogi and the Commissar* (New York, Macmillan, 1945).
43. *Idem*, p. 235.
44. *E.A.K.*, Vol. II, 579 ff.
45. *E.A.K.*, Vol. II, 649.
46. *D.L.W.*, 184.
47. *E.A.K.*, Vol. II, 290.
48. *E.A.K.*, Vol. II, 630.
49. *E.A.K.*, Vol. II, 622.
50. *Posthumous Tracts*, tr. by J. J. Garth Wilkinson (London, 1847).
51. *E.A.K.*, Vol. II, 310.
52. *E.A.K.*, Vol. II, 251.

CHAPTER TEN: ANATOMY OF SOUL

1. Rufus Jones, *Studies in Mystical Religion* (New York, Macmillan).
2. *E.A.K.*, Vol. II, 356.
3. E. S. had Stiernhjelm's copy of Plotinus.
4. *E.A.K.*, Vol. II, 250.
5. See E. A. Hitchcock, *Swedenborg, A Hermetic Philosopher* (New York, Appleton & Co., 1858).
6. See S. Radhakrishnan, *Indian Philosophy* (London, Allen & Unwin) for best general account.
7. See Grace H. Turnbull, *The Essence of Plotinus* (Oxford Univ. Press), extracts from Enneads, based on the McKenna translation.
8. Aldous Huxley, *The Perennial Philosophy* (New York, Harper).
9. *E.A.K.*, Vol. II, 208.
10. *E.A.K.*, Vol. II, 209, 210.
11. *E.A.K.*, Vol. II, 213.
12. *E.A.K.*, Vol. II, 273.
13. *E.A.K.*, Vol. II, 274.
14. *E.A.K.*, Vol. II, 269.
15. *E.A.K.*, Vol. II, 277.
16. *E.A.K.*, Vol. II, 304.
17. *E.A.K.*, Vol. II, 277.
18. *E.A.K.*, Vol. II, 294.
19. *E.A.K.*, Vol. II, 279.
20. *E.A.K.*, Vol. II, 281.
21. *Ibid.*
22. *Ibid.*
23. *E.A.K.*, Vol. II, 317.
24. *E.A.K.*, Vol. II, 320.
25. *E.A.K.*, Vol. II, 322.
26. *E.A.K.*, Vol. II, 323.
27. *Ibid.*
28. *Ibid.*
29. *Ibid.*
30. *E.A.K.*, Vol. II, 329.

31. *E.A.K.*, Vol. II, 330.
32. *Ibid.*
33. *Ibid.*
34. *E.A.K.*, Vol. II, 331.
35. *E.A.K.*, Vol. II, 366.
36. *E.A.K.*, Vol. II, 331.
37. *E.A.K.*, Vol. II, 327.
38. *E.A.K.*, Vol. II, 323.
39. *E.A.K.*, Vol. II, 324.
40. *Psychological Transactions*, p. 48.
41. *E.A.K.*, Vol. I, 22.

CHAPTER ELEVEN: STRANGE DREAMS AND "TEMPTATIONS"

1. *A Philosopher's Notebook*, tr. and ed. by Alfred Acton (Philadelphia, Swedenborg Scientific Association, 1931).
2. *Idem*, p. 37.
3. *Tafel*, doc. 163.
4. *N.P.*, October, 1931.
5. *Tafel*, doc. 127.
6. *E.A.K.*, Vol. II, 352.
7. "Subconscious Reasoning," by Wm. Romaine Newbold, *Proceedings S.P.R.*, Pt. 30, p. 11.
8. *E.A.K.*, Vol. II, 10, 42.
9. *Swedenborgs Drömmar* (Stockholm, J. and A. Riis, 1860), p. 62. This is the edition of Swedenborg's "Dream Diary" (*D.D.*) to which references are made in this biography.
10. "Corpuscular Philosophy," *Scientific and Philosophical Treatises*, Pt. 2.
11. *W.E.*, 6905.
12. *Sp.D.* 2951
13. *The Fibre*, tr. by Alfred Acton, 525 ff.
14. *Ibid.*
15. K. T. Behanan, *Yoga* (New York, Macmillan, 1937).
16. Theos Bernard, *Hatha Yoga* (New York, Columbia University Press, 1945).
17. Behanan, *op. cit.*, p. 199.
18. See pages 218–219.
19. *A.K.*, 22.
20. *A.K.*, 20.
21. *Swedenborgs Drömmar* (Stockholm, P. A. Norstedt & Söner, 1858), ed. by G. E. Klemming, published privately for the first time in 1858.
22. *The Philosopher's Notebook*.
23. *E.A.K.*, Vol. II, 265.
24. *The Fibre*, 507.
25. *Ibid.*
26. *A.K.*, Vol. I, 13.
27. *A.K.*, Vol. II, 463.
28. *Tafel*, doc. 164 B.
29. *D.D.*, p. 17.
30. *The Fibre*, 488.

CHAPTER TWELVE: THE GREAT VISION

1. *D.D.*
2. *D.D.*, p. 3.

3. *Generation*, tr. by Alfred Acton.
4. *D.D.*, p. 30.
5. *D.D.*, p. 37.
6. *The Soul*, tr. by Frank Sewall, 208.
7. *D.D.*, pp. 19, 20.
8. *W.E.*, 541.
9. *D.D.*, p. 42.
10. *Ibid.*
11. *D.D.*, p. 17.
12. *D.D.*, pp. 10 ff.
13. "Fac et spera."
14. *A.K.*, Vol. I, 12.
15. *D.D.*, p. 43.
16. Alfred Acton, Intro. to *W.E.*, p. 83.
17. *D.D.*, p. 46.
18. *A.K.*, Vol. II, 565.
19. *A.K.*, Vol. II, 566 n.
20. Acton, Intro. to *W.E.*, p. 84.
21. *The Soul*, 31.
22. *A.K.*, Epilogue, 458.
23. *The Senses*, tr. by Enoch S. Price, 592.
24. *Idem*, 601.
25. *Idem*, 581.
26. *Idem*, 534.
27. *Idem*, 641.
28. *W.L.G.*, tr. by A. H. Stroh and F. Sewall, 80.
29. *W.L.G.*, 56.
30. *Ibid.*
31. Rufus M. Jones, *Spiritual Reformers of the 16th and 17th Centuries* (London, Macmillan & Co.), p. 101.
32. *Ibid.*
33. *Tafel*, doc. 5, par. 15.
34. *Sp.D.*, 397.
35. Gustave Géley, *From the Conscious to the Unconscious* (1920).
36. *W.E.*, 3557.
37. *W.E.*, 1003.
38. *Tafel*, Vol. II, Pt. 2, n. 168.
39. *W.E.*, 541.
40. *W.E.*, 475.
41. *D.D.*, pp. 32, 34.
42. *Tafel*, docs. 165, 166.

CHAPTER THIRTEEN: SWEDENBORG'S SANITY

1. *Tafel*, doc. 129.
2. W.E., 3347.
3. *Tafel*, doc. 167 B.
4. *Tafel*, 270.
5. C. D. Broad. Presidential Address, *Proceedings S.P.R.*, vol. XLIII, p. 398.
6. Jones, *Spiritual Reformers*.
7. Martin Lamm, *Swedenborg* (Stockholm, 1913).
8. Hitchcock, *op. cit.*
9. *The Soul*, 522.
10. William James, *Varieties of Religious Experience*.

11. Th. Flournoy, *From India to the Planet Mars* (New York, Harper & Bros.).

12. F. W. H. Myers, *Human Personality* . . .

13. *Finsk Tidsskrift* (1923), p. 281.

14. Cited by H. D. Spoerl, in *New Christianity,* Winter, 1937, p. 14.

15. Karl Jaspers, *Strindberg und van Gogh* (Berlin, Springer, 1926).

16. See "Psychoanalysis in Modern Literature," *Columbia Dictionary of Modern European Literature,* p. 657.

17. *Sp.D.,* 1166.

CHAPTER FOURTEEN: PSYCHICAL RESEARCH

1. See Gardner Murphy, "Parapsychology," *Enc. of Psych.,* p. 422, for criticism of methods.

2. See for example, Hodgson and Davey, "The Possibilities of Malobservation and Lapse of Memory . . . ," *Proceedings S.P.R.,* Pt. 11; and Th. Bestermann, "The Psychology of Testimony," *Proceedings S.P.R.,* Pt. 124.

3. *Book List* 75, compiled by the (English) National Book Council, contains a selected list of books on psychical research, with prices. Price one penny from the Society for Psychical Research, 31, Tavistock Sq., London, W.C. 1, England. For technical reports of experiments, see *Enc. of Psych.,* p. 434. An excellent general bibliography is included in G. N. M. Tyrrell's *The Personality of Man* (Pelican Book, Harmondsworth, Middlesex, England, Penguin Books, 1946). This book, together with Mr. Tyrrell's *Science and Psychical Phenomena* (London, Methuen, 1938), Whately Carington's *Thought Transference* (New York, Creative Age Press, 1946. London, Methuen, 1945, under title *Telepathy*), and J. B. Rhine's *The Reach of the Mind* (New York, William Sloane, Associates, 1947) will provide a good introduction to the subject.

4. See Murphy, "Parapsychology," *Enc. Psych.*

5. Tyrrell, *op. cit.*

6. *Ibid.*

7. *Proceedings S.P.R.,* Vol. XLVII, pp. 21–150.

8. *Ibid.,* p. 107.

9. Murphy, "Parapsychology," *Enc. Psych.*

10. "Experiments on the Paranormal Cognition of Drawings, IV," *Proceedings, S.P.R.,* Pt. 168 (July, 1944).

11. Overton Luhr, *Physics Tells Why* (Lancaster, Pa., The Jacques Cattell Press, 1943), p. 269. See, however, "Telepathy and Electromagnetic Waves," by A. J. B. Robertson, *Journal S.P.R.,* No. 631–632, p. 7, for a technical discussion seeking to prove that telepathy has a relation to electromagnetic radiation. According to Mr. Robertson, no "code" would be necessary, if the process were conceived as resembling television broadcasting.

12. *The Soul,* 31.

13. *Idem,* 110.

14. Sidis and Goodheart, *Multiple Personality;* W. McDougall, *Outline of Abnormal Psychology.* For the most noted case, see the report on the Misses Beauchamp, by Morton Prince, *Proceedings S.P.R.,* Pt. 11, Vol. XV (February, 1901).

15. John Layard, "Psi Phenomena and Poltergeists," *Proceedings S.P.R.,* Pt. 168 (July, 1944). Payne and Bendit, *The Psychic Sense* (London, Faber and Faber, 1943).

15a. J. B. Rhine, "Pierre Janet's Contribution to Parapsychology," *The Journal of Parapsychology,* September, 1947, p. 155.

16. G. N. M. Tyrrell, *Apparitions* (London, Society for Psychical Research, 1942). Publications of the Society for Psychical Research (English) can be ordered from F. W. Faxon, 83 Francis St., Boston, Mass.

17. *Sp.D.,* 4250.

18. *Sp.D.,* 2898.

CHAPTER FIFTEEN: SWEDENBORG'S CLAIRVOYANCE

1. *N.C.L.*, January, 1927, p. 3; and *N.P.*, April, 1943, p. 303.
2. *D.D.*
3. *Idem*, pp. 15, 30.
4. *Idem*, p. 62.
5. *Idem*, p. 37.
6. *Idem*, p. 28.
7. *Idem*, p. 53.
8. See Jolan Jacobi, *The Psychology of Jung* (New Haven, Yale University Press, 1943), p. 87.
9. *Idem*, p. 59.
10. *Journal A.S.P.R.*, January, 1944, pp. 18, 19.
11. *The Fibre*, 526.
12. Murphy, "Parapsychology," *Enc. Psych.*, p. 417.
13. *Tafel*, doc. 272, p. 625.
14. *Tafel*, doc. 273 A. The dates in brackets are not those of what purports to be the original letter, but Tafel, in his doc. 272, p. 620 ff., convincingly explains that the latter dates have been falsified. The letter, as published in Borowski's *Life of Kant*, is dated 1758. In it, as cited, Kant assures his esteemed correspondent, Charlotte von Knobloch, that the authenticity of the Gothenburg story could not be questioned. In 1766, Kant published *Dreams of a Spiritseer*, in which he made fun of "Schwedenberg" for his credulity. The inference would be that Kant later on, after he had presumably investigated still further, had changed his mind about Swedenborg's powers.

   But the Stockholm fire and Swedenborg's perception of it while he was in Gothenburg did not take place till 1759. In the letter to C. von Knobloch, thus wrongly dated (or rather re-dated by persons unknown) where Swedenborg's name is correctly spelled, there is still more overwhelming evidence that it could not have been written till after 1766, most probably in 1768.
15. *Tafel*, doc. 271, p. 616 n.
16. *Tafel*, doc. 291, p. 724.
17. *Tafel*, doc. 257 B.
18. Carington, "Experiments on the Paranormal . . . ," *Proceedings S.P.R.*, Pt. 168 (July, 1944); J. Hettinger, *The Ultra-Perceptive Faculty* (London, 1940), and J. Hettinger "Psychometric Telepathy Across the Atlantic," *Journal A.S.P.R.*, July, 1947, p. 94.
19. Murphy, "Parapsychology," *Enc. Psych.*, p. 419.
20. Ludvig Holberg, *Udvalgte Epistler*, ed. by Fr. Winkel Horn (Copenhagen, Chr. Steen, 1884).
21. Carl Grimberg, *Svenska folkets underbara öden*, Vol. IV, p. 415.
22. *Tafel*, doc. 275 H.
23. S. C. Odhner, "New Documents Concerning Swedenborg," *N.C.L.*, February, 1916, p. 99.
24. *Tafel*, doc. 275 P.
25. *Tafel*, doc. 275 F.
26. *Tafel*, doc. 274 B.
27. *Proceedings S.P.R.*, Pt. 103.
28. *Proceedings S.P.R.*, Pt. 99, p. 299.
29. *Proceedings S.P.R.*, Pt. 168.
30. J. G. Pratt, *Towards a Method of Evaluating Mediumistic Material* (Boston Society for Psychic Research, 1936).
31. For summaries of these complicated cases see Tyrrell, *Science and Psychical Phenomena*, p. 230; also Kenneth Richmond, *Evidence of Identity* (London, G. Bell & Sons, 1939). Complete reports in the *Proceedings S.P.R.*

32. See Anita Mühl, *Automatic Writing* (Dresden and Leipzig, Steinkopf, 1930).
33. *Journal A.S.P.R.*, October, 1945.
34. *Ibid.*

CHAPTER SIXTEEN: AUTOMATIC WRITING

1. *Tafel*, doc. 92.
2. *The Word Explained*, ed. and tr. by Alfred Acton (Bryn Athyn, Pa., Academy of the New Church).
3. *D.D.*
4. "Origen," *Enc. Brit.*, 13th ed.
5. C. Th. Odhner, in *N.C.L.*, March, 1903, p. 136.
6. *N.C.L.*, April, 1903.
7. "Origen," *Enc. Brit.*, 13th ed.
8. *W.E.*, 378.
9. *The Philosopher's Notebook*, p. 275.
10. Acton, Intro. to *W.E.*, p. 122.
11. See Mühl, *Automatic Writing*.
12. *W.E.*, 459.
13. *W.E.*, 1150.
14. *W.E.*, 7006.
15. *W.E.*, 4812.
16. *W.E.*, 4849.
17. *W.E.*, 1511.
18. *W.E.*, Vol. II, pp. 493, 494, footnotes to 1511.
19. *Ibid.*
20. *Ibid.*
21. *W.E.*, 1892.
22. *W.E.*, 5652.
23. *W.E.*, 6389.
24. *W.E.*, 7425.
25. See Rufus M. Jones, *Studies in Mystical Religion* (Macmillan, 1909).
26. *W.E.*, 1510.
27. *W.E.*, 1712.
28. *The Philosopher's Notebook*.
29. *W.E.*, 6257.
30. *W.E.*, 6232.
31. *W.E.*, 932.
32. Codices 59, 60, 61.
33. Codex 74.
34. Codex 59, pars. 979–997.
35. Else F. Kronheimer, 26 St. Margaret's Road, Oxford, England. (B. Sc., thesis: "Personality Development in the Light of Graphological Inquiry.")
36. *Sp.D.*, 2962.
37. Codex 2.
38. Codex 88.
39. Codex 3.
40. *C.L.*
41. *The Spiritual Diary of Emanuel Swedenborg*. Vol. I, tr. by J. H. Smithson (London, 1846); Vol. II, tr. by George Bush (Boston 1886); Vol. III, tr. by Bush and Smithson (London, 1883); Vol. IV, tr. by George Bush and James F. Buss (London, 1889); Vol. V, tr. by James F. Buss (London, 1902).
42. *W.E.*, 5292.
43. *Ibid.*

44. *Ibid.*
45. *W.E.*, 968.

CHAPTER SEVENTEEN: "WHAT IS A SPIRIT?"

1. *Sp.D.*, 281.
2. *Sp.D.*, 1499.
3. *Sp.D.*, 3317.
4. *Sp.D.*, 3464.
5. *Ibid.*
6. *Sp.D.*, 1613–1615.
7. *Sp.D.*, 3320.
8. *Sp.D.*, 1612–1615.
9. Bernard, *Hatha Yoga*, p. 47.
10. See Dr. Th. Brosse in *Bulletin du Centre Homéopathique de France*, February, 1937; cited in *Main Currents in Modern Thought*, July, 1946.
11. *Sp.D.*, 402.
12. *Sp.D.*, 651.
13. *A.C.*, 1884–1885.
14. *Ibid.*
15. *Sp.D.*, 651.
16. *Tafel*, doc. 255.
17. *W.L.G.*, p. 229.
18. *Sp.D.*, 651.
19. *Sp.D.*, 2894.
20. *W.E.*, 5004.
21. *A.C.*, 68.
22. *Sp.D.*, 3470.
23. *Sp.D.*, 2366.
24. *Sp.D.*, 2386.
25. *Sp.D.*, 2355.
26. *A.C.*, 444–445.
27. *A.C.*, 447.
28. *D.L.W.*, 257.
29. See C. Th. Odhner, "The Limbus," *N.C.L.*, April, May, June, 1903; Henri de Geymuller, *Swedenborg et les Phenomènes Psychiques* (Paris, Librairie Ernest Leroux, 1934) and, for a modern theory of a "non-physical but real" body, C. Drayton Thomas, "A New Hypothesis Concerning Trance Communications," *Proceedings S.P.R.*, Pt. 173, May, 1947.
30. *Sp.D.*, 242, 3472.
31. *W.E.*, 1150 B.
32. *Sp.D.*, 2251.
33. *Sp.D.*, 1564–1565.
34. *Sp.D.*, 2440–2441.
35. *Sp.D.*, 2037.
36. *Sp.D.*, 438.
37. *Sp.D.*, 192.
38. *Sp.D.*, 1399.

CHAPTER EIGHTEEN: "ARCANA CELESTIA"

1. Acton, Intro. to *W.E.*
2. *Tafel*, doc. 258.

3. *W.E.*, 378.
4. *A.C.*, 3412.
5. *Sp.D.*, 1647.
6. *W.E.*, p. xvii, n.
7. Jones, *Spiritual Reformers.*
7a. The auctioneer's list of Swedenborg's books to be sold after his death has been published in facsimile as *Catalogus Bibliothecae, Emanuelis Swedenborgii,* ed. Alfred H. Stroh, Stockholm, 1907. It contains few "occult" books, but all his books may not have been sold, and he spent much time in foreign libraries.
8. *D.L.W.*, 257.
9. *Sp.D.*, 480.
10. See Jacob Boehme, "Of Heaven and Hell," in *The Signature of All Things,* Everyman's Library, no. 569.
11. See P. D. Ouspensky, *A New Model of the Universe* (Knopf, 1934), p. 142.
12. Tyrrell, *The Personality of Man.*
13. Acton, Intro. to *W.E.*, p. 134.
14. Unless otherwise stated, the quotations that follow in this chapter are from *Heaven and Hell.*
15. Jacobi, *The Psychology of Jung,* p. 19.
16. *Sp.D.*, 4731.
17. *Sp.D.*, 1313–1314.
18. *Sp.D.*, 5546.
19. *Sp.D.*, 4677.
20. *Journal A.S.P.R.*, October, 1945, p. 181.
21. *Sp.D.*, 306.
22. *Sp.D.*, 400.
23. *Sp.D.*, 187.
24. *Sp.D.*, 293.
25. *Sp.D.*, 1484.
26. *Sp.D.*, 3641.
27. *H.H.*, 203.
28. *Sp.D.*, 2406.
29. *Sp.D.*, 1928.
30. *Sp.D.*, 4337.
31. *Sp.D.*, 3624.
32. *Sp.D.*, 2176.
33. *Sp.D.*, 159, 160.
34. *Tafel*, doc. 270.
35. *W.E.*, 4949.
36. *Sp.D.*, 2772.
37. *Sp.D.*, 192.
38. *Sp.D.*, 2659.
39. *Sp.D.*, 3858.
40. *Sp.D.*, 1755.
41. *Sp.D.*, 2392, 479.
42. *Sp.D.*, 1907.
43. *Sp.D.*, 2203.
44. *Sp.D.*, 557.
45. *A.C.*, 448.

CHAPTER NINETEEN: SPACE, TIME, AND MEMORY

1. *A.C.*, 1275.
2. *A.C.*, 1376.

3. *A.C.*, 1277.
4. *A.C.*, 1378.
5. Tyrrell, *Apparitions*.
6. *A.C.*, 1379.
7. Tyrrell, *op. cit.*, p. 114.
8. *Ibid.*
9. *H.H.*, 193.
10. *H.H.*, 194.
11. *Sp.D.*, 5646.
12. *A.C.*, 5605.
13. *Sp.D.*, 5623.
14. *Ibid.*
15. *The Fibre*, 519 ff.
16. *The Five Senses*, 601, 602.
17. *Idem*, 601.
18. Henri Bergson, *Matière et mémoire* (Paris, Alcan, 1900), p. 264.
19. *Sp.D.*, 887.
20. *Sp.D.*, 353.
21. *Sp.D.*, 887.
22. *Sp.D.*, 4410.
23. *Sp.D.*, 1662.
24. *Sp.D.*, 1932.
25. *Sp.D.*, 1662.
26. *Sp.D.*, 1622.
27. *Sp.D.*, 2593.
28. Bergson, *op. cit.*, pp. 270, 266.
29. *Sp.D.*, 2989.
30. *Sp.D.*, 2594; cf. 4556.
31. See n. 14 to Chap. XIV.
32. Hans Driesch, *Psychical Research,* (London, Bell, 1933).
33. *Sp.D.*, 295.
34. *Sp.D.*, 2156.
35. *Sp.D.*, 889.
36. *Sp.D.*, 890.
37. *Sp.D.*, 4560 m.
38. *Sp.D.*, 4115 ff.
39. *Sp.D.*, 1776.
40. *Sp.D.*, 3869, 4166.
41. *Sp.D.*, 4558 m.
42. *Sp.D.*, 4553 m.
43. *Sp.D.*, 4313.
44. *Sp.D.*, 1983, 1077, 885–891.
45. *Sp.D.*, 1078.

CHAPTER TWENTY: SPEECH, ODORS, AURAS

1. G. W. Balfour, "A Study of the Psychological Aspects of Mrs. Willett's Mediumship and the Statements of the Communicators Concerning Process," *Proceedings S.P.R.,* Vol. XLIII, p. 41.
2. *Idem*, p. 161.
3. *Sp.D.*, 1342.
4. *Sp.D.*, 1343, 2308.
5. *Sp.D.*, 2309.
6. *Sp.D.*, 5585, 5589.
7. *Sp.D.*, 5585, 5590.

8. *Sp.D.*, 5592½.
9. *Sp.D.*, 5596, 987.
10. *Sp.D.*, 5564.
11. *Sp.D.*, 5565.
12. *H.H.*, 255.
13. *H.H.*, 240.
14. *H.H.*, 269.
15. *Sp.D.*, 3308.
16. *Sp.D.*, 1584.
17. *A.C.*, 1504.
18. *A.C.*, 1514.
19. *Tafel*, doc. 302 I.
20. *Ibid.*
21. *Ibid.*
22. *Sp.D.*, 1846.
23. *A.C.*, 1505.
24. *A.C.*, 1511; *Sp.D.*, 4202.

CHAPTER TWENTY-ONE: GARDENER, STATESMAN, AUTHOR

1. *Tafel*, doc. 213.
2. Henrik Alm, *Swedenborgs hus och trädgård* (Stockholm, 1938).
3. C. L. Odhner, "Swedenborg's Hobby," *N.C.L.*, February, 1923.
4. *Sp.D.*, 2072.
5. *Tafel*, doc. 5.
6. *Tafel*, doc. 492.
7. *Tafel*, doc. 173.
8. *Ibid.*
9. *Tafel*, doc. 178.
10. *Tafel*, doc. 180.
11. *H.H.*, 64.
12. *Sp.D.*, 2451.
13. Cf. *Sp.D.*, 2652.
14. *Sp.D.*, 2470.
15. *H.H.*, 475.
16. *H.H.*, 478, 524.
17. *H.H.*, 534.
18. "Charity," *The Coronis* (London, W. Newbury, 1843), pp. 127, 128.
18a. W. Y. Evans—Wentz, *The Tibetan Book of the Dead* (Oxford Univ. Press), 1927.
19. *Sp. D.*, 2413.

CHAPTER TWENTY-TWO: INTERWORLD "CORRESPONDENCE"

1. *The Fibre*, 378.
2. *D.L.W.*, 339.
3. *Ibid.*
4. *D.L.W.*, 344.
5. *A.K.*, 293.
6. *A.C.*, throughout.
7. *Sp.D.*, 1145½.

8. *The Philosopher's Notebook*, p. 160.
9. See "Kabbalah," *Enc. Brit.* (13th ed.), p. 621.
10. *Sp.D.*, 367.
11. *Sp.D.*, 670.
12. *Sp.D.*, 1145⅛.
13. *A.C.*, 3644.
14. *Sp.D.*, 1741, 1772.
15. *Sp.D.*, 1701, 1703.
16. *Sp.D.*, 986.
17. *Sp.D.*, 1793.
18. *Sp.D.*, 1743, 1744.
19. *Sp.D.*, 1063.
20. *Sp.D.*, 519.
21. *Sp.D.*, 1558.
22. *The Philosopher's Notebook.* See Lynn Thorndike, "The Latin Pseudo-Aristoteles and Medieval Occult Science," in *English and Germanic Philology*, Vol. XXI (1922). *Die sogenannten Theologie des Aristoteles,* ed. and tr. by Fr. Dieterich (Leipzig, 1883).
23. For drawing see *Sp.D.*, Vol. IV, p. 355; for text see p. 213. For Indian hut see C. Grimberg, *Världshistorie* (Stockholm, Norstedt), Vol. XI, p. 195.
24. *Sp.D.*, 6013; see also 6045.
25. *Tafel*, doc. 199.
26. *Sp.D.*, 4742.
27. *Sp.D.*, 5099.
28. *Sp.D.*, 2542.
29. *Sp.D.*, 6064.
30. *Sp.D.*, 5980.
31. *Tafel*, Vol. II, p. 1312.
32. *Sp.D.*, 5999.
33. *Sp.D.*, 4354.
34. *Sp.D.*, 592, 593.
35. *Sp.D.*, 4315.
36. *Sp.D.*, 4107, 4233.
37. *Sp.D.*, 1996.
38. *Sp.D.*, 5176.
39. Personal statement to the writer, Sennen Cove, England, November, 1946.

CHAPTER TWENTY-THREE: STORIES FROM BEYOND

1. *Tafel*, doc. 313, p. 995.
2. *Chronological List of the Works of Emanuel Swedenborg* (Upsala and Stockholm, Royal Swedish Academy, 1938).
3. *Ibid.*
4. *Tafel*, doc. 313.
5. *Sp.D.*, 5629.
6. *Sp.D.*, 5043, 5046.
7. *Sp.D.*, 843.
8. *Sp.D.*, 5711.
9. *Tafel*, docs. 249, 250, 251.
10. *Tafel*, doc. 252.
11. *Tafel*, doc. 252 E.
12. *Tafel*, doc. 6, p. 58.
13. *The Intercourse between the Soul and the Body* (Rotch ed.), 19.

CHAPTER TWENTY-FOUR: MARRIAGES IN HEAVEN

1. *Tafel,* doc. 234.
2. *C.L.,* 92.
3. *C.L.,* 93, 94.
3a. Gershom G. Scholem, *Major Trends in Jewish Mysticism.* Schocken Books (New York, 1946).
4. *C.L.,* 79.
5. *C.L.,* 44.
6. *C.L.,* 54.
7. *C.L.,* 49.
8. *C.L.,* 326.
9. *Sp.D.,* 6096.
10. *C.L.,* 470, 472.
11. *C.L.,* 42.
12. *C.L.,* 183.
13. *C.L.,* 488.
14. *Sp.D.,* 2622.
15. *C.L.,* 505.
16. *C.L.,* 507 ff.
17. *C.L.,* 512.
18. *C.L.,* 231.
19. *C.L.,* 263.

CHAPTER TWENTY-FIVE: SWEDENBORG IN DAILY LIFE

1. *C.L.,* 28.
2. *Tafel,* doc. 253.
3. Original manuscript, Swedenborg Society, Inc., London.
4. *Tafel,* doc. 291.
5. *Tafel,* doc. 243.
6. *Tafel,* doc. 255.
7. A. P. Tuxen, *Slægten Tuxen* (Copenhagen, 1928).
8. S. C. Odhner, "A New Document Concerning Swedenborg," *N.C.L.,* January, 1914, p. 45.
9. *Tafel,* doc. 6, p. 59.
10. *Tafel,* doc. 245 B.
11. *Tafel,* doc. 314, p. 1035.
12. *The Fibre,* 519 ff.
13. *Proceedings S.P.R.,* Pt. 11, p. 387 (on memory lapses and substitution).
14. *Tafel,* doc. 301, no. 8, p. 757.

CHAPTER TWENTY-SIX: AMSTERDAM REPORT

1. August Scherer, *Aufzeichnungen einer Amsterdammer Bürgers* (Brussels). Tafel's translation compared with original and found correct, which is not always the case with his translations from the Swedish.
2. *Summary Exposition of the Doctrine of the New Church,* 107.
3. *Tafel,* doc. 245 X.
4. *The Intercourse between the Soul and the Body.*

CHAPTER TWENTY-SEVEN: BALM IN ENGLAND

1. See *Tafel*, doc. 272 ff.
2. *Journal A.S.P.R.*, October, 1946, p. 189.
3. *Tafel*, doc. 281.
4. *Tafel*, Biographical Notes.
5. *Tafel*, doc. 1.
6. *Tafel*, doc. 261.
7. *Tafel*, doc. 261, pp. 529 ff.
8. *Tafel*, doc. 263 A.
9. *Tafel*, doc. 264 D.
10. *Tafel*, doc. 264 A.
11. Cuno's diary.

CHAPTER TWENTY-EIGHT: SWEDENBORG'S RELIGION

1. *Tafel*, doc. 313, p. 1015.
2. *T.C.R.*, 370.
3. *T.C.R.*, 125.
4. *T.C.R.*, 163 ff.
5. *T.C.R.*, 73.
6. *T.C.R.*, 126.
7. *T.C.R.*, 134, no. 3.
8. *Sp.D.*, 948.
8a. *Sp. D.*, 2043, 2044.
9. *Divine Providence*, 234.
10. *T.C.R.*, 482.
11. *Sp.D.*, 6101.
12. *T.C.R.*, 333.

CHAPTER TWENTY-NINE: A HAPPY END

1. *The Coronis.*
2. *Tafel*, doc. 269 C, p. 577.
3. *Tafel*, doc. 267.
4. *Tafel*, doc. 264, no. 11.
5. *Sp.D.*, 3623.
6. *The Five Senses*, p. 287.
7. *Tafel*, doc. 265, no. 8.

Index

289.4092
T646

71591